to learn and teach

been involved in the Charismat

in Scotland and overseas. His recently completed

on ancient/future spirituality relates post-modern discipleship to the perennial themes of story, journey and encounter.

The Watkins dictionary *of* SAINTS

Revd Philip D. Noble

WATKINS PUBLISHING

LONDON

This edition published in the UK 2007 by
Watkins Publishing, Sixth Floor, Castle House,
75–76 Wells Street, London W1T 3QH

1 3 5 7 9 10 8 6 4 2

Designed by Jerry Goldie

Typeset by Dorchester Typesetting

Printed and bound in Great Britain

British Library Cataloguing-in-Publication data available

ISBN 978-1-905857-20-3

www.watkinspublishing.com

Acknowledgements

It is never possible to thank everyone who has helped to form us. I will thank some in the hope that they will symbolize the many that remain anonymous.

I thank my late father who wrote a small book on the saints for Brechin Diocese some 30 years ago, which gave me a start on the present project; and my mother who introduced me to St Christina the Astonishing.

I am grateful to those dear friends, George Bosworth, Robert Forrest, Alison Killen, Mary MacDonell, Mary Noble and Bob Smith, who have patiently read parts of the manuscript and provided suggestions and corrections, and to the saints of St Ninian's Episcopal Church in Prestwick who have attentively listened to my retelling of the stories of saints of previous ages; they continue to give me much inspiration. I also wish to thank Doreen Montgomery of Rupert Crewe Ltd for her careful and tireless encouragement.

Finally, I thank God for Rosalind who lived through every day of this book with me and without whose help it could never have been completed.

Contents

Acknowledgements   vi

Introduction   ix

Dictionary of Saints A-Z   1

Appendix I: Heresies   256

Appendix II: Apostles' Creed   261

Appendix III: Symbols of the Saints   262

Appendix IV: Saints in Waiting   264

Appendix V: Alphabetical Index of Saints   268

Appendix VI: Index of Feast Days   288

Appendix VII: Index of Patron Saints   297

Notes   302

Map of Ireland   303

Map of Mainland Britain   304

Map of Europe   305

INTRODUCTION

'A story told with pathos, humour or drama opens the imagination and invites the reader and hearers to imagine themselves in similar situations, offering new insights about God and human beings which enable them to order their own lives more wisely.'[1]

To study the life of even one of the saints can be a lifetime's work and many of the books written about them are being regularly updated to keep pace with the latest developments in scholarship. The rise of modernism brought with it a concentration on the historical critical method which sought to establish as accurately as possible the dates, places and events of the lives of the saints and to identify and weed out those stories which appeared to be of a fanciful nature.

The Penguin Dictionary of Saints sums up the modernist view well in its summary of St Catherine: 'St Catherine is in the Roman martyriology, but there is no other positive evidence that suggests she ever existed outside the mind of some Greek writer who first composed what he intended to be simply an edifying romance.'[2]

And again: 'Most of what is related about him [St Ciaran] however entertaining or edifying has no value as sober history.'[3]

This particular dictionary is an attempt to complement such academic studies and to respond to a rediscovered interest in the actual stories of the saints that has arisen in the latter part of the twentieth century and early twenty-first century. As postmodernism has grown in influence in Western society, there has been a corresponding interest in spirituality in general, and the lives of the saints have become the subject of curiosity far beyond the confines of the Christian church. Given the influential and edifying role of the lives of the saints, their stories provide a thought-provoking challenge and encouragement for us all to review our own spiritual formation.

It is not so much that historical accuracy is unimportant, but rather that it is only one aspect of the whole. Chief Bromden, the narrator in Ken Kesey's novel *One Flew Over the Cuckoo's Nest,* explains, 'It's hard for me to have a clear mind thinking on it. But it's the truth even if it didn't happen.'[4] There is at the heart of each story a truth that resonates beyond simple historical detail. There is no such thing as 'mere story'; a story is its own fact.

John Cassian, one of the saints referred to in the following selection, actually talks about a four-fold reading of scripture, namely the historical, allegorical, moral, and the mystical.

It is not surprising that some stories are thought to be conflations of several different saints, since the Roman martyriology alone lists over 66 different saints called Felix.

St Jerome is credited with having taken the thorn out of a lion's paw when it seems likely that St Gerasimus was in fact the person associated with this. Also problematic is the precise spelling of the names of the early saints, some occur in several alternative spellings and this has given rise to further confusion.

Communities of faith shared the stories of their ancestors and built up a powerful spiritual formation 'book' that went beyond the Acts of the Apostles, from which they drew inspiration.

St Ignatius of Loyola, for example, after being wounded in the siege of Pameluna, was invalided for several months and passed the time in reading the lives of the saints. He was so moved by their exploits that he wanted to join them in their mighty quest of holiness and faithful service.

St Nicodemos of the Holy Mountain, who made three collections of the lives of the saints, wrote, 'Illuminates, warms, revives, and activates the creativity of virtues in the Church', and asked that his first collection of saints be made available in larger print so that 'old people could read it especially during the night hours.'[5]

Due to the constraints of space, it has been necessary to be highly selective and some fairly well-known saints have had to be omitted from this book. In the interest of simplicity I have also omitted the words 'probably' and 'possibly' where they would deter from the flow of the story; similarly most dates are given without stating that these are often approximations or 'best guesses', especially in the first few centuries.

The study of the relics of the saints, which now occupies a fascinating place in modern scholarship, lies beyond the scope of this dictionary.

Many saints became identified as such because they stood out against the prevailing culture and novel belief systems of their day, and an Appendix has been added which summarizes the main heresies they opposed. Where they appear in the text, these heresies are marked with an asterisk.

Saints and their stories make constant reference to places, people and revolutionary new works of God. Today holy places such as Iona, Lourdes and Santiago de Compostela attract increasing numbers of pilgrims. These places have been meeting points for many saints in the past and act as magnets for those seeking a deeper experience of things spiritual.

Following continued persecution, the custom arose of holding a feast in celebration of the life of martyrs on the anniversary of their death. From the origins of this custom in second-century Smyrna, it is clear that the glory was given not so much to the individual saint but to God. Local saints grew up in different places and this practice continued for the first thousand years of the Christian Era.

A brief look at the dictionary will show that many lives of the saints exhibit a web-like inter-connectedness, so to allow for easy cross-referencing, those who had influence in the lives and works of others have been written in bold type.

Completely new works of God are typified in saints such as St Antony and St Francis who were to become the inspirational source for new communities and ways of living, or stood as the first in line to oppose the worldliness and shallowness of the religious practice of their day.

These however are only special examples of a much more general understanding, for sainthood stands at the very heart of the church, and the early church regarded all members as saints. For example, St Paul writes to the saints at Corinth and Collossae (1 Cor 1:2 ; Col 1:2), and St Peter (1 Peter 2:9) calls the faithful a chosen race, a royal priesthood, a dedicated nation.

The original purpose of canonization[6] was not to give a small number of faithful people special status but was rather an attempt to limit the excessive and untested claims of some local communities.

The Eastern Orthodox Church's understanding of sainthood differs slightly from the rest of Christianity, and they never adopted such a centralizing system of canonization. Most of their saints were locally recognized and some more widely accepted. A few examples of these Orthodox 'saints' such as St Theophan are also included in the following pages.

The primary requirement for canonization in the Western Church has always centred on the holiness and Christ-likeness of the individual, this being attested to by all who knew them. They stand as witnesses to the glory of God breaking in on the world. Only after this initial condition has been met are other factors considered. A short Appendix of a few saints 'in waiting' has been included to illustrate this point.

The world cannot understand, and our minds scarcely comprehend, but our spirits resonate to the heroic acts of the faithful ones. In the mid-twentieth century there was an initial liberation and relief in the discovery of the anti-hero character, and as a consequence Dustin Hoffman and Woody Allen replaced John Wayne and Gregory Peck. But the situation has now palled somewhat, and again there is a yearning for real heroes.

The beginning of the twenty-first century sees politicians expressing surprise at any suggestion that their 'private lives' could in any way affect their public decisions. The saints would have been astonished that anyone could suggest that it could possibly be otherwise. For in discovering that all of us have feet of clay, we have been lulled into living with anti-heroes and have thus become accustomed to tolerating mediocrity. However, contrary to popular belief, it is this latter world-view and not that of the faithful saints that has been shown over and over again to be tainted, unreal and ultimately destructive.

We all possess the spark of divine love that awaits rekindling and the stories of the saints present us the challenge that this spark should be blown into a flame of passionate adventure for abandoned selfless living. Their stories tell us how this happened for them and also give some clues as to how this can happen again for others, including ourselves, today.

Cardinal Suenens wrote in the 1970s book *A New Pentecost*: 'God writes extraordinary novels for those of us who are ready "to play his game", willing to be open to the unexpected, on the alert to hear the whispers of grace and the promptings of the Spirit.'[7]

So it will always be with the saints of every age.

Philip Noble, Prestwick
St Cuthbert's feast day, 2006

A

St Abban *Feast day: 16 March. Born in Ireland; died in Leinster, Ireland c. 630.* Abban was the son of King Cormac of Leinster. He founded many churches in the district known today as County Wexford in Ireland. Latterly, he served as Abbot of Killabban Abbey in Leinster. The present Adamstown was once called Abbanstown in honour of his life and work.

St Abbo *Feast day: 13 November. Born in Orléans, France, 945; died in Gascony, France, 1004.* After studying in Paris and Rheims, Abbo entered the Benedictine order at Fleury. **St Oswald,** who stayed for a time at the same monastery, was greatly impressed by Abbo's talents and brought him to England in 986 to work as director of his school at Ramsey. Abbo returned to Fleury two years later intending to continue his studies, but instead found himself chosen as abbot.

Abbo was highly educated and was particularly interested in astronomy and mathematics. His calming influence helped avert mass riots, which were being whipped up by those who believed the world would come to an end in the year 1000. His readiness to intervene, in the hope of bringing reconciliation, resulted in his death four years later at the monastery of La Réole in Gascony. He died of stab wounds received while trying to quell a violent riot between monks and armed servants.

Sts Abdon and Sennen *Feast day: 30 July. Born in Persia; died in Rome, c. 250.* Abdon and Sennen were two Persian noblemen brought in chains to Rome during the persecution by Emperor Diocletian. They had been found guilty of ministering to the persecuted Christians and of burying the bodies of the martyrs. Though put in an arena with wild animals, they were left unscathed and, finally, gladiators had to be ordered to hack them to pieces. A group of Christians in Rome carried away their bodies at night for secret burial next to the house of a subdeacon called Quirinus.

St Abel *Feast day: 5 August. Born in Ireland; died in France, c. 751.* Abel was a Benedictine monk who accompanied **St Boniface** on his missions to mainland Europe. Chosen as Archbishop of Rheims by Pope St Zachary in 744, he was unable to take over the see due to the interference of hostile forces supporting the self-appointed bishop Milo. He graciously retired to a monastery of which he was later made abbot.

St Abercius Marcellus *Feast day: 22 October. Born in Phrygia; died in Hieropolos, c.200.* Little is known of Abercius before the age of 72. He was Bishop of Hieropolos at the time and was summoned to Rome to exorcise a demon from Lucilla, the daughter of Emperor Marcus Aurelius. He succeeded and returned to his see, travelling home via Syria and the Euphrates River valley. He was passionate in his commitment to Christian unity and regarded the sacrament of baptism as the essential element required to achieve this. The English archaeologist W.M.

Ramsay discovered an epitaph from his tomb that described Abercius' journey and the hospitality that he received from fellow Christians along the way.

St Abraham *Feast day: 15 June. Born in Euphrates River region of modern Iraq; died in Gaul, c. 480.* Taken prisoner by bandits while travelling to Egypt to visit monastic communities, Abraham was held as a slave for five years. He escaped and made his way to Gaul, where he became a hermit. Recognized for his sanctity, he was later ordained priest, and in due course, became Abbot of St Cyriacus Abbey.

St Abraham Kidunaja *Feast day: 16 March. Born c sixth century. Born in Edessa, Mesopotamia in the sixth century.* Abraham was the dutiful son of wealthy parents. On the day before the marriage his parents had arranged for him, he fled to the desert and remained there, much distressed by his own disobedience. Making his home in a cave he sealed up the entrance, leaving only a small opening through which he could be fed. Abraham lived as a monk, wearing the same goatskin coat for all his 50 years, and was never seen to smile.

The Bishop of Edessa sought Abraham's help in converting the troublesome people of Beth-Kiduna. Abraham agreed but asked the bishop to arrange for a church to be built there. When it was completed he went and broke down all the pagan idols and altars he could find in that place, whereupon he was attacked, beaten and thrown out by the furious inhabitants. That night he returned to the church and after Morning Prayer went about the streets haranguing the people and calling on them to repent. This time the people treated him even more severely, throwing him out of town, stoning him and leaving him for dead. He returned again and again and, though the beatings continued for a time, after three years the tide turned and many people were converted. This was the fruit of his holy and persistent example. He lived to be over 70 years old.

Abraham also rescued his niece Mary from a life of prostitution by disguising himself as a soldier in need of her services, and then persuading her to return to a chaste life.

St Abraham of Rostov *Feast day: 29 October. Born in Galicia, Russia in the twelfth century.* Brought up in a pagan household, Abraham became a Christian when his prayer to God for healing from a chronic illness was answered. Soon thereafter he answered the call to the monastic life and travelled to Rostov in order to preach to the heathen. He worked diligently to build two parish churches for his new converts and founded a monastery in the second of these, but he did not allow this community to distract him from his work of evangelism and care for the poor and needy.

St Abraham of Smolensk *Feast day: 21 August. Born in Smolensk, Russia; died, c.1221.* At an early age, Abraham entered the Monastery at Bogoroditakay and became famous as a biblical scholar and a skilled copier of manuscripts. As an ordained priest, his simplicity, and tireless insistence on repentance made him many enemies amongst the less fervent members of his religious community. Abraham painted two icons, both representing the Last Judgement. His abbot forbade him to preach and he eventually left to join a different order of monks.

He fared no better there and charges of heresy, immorality, and hubris were brought against him. As a result, Bishop Ignatius of Smolensk ordered him to return to his original monastery and forbade him from celebrating the Holy Eucharist. St Abraham's holiness of life was well known to the citizens of Smolensk and, when a terrible drought afflicted the region, they demanded that the case against Abraham be re-examined. The bishop exonerated him, apologized for the way he had been treated, and requested that Abraham pray for the city.

Before he had returned to his cell, the heavens had opened in a deluge of rain.

Ignatius appointed him Abbot of the Mother of God Monastery, where he happily spent the rest of his days in humble and committed service.

St Acacius *Feast day: 31 March. Born in Antioch in the third century.* Acacius was a priest who worked hard to support the Christian community during the time of persecution. He encouraged Christians to pray for the emperor but was arrested, tried and sentenced to death for refusing to take part in emperor worship. When the Emperor Decius read a transcript of the trial, he could not help smiling at the wit and wisdom of Acacius' responses. The governor Maximus was so impressed by his faithful witness that he too became a Christian and suffered the same fate.

St Acca *Feast day: 20 October. Born in Northumbria; died, c.740.* Acca was educated by **St Bosa** and became a Benedictine monk. **St Wilfrid** appointed him Abbot of Hexham Abbey. A highly regarded scholar and supporter of Christian arts and music, he brought Maban, a cantor from Kent, north in order to teach his clergy the Roman style of monastic chanting. He encouraged the writing of a life of Wilfrid and was well thought of by **St Bede**, who dedicated some of his work to him. Driven out of Hexham in 732 for unspecified reasons, he retired to a hermitage at Whithorn, Galloway, but returned to Hexham just before his death. One of the Celtic crosses that marked his grave still stands there.

St Acepsimas *Feast day: 3 November. Born in Syria in the fifth century.* Acepsimas lived as a hermit in a cave near Cyrohas, in Syria. Though he had always longed to be a priest, he spent nearly all his life in faithful prayer and penance as a layman. After almost 60 years, he was allowed to undergo training and was ordained. He died shortly after in a state of happiness.

St Acestes *Feast day: 2 July. Born in the first century.* Acestes was one of three soldiers who escorted **St Paul** to his death. They were all converted during their brief encounter and, declaring their new-found faith, protested against Paul's execution. All three were immediately beheaded.

St Achatius *Feast day: 31 March. Born in Antioch, Phrygia; died, 251.* Achatius was a prominent Christian who became Bishop of Antioch. Under examination by the authorities, he assured the local Roman official Martian that he was faithful to the emperor and prayed constantly for him. He also took the opportunity to explain the merits of Christianity.

Achatius was imprisoned for his refusal to sacrifice to pagan gods or to give the names of other Christian believers. However, when Emperor Decius read the trial report he was so impressed that he promoted Martian and pardoned Achatius.

St Achillas *Feast day: 7 November. Born in North Africa; died, 313.* Achillas was bishop of Alexandria, Egypt. Though he ordained Arius, who later fell into heresy, he continued to defend the faith and was praised by **St Athanasius** for his purity. Achillas experienced severe criticism from Arius and his followers and he died before Arius was finally condemned and forced to flee to Palestine.

St Adalbert of Prague *Feast day: 23 April. Born in Bohemia, 956; died in Pomerania, 997.* Adalbert was born into a princely family. Educated at Magdeburg, he had grand visions for missionary work and reform and, while still under 30 years old, became the second Bishop of Prague.

He set high moral and intellectual standards and divided his revenues along the lines suggested by **St Gregory the Great**. He came into conflict with the authorities over his plans to convert Hungary and Bohemia and, in 990, he withdrew to Rome to enter the Benedictine monastery of **St Boniface** and Alexius on the Aventine. Two years later, he was ordered back to Prague by Pope John XV.

Adalbert founded various abbeys and, though he had little outward success, he and his companions continued to evangelize in several countries of Eastern Europe until they were killed by a group of Prussians who suspected them of being Polish spies.

St Adamnan *Feast day: 23 September. Born in Donegal, Ireland, 624; died, 704.* Adamnan became a monk at the monastery in Donegal and later became ninth abbot of Iona. Adamnan worked ceaselessly to reconcile Irish and Scottish monks, and to encourage the peaceful readjustment of their Celtic practices with those of Rome. He helped bring about a new level of moderation to tribal disputes at the Council of Birr where it was agreed that, in war, women and children should be neither imprisoned nor killed. This became known as Adamnan's Law.

He wrote a life of **St Columba**, the first Abbot of Iona.

St Adelaide *Feast day: 16 December. Born in Burgundy, 931; died, 999. Canonized 1097 by Pope Urban II.* Adelaide was described as 'a marvel of beauty and goodness'. In her mid-teens she married King Lothair of Italy, but on his death, was imprisoned by his successor, Berengar of Ivrea. He attempted to force her to marry his son but Adelaide escaped and sought help from King Otto of Germany who invaded Italy and married her in 951. After Otto died Adelaide quarrelled with their son, Otto II, and moved to live with her brother in Burgundy. Being greatly concerned with evangelism, she set about establishing many monasteries and churches. She was reconciled with her son in 983, and acted as regent for her young grandson Otto III. She died at the convent she had founded in Seltz.

St Adrian *Feast day: 4 March. Born in Pannonia, Hungary; died, 875.* Adrian was a member of the Hungarian royal family and was appointed bishop of the local diocese there. He resigned to come to Fife in Scotland in order to evangelize the Picts, but was forced to retire to the Island of May after a Viking attack. He and his companions were eventually killed there by marauding Danes. King David I of Scotland founded a monastery on the Isle and this became a centre for pilgrims.

St Aelred of Rievaulx *Feast day: 3 February. Born in Hexham, England, in 1109; died in 1167. Canonized in 1191 by Pope Celestine III.* Aelred's father and grandfather were both Saxon priests. He received a wide education at Durham, and became a steward to **St David I**, the king of Scotland, at the age of 20, just as the new king was beginning his reign. Aelred left to join the Cistercian community at Rievaulx and later became abbot in 1147. In response to a request from **St Bernard of Clairvaux** he wrote 'The Mirror of Charity', and in his later life, though he suffered much ill health, he wrote further books on spirituality and the lives of **Sts Ninian and Cuthbert**.

St Agatha *Feast day: 5 February. Born in Catania, Sicily; died in 251.* Patron of bell-founders. Agatha was famous for her beauty and gentleness. She refused to marry the Sicilian consul Quintinian, since she had dedicated her life to God. He tried many different ways of forcing her to change her mind which included installing her in a brothel for a month. Agatha refused to give way and was brought to trial on the charge of belonging to an outlawed sect.

Even though she was ruthlessly persecuted and suffered sexual assault and indignity, her faith did not waver. Following a period of imprisonment, she was horrifically tortured to death.

St Agnes *Feast day: 21 January. Born in Rome, 291; died in 304.* Agnes was a beautiful young girl who rejected the advances of the Governor's son saying, 'Jesus Christ is my only Spouse.' Though she was offered many inducements to deny her faith, she refused and even imprisonment could not persuade her. She went to her death by the sword with her face shining. She was only 13 years old.

St Agnes of Assisi *Feast day: 16 November. Born in Assisi, 1212; died in 1253. Canonized in 1753 by Pope Benedict XIV.* Agnes was the daughter of Count Favorino Scifi, and younger sister of **St Clare**. She was one of the first to join the Franciscan order of the Poor Clares, despite her father's efforts to prevent her from doing so.

Other noblewomen of Assisi also joined them and Agnes was eventually chosen by **St Francis of Assisi** to found and become abbess of a community at Monticelli, near Florence. Full of energy and zeal, she went on to establish communities of Poor Clares in Mantua, Padua, and Venice. She was especially known for her love of poverty and her loyalty to the teachings of Francis and Clare.

St Aidan of Lindisfarne *Feast day: 31 August. Born in Ireland; died in Bamborough, 651.* Aidan was an Irish monk who had studied under **St Senan**, at Iniscathay (Scattery Island). He became a monk at Iona about 630. Five years later he was selected as first Bishop of Lindisfarne. **St Bede** had a high regard for Aidan and described him as 'inspired with a passionate love of virtue, but at the same time full of a surpassing mildness and gentleness'.

During his later life, King Oswald of Northumbria, who had studied in Ireland, did all he could to support Aidan and his companions.

St Ailbhe *Feast day: 12 September. Born in Ireland; died in 541.* Patron of Munster. Ailbhe was a missionary in Ireland before **St Patrick**, having been converted by British missionaries, he later became Patrick's disciple. He was the first Bishop of Emly in Munster and was known for his eloquent sermons, charity and kindness. One story tells of how an old she-wolf came to him for protection from a hunting party, laying her head on his chest. Ailbhe especially loved to pray in front of the sea and King Aengus of Munster gave him the Aran Islands (Co. Galway) on which Ailbhe encouraged **St Enda** to found a great monastery.

In his later years, he wanted to resign, retire to the solitude of a northern island and prepare for his death, but the king stationed guards at the ports to prevent his flight. Thus Ailbhe died while still in office.

St Alban *Feast day: 22 June. Born in England; died c. 304.* During Diocletian's persecution, Alban, though still a pagan, hid a priest in his home. He was so moved by the priest's devotion and prayer, that he sought instruction in the Christian faith and was baptized. When news leaked out that a priest was being concealed, soldiers came to arrest him. Alban took the priest's cloak and allowed himself to be arrested in his place, thus allowing the priest to escape.

He was questioned and harshly beaten in order to make him worship the pagan gods. When he still refused, the order was given for him to be taken out and beheaded. The crowd that accompanied him was so large that they blocked the only bridge to the execution site. Alban prayed and the river dried up at his feet allowing him to pass over to the other side. Witnessing this, the soldier who had been assigned to kill him was converted and martyred with him. **St Bede** records that the man who cut off Alban's head did not witness the event, since his eyes and the saint's head, fell to the ground together. Alban was the first English martyr.

St Alberic *Feast day: 26 January. Died in Citeaux, 1109.* Alberic was a Benedictine hermit who in 1075 co-founded a monastery at Molesmes and became its first prior. He tried twice to reform the monastery but monks rebelled and imprisoned him. On his release he left and helped found a new monastery at Citeaux, from which the Cistercian Order traces its origins.

The additional austerities that he introduced into Molesmes gave it a true Cistercian character, and the order began to flourish and grow, becoming one of the most influential monastic orders.

St Albert the Great *Feast day: 15 November. Born in Lauingen, Swabia, (south west Germany) in 1206; died in Cologne, 1280.* Albert studied at various universities including those of Padua and Paris, before becoming a Dominican monk. He was among the first of the natural scientists, and organized the study programme for the whole Dominican order. His encyclopaedic knowledge included such varied topics as biology, chemistry, physics, astronomy, geography, metaphysics, mathematics, biblical studies and theology.

Albert was appointed Bishop of Ratisbon in 1260, even though Humbert de Romanis, Master General of the Dominicans, being loath to lose the services of the great Master, endeavoured to prevent the nomination. Albert governed the diocese until 1262, when he voluntarily resumed the duties of a professor in Cologne.

He greatly admired **St Thomas Aquinas** who was one of his students, and he defended his teachings when attacks were made upon them following Thomas' untimely death, in1274.

In 1278, Albert wrote an account of his life, but soon after his outstanding intellect gradually became clouded, his bodily strength gave out, and in a greatly weakened state, he died.

St Aldhelm *Feast day: 25 May. Born in Wessex, 639; died in 709.* As a young man, Aldhelm lived for a time as a hermit. His custom was to gather the children of the neighbourhood for instruction and eventually his hermitage became a school. He was made Abbot of St Augustine's, Canterbury and of Malmesbury, where he practised great austerity. During his term in office the abbey prospered and after his death it became widely known as a centre for scholars.

He was a skilled communicator, a poet and a scholar. He would attract people to church by reciting his verses interspersed with hymns while accompanying himself on the harp. He gained the attention of his audience with bits of clowning and reading short passages from the Gospels and in this way was able to speak to their souls. In 857, King Ethelwulf erected a silver shrine at Malmesbury in his honour.

St Alexander *Feast day: 18 March. Died in Caesarea, 251.* Alexander was a student with Origen at Alexandria, became Bishop of Cappadocia, and was imprisoned for seven years for his faith. Upon his release, this mild man made a pilgrimage to Jerusalem where he was compelled by the aged bishop, **St Narcissus**, to remain in order to assist him in the government of that see. While there he developed a famous theological library and encouraged Origen, while still a layman, to teach in church.

Alexander suffered many tortures during the persecution of Decius, but survived them all. He was thrown to the wild beasts but they refused to attack him, some licking his feet, and others his footprints in the sand of the arena. Worn out by his sufferings, he died in prison.

St Alexander of Constantinople *Feast day: 28 August. Born in 244; died in 337.* Widely known for his wisdom and holiness, Alexander was elected Bishop of Byzantium at the age of 73. He attended the Council of Nicea in 325 and joined in the condemnation of Arius* and his heretical teachings. Emperor Constantine the Great commanded that Arius be received back into the Church but Alexander refused and shut himself up in a church to pray for the strength to continue his resistance. Arius died the day before Alexander was to be exonerated.

St Alexander Nevski *Feast day: 30 August. Born in Russia, 1220; died in Gorodets, 1263.* Alexander was the son of Grand Prince Yaroslav II of Vladimir who became a famous ruler and defender of Russia against many attacks from invading forces. He was elected Grand Prince of Novgorod in 1236, and in 1242 he defeated the Teutonic knights whom Pope Gregory IX had commissioned to bring Western Christianity to the Baltic. He was known for his prayerful attitude and became a monk shortly before his death. His firm diplomacy with the Mongols protected the Russian people from the usual ravages of occupation.

St Alexis *Feast day: 17 July. Born in the fifth century.* Alexis was the only son of a Roman senator. He learned to be charitable to the poor from his devout Christian parents, and allowed himself to be betrothed to an heiress who was related to the emperor. With the consent of his wife, Alexis fled from the church as soon as the marriage ceremony was completed, leaving behind all his worldly wealth and honours. He later returned as a beggar and, unrecognized by his parents who always showed kindness to the poor, was allowed to stay in a corner of their house, under the stairs. After his death a note was found, explaining who he was.

St Alfrick *Feast day: 16 November. Died in 1105.* Alfrick was a monk in the Benedictine Abbey of Abingdon who was noted for his holiness and charity. He was appointed Bishop of Wilton in 990, then Archbishop of Canterbury five years later. He cared for the Church in the difficult years of the Norse invasion of England.

St Alfwold *Feast day: 26 March. Died in 1058.* Alfwold became a monk and companion of **St Swithun** in Winchester, England. His ascetic lifestyle was in great contrast to the riotous living of the Danish kings of that day and made a deep impression on local leaders. Alfwold had a special devotion to **St Cuthbert**, and made a pilgrimage to visit him in Durham. He died with the special antiphon of St Cuthbert upon his lips.

St Alipius *Feast day: 15 August. Born in Tagaste, North Africa; died in 430.* Alipius became a magistrate in Rome and was a longstanding friend and companion of **St Augustine** from their youth in North Africa. They were both baptized in Milan by **St Ambrose** and the two were later ordained in Hippo, North Africa. Subsequently, Alipius became bishop of his home town and faithfully served there for 30 years.

St Alphege *Feast day: 12 March. Born in Weston near Bath, England, 953; died in 1012.* Alphege was known as 'the Elder' or 'the Bald', and was reluctantly made Bishop of Winchester, England, where he ordained **St Dunstan**. The country was subject to regular attacks from Viking raiders and Alphege sought to win these wild men to the Christian faith.

King Aethelred sent Alphege and a companion to visit King Olaf in Norway and sue for peace. Olaf was a Christian but he was unconfirmed, so Alphege negotiated a peace treaty by agreeing to confirm Olaf and have King Aethelred adopt him as his son. In return, Olaf promised that he would never again invade England.

Alphege is credited with helping to restore monasticism to England.

St Alphonsus Marie Liguori *Feast day: 1 August. Born in Marianella, near Naples, 1696; died in 1787. Canonized in 1753 by Pope Benedict XIV.* Alphonsus' father was a naval officer and Captain of the Royal Galleys. He was a skilled musician who trained as a lawyer before becoming a priest and moving to live with a group of secular missionaries. In 1732, Alphonsus founded the Redemptorist congregation, at Scala, near Amalfi, Italy with the intention of ministering more effectively among the neglected country people in the neighbourhood of Naples. Inner rivalries quickly appeared and he was tricked into signing a document which excluded him from having any authority over the future of the order. Though by this time Alphonsus was suffering severely from rheumatic fever and depression, he persevered and still experienced prophecies, miracles and visions.

St Altman *Feast day: 8 August. Born in Paderborn, Westphalia, Germany; died in 1091.* Altman studied in Paris and was ordained there. He took part in a pilgrimage to Jerusalem along with 7,000 others. This ill-fated group was held hostage by Muslim Saracens for some months, and were only released when a friendly emir intervened on their behalf. They returned home much depleted in numbers, due to the privations and dangers of their perilous journey. Such tragic events as these provided a trigger for the Crusades.

On his return Altman was named Bishop of Passau. He founded an Abbey at Gottweig, Austria, and became active in Church reform. His vigorous support for the Pope's teaching on celibacy, and his fight against clergy corruption, made him extremely unpopular, and finally he was driven out of his diocese.

Temporarily banished to Rome, he was appointed Apostolic Delegate to Germany. On his return to Passau, he continued to maintain the call for reform and was driven out once again. He spent his remaining years in exile in the Abbey at Gottweig.

St Alto *Feast day: 9 February. Born in Ireland; died in 760.* Alto lived for many years in a hut near Augsburg, Germany. His reputation for holiness and austerity reached King Pepin, who made him a gift of some land. Alto cleared this and founded an abbey in the Celtic tradition. Even though **St Boniface** was unable to persuade him to bar women from its precincts, he still dedicated a church for the abbey. This church was destroyed by the Huns soon after Alto's death, but later restored and taken over by the followers of **St Bridget**, who were known as the Bridgettines.

St Alvarez *Feast day: 19 February. Born in Lisbon, Portugal; died in 1430.* Alvarez entered the Dominican convent at Cordova and his gift for preaching soon became widely recognized. He was an advisor to the court and helped initiate several reforms.

He became over-involved in various court intrigues and decided to withdraw to construct a spiritual centre that he named 'Escalaceli' (literally 'ladder of heaven') in the mountains near Cordova. It is reported that angels helped with the building by bringing raw materials, under cover of darkness, to where workmen could easily gather them. The Escalaceli, which was completed in a remarkably short time, became the most famous centre of religious devotion in the region.

He skilfully and successfully encouraged people of every social standing to oppose the man appointed to be pope by a Church schism, Benedict XIII (Peter de Luna). He was known as the Antipope. Alvarez undertook extreme practices of penance and was known to be a miracle worker.

St Amalberga *Feast day: 10 July. Born in 770; died in 825.* Amalberga refused a proposal of marriage from the Emperor Charlemagne, who attempted to take her by force, breaking her arm in the process. When Charlemagne withdrew his demands, Amalberga miraculously cured him from an illness. She was known for such miracles throughout the region.

St Amand *Feast day: 6 February. Born in the lower Poitou in 584; died at Elnone in 679.* At the age of 20 Amand retired to a small monastery, totally disregarding his father's threats that he would lose his inheritance if he did not return home.

Moving to Tours, Amand was ordained, then travelled to Bourges, where he lived for 15 years, in a cell near the cathedral, under the direction of the Bishop St Austregisulus.

After pilgrimage to Rome, he returned and was consecrated bishop, receiving a roving commission to teach the Faith to the heathens, which he did with great diligence. Learning of the ferocious hostility to the Christian religion amongst the people of Ghent, he decided to make this district his special project. Though he was sometimes beaten, and even thrown into a river, he persevered even though his preaching had little apparent effect. Eventually, crowds flocked to him to be baptized. He continued his missionary work well into his ninetieth year, till ill health caused him to withdraw to Elnone, where he died four years later.

He was the father of monasticism in Belgium, and established several foundations there.

St Amata *Feast day: 20 February. Born in Assisi; died in 1250.* Amata, a niece of **St Clare** of Assisi, was miraculously cured of an illness by her aunt and, as a result, went on to enter one of the monasteries of the Poor Clares.

St Amator *Feast day: 1 May. Born in Auxerre, France; died in 418.* Amator was the only son of wealthy parents, who arranged a wedding for him by bringing in the ageing Bishop Valerian to conduct the ceremony.

Whether by accident or divine purpose, the bishop read the words of the ordination ceremony for deacons, instead of the marriage service. Neither Amator nor his bride had wanted to be married, and therefore welcomed this opportunity to enter the service of the Church. His wife entered a convent and he was ordained, eventually becoming Bishop of Auxerre.

In advanced years, Amator cut down the sacred tree in the city centre where Germaus, the young Christian Governor of Auxerre, displayed the heads of his hunting kills. He then withdrew for a time to escape Germaus' anger but, on his return, summoned all Christians to the cathedral. With the help of some clergy, he had the governor stripped of his secular clothing, tonsured and installed as bishop designate of Auxerre.

His life work completed, Amator died peacefully a few days later.

St Amatus *Feast day: 13 September. Born in Grenoble, France; died c. 630.* Placed into St Maurice Abbey as a small child, Amatus duly became a Benedictine monk and then lived as a hermit for a season. In 620 he converted a Merovingian noble named Romaric, who went on to found a double monastery. Amatus was appointed as its first abbot.

St Ambrose of Milan *Feast day: 7 December. Born in Trier, Germany, 340; died in Milan, 397.* His father Ambrose was the Praetorian Prefect of Gaul. Ambrose had one brother, and a sister, **St Marcellina**, who became a nun even though she continued to live as a religious at home. Ambrose was tutored by a Roman priest named Simplician, who later succeeded him as Bishop of Milan.

Highly proficient in both law and oratory, Ambrose attracted the attention of the Emperor Valentinian and, when he was still only 30, he was appointed Governor of Aemilia and Liguria in north Italy.

When the Arian Bishop Auxentius of Milan died in 374 a violent dispute arose between rival factions and Ambrose went to the cathedral to exhort the people to be restrained and to resist violence. In the middle of his speech, a child cried out, 'Ambrose for bishop!' This was taken up by the crowd, and Ambrose was unanimously elected by popular acclaim. He resisted at first, but finally agreed and was baptized and consecrated bishop within two weeks.

Ambrose was a supporter of **Athanasius**, defended the Church against heresy and was widely respected because of his dedication to the poor and needy. As bishop, Ambrose felt he was primarily responsible for the instruction of catechumens, and when he baptized new Christians, he always washed their feet.

He sold church silver to ransom prisoners, is credited with the introduction of communal singing with rhyming verses, and was a close friend of **St Monica** being instrumental in the conversion of **St Augustine of Hippo** in 387.

In 390, when Emperor Theodosius I ordered the massacre of a crowd of 7,000 in Thessalonica (Salonica), in reprisal for murdering the Roman governor, Ambrose demanded a public expression of repentance. Theodosius agreed, and was readmitted to communion with the Church at Christmas. Following this, Ambrose and his emperor became firm friends.

Ambrose was a consistent defender of orthodoxy and at the request of the Emperor Gratian wrote '*De fide*' to counter Arian arguments. He was the first bishop to be used by the state in peace negotiations and died on Easter Eve 397, after 23 years as bishop.

St Ammon *Feast day: 20 December. Died in Alexandria c. 250.* Ammon was a Christian soldier in Alexandria during the time of persecution by Emperor Decius. During the trial of Egyptian Christian believers, Ammon and some other Christian soldiers were among the guard. When they sensed that the accused showed signs of wavering, they encouraged them to stand firm with nods and gestures.

The judge noticed their unusual behaviour and confronted the guard, whereupon five soldiers, Ammon, Ingenes, Ptolemy, Theophilus, and Zeno, came forward and declared that they were Christians.

Though imprisoned and tortured, they showed the same Christian steadfastness as their former prisoners and they too were beheaded. These soldiers are known collectively as the Theban Martyrs.

St Amphianus *Feast day: 2 April. Born in Lycia, Turkey; died in 305.* Amphianus was a fervent young Christian man. He could not keep silent about his faith and bravely entered the official residence of the Roman governor to protest against the pagan sacrifices he saw there. Even though he was arrested, he continued to rebuke the governor for his idolatrous practise and was eventually tortured to death.

St Amphilocus *Feast day: 23 November. Born in Cappadocia; died c. 400.* A cousin of **St Gregory of Nazianzus**, he studied in Constantinople and, in 374, became Bishop of Iconium. He was a close friend of **St Basil** and a strong opponent of the Arian* heresy. When the Emperor Theodosius I refused to keep Arians away from the Council of Constantinople in 381, Amphilocus devised a plan in order to show his displeasure: he waited a little and then went to visit the emperor, giving him the usual greeting of respect due but totally ignoring his son who stood right by his side. When the emperor pointed out his omission, Amphilocus apologized and patted the boy on the cheek. Theodosius lost his temper but was deeply affected by the bishop's next remark, 'You cannot bear a slight against your own son, what about those who dishonour the Son of God?'

Soon after this, the emperor made a law forbidding the Arians to hold meetings.

The original correspondence between St Amphilocus and **Sts Gregory and Basil** has been preserved to this day.

St Anastasius I *Feast day: 19 December. Born in Rome; died there in 401.* Anastasius, the son of Maximus, was elected pope in 399 and served in this role for two years. His pontificate was marked by his condemnation of Origen and his determination to stop the errors of those who followed and expanded upon Origen's teachings. He urged the African bishops to continue their opposition to Donatism*, and his personal holiness and piety was recognized by **St Jerome**. **Sts Augustine** and **Paulinus of Nola** also praised his sanctity. Pope Anastasius was the first to introduce the rule that priests should stand to read the Gospel. He was a man of extreme poverty and humility.

St Anatolia *Feast day: 9 July. Born in Italy; martyred in 250.* During Emperor Trajanus Decius' persecutions, Anatolia rejected her suitor, Aurelius, because she felt called to the single life. The young man asked her sister Victoria to persuade her; not only was Victoria unsuccessful in this, but she also decided to break off her engagement as a result of their conversations.

Both sisters were arrested and attempts were made to starve them into submission. Anatolia was locked in a room with a poisonous snake but remained unmoved, even the threat of death could not shake their convictions.

Their executioner was so moved by their unwavering faith that he was converted to the Christian faith and soon after died a martyr's death by the sword.

St Anatolius *Feast day: 3 July. Born in Alexandria, Egypt; died in 283.* Well known as a philosopher, mathematician and scientist, Anatolius conducted a school of philosophy in Alexandria when the Romans had part of the city under siege.

He skilfully negotiated with their general to have the most vulnerable people released, after which the rebels surrendered. Anatolius was later made Bishop of Ladies in Syria by popular acclaim.

St Andochius *Feast day: 24 September. Born in Smyrna in the second century.* **St Polycarp** sent Andochius to Gaul along with a deacon named Thyrsus. When they arrived at Autun, they converted a merchant named Felix with whom they were staying. All three were arrested, tortured, and put to death by the Romans because they would not deny Christ.

St Andrew *Feast day: 30 November. Born in Palestine in the first century.* Patron of fishermen, Russia and Scotland. Andrew was a follower of John the Baptist and became the first disciple of Jesus Christ. He brought his brother Simon to meet Jesus and he also became a disciple. They were both fishermen but left their nets to follow Jesus for three years, and were then commissioned by the risen Lord for missionary work. St Andrew went to Greece to preach the Gospel where he was martyred, having been tied to a cross. He lived for two days in a state of suffering, still preaching to the people who gathered, before he finally died.

Sts Andrew Kim Taegon, Paul Chong Hasang, and Companions *Feast day: 20 September. Born in Korea; died in 1846. Canonized 1984 by Pope John Paul II.* Andrew Kim Taegon was a member of the Korean nobility and the first Roman Catholic priest in that land. After attending a seminary in Macao he returned home and, during a time of severe persecution of the Church, was tortured and finally beheaded at Seoul. One hundred and three others were also martyred, most of whom were lay folk of all ages.

St Andronicus *Feast day: 9 October. Born in Alexandria, Egypt in the fifth century.* Andronicus was a silversmith who travelled with his wife Athanasia to Antioch. After both of their children had died in a plague, they returned to Egypt to become hermits in the desert. Athanasia dressed as a man and lived in a separate hermitage. Some years later, they went on pilgrimage to Jerusalem and upon their return, joined a monastery near Alexandria.

St Angadresma *Feast day: 14 October. Born in France, 615; died in 695.* Though betrothed, Angadresma dreaded the thought of marriage and prayed for a miracle that would allow her to follow a religious vocation. She contracted leprosy, whereupon her fiancé broke off the engagement and married someone else. As soon as she entered holy orders the disease disappeared and her skin was fully restored. In time, she became the abbess of the Benedictine monastery near Beauvais, France, and became well known for working miracles.

St Angela de'Merici *Feast day: 27 January. Born in Desenzano, Lombardy, Italy, 1470; died in Brescia, Italy, 1540. Canonized 1807 by*

Pope Pius VII. Orphaned at age ten, Angela and her sister and brother were raised by their wealthy uncle. She became a Franciscan tertiary at the age of 13. Her uncle died in 1490 and Angela returned to Desenzano to teach catechism. Angela had an extremely retentive memory, spoke Latin well and had a deep understanding of scripture.

On a pilgrimage to the Holy Land, she lost her sight, while staying at Crete, but she continued undeterred. On the return trip she found her vision was totally restored at the very spot where she'd lost it.

During a visit to Rome in 1525, Pope Clement VII gave her permission to form a community. Shortly, thereafter, **St Ursula** appeared to her in a vision and she formed the Company of Saint Ursula (Ursuline nuns), the first teaching order of women. The nuns wore simple black dresses, took no vows, but worked to oversee the religious education of poor girls, and to care for the sick.

The Ursulines were formally recognized by Pope Paul III in 1544, four years after Angela's death

St Angelo *Feast day: 5 May. Born in Jerusalem; died at Leocata in 1220.* One of twins, and a son of Jewish converts to Christianity, Angelo entered the Carmelite Order at 18. As a result of a vision, he set out for Sicily and on his journey many were converted by his teaching and miracles, including over 200 Jews at Palermo.

While preaching at Leocata, he was mortally wounded by a gang who were offended by his outspoken criticism and died there, still praying for his murderers.

St Angilbert *Feast day: 18 February. Died in 814.* Angilbert was brought up in the court of the Emperor Charlemagne. He studied under the great English scholar Alcuin, and gained the nickname 'Homer' because of his literary and linguistic skills.

He fathered two children with Bertha, Charlemagne's daughter. When his prayers for a successful resistance to a Danish invasion were answered, and a storm scattered the Danish fleet, Angilbert, with his wife's agreement, decided to become a monk. He became the Abbot of Saint-Riquier in Picardy, France, where he restored the abbey and endowed it with over 200 books. Meanwhile Bertha entered a convent.

St Annemund *Feast day: 28 September. Born in Lyon, Gaul; died at Mâcon in 658.* Annemund was raised in the court of King Dagobert I. When Clovis II succeeded to the throne, Annemund was appointed his advisor and later was made Bishop of Lyon. **St Wilfrid** of York, who was on his way to Rome with **St Benedict Biscop**, stayed with Annemund for some time while visiting Lyon and a close friendship developed between them.

In the disturbances that followed the death of King Clovis, Annemund was slain by soldiers in Mâcon.

St Ansanus *Feast day: 1 December. Born in Rome; died in 304.* Ansanus became a Christian at the age of 12 and he was denounced to the Roman authorities by his own father. He was able to skilfully elude capture and began missionary outreaches in both Siena and Bagnorea, Italy, becoming known by the title 'the Baptizer'. During the persecution by the Emperor Diocletian, he was eventually arrested and beheaded along with many others believers. The place of his execution was carefully noted and a church was later built upon the site.

St Anselm of Canterbury *Feast day: 21 April. Born in Aoust, in Piedmont, 1033; died in 1109. Canonized in 1720 by Pope Clement XI.* Anselm was called to the monastic life at the age of 15 and at 30 was made Prior of Bec Abbey in Normandy, which was famous as a centre for scholarship.

Later he was appointed Abbot of Bec, and travelled to England. He was greatly distressed by the many abuses in Church and state life he found there, including the deliberate refusal of King William Rufus to create certain Church positions in order that he might gain financially.

Anselm willingly accepted his appointment as Archbishop of Canterbury in 1093, and continued to oppose the king's interference in spiritual affairs, though in due course they did manage to reach a compromise.

He also helped to settle a dispute amongst the Greek bishops of southern Italy over the filioque clause in the creed. The Western Church had added the words 'and the son' without consultation in an attempt to safeguard Trinitarian teaching. Anselm is rightly regarded as the founder of scholastic theology and was one of the first Church leaders to openly oppose the slave trade.

St Antoninus *Feast day: 2 September. Born in Syria, in the fourth century.* Antoninus rebuked those who worshipped stone idols, despite the fact that he was a stonemason by trade and the practice would have been to his financial advantage. He retired for two years to live as a hermit before feeling compelled to return to his village and destroy the pagan idols there. He was chased out of town and went to Apamea where the bishop asked him to build a church. Antoninus did so, but this so infuriated the pagan population that a riot broke out and he was brutally killed.

St Antony of Egypt *Feast day: 17 January. Born in Aama, south of Memphis, near Thebes, 251; died in 356.* Patron of swineherds. Antony led a sheltered life as a child, but upon the death of his parents he gave away most of his considerable inheritance to the poor, keeping only a little for himself and his sister to live on. He spent most of his time in manual labour, prayer and reading. Antony would also seek out holy hermits wherever he could find them, so as to learn from their example and teaching.

He retreated into the desert in 272 and lived an ascetic life in solitude. He occupied himself by gardening and making mats, but was sought out by many who were seeking spiritual advice. Though he greatly preferred the solitary life, in 305 he founded his first monastery at Fayum, consisting of a group of cells for those who wished to live in a similar way.

He was a great friend of a fellow ascetic and desert dweller **St Paul the Hermit**. They would meet annually and share a meal, which was miraculously provided by ravens. At the time of Paul's death, when Antony came to visit, he found that two lions had dug a hole for Paul's grave so that the aged Antony would be saved this labour.

When Antony died he had asked that his burial place be kept secret but some two centuries later his relics were discovered and taken to Alexandria. **St Athanasius** greatly respected Antony and wrote an account of his life.

St Antony of Padua *Feast day: 13 June. Born in Lisbon, Portugal, 1195; died in 1231. Canonized in 1232 by Pope Gregory IX.* Patron of lost objects. Antony was a prayerful and studious young man. Deeply moved by the sight of the mutilated bodies of five Franciscans who had been killed in Morocco, he decided to go there and become a martyr also, if God so willed.

His ship, however, was blown off course to Sicily and from there he travelled to Assisi, where he joined the Franciscan brothers. His attractive personality and gift of simplicity made him an ideal communicator, and he would profess his faith at every opportunity. The Pope had a high regard for his holiness and learning, and he acted as envoy to the Holy See on behalf of the Franciscan order.

Antony died in Padua where he had experienced a sympathetic response to his preaching.

St Anysia *Feast day: 30 December. Born in Salonika, Greece; died in 304.* Anysia was a wealthy young Christian woman who gave generously to the poor. While on her way to worship, she was confronted in the street by a soldier who asked where she was going. Startled by the roughness of his approach, she made the sign of the cross on her forehead and he angrily tried to compel her to attend a pagan sacrifice. When she resisted, he killed her with his sword.

St Aphraates *Feast day: 7 April. Born in Persia; died in 345.* Aphraates was a Christian convert who travelled to Edessa in Mesopotamia seeking to serve God more fully there. This led him to become a hermit and lead a solitary life. The rise of Arianism* caused him to leave his cell to help in ministering to the faithful remnant that had been expelled from the churches. He survived attempted murder for this public stance.

He earned the nickname 'the Persian sage' and wrote extensively in defence of the faith. His best know work, entitled 'Demonstrations', is the oldest existing document of the Syrian Church.

St Apollinaris *Feast day: 8 January. Born in Phrygia; died in 179.* Apollinaris was Bishop of Hieropolos, famous for his writings in defence of the Christian religion. He beseeched the Emperor Marcus Aurelius to discontinue the persecution of the Church, reminding him of the famous victory that his own 'Thundering Legion' had won. This legion, which consisted almost entirely of Christian soldiers, had been trapped by barbarians in a waterless plain and was in danger of dying of thirst when, after much prayer, a mighty thunderstorm came to their aid. Not only did this provide the soldiers with much needed drinking water, but the lightning also blinded and confused the opposing force, causing them to flee.

The emperor subsequently published an edict forbidding anyone to be persecuted because of his or her Christian religion. This was not totally effective but the situation improved markedly for Christian believers for a time.

St Apollo *Feast day: 25 January. Born in Egypt, 300; died in 395.* Apollo was a hermit who spent 40 years in the desert region around Thebes, before going on to found a strong monastic community, which by 380 had grown to include 500 members. The monks dressed in coarse white habits and received daily exhortations to holy living along with Holy Communion.

Well known as a miracle worker, Apollo was able to produce a continuous multiplication of bread for his community and the surrounding population during a period of desperate famine.

St Armogastes and Companions *Feast day: 29 March. Died in 455.* Armogastes was the Christian servant of the son of the Vandal king, Geiseric. When the monarch renounced his Christianity and returned to his pagan roots, he insisted that Armogastes renounce his faith also. When he refused, he was tortured many times but refused to recant. Geiseric, who had been warned of the dangers of making a martyr of him, duly banished him to the mines. Armogastes was later ordered to become a cowherd near Carthage. He remained there for the rest of his days living a humble and prayer-filled life.

St Arnulf *Feast day: 18 July. Born in France; died in 640.* Arnulf took Doda to be his wife. They had a son called Ansegilius who when he grew up married **Begga**, the daughter of Pepin of Landen, thus starting the Carolingian dynasty of France. Doda became a nun and Arnulf had made plans to enter a monastery but before he could fulfil his plan, he was named Bishop of Metz around 616. He continued his court services, making Clotaire of Neustria the King of Austrasia. He also served as counsellor to Dagobert, King Clotaire's son. In 626 Arnulf retired to a hermitage at Remiremont, France.

St Arnulf *Feast day: 15 August. Born in Flanders, Belgium, in 1040; died in 1087.* Arnulf had a distinguished military career in the service of the kings of France. Retiring to France as a hermit, he attached himself to the monastery of Saint-Michel in Soissons. Reluctantly he became abbot and, with similar reticence, was later appointed Bishop of Soissons in 1081. He tried his best but the position proved to be a great burden to him. When a rival made a claim to the see, Arnulf regarded this as a divine sign and returned to the monastic life. He founded the Abbey of Onendbourg in France.

St Arsacius *Feast day: 16 August. Born in Persia; died in 358.* Arsacius was a member of the Roman army and keeper of the royal zoo. He was imprisoned for a time because of his Christian faith and following release, retired to a small tower near Nicomedia. He had a vision concerning an impending earthquake and rushed immediately to warn the authorities and to beseech the clergy and people to pray for their town.

On August 24, 358 an earthquake did indeed occur destroying most of Nicomedia and Arsacius' tower was one of the few buildings left standing. Some sought refuge there and his dead body was discovered, still in the attitude of prayer.

St Arsenius the Great *Feast day: 19 July. Born in Rome, Italy, 354; died in 450.* Arsenius was a Roman deacon and tutor of the children of Emperor Theodosius I. He served at Theodosius' court in Constantinople for about ten years before becoming a monk in Alexandria, Egypt. After inheriting a fortune from a relative, Arsenius studied with St John the Dwarf who initially treated him extremely rudely. When the former courtier accepted this treatment graciously and without complaint, he was then formally and respectfully received. He became a hermit in the desert of Egypt and, while never refusing to give spiritual help, generally avoided the company of his fellow monks. In 434 he went to the rock of Troe near Memphis, Egypt, and finally moved to the island of Canopus near Alexandria, where he remained until he died. He was known to frequently exhibit the spiritual gift of tears.

St Artaldus *Feast day: 7 October. Born in the castle of Sothonod in Savoy, 1101; died in 1206.* Artaldus became a Carthusian monk at Portes. After spending many years there, both as a priest and an experienced monk, he was sent to found a charterhouse near his home. The Pope used to consult with him on difficult matters much as he had done his master **St Bruno** before. He was called from his monastery to be Bishop of Belley, in spite of his being over 80 years old. He resigned two years later and returned to Arvieres, where he lived in peace for the rest of his days.

During his last years he was visited by **St Hugh of Lincoln** who gently rebuked him for taking an undue interest in political gossip. Hugh reminded Artaldus that he was in a community that had turned its back on the world, and did not respond to any of his enquires about non-spiritual matters.

St Artemius *Feast day: 20 October. Died in 363.* Even though Artemius was a supporter of the followers of the heretic Arius for a time he is still considered a saint.

Artemius was an army officer in Constantine's army and was made imperial prefect of Egypt. When the Arian* supporter George the Cappadocian was placed on the Episcopal throne of Alexandria, **Athanasius** went into hiding. Artemius' duty was to find him, which he tried exceedingly hard to do, persecuting many orthodox believers in the process.

However as Governor of Egypt he was no less zealous against paganism, destroying many of their temples, images and idols. When Julian the Apostate became emperor, he received many complaints about Artemius and thus the very man who had led the persecution against the orthodox Christians now found himself persecuted, and eventually was regarded as a hero by faithful believers. Latterly he was deprived of his property and beheaded.

St Asaph *Feast day: 1 May. Born in Wales; died in 600.* Asaph lived in a hermitage in Tenegel, near Holywell. While still a youth, Asaph served Kentigern and, when asked to bring Kentigern a piece of wood for the fire, Asaph brought live coals in his apron instead. This event first drew Kentigern's attention to Asaph's special gifts. He became the successor to **St Kentigern** as Bishop of Llanelwy, when the former was recalled to his role as bishop in Strathclyde in 573.

St Asclas *Feast day: 23 January. Born in Egypt; died in 287.* Asclas was tortured and imprisoned by Arrian the Governor of Egypt during the persecutions of Emperor Diocletian for boldly confessing his Christian faith. Later, when Arrian tried to cross the Nile in a boat, he found himself unable to do so. Asclas got a message to him that unless he acknowledged Christ in writing, he would never cross the Nile. Frustrated at his lack of progress, Arrian complied, acknowledging the God of the Christians as the only true God, and the boat quickly reached the other bank. Once safe, however, Arrian commanded that Asclas be tortured again, tied to a stone, and thrown into the Nile.

St Asicus *Feast day: 27 April. Born in Ireland; died in 490.* Asicus, a coppersmith, became one of **St Patrick**'s first disciples and was appointed as the first Abbot-Bishop of Elphin Monastery in Roscommon, Ireland. Believing himself unworthy of the office because he had told a lie, he resigned and retired to become a hermit on an island in Donegal Bay. After seven years of searching, his brother monks discovered where he had hidden himself and persuaded him to return to Elphimbut. Sadly Asicus died on the return journey.

St Astius *Feast day: 7 July. Born in Macedonia; died in 117.* Astius was the Bishop of Dynhachium in Macedonia during the reign of Emperor Trajan. He was seized by the Roman authorities and crucified for his faith. A group of believers who expressed sympathy for him were arrested and also martyred by being wrapped in chains and thrown into the sea from the deck of a galley.

St Athanasia *Feast day: 15 August. Born on the Island of Aegina, Greece; died in the eighth century.* Athanasia was drawn to the religious life at an early age but, at her parents' request, she agreed to marry an army officer. Her husband was killed in battle against the Saracens only 16 days after the wedding.

Her second marriage was to a deeply religious layman; they led Bible studies in their home and cared for the destitute, sick and poor. By mutual agreement, her husband became a monk and she a nun. The small community she had joined later moved to Timia where she became widely known for miraculous healings. In order to escape those who constantly sought her out demanding help, Athanasia had to flee to Constantinople and it was while there she became an advisor to Empress Theodora.

In later life she heeded the appeals of her sisters and returned to join them at Timia, staying with them until she died.

St Athanasius *Feast day: 2 May. Born in Alexandria, Egypt in 296; died in 373.* Athanasius was educated in his hometown by various scholars, including Alexander, who in 313 succeeded **Achillas** as Bishop of Alexandria. Two years after this, Athanasius went to the desert to spend some with **St Antony of Egypt** and other desert fathers.

Even as a deacon he was active against the Arian heresy* which was openly taught in Egypt from about 323, and he continued this struggle for orthodoxy, sometimes without almost any support, for most of his long life. The supporters of Arius cleverly embodied his doctrines in songs and hymns set to popular tunes and these became widely popular.

Athanasius attended the council of Nicea in 325 as an assistant to his bishop and when Alexander died the following year, he was the obvious and unanimous choice to succeed him.

His opposition to the Arian heresy involved him in much hardship and his opponents tried to have him removed from office several times by bringing false charges against him, including sedition, theft, and even murder. Though Athanasius was clearly innocent his outspoken defence seems to have upset the emperor and as a result he was forced to flee to the safety of the desert and live among the monks there. He was exiled on five occasions and spent 17 of the 46 years of his episcopate in exile.

Despite several close encounters with the authorities, he always managed to evade capture. On one occasion, when he and his companions were on a boat on the Nile they noticed an imperial galley coming towards them. Unflustered Athanasius ordered that the boat be turned round and rowed towards it. The pursuers called out asking for information about the fugitive.

'He is not far off,' was the reply. 'Row fast and you will overtake him.' His bold tactic proved to be successful and he was able to escape capture once again.

Athanasius wrote a theological treatise entitled 'The Incarnation' in his younger days and towards the end of his life compiled an account of the life of his great friend and mentor St Antony of Egypt. After a life of virtue and suffering, which established his reputation as one of the greatest men of his time, he died in peace with the victory of orthodoxy assured.

St Athenodorus *Feast day: 18 October. Born in Neocaesarea, in Cappadocia; died in 269.* Athenodorus and his brother **St Gregory Thaumaturgus** were members of a prominent pagan family. They travelled to Caesarea with their sister in 223, planning to study law in Beirut, Lebanon. Origen was in Caesarea at the time, and he converted both Athenodorus and Gregory. Athenodorus was named bishop of a see in Pontus late in his life and was martyred in the persecutions of Emperor Aurelian.

St Attalas *Feast day: 10 March. Born in Burgundy, France; died in 627.* Attalas entered the monastic life under **St Columban**'s strict rule at the monastery of Luxeuil. The abbot selected him to go with him to Bobbio in Italy, where they founded a monastery on land donated by the King of Lombardy. On Columban's death, Attalas succeeded him as abbot but, once the authority of Columban was removed, the monks rebelled against the severity of the monastic discipline, which made life difficult for Attalas.

Towards the end of his life Attalas had a clear premonition of his death. This enabled him to prepare himself and his brother monks for his passage to eternity. He is best remembered for performing miracles and for his opposition to Arianism*.

St Atticus *Feast day: 8 January. Born in Sebaste; died in 425.* Atticus, who had been brought up in a heretical sect, was converted and ordained in Constantinople. He helped to depose **St John Chrysostom** from the see of Constantinople at the Council of the Oak in 405, becoming bishop in his place a year later. Eventually realizing his errors Atticus repented and submitted himself to the authority of the Pope.

He became a faithful servant of the people and a tireless foe of heretics. Pope **St Celestine I** was extremely impressed by his gifts and energy, and described him as 'a true successor of Chrysostom'.

St Atto *Feast day: 22 May. Born in Badajoz, Spain,1070; died in 1153.* Atto joined the Benedictine monastery at Vallambrosa, Italy, and eventually became the Abbot-General of the Vallambrosans and Bishop of Pistoia. He wrote the lives of St Gualbert and St Bernard of Parma, and a history of the shrine of Compostela in Spain.

St Attracta *Feast day: 11 August. Born in Ireland, sixth century.* Attracta was the strong-willed daughter of a noble Irish family. When her father opposed her religious vocation, she fled to **St Patrick** at Coolavin and made her religious vows to him. She founded a hospice at Killaraght on Lough Gara, where seven roads met, and became a hermit at Drum, near Boyle. She performed many miracles, including parting the waters to allow soldiers to escape, and using human hair to harness deer so they could do the heavy work that had been unjustly assigned to her.

St Aubin *Feast day: 1 March. Born in Brittany in 469; died in 549.* Aubin entered the monastery of Tincillac as a youth, was elected abbot at the age of 35, and went on to become the Bishop of Angers in 529. He was well known for his work in ransoming slaves and for his generosity to the poor and sick.

On one occasion Aubin pled with the local judge for the release of some criminals in the local prison but he was refused. Not to be defeated by mere words, he went to the front of the prison and prayed openly for their release. After several hours a landslide brought down part of the wall. The captives escaped, followed Albin to church, and repented of their former ways. He was known for his holiness and the many miracles he performed.

St Augustine of Canterbury *Feast day: 28 May. Born in Rome, Italy; died in 605.* Augustine was sent by **St Gregory the Great** to evangelize the British Isles in 597. Forty brother monks, including **St Lawrence of Canterbury**, accompanied him. On their journey to this new area of mission they heard terrifying stories of the ferocity of the Celts and this caused the group to hurry back to Rome in fear. But Gregory told Augustine that he had no choice but to go and so he set off again.

Once there Augustine spread the faith throughout England and one of his earliest converts was King Ethelbert who was baptized within a year of their arrival. Many of Ethelbert's subjects joined him in becoming Christians.

Augustine was ordained Bishop of Gaul by the Archbishop of Arles, and appointed as the first Archbishop of Canterbury. Although he was unable to reconcile the differences that existed between the customs of the Celtic and Latin Churches, he was one of the first to encourage meaningful contact between these two traditions.

Anglican Archbishops of Canterbury are still referred to as occupying the Chair of Augustine.

St Augustine of Hippo *Feast day: 28 August. Born in Tagaste, North Africa in 354; died in Hippo, North Africa, 430.* Patron of brewers. Augustine was brought up as a Christian under the influence of his devout mother, **St Monica**. He abandoned his faith at an early age and led a wild life, full of false beliefs. Augustine moved to the city of Carthage, 'a cauldron of unholy loves', to become a teacher of rhetoric. There he began his quest for absolute wisdom. He attempted to read the scriptures but, due to a combination of a poor translation and personal arrogance, he dismissed them as worthless. During this period he took a Carthaginian woman as his concubine and remained faithful to her for 15 years, having a son by her.

After investigating and experimenting with several philosophies, he became a Manichaean*. Disturbed by the behaviour of the students in Carthage, he moved to Rome. Here he again became disillusioned with the emptiness of his life, and turned to the philosophy of Platonism. He found this also to be an unsatisfying answer to his quest.

Though he was by now being gradually drawn towards the Christian faith, conversion was no simple process for Augustine. On moving to Milan he met **St Ambrose**, then bishop of that city, and was impressed by his kind demeanour and rhetorical skills. He was intellectually convinced by Ambrose's preaching but his passions remained untamed.

Augustine graphically described his conversion, which took place under a fig tree in a spacious garden in Rome, in his book *The Confessions*. He had been weeping profusely out of desperation, when he heard a voice say, 'Take up and read.' On opening the Bible, his eyes fell on the verses from Paul's letter to the Romans 13:13–14. Before he had finished reading, the darkness of doubt had vanished, and soon after Bishop Ambrose baptized him. This was in the year 387. Augustine was ordained priest at Hippo in North Africa in 391 and consecrated as bishop four years later.

He was especially renowned for two books, *The Confessions* and *The City of God*. His collected sermons and Bible commentaries still attract attention and he is much quoted by preachers.

St Austreberta *Feast day: 10 February. Born in Therouanne, Artois, France, 630; died in 704.* Austreberta was the daughter of the Count Palatine Badefrid and St Framechildis. Faced with an unwanted marriage, Austreberta went secretly to **St Omer** who gave her the veil, the symbol of the consecrated virgin. She convinced her family that her vocation was genuine and with their permission entered the convent of Abbeville, Port-sur-Somme. In the course of time she was elected abbess and helped reform the convent of Pavilly. She was widely known for her visions and miracles.

St Autbert *Feast day: 10 September. Born in France; died in 725.* Autbert, the Bishop of Avranches, France, had a vision of **St Michael the Archangel** bidding him to found the now famous monastery of Mont St Michel on the Normandy coast. The work was exceedingly difficult and tiring but, with the encouragement of subsequent confirming visions, he was encouraged to go on and complete the building. The church was finally completed in 709 and dedicated to St Michael and to those in peril on the sea.

St Auxentius *Feast day: 14 February. Born in Persia; died in 473.* Auxentius was son of a Persian named Addas, and a member of the entourage of Emperor Theodosius II in Constantinople. He retired from military service and became a monk in Constantinople. When people began to praise him he became greatly distressed and withdrew to Mount Oxia near Chalcedon to become a hermit. But peace and solitude eluded him there as people continued to flock to him, bringing their sick for his prayers – through which many experienced healing. When asked to pray for someone's healing Auxentius would turn aside and object: 'I also am a sinful man.' But if pressed, he would encourage everyone present to pray for the healing of the sick person or, failing that, he would say over the head of the patient: 'The Lord Jesus Christ heals you.'

He was accused of heresy and summoned to the Council of Chalcedon for examination. After giving evidence on his own behalf he was cleared of all charges. Following this he withdrew to Mount Skopa, near Chalcedon and set up his hermitage there. Many disciples found their way there, drawn by his holy life and profound teaching.

St Aventanus *Feast day: 25 February. Born in Limoges, France; died at Luca, Italy in 1380.* Aventanus joined the Carmelites as a lay brother. He began a pilgrimage to the Holy Land, along with another Carmelite brother called Romaeus. Unfortunately, while crossing the Alps, they encountered many severe difficulties, including an outbreak of plague, which fatally infected Aventanus and he died soon after. Aventanus was known to have had a gift of ecstasies, miracles, and visions.

B

St Babylas *Feast day: 24 January. Born in Turkey; died in 250.* Babylas became the Bishop of Antioch, Turkey, about 240. **St John Chrysostom** records that Babylas refused permission for Emperor Philip the Arab to enter his church until he had done penance for having murdered his predecessor, Gordian III.

Babylas was arrested during the persecutions of Emperor Trajanus Decius, and died while awaiting execution. In 351 his relics were taken to Daphne, a few miles away, to counter the influence of the cult of Apollo that thrived there. This proved successful, and the relics were returned to their original resting place a dozen years later.

St Bagnus *Feast day: 20 June. Born in northern France; died in 710.* Bagnus was a disciple of St Wandrille, and became a Benedictine monk at Fontenelle Abbey in France. In 689 he was named as Bishop of Thérouanne and set about evangelizing the northern coastal region around modern Calais. After 12 years he resigned his See and returned to Fontenelle to live the simple monastic life. After only three years' respite, however, he was obliged to accept the role of abbot there and he also went on to govern Fleury Abbey.

St Baldomerus *Feast day: 27 February. Born in Lyon, France; died in 650.* Patron of locksmiths. Baldomerus was a locksmith who lived in great poverty and spent his spare time in prayer and spiritual reading. He gave generously to the poor and, on at least one occasion, sold his tools to provide succour for the poor. Abbot Viventius of the monastery of St Justus in Lyon was much impressed by his sanctity and invited him to join the brothers there. Baldormerus was regularly visited by wild birds; they showed no fear of him and readily ate directly from his hand.

St Baldred *Feast day: 6 March. Born in Ireland; died at Aldaam, Scotland, 756.* Baldred was an Irish Benedictine hermit from Lindisfarne who spent a solitary life in the border regions of northern England. At one time he lived in a cell on the Bass Rock in the Firth of Forth. Legend tells of a dangerous rock which was the cause of many shipwrecks in the Firth. Out of compassion, Baldred went out to the rock and stood upon it till it began to float to the shore like a small boat blown by the wind. A rock, known as St Baldred's rock, is still identifiable today on the shore of the Firth.

He lived a life of great asceticism and went to Tynningham on the Scottish border to live in retirement.

St Balin *Feast day: 3 September. Born in Saxony in the seventh century.* Balin was the handsome and well-beloved son of an Anglo-Saxon king, a disciple of **St Colman** of Lindisfarne, and a brother of St Gerald of

Balm. He accompanied Colman to Iona, in Scotland, and then took up residence in Connaught, Ireland.

St Bandaridus *Feast day: 9 August. Born in France; died in 556.* Bandaridus was made Bishop of Soissons, France in 540. He founded Crepin Abbey and diligently served his see until he was banished as a result of a dispute with the ruling authorities. He travelled to England and became a gardener in an abbey, living there anonymously. After seven years he was recognized, recalled by the king, and instructed to resume his ministry, which he obediently did.

St Barbara *Feast day: 4 December. Born in the fourth century.* Barbara was very beautiful in both appearance and nature. Her jealous and demented father kept her in a secluded tower which he had built especially for that purpose. During her period of captivity she devoted herself to prayer and to the study of scriptures, and was able to receive baptism in secret.

This was in a time of persecution for Christians, and when her father discovered that she was a Christian, he was furious and betrayed her to the authorities. Barbara was horribly tortured, and then beheaded, her own father acting as executioner. He was killed moments later by a flash of lightning.

St Barbasymas *Feast day: 14 January. Born in Persia; died at Ludan in Huzistan in 346.* Barbasymas was made Bishop of Seleucia and Ctesiphon in 342 during the persecution of the Sassanid King Shapur II, and was arrested along with 16 of his priests. They were imprisoned and tortured in an attempt to try to persuade them to take part in sun worship. Barbasymas was offered a cup filled with gold coins, and even a governorship, in return for his renunciation of the Christian religion, but he and all the others steadfastly refused every attempt to bribe or coerce them. All 17 were beheaded.

St Barbatus *Feast day: 19 February. Born in Benevento, Italy, 612; died in 682.* After being ordained in Marcona, Barbatus was sent to Benevento, which was, at that time, a place steeped in pagan practices. He confidently predicted that the siege by Byzantine Emperor Constans II in 663 would end when the city rejected their pagan ways. He felled a sacred tree then melted down a golden snake, which had been an object of worship, and fashioned it into a chalice. Just as he had foretold, the siege ended. Barbatus was named Bishop of Benevento in succession to St Hildebrand. He attended the Council of Constantinople in 680.

St Bardo *Feast day: 15 June. Born in Oppershafen, Wetterau, Germany, 982; died in 1053.* Bardo was educated at Fulda Abbey, and went on to become a Benedictine monk and the abbot of two monasteries. He was appointed Archbishop of Mainz in 1031, and also served as chancellor and chief distributor of alms for the empire. He was so serious and strict that the Pope (**St Leo IX**) urged him to work less hard and to relax some of his personal austerities and mortifications. He was not without humility and on one occasion, overhearing a young man at his table making fun of his earnestness, he stopped the conversation, fixed the youth with his gaze, and then presented him with a special gift of some choice food.

St Barhadbescaba *Feast day: 20 July. Born in Persia; died in 355.* Barhadbescaba was a deacon in Arbela who was caught up in the persecution conducted by the Sassanid King Shapur II, which began in 340. He was tortured by the governor of Adiabene region (modern Iran) but refused to renounce his faith. Aggai, an apostate Christian, was ordered to behead Barhadbescaba, but he trembled so much that even after seven attempts he could not sever the head. Finally Aggai had to slay him by running him through with a sword.

St Barlaam *Feast day: 19 November. Born in Antioch, Cappadocia; died in 304.* Barlaam was a strong and fervent Christian of uncouth and rough appearance who lived in a small village near Antioch. He was arrested and imprisoned because of his continual refusal to offer sacrifices to the pagan deities. The prefect, desperate not to be beaten by such an uncouth fellow, devised a plan: he filled Barlaam's hand with hot coals covered with incense, and forced him to hold them over the pagan altar. His intention was that Barlaam would be forced to shake the coals out of his hand and spill incense onto the altar, thus being said to have paid tribute to the gods. To his persecutor's frustration, Barlaam refused to release the coals allowing them to burn deep into his hands instead. His persecutors were finally forced to slay him.

St Barlaam *Feast day: 6 November. Born in Novgorod, Russia; died in 1193.* Barlaam was born into a wealthy family and was christened Alexis. Following the death of his parents, he became a hermit at Khutyn near the Volga.

As his fame spread so many disciples wanted to join him there that he felt obliged to found a monastery. His original wooden chapel was rebuilt in stone to serve as a church for the community and it was dedicated to the Transfiguration. Following the completion of the construction Barlaam nominated a fellow monk, named Antony, to succeed him and died soon after.

St Barnabas *Feast day: 11 June. Born in Cyprus; died at Salamis, 61.* Barnabas was originally called Joseph. He is first mentioned in the Acts of the Apostles because of his willingness to sell some of his property and give the whole amount to the Apostles. They gave him the name Barnabas which means 'son of encouragement'.

He accompanied **St Paul** on some of his missionary journeys. Following a dispute concerning the reliability of his cousin John Mark, they parted company. Paul continued with his travels leaving Barnabas and Mark to return to Cyprus. Barnabas founded the Cypriote Church and went on to preach in both Alexandria and Rome before finally being stoned to death.

St Barnard *Feast day: 23 January. Born in Province of Lyonnais, France, 777; died in 841. Canonized in 1907 by Pope Pius X.* Barnard was educated at the court of Charlemagne, before becoming a Benedictine monk. He restored Ambronay Abbey and eventually became abbot there. Barnard was made Archbishop of Vienne, in the Rhône valley, and while he did not always act wisely in relation to political disturbances, his integrity, discipline and faithfulness were never called into question. He founded Romans Abbey in 837, and ended his life there.

St Barsanuphius *Feast day: 11 April. Born in Egypt; died in 550.* Barsanuphius maintained his hermitage near a monastery in Gaza. He was renowned for his holiness and wisdom, and communicated only in writing. Though leading an austere life himself, he counselled others always to eat, drink, sleep and clothe themselves in moderation. A constant theme of his writings was the forgiveness of sins.

St Bartholomew *Feast day: 24 August. Born in Cana, Israel in the first century; died at Abanopolis, on the Caspian Sea.* Bartholomew was one of the 12 disciples of Jesus. His name means 'son of Tolomai', and he was also known as Nathanael. After the outpouring of the Holy Spirit at Pentecost (Acts 2), he preached in India and Greater Armenia, and also in Mesopotamia, Persia and Egypt. While on a mission at Derbend, on the west coast of the Caspian Sea, Bartholomew was taken prisoner by King Astyages, flayed and finally beheaded.

St Basil the Great *Feast day: 14 June. Born in Caesarea of Cappadocia, 330; died in 379. Doctor and Patriarch of the Eastern Church.* Basil was one of ten children of St Basil the Elder and St Emmelia. His siblings included **St Gregory of Nyssa**, **St Macrina the Younger** and St Peter of Sebastea.

After being educated in Caesarea, Constantinople and Athens, where he became firm friends with his fellow student **St Gregory of Nazianzus**, Basil opened a school of oratory in Caesarea and practised law there before becoming a monk and founding a monastery in the wilderness at Pontus.

His monastic rule proved to be the most lasting of those developed in Eastern Christianity. He was ordained in 363 and made Bishop of Caesarea in 370, playing a major part in the defeat of Arianism* at the Council of Constantinople in 381. A man of great personal holiness, he fought corruption of all sorts vigorously, and is revered as one of the greatest orators in the history of the Christian Church.

St Bathildis *Feast day: 30 January. Born in England; died at Celles, France, 680.* Bathildis was an Anglo-Saxon slave girl in the household of

Erchinoald, the mayor of the Frankish Imperial Palace. She quickly won the favour of the prince, and also of the older women of the court as she washed their feet, looked after their daily needs, and generally cared for them in every way.

Bathildis attracted the attention of the King of France, Clovis II, and in the year 649, they were married. She bore him three sons. As queen, Bathildis used her influence to aid Abbot Genesius, who later became Bishop of Lyon, and she gave generously to the poor.

On the death of King Clovis in 657, she acted as regent for their eldest son Clotaire III, founded the monasteries of Corbie and Chelles, and helped end the practice of selling Church appointments. Bathildis also suppressed the slave trade, of which she herself had been a victim, and redeemed many slaves.

As a result of a plot by Bishop Sigebrandus, in 667, she retired to the Monastery of Chelles, and remained there under the authority of Abbess Berthille until her death 13 years later.

St Baudelius *Feast day: 20 May. Born in Orleans, France; died in 380.* Baudelius was a married missionary who preached the gospel in the region of Nimes in France. Baudelius was beheaded for daring to interrupt a festival in honour of the Roman deity, Jupiter.

St Bavo *Feast day: 1 October. Born in Hesbaye, Brabant; died in 655.* Bavo was a nobleman who as a youth had lived a wild, selfish, undisciplined life. On hearing **St Amand** preach at Ghent, he was converted, gave all his money to the poor, and entered the monastery there.

Bavo accompanied Amand on his missionary journeys in France and Flanders, and was known especially for his humble heart, and strong self-discipline. When Amand eventually gave him permission to live as a hermit, he chose the hollow trunk of a large tree for his cell and survived mainly on vegetables. It was only later that he built a more permanent hermitage at Mendonck. Before his conversion Bavo had sold several of his servants as slaves to other nearby estates in the area. As a sign of public penance for having done so he sought out one of his former servants and had the man lead him by a chain to the local jail.

Bavo built himself a new cell in a wood near to the monastery and died there peacefully some years later.

St Beatus *Feast day: 9 May. Born in England; died in 112. Designated as Apostle of Switzerland.* A monk and hermit who had been baptized by **St Barnabas** and ordained by **St Peter**, Beatus went to Switzerland where he lived and died in a cave on Mount Beatenburg above Lake Thun. It was at this site that Beatus had a legendary battle with a dragon, and it became a popular pilgrimage site.

The Venerable Bede *Feast day: May 25. Born in Wearmouth-Jarrow, England; died in 735. Canonized in 1899 by Pope Leo XIII.* At the age of seven Bede was entrusted to the care of monks. He was made a deacon at the age of 19 and was ordained when he was 30. Most of his life was devoted to teaching and writing and the study of Scripture. One of the most learned men of his time, he is best known for the *Historia Ecclesiastica* that contains his account of Christianity in England up to 729.

Bede was called 'Venerable' because of his wisdom and careful scholarship; he was the first to date events *Anno Domini* (AD).

St Bega *Feast day: 31 October. Born in Ireland in the seventh century; died in England.* A princess of Ireland, Bega chose to flee the royal court rather than marry a prince from Norway. She was miraculously transported to Cumberland, England where she lived for a time as an anchoress, being fed by the wild birds, but the king of Northumbria, concerned for her safety, advised her to consider being part of a religious community. **St Aidan** received her vows as a nun and Bega founded St Bee's Monastery, which became a cell of the Benedictine Abbey of St Mary of York. She served as abbess there until she died.

St Begga *Feast day: 17 December. Born in Landen, near Brussels; died in 691.* The daughter of the palace mayor and his wife St Itta, Begga married Ansegilius, son of **St Arnulf** of Metz. Their son, Pepin of Herstal, was the founder of the Carolingian dynasty of rulers in France.

Following a long and happy marriage Ansegilius died. Begga built seven chapels representing the seven churches of Rome and established a convent at Andenne on the River Meuse where she became the abbess. She lived out the rest of her days there.

St Benedict *Feast day: 21 March. Born in Nursia in Sabine, Italy, 480; died in 547.* Patron of speleologists (cave explorers). Named Patron Protector of Europe by Pope Paul VI in 1964. Benedict was sent to Rome to study rhetoric but was appalled at the degradation he found there. He fled the city for a life of prayer and the pursuit of holiness as a hermit.

Three years later a group of monks persuaded him to become their leader, but his rule of discipline proved too strict for them and they attempted to get rid of him by poisoning his drink. On sitting down at table, however, Benedict followed his usual custom of making the sign of the cross over his food, and the cup broke into pieces. He left the others and returned to his cave, but in the following years many more asked for his help, and in due course he set up 12 monastic institutions with a dozen monks in each.

Yet again jealous outsiders verbally attacked his leadership and Benedict moved away once more, this time to found a monastery at Monte Cassino. He set about this new work with a 40-day fast, and then began to preach the gospel to the local population. With their help, he pulled down a temple to Apollo which topped the nearby hill. Benedict gathered his disciples into a single community and his new enterprise became the centre of the Church's monastic system. His twin sister, **St Scholastica**, settled nearby to live a solitary religious life.

Benedict's simple rule involved a life of moderate asceticism, study and work, all based around regular periods of prayer. Benedict strongly encouraged Scripture memorization and used the Psalms as prayers. He regarded prayer as a 'work of God' and instructed his followers to practise sacred reading known as *lectio divina* for up to six hours a day. He foretold his own death and was buried in the same grave as his sister **St Scholastica**, on the site of the altar of Apollo which he had torn down.

St Benedict II *Feast day: 7 May. Died in Rome, 685.* Benedict was known for his humility and generosity. He was an ordained priest and gained great fame for his knowledge of the Scriptures and his singing voice. Following the death of Pope Leo II in 684 he was chosen to be Pope. Benedict obtained a decree from the Emperor Constantine Pogonatus that freed the Church from some state controls, and adopted Constantine's two sons. He helped to suppress Monothelitism*, and was a strong supporter of **St Wilfrid** of York.

St Benedict Biscop *Feast day: 12 January. Born Northumbria England, 628; died in 690. Canonized in 1807 by Pope Pius VII.* Biscop Baducing served as a soldier in the army of King Oswui of Northumbria until he was 25. He then made the first of what were to be four pilgrimages to Rome.

Returning from his second visit, he brought with him **Theodore of Canterbury**, the newly appointed Archbishop of Canterbury, and it was after this trip that he took the monastic name Benedict.

On his fourth trip, he recruited stonemasons and glass workers and brought them back with him to begin work on the building of his first monastery at Wearmouth. He also created cultural ties between Britain and the Continent by collecting books and pictures on his travels and bringing them back to England.

St Benedict the Black *Feast day: 4 April. Born in Messina, Italy; died c.1589. Canonized in 1807 by Pius VII.* Patron of African Americans. Benedict was the son of African slaves working in Italy. Freed by his master, he decided to follow a life of prayer, and eventually settled with a group of hermits at Montepellegrino. In due course he was appointed to be their new leader. However Pope Pius IV gave instructions that this group be disbanded and Benedict became a Franciscan lay brother and cook at a convent near Palermo. Though illiterate, he was appointed against his will to be superior of the convent at Palermo and then to the role of novice master. He requested permission to return to being the cook and after he had served his term, this request was granted. Benedict never referred to possessions as 'mine' but always 'ours'. His humble approach to the monastic life only served to increase his reputation for sanctified wisdom, and people flocked to visit him in increasing numbers.

St Benedict the Hermit *Feast day: 23 March. Died in Italy, 550.* Benedict was a solitary monk who lived in the Italian countryside at the time of **St Benedict** of Nursia. He was captured by the Goths when they invaded Italy under the leadership of Totila. Benedict was shut up in an oven but survived the ordeal and was liberated the next day, totally unharmed.

St Benignus *Feast day: 9 November. Born in Ireland; died at Feringmere, England in 467.* Benignus was the son of Sessenen, who was a disciple and psalm singer to **St Patrick**. He was superior of the Abbey at Drumlease, and succeeded Patrick as Chief Bishop of Ireland. His missionary endeavours took him throughout counties Clare, Kerry and Connaught. Benignus resigned in 460 and followed Patrick to England. He retired to a solitary place, stuck his staff into the ground and when it burst into leaf and bud, built his hut there.

St Benjamin *Feast day: 31 March. Born in Persia; died in 421.* A zealous Christian bishop in Persia named Abdas was scandalized by the worship of false gods at the so-called 'Temple of Fire', and burned it to the ground. King Isdegerd was furious, and threatened to destroy all the churches unless the bishop agreed to rebuild the temple. He steadfastly refused, whereupon the churches were demolished, he was put to death, and a period of 40 years of persecution began. Christians were subjected to the cruellest tortures, and Benjamin was among those who suffered violent persecution. He was a deacon who had been imprisoned for his faith and was released on condition that he did no more Christian proselytizing.

However Benjamin believed that it was his duty to preach about Christ and continued to do so. He was rearrested and brought before the king. Though horribly tortured, he refused to deny his faith, and finally a knotted stake was inserted into his bowels to tear him apart and he died in terrible agony.

St Bercharius *Feast day: 16 October. Born in Aquitaine, France; died c.696.* Archbishop St Nivard of Rheims recognized the potential of Bercharius and urged his parents to encourage his obvious faith. He became a Benedictine monk at Luxeuil, was ordained, and appointed to be the first abbot at Hautvilliers monastery that St Nivard had founded. He went on to found the monastery at Moutier-en-Der and a convent at Puellemontier. Bercharius' death was a tragic affair; he was stabbed in his sleep by Dagnin, a deranged monk whom he had disciplined. He died two days later, having personally forgiven his attacker.

St Berhtwald *Feast day: 9 January. Born in England: died in 731.* Berhtwald was an Anglo-Saxon, educated at Canterbury, who became a monk and later abbot of Reculver in Kent. He was elected Archbishop of Canterbury in 692 and consecrated at Lyon.

In 703, Berhtwald presided over the Synod of Austerfield (West Yorkshire), which deposed **St Wilfrid** from his See of York and forced him to hand over the monasteries under his control. Wilfrid appealed to the Pope and was eventually reinstated at the Synod of the River Nidd in 705.

St Bernadette *Feast day: 16 April. Born in Lourdes, France, 1843; died in 1879. Canonized in 1933 by Pope Gregory XVI.* Bernadette was a frail child, born into a poor family. She suffered from several ailments including digestive problems and painful attacks of asthma. At the age of 15 she had a vision of the Blessed Virgin Mary near the Massabielle grotto when gathering firewood with her sister and a friend. Bernadette experienced 17 further apparitions, during which she was told that she should pray for sinners, do penance and have a chapel built there. Many were sceptical at first, but following a vision, Bernadette uncovered a spring of water which began to flow strongly, and miracles were recorded by some of those who used the spring.

Always very humble and self-effacing, Bernadette became a nun in 1866. She likened herself to a broom, always ready to be used or set in a corner as required. She remained childlike all her life and did everything she could to avoid publicity.

St Bernard of Clairvaux *Feast day: 20 August. Born in Dijon, France, 1090; died in 1153. Canonized 1174 by Pope Alexander III. Doctor of the Church 1830.* Bernard was born into a large, well-off family. As a child he was extremely shy, but loved learning. He was sent to study as a secular canon at an early age. His winsome and powerful personality so attracted others to him that mothers hid their sons, wives their husbands, and companions their friends, for fear that they would be drawn away by his persuasive earnestness. Even so when Bernard decided to enter the monastic life, 31 companions, including four of his brothers, travelled to Citeaux to enrol in the Cistercian order along with him.

Three years later Bernard was sent with 12 others to found a new monastery at Langres in Champagne. Tireless in his pursuit of the Gospel, Bernard never lost his love of the solitary life although he was involved in controversy when Peter Aberlard, accused him of pride. Several bishoprics were offered to him, but he refused them all. His reputation spread far and wide, and he was invited to preach during the Second Crusade.

The expedition was ill-conceived and much criticism followed, but Bernard attributed this failure to the sins of the Crusaders. Bernard was known to exhibit the gift of miracles and, along with reform of the monastic system, he expressed a practical spirituality through his hymns and writings. His motto was 'To know Jesus and Jesus crucified'.

St Bernard of Parma *Feast day: 4 December. Born in Florence, Italy; died in 1133.* A member of the great Umberti family, Bernard chose to renounce excellent secular prospects in order to become a monk. He was abbot of the monastery San Salvio and was later chosen by Pope Paschal

II to be Bishop of Parma. This was at a time of great disturbance and conflict in the Church as a result of the informal appointment of two antipopes. Bernard was deposed by rivals and exiled from his see for two years.

Previous bishops of Parma had gradually accumulated temporal power and Bernard reversed the trend by ridding the Church of such distractions.

In 1127 the leaders of the Hohenstaufens proclaimed Conrad King of Germany. Bernard protested and was forced to flee once more.

St Bernardino Realino *Feast day: 2 July. Born in Capri, Italy, 1530; died in 1616.* Bernardino was given a Christian education by his devout mother before studying medicine at the University of Bologna, later switching to law. His reputation as a brilliant and dedicated student spread far and wide, and Bernardino was appointed auditor and lieutenant general to Naples at the early age of 24. Ten years later he felt called to join the Jesuit order and was ordained a priest in 1567.

A compassionate confessor and a powerful preacher, Bernardino's sincere and humble approach gained him great respect. He became rector of the Jesuit College in Lecce and also superior of the community until his death 42 years later. His kindness and compassion helped to end many of the vendettas and public scandals that had become all too common in Church circles.

On his deathbed, the city's magistrates requested that he would take the city under his protection. St Bernardino was too weak to respond but bowed his head in assent.

St Bernardino of Siena *Feast day: 20 May. Born in Massa Marittima, Tuscany, Italy, 1380; died in 1444.* Bernardino was a simple and chaste child known for his goodness. He was orphaned at the age of seven and brought up by a devout aunt.

When Siena experienced an outbreak of the plague in 1400, Bernardino immediately went to the largest hospital and began to help care for the victims. His selfless example encouraged other young men also to offer to tend the dying. However, Bernardino threw himself so completely into every task that he undertook that after four months he collapsed with exhaustion.

He joined the Franciscans in 1403 and was ordained a priest a year later. Even though his voice was naturally soft and weak, through prayer and perseverance he developed into a fine strong orator.

At the close of one of his missions in Milan, he was not allowed to leave without promising to return. Pius II called him a second Paul. He travelled throughout Italy on foot, preaching for hours at a time.

He became vicar general of the Franciscans in 1430 and worked hard to reform and renew that order. He then became a travelling preacher and teacher once again. During his last visit to his home town he preached for 50 days consecutively and died soon after on the way to another preaching engagement.

St Bernward *Feast day: 20 November. Born in Saxony, 987; died in 1022. Canonized in 1193 by Pope Celestine III.* Bernward was orphaned at an early age and brought up by his uncle Bishop Volkmar of Utrecht. He studied at the cathedral school of Heidelburg and at Mainz, before being ordained in 987. Appointed chaplain and tutor to the child of Emperor Otto III, Bernward was elected Bishop of Hildesheim in 993.

He had an interest in architecture and art, and created several metalwork pieces for St Michael's Church and monastery.

Bernward was in dispute for years with Archbishop Willigis of Mainz over Episcopal rights to the Gandersheim convent. Eventually Rome ruled in his favour and he became a Benedictine monk late in life.

St Bertharius *Feast day: 22 October. Born in France; died in 884.* A member of the royal house of France, Bertharius became the Benedictine Abbot of Monte Cassino, Italy in 856. He and several others were martyred in the monastery chapel by invading Saracens.

St Berthold *Feast day: 29 March. Born in Limoges, France c. 1195.* Berthold was a brilliant student at the University of Paris. After ordination, he joined the Crusades along with his brother, Aymeric, the Latin patriarch of Antioch, in Turkey.

Finding a group of hermits on Mount Carmel, he joined them, and established a rule which was to become the Carmelite Order. Berthold strived for the reform of the Christian soldiers in the region. His brother Aymeric appointed him the first superior general of the Carmelite order, a position which he held for 45 years.

St Bertinus *Feast day: 5 September. Born in Constance, France; died in 700.* Bertinus trained at the abbey of Luxeuil under the strict rule of **St Columban**. In 639, together with two other monks, he joined **St Omer**, Bishop of Therouanne, who had for two years been evangelizing the pagan Morini in the low-lying marshy country of the Pas-de-Calais. Here they founded the monastery of St Mommolin, and eight years later a second at Sithiu. Bertinus was abbot there for nearly 60 years during which time it gained a great reputation. Accordingly, after his death, it was called St Bertin and gave birth to the town of St Omer.

Bertinus practised the greatest austerities and was constant in prayer. He travelled widely, training others to preach, and chose **St Winoc** to found a monastery at Wormhoudt, near Dunkirk. Bertinus lived to be over 100 years old, and he died surrounded by his sorrowing brother monks.

His liturgical emblem is a small ship.

St Bessarion *Feast day: 17 June. Born in Egypt in the fourth century.* Bessarion was a disciple of **St Antony** and later of **St Macarius**. He wandered about without a permanent home, observing silence and undertaking frequent fasts. He once went 40 days without food, standing in prayer in the middle of a bramble patch.

He performed many miracles, including making salt water fresh, bringing rain during drought, and walking on the River Nile. In common with many other desert fathers, he wrestled with demons and lived to a great age.

St Bettelin *Feast day: 9 September. Born in Croyland, England, in the eighth century.* Patron of the town of Stafford. Bettelin was of noble birth and married an Irish princess. His wife went into labour and gave birth while they were travelling through a forest and when he went for help, a pack of wolves attacked and killed both mother and child. Following this traumatic event Bettelin became a hermit, learning much from the saintly **St Guthlac**, who gave him precious instruction. Bettelin left his hermitage only once to drive away usurping invaders.

St Bibiana *Feast day: 2 December. Born in Rome in the eighth century.* Bibiana was the daughter of Christian parents who were martyred for their faith. She and her sister Demetria were left destitute and remained in their house, spending their time in fasting and prayer.

Hunger appeared to have no effect on them, but when the two were brought to trial, Demetria bravely confessed her faith before falling dead at the feet of the judge. Bibiana was placed in the hands of an artful and scheming woman called Rufina, who used every conceivable means to destroy her faith, but failed completely. The frustrated authorities finally ordered that Bibiana be tied to a pillar and beaten, with scourges laden with lead plummets until she was dead.

St Bilfrid *Feast day: 6 March. Born in England in the eighth century.* Bilfrid was a Benedictine hermit on Lindisfarne, Northumbria, and a silversmith by trade. He aided Bishop Eaddfrid in preparing and binding the Lindisfarne Gospels (the Gospels of St Cuthbert), using gold, silver, and gems.

St Blaise *Feast day: 3 February. Born in Armenia in the fourth century.* Patron of throat illnesses, and wild animals. Blaise was born into a noble family and raised as a Christian. He was ordained priest and later became Bishop of Sebastea in Armenia. In a time of persecution, he fled to the mountains to live in a deserted cave. He was surrounded by wild animals and many of those who were sick or wounded were healed by Blaise. He was eventually tracked down and arrested by a group that was on an expedition to capture wild animals for the amphitheatre.

Blaise was tried and sentenced to be starved to death, but he received sustenance from those to whom he had previously shown mercy. He continued to strengthen his fellow prisoners, praying for them and healing them. On one occasion he resuscitated a child who was choking on a fish bone.

Since the lack of food did not seem to be weakening him, the governor had his flesh torn with wool combs, then he was beaten and beheaded. Blaise's symbol is a wool comb.

St Blandina *Feast day: 2 June. Born in Vienne, France; died in Rome, 177.* Patron of young girls. Blandina was a young slave girl who was arrested because of her faith during a time of violent Roman persecution of Christians in the region around Vienne and Lyon. **St Irenaeus,** who was a priest by this time, had been sent there by **St Polycarp** from Asia.

Blandina's mistress, who was a Christian also, had feared that Blandina lacked the strength to brave the torture, but she was proved very wrong. For though she was tortured for a whole day, her tormentors eventually gave up and she was bound up in a net and thrown before a wild bull. Her remains were burned and the ashes thrown in the River Tiber.

St Blane *Feast day: 11 August. Born on the Island of Bute, Scotland; Died in 590.* Blane studied in Ireland for seven years, and became a monk there. On his return to Scotland he was ordained and devoted himself to missionary work. He was consecrated bishop, made a pilgrimage to Rome, and is credited with performing miracles. He died at Kingarth, on Bute.

His monastery became the site of the cathedral of Dunblane, Scotland and the monastery bell is still preserved in that town.

St Bonaventure *Feast day:15 July. Born in Bagnorea in Tuscany, Italy, 1221; died in 1274. Canonized 1482 by Pope Sixtus IV.* Bonaventure received his name as a result of the joyful exclamation of **St Francis of Assisi,** '*O buona ventura*' (O good fortune). This happened as a result of a successful prayer that Francis had made for his deliverance from a dangerous childhood illness.

St Bonaventure entered the Franciscan Order at the age of 22.

He studied under the famous doctor, Alexander of Hales in Paris, earning for himself the title 'Seraphic Doctor'. He taught theology and Holy Scripture in Paris from 1248 to 1257 at a time when there was much rivalry between the monks and the more worldly clerics. Bonaventure defended the poverty of life of the Friars and was finally vindicated by Pope Alexander IV.

He studied alongside **St Thomas Aquinas** and they received their Doctorates of Theology together. Aquinas centred on academic theology while Bonaventure was more concerned with spiritual formation. His writings form the basis of the Franciscan theology, and he is considered the Second Founder of that Order.

Bonaventure was elected Minister General of the Franciscans in 1257 and he set out a constitution for the Order, so as to guard against lax practice.

He refused the role of bishop, but was eventually persuaded to be a cardinal in 1273. His contribution to the General Council of Lyon proved crucial in reuniting the Greek and Latin delegates, but he died suddenly in the night soon after the gathering had dispersed.

St Boniface (Wynfrith) *Feast day: 5 June. Born in Crediton, Devon, England, 680; died in 754.* Patron of Germany. Wynfrith was an Anglo-

Saxon of farming stock who was educated at Exeter, and then at Nursling Monastery. He compiled the first Latin Grammar in English and was known for his love of poetry and word puzzles. At the age of 30, having declined the office of abbot, Boniface set out for Rome where he was ordained, and called to mission work in central Germany. He changed his name from Wynfrith to Boniface at this time.

Miracles accompanied his primary missionary work. He destroyed pagan idols, baptized converts and asked English monasteries to send teachers to help establish churches. On one occasion in Bavaria, in order to show his disdain for the pagan gods, he felled a pagan sacred oak and preached to such great effect that many were converted. Even after he was appointed Archbishop of Mainz, his missionary zeal was not dampened.

By 741 the Church in France had fallen into great disarray and Boniface gladly accepted the opportunity to oversee its restoration. Within five years of his appointment the situation had been largely turned round.

He was a major influence on the history of the European Church and made sure of continuity by appointing his disciple St Lull to follow him.

While on a mission trip down the Rhine in 754, Boniface and a small group of his followers were set upon and murdered by a pagan rabble.

St Bosa *Feast day: 9 March. Born in Yorkshire, England; died in 705.* Bosa was a Benedictine monk of the monastery of **St Hilda** in Whitby, England. In 678, he was consecrated bishop by **St Theodore**. He was involved in **St Wilfrid**'s refusal to accept the division of the See of York and when Wilfrid was exiled by King Aldfrid in 691, Bosa became the bishop. The **Venerable Bede** described him as a man of 'singular merit and holiness' and 'a man beloved of God'.

St Botulph *Feast day: 17 June. Born in East Anglia; died in 680.* Sts Botulph and Adulph were two noble English brothers who travelled into Belgic Gaul to be educated in religious houses there. Adulph was made Bishop of Maestricht, which he administered in an effective and holy manner, while Botulph returned home and asked King Ethelmund for land on which to found a monastery. The king responded positively to his request and gave him Ikanho, a barren spot almost surrounded by water.

Botulph was a humble, mild, and affable man who was loved by everyone. He lived to a good age before dying peacefully. The Danes later destroyed his monastery, and so his relics transferred to the monastery of Ely.

Botulph's town, now Boston, in Lincolnshire, England, is named after him.

St Braulio *Feast day: 26 March. Born in Spain; died in 651.* Braulio was of noble birth, and studied at the college founded in Seville by **St Isadore**. He grew up to be so eminent a scholar that Isadore regarded him as a friend rather than a pupil, and used to send him his own writings to correct and revise. A faithful and successful pastor, he was chosen to be Bishop of Seville in 631.

He kept in close touch with Isadore, with whom he worked to restore Church order and discipline, and he took part in the fourth Council of Toledo. Braulio was a convincing and eloquent preacher who genuinely cared for the poor and needy.

Though he experienced failing eyesight in later life, his fine memory did not desert him and the last day of his life was spent reciting the Psalms.

St Brendan *Feast day: 16 May. Born in Tralee, Ireland, 486; died in 583.*
Educated by **St Ita** at Killeedy, Brendan was ordained by Bishop Erc. He became a monk and in 559 founded a large monastery at Clonfert in Galway, which quickly grew to over 3000 members.

Brendan is often referred to as 'the Navigator', and is best known because of a famous manuscript entitled 'Brendan's Voyage' which dates from the eighth century. This details the adventures that he and some of his monastic companions had while sailing in search of a beautiful land of promise known as 'the isles of the blessed'.

They made several voyages in skin-covered coracles to the islands of the West coast of Scotland, and beyond. He visited **St Columba** on Iona and also **St Gildas** in Britain, and it is quite possible that the monks did indeed manage to reach the shores of North America.

Brendan foresaw that he would not die at Clonfert and left clear instructions that should this happen, his body should be returned secretly to his home community disguised as luggage, and these orders were dutifully obeyed.

St Brice *Feast day: 13 November. Born in Toiraine, France; died in 444.*
St Brice was raised by **St Martin of Tours** at Marmoutier. He struggled with ambition, pride and self-interest for most of his life. St Martin was most patient with him and in time he regretted his worldly actions and asked Martin's forgiveness for his attitude. Brice succeeded Martin as Bishop of Tours in 397, but quickly returned to his old habits and became so neglectful and lazy that he was dismissed.

He spent seven years in exile in Rome during which time he deeply repented and completely changed his lifestyle. When the administrator of his See died, he returned and ruled with great humility and holiness, and was venerated and respected as a true saint by the time of his death.

St Bridget *Feast day: 23 July. Born in Sweden, 1303; died in 1373.*
Bridget married a Swedish nobleman when she was 14 and they had eight children. After the eighth child was born, her husband retired to the Cistercian Monastery at Alvostra.

When he died, Bridget founded an order at Vadsterna for monks and nuns who lived separately but shared the same church. This order became an important religious centre and the members were known as the Bridgettines. After going to Rome to obtain papal approval for the order,

Bridget went on a pilgrimage to the Holy Land before returning to spend the rest of her days at Vadsterna, ministering to the sick and poor and attending to visiting pilgrims.

St Brigid *Feast day: 1 February. Born in Faughart near Dundalk, Louth, Ireland, 450; died in 523.* Co-patron of Ireland with St Patrick. Brigid's father was Dubhthach, an Irish chieftain of Leinster, and her mother, Brocca, was a slave at his court. She was a very attractive young girl, but on learning that her father was preparing to marry her off, she prayed fervently to God to make her plain, a prayer that God granted. Even as a young girl, she was drawn to the religious life, and was professed by **St Mel of Armagh**. Brigid and seven companions formed a community near Croghan Hill in the year 468, before following Mel to Meath.

In 470 she founded a double monastery at Kildare and was abbess of the first convent in Ireland. This foundation developed into a centre of learning and spirituality which included a school of art whose illuminated manuscripts became famous. The cathedral city of Kildare grew up around this centre.

Throughout her life Brigid showed boundless charity and compassion for those in distress. She died at Kildare and was buried at Downpatrick with **St Columba** and **St Patrick**.

St Bruno *Feast day: 6 October. Born in Cologne, Germany, 1033; died in 1101.* Bruno studied at the Cathedral School at Rheims, and on his return to Cologne in about 1055, was ordained and became a Canon at St Cunibert's.

He returned to Rheims in 1056 as professor of theology, and became head of the school the following year, remaining there until 1074. Though the people of Rheims wanted to make Bruno archbishop, he decided to pursue the solitary life. He became a hermit under Abbot **St Robert of Molesmes** and in 1084 moved on to Grenoble with six companions, where they were assigned a place in a desolate, mountainous, alpine area called La Grande Chartreuse. There they built an oratory and individual cells, adopting a life of poverty, manual work, prayer, and transcribing manuscripts. Though as yet they had no written rule, this was the beginning of the Carthusian Order.

The fame of the group spread and in 1090 Bruno was brought to Rome by Pope Urban as Papal Advisor, but once there, Bruno persuaded Urban to allow him to resume his monastic calling. He founded St Mary's at La Torre in Calabria, where he remained until his death. He wrote several commentaries on the Psalms and on St Paul's Epistles. Bruno was never formally canonized because of the Carthusians' aversion to public honours.

St Bruno of Würzburg *Feast day 27 May. Born in Germany; died 1045.* Bruno was a man of great wealth who was consecrated Bishop of Würzburg, Germany in 1033. He spent all his considerable private fortune building churches throughout his diocese. While Bruno was dining with Emperor Henry III at Bosenburg, a gallery collapsed and he was killed instantly.

St Burchard *Feast day: 14 October. Born in Wessex, England; died in 754.* Burchard was a priest in England, a Benedictine monk, a disciple of **St Boniface** and a missionary to Germany. In 732, he went to Germany to serve under St Boniface who in due course consecrated him as the first Bishop of Würzburg. He worked energetically alongside the ruling powers and in 749 negotiated the Pope's approval for King Pepin the Short's accession to the Frankish throne. He founded several Benedictine abbeys. Burchard resigned from his See around 753 and retired to Hamburg, Germany, to pursue the monastic life. He died soon after.

C

St Cadoc *Feast day: 24 January. Born in Wales; died in 580.* Cadoc was the son of a Welsh king and known for his wild and warlike nature. When Cadoc stole a cow from an Irish monk, the holy man was bold enough to protest to the king and to demand its return. The monarch wisely placed his son in the care of that same monk and Cadoc learned much from him, including the rudiments of Latin. After pursuing his studies in Ireland, he was ordained a priest and founded Llancarfan Monastery near Cardiff, Wales, before becoming a missionary on the coast of Brittany.

Returning to Britain, Cadoc was involved in the Saxon occupation of the British lands and a companion of **St Gildas**. He was consecrated a bishop in Wales and later martyred at Benvento.

St Cadwallader *Feast day: 12 November. Born in Saxony, 659; died in Rome, 689.* Cadwallader became King of the West Saxons in 685. He was a peace-loving and holy prince who expanded his kingdom to Sussex, Surrey, and Kent. His noble desire to avoid war at all costs had earned him the nickname 'the battle-shunner'. He suffered a terrible defeat at the hands of the Wessex army, which was due in part to his lack of willingness to make the first aggressive move.

On his conversion to the Christian faith, he resigned as king and went to Rome, and was baptized there by Pope Sergius on Easter eve. He died a few days later and was buried, still in his baptismal clothes, in St Peter's, Rome.

St Caedmon *Feast day: 11 February. Born in England; died in 680.* Caedmon was a herdsman who came to work at Whitby Abbey to tend the animals. Though he had a deep love of life, poetry and song, his shyness and diffidence meant that he did not join in the times of communal singing after meals. Instead, his custom was to withdraw with the excuse that the animals needed tending.

St Bede recounts that one night while asleep, Caedmon was given the words of a hymn, which he was able to remember perfectly. When he shared this with **St Hilda** she encouraged him to consider becoming a monk.

Though Caedmon could neither read nor write, he would listen attentively to the lessons read at daily services and then retell them using the traditional oral form of Anglo-Saxon verse. Among his many compositions were poetic versions of the Exodus from Egypt, and the life, death and resurrection of Christ. The only poetic work which survived him is his 'Hymn of Creation'. It was recorded in Latin by Bede, and was the very first poem that he received while asleep.

St Caesaria *Feast day: 12 January. Born in France; died in 529.* Caesaria was the sister of Bishop **St Caesarius of Arles**, Gaul. She became first abbess of a convent that he founded about 512, and ruled over 200 nuns who were devoted to the care of the poor, the sick, and their children. The sisters made their own clothes and created ornamentation for their church out of plain woollen or linen cloth. Though enclosure was permanent and complete, the nuns would mend and weave clothing for those in the outside world.

St Caesarius of Arles *Feast day: 27 August. Born in Chalons-sur-Salone, Burgundy, France, 470; died in 542.* Caesarius was born into a French-Roman family and spent a brief time as a monk in Lerins following which he was ordained by his uncle, the Bishop of Arles. He was sent to reform a local monastery, which had fallen into lax practice, and he did this with great success.

Caesarius developed careful and energetic pastoral and preaching skills and in 503, he succeeded his uncle, Fonus, as Bishop of Arles. He instituted many reforms, including the daily celebration of the liturgy. He insisted that this was not a matter of mere observance, but rather a real raising of the mind and heart to God. Caesarius also founded a convent at Arles, and appointed his sister St Caesaria as abbess.

He presided over the Council of Orange in 529. During this particular gathering the theology of predestination to hell was discussed and declared to be mistaken. In 505, because of the deceit of his enemies, Caesarius was banished by the Gothic King Alaric II, but was soon after restored.

After this, Theodoric the Great, King of Italy, laid siege to Arles, and arrested Caesarius but soon released him. Theodoric was so impressed by his holiness that he gave him a valuable silver basin and 300 pieces of gold, which Caesarius used to ransom other captives.

He then went to Rome where Pope St Symmachus made him the apostolic delegate to France. When the Franks captured Arles in 536, Caesarius retired to the convent he had instituted, made a will in its favour and died soon after.

St Caesarius of Nazianzus *Feast day: 25 February. Born in Nazianzus, Asia Minor; died in 369.* Caesarius was the brother of the theologian **St Gregory of Nazianzus**. Caesarius studied medicine and philosophy in Alexandria, Egypt, and in Constantinople. He became well known and respected as a physician, and was appointed to an influential position in the court of Emperor Julian the Apostate.

Caesarius was under instruction in the Christian faith though he had not been baptized. In spite of extreme pressure from the emperor to give up his faith, he resigned from the court rather than do so. He went on to serve as physician to Emperor Jovian, and later Emperor Valens appointed him to be his treasurer.

In 468 after a traumatic experience during an earthquake in Bithynia, Caesarius eventually underwent baptism.

St Gregory gave a full account of his brother's life and work when he conducted his brother Caesarius' funeral.

St Cajetan *Feast day: 7 August. Born in Vicenza, Italy, 1480; died in 1547. Canonized in 1671 by Pope Clement X.* Educated at Padua University in law and theology, Cajetan went to Rome believing he was called to some great work there, but after a few years he returned to his hometown disappointed and began to study for the priesthood. He was ordained in 1516, and conscious of the widespread corruption and notorious laxity amongst the clergy, he began a reform movement from within the Church in order to bring renewal and restoration.

Along with the more fanatical Pietro Caraffa, who later became Pope Paul IV, he founded the Theatine order in 1523. The name was taken from the Latin form of bishop in Pietro's diocese. Together they established confraternities of clergy and laity for the promoting of God's glory and care for the poor. Cajetan told his brothers, 'In this oratory we try to serve God by worship; in our hospital we may say that we actually find him.'

These communities specialized in the study of Christian doctrine, the restoration of dignity and spirituality in worship, and pastoral care. When Rome was sacked by imperial troops in 1527 they moved their headquarters to Naples.

It was here, and later in Verona and Venice, that the movement established the first of a new kind of pawn shop, designed to help rather than exploit the poor. They persevered even when openly opposed by both laity and clergy. Their holy lifestyle and humble living converted as many as did their preaching. Cajetan was admired and well-liked, and the order was in many ways a pioneer in badly needed reform.

Unfortunately, due to the unpopularity of his co-founder Caraffa, their movement was soon eclipsed by similar reforming orders with superior organization such as the Jesuits founded by **St Ignatius Loyola**.

In his final illness, when doctors tried to get him to move from the wooden boards where he slept to a comfortable bed, Cajetan, humble to the last, responded, 'My saviour died on a cross. Let me die on wood at least.'

St Calepodius *Feast day: 10 May. Born in Rome, Italy; died in 250.* Calepodius was a priest who was martyred during the reign of Emperor Severus Alexander. Martyred along with him in this particularly severe persecution were husband and wife Sts Felix and Blanda, the senator St Simplicius and his entire family. St Palmatius who was of consular rank also died, along with 65 members of his family and household.

Calepodius was decapitated and his body was thrown into the river Tiber from whence a fisherman captured it in his nets and brought it to Pope **St Callistus** I. Calepodius founded the cemetery in Rome which bears his name.

St Calimerius *Feast day: 31 July. Born in Greece; died in 190.* A Greek who was educated in Rome, Calimerius was a disciple of Pope St Telesphorus. He was appointed Bishop of Milan, preached in the area, and was known as 'the Apostle of the Valley of the Po River'. In the persecutions started by Emperor Commodus, Calimerius was flung head-first into a well. He was buried under the high altar of his church in Milan.

St Callistus *Feast day: 14 October. Born in Rome; died in 222.* Callistus was the slave of a Christian master named Carpophorus who unwisely appointed him to be in charge of a bank for fellow believers. This venture was a failure; Callistus lost all the money and fled from Rome. When he was finally arrested he was found guilty and sentenced to the treadmill. His creditors obtained his release in order to try to recover the lost money, but Callistus was soon rearrested and sentenced to hard labour in the quarries of Sardinia.

On his release a second time, **Pope Zephyrinus** appointed Callistus manager of the main Christian cemetery of Rome. He did this job well, was made a deacon, and in a mercurial rise, he was appointed Pope within 17 years.

Callistus' reign as pope lasted only five years and he had to deal with several difficult theological issues, which resulted in him being accused of laxity and heresy. His proposal, that the Church should recognize the marriage of slaves and free persons, resulted in his long-term opponent Hippolytus leading a schism in the Roman Church.

Callistus was killed during a popular uprising in Rome, and his body was thrown down a well.

St Camillus de Lellis *Feast day:18 July. Born in Bocchianico, in Abruzzi, Italy, 1550; died in 1614. Canonized in 1746 by Pope Benedict XIV.* Patron of doctors, nurses and nursing groups. St Camillus de Lellis was a soldier of fortune who fought for the Venetians against the Turks. He was a compulsive gambler and in 1574 he found himself penniless in the city of Naples as a result of his addiction. Out of remorse he accepted work as a labourer on the new Capuchin buildings at Manfredonia. He was finally converted as a result of a moving sermon given by the guardian of that community.

He tried twice to join the Capuchins, but on both occasions he was prevented from being finally professed due to a diseased leg which he had contracted while fighting the Turks.

Aware from first-hand experience of the desperate plight of many hospital patients, he committed himself to caring for the sick, initially by becoming bursar of St Giacomo Hospital in Rome. After further prayer and consideration he received permission from his confessor **St Philip Neri** to be ordained, and with two companions, he founded his own congregation, the Camellians, dedicated to the care of the sick.

The Camellians ministered to the sick of Holy Ghost Hospital in Rome, and founded a new house in Naples in 1588. They also cared for those stricken by the plague aboard ships in Rome's harbour and ministered to wounded troops in Hungary and Croatia, forming the first field medical unit. Camillus resigned as superior of the Order in 1607 and died in Rome.

St Canice *Feast day: 11 October. Born in Glengiven, Ireland, 525; died in 600.* Canice became a monk under **St Cadoc** at Llancarfan, Wales, and was ordained there. After a trip to Rome, he studied under **St Finnian** at Clonard, Ireland, and preached for a time in Ireland, before going to do mission work in Scotland visiting his close friend **St Columba** on Iona. They visited King Brude of the Picts together and he was converted as a result of their visit.

Though Canice was a most successful and active missionary, he highly valued his times of retreat and communion with the natural world. He was known to politely ask the birds to make less noise on Sundays, and on one occasion he rebuked mice for nibbling at his sandals. He used these times of solitude to copy spiritual texts, including a manuscript of the four Gospels.

Canice built monasteries at Aghaboe, and Kilkenny in Ireland and his principle church was at Inchkenneth on Mull.

St Canute IV *Feast day: 19 January. Born in Odense, Denmark; died in 1086.* Canute was the illegitimate son of King Swein Estrithson of Denmark who succeeded his brother Harold as king in 1081. He married Adela, the sister of Count Robert of Flanders.

Denmark had been nominally evangelized by English missionaries, but it was Canute who gave the greatest encouragement to the clergy by passing several laws in their favour.

In 1085, he planned an invasion of England, but a rebellion against his taxation plans forced him to flee to the Isle of Funen. Canute, his brother Benedict and 17 companions sought refuge in the church of **St Alban**, but were slain there while kneeling in prayer before the altar.

St Canute Lavard *Feast day: 7 January. Born in Roskilde, in 1096; died in 1131. Canonized in 1169 by Pope Clement XI.* Canute Lavard was the nephew of **St Canute** and son of King Eric the Good of Denmark. He was brought up in the Saxon court, and when he came of age was made Duke of Jutland.

Canute supported the efforts of **St Vicelin** and defended his land against Viking raids. In 1129, when King Lothair III recognized Canute as king of the Western Wends, his own uncle, King Nils of Denmark, was furious and plotted his death. He was slain by Magnus Nielsen and Henry Skadelaar, his cousins, near Ringsted, and thus regarded as a martyr.

St Caprasius *Feast day: 20 October. Born in Agen, France, 1521; died in 1597.* Caprasius was the first Bishop of Agen, France. During Emperor Diocletian's persecution, he went into hiding, but on learning of the death of St Faith he was emboldened to reveal his identity. His mother, Alberta, his brothers Primus and Felician, and other believers joined him and when they refused to deny their faith, they were all executed.

St Caradoc *Feast day: 14 April. Born in Brycheiniog, Wales; died in 1124.* Caradoc was a harp player and well-respected member of the court of a local prince in southern Wales and was responsible for caring for the royal greyhounds. One day these escaped, through no fault of Caradoc's. The angry prince overreacted so much to this that Caradoc chose to leave the court rather serve a ruler who preferred greyhounds to men.

In a gesture of remorse, he broke the top off his lance and turned the staff into a walking stick then travelled to Llandaff and entered the service of the local bishop. Later he became a hermit at St Cendydd's Church in Gower, and eventually taking up residence on Barry Island at St Issels.

Caradoc was forced into exile when Henry I invaded the region and was briefly taken prisoner by Viking raiders. Following his release he retired to Haroldston, where he occupied the cell of St Ismael till his death of natural causes.

Sts Carpus, Papylus, Agathonica and Agathodorus *Feast day: 13 April. Born in Pergamum, Asia Minor; died in 170.* Carpus was the Bishop of Gurdos, and was martyred along with Lydia, Papylus, Agathonica, Agathodorus, and others. Papylus was a deacon. Agathonica was Papylus' sister, and Agathodorus was their servant.

The request had come from the proconsul to offer sacrifices in the name of the emperor but the whole household refused, even when Carpus was hung up to be tortured with iron claws that flayed the skin from his sides. He continued to proclaim his faith until the pain overcame him. The last words of Carpus were: 'Blessed are You, Lord Jesus Christ, Son of God, because You judged me, a sinner, worthy to have this part in You!'

St Casimir *Feast day: 4 March. Born in Poland, 1461; died in Vilna, 1484. Canonized 1521 by Pope Leo X.* Patron of Poland and Lithuania. Casimir was the second son of King Casimir I of Poland and Elizabeth of Austria; the third of 13 children, he was committed to God from an early age. Rejecting the rich trappings of a prince, he clothed himself in plain attire and adopted a simple lifestyle.

When Casimir was 14 years old, his father, insisted that he lead an army to take over the throne of Hungary. This was in response to a request of some disgruntled nobles. But when this invasion force met with unexpected opposition the soldiers, who had not been paid, began to desert in large numbers. On the advice of his officers, Casimir returned home only to discover that Pope Sixtus IV had expressly opposed the invasion. Consequently he refused to try again.

His father was furious and had his son imprisoned in a castle in Dobzki.

The time of enforced confinement gave Casimir time for reflection, prayer and study and only helped to strengthen his resolve to live his life as a faithful Christian and keep his self-imposed vow of celibacy.

When his father died, Casimir became king but died within three years of taking office from a lung disease which had been exacerbated by his austere lifestyle. A copy of his favourite song, a Latin hymn to Mary written by St Bernard of Cluny, was interred with him.

St Cassian *Feast Day: 3 December. Died in 298.* Cassian was the court recorder at the trial of **St Marcellus** at Tangier in North Africa. As he was writing down a record of the proceedings he became so indignant at the injustice being done to Marcellus that he threw down his pen and declared himself to be a Christian also. He was arrested immediately and martyred a few weeks later.

St Cassian of Imola *Feast day: 13 August. Born in Italy; died in 250.* Cassian was a teacher at Imola, near modern Ravenna, Italy. He was arrested for being a Christian and stripped naked before his students, who numbered about 200. They were encouraged to attack him, which they did without remorse, throwing their tablets, pens and knives at his face and head and then cutting and stabbing his body with their iron pens till he was dead.

St Catherine of Alexandria *Feast day: 25 November. Born in Alexandria, Egypt; died in 310.* Patron of philosophers and preachers. Catherine was born into a noble family and converted to Christianity through a vision. When Emperor Maxentius began his persecutions, the 18-year-old Catherine, who was very beautiful, went to the emperor and rebuked him publicly. Unable to answer her arguments, he called in 50 philosophers to refute her claims. Catherine demolished their arguments with consummate ease and they were converted on the spot. In a fury Maxentius ordered that they all be burned to death.

Catherine's refusal of a royal marriage led to her being arrested and imprisoned. However, while Maxentius was absent, Catherine was able to speak to his wife and 200 of his soldiers and they were all converted. On his return, the emperor had them all killed.

Catherine was condemned to die a dramatic and torturous death on a spiked wheel, but the wheel broke and splinters flew off, killing some of the assembly. In a blind rage Maxentius had her beheaded.

Her shrine was established at the Orthodox monastery on Mount Sinai.

St Catherine was one of the voices heard by **St Joan of Arc** in her vision.

St Catherine Labouré *Feast Day: 28 November. Born in the Cote D'Or in France, 1806; died in 1876. Canonized in 1947 by Pope Pius XII.* The only one of her large family to go to school, Catherine (previously named Zoe) worked as a waitress in Paris before entering the community of the Daughters of Charity in that city. As a young nun Catherine experienced several visions of saints but due to her humility she kept the full extent of these apparitions secret until very near to her death. One of these visions included the description of a medal, which was to become known as the 'Miraculous Medal'. In 1832 she arranged for some to be struck and, two years later, over 130,000 medals had been produced and distributed.

St Catherine de Ricci *Feast day: 13 February. Born in Florence, 1522; died in 1589. Canonized 1747 by Pope Benedict XIV.* When she was 13, Catherine's father placed her in the convent of Monticelli in Florence, where her aunt, Louisa de Ricci, was a nun. A year later she entered the convent of the Dominican nuns at Prat in Tuscany, and by the age of 25 she was appointed perpetual prioress. Catherine's passion for holiness led her into lengthy correspondence with several influential people, including **St Philip Neri** and three men who would later become pope. Apart from her letter writing she is best remembered for her disciplined and ordered approach to the spiritual life. Even her visions, in which she relived Christ's passion, occurred regularly for 12 years beginning at noon on every Thursday and lasting till 4.00 pm on Friday.

A miraculous sign would appear from time to time on the fourth finger of Catherine's left hand; a symbol of her espousal to Christ.

She died after a long period of illness.

St Catherine of Siena *Feast day: 30 April. Born in Siena, Italy, 1347; died in 1380. Canonized 1461 by Pope Pius II.* As a small child Catherine was deeply spiritual and experienced visions from early childhood. She took no interest in her personal appearance despite the urgings of her parents, and even cut off her hair when her parents tried to find her a husband. Nothing could shake her resolution and eventually they permitted her to follow a life of spiritual devotion and discipline.

Gradually she gathered a band of friends, which included some notable spiritual directors of the time. Following accusations made against her she was summoned to the Dominican order in Florence, but was found to have no case to answer. On return to Siena Catherine and her friends once again involved themselves in caring for prisoners and those stricken by the plague.

In 1375, following more visions and miraculous events, Catherine was invited to Pisa where her very presence brought about a religious revival. While praying in the church of St Christina in Pisa she received the stigmata, signs of the wounds of the crucified Christ, and these were clearly visible to all who saw her body after her death.

Catherine was a gifted and sought-after conciliator and was instrumental in enabling Pope Gregory XI to return to Rome from Avignon. Despite continuing troubles she persisted to work for peace among political and spiritual leaders and much of her correspondence with them still survives today.

At the age of 33, Catherine suffered a paralytic stroke which disabled her from the waist down. She died eight days later.

St Catherine of Sweden *Feast day: 24 March. Born in Sweden, in 1330; died in 1381.* The daughter of **St Bridget**. Catherine married, but with the agreement of her husband the marriage was never consummated.

She went to Rome in 1348, where her mother had gone to live after being widowed. Catherine's husband died soon after her arrival in Rome, and she continued to work alongside her mother for the next quarter of a century.

They travelled widely on pilgrimage to many places, including Jerusalem, but regarded their main work as prayer and meditation, caring for the poor and instructing others in the Faith. Though many were attracted by Catherine's beauty and gentle nature, God's providence kept her safe from all these unsought-for advances.

Following the trip to Jerusalem, St Bridget died and Catherine took her mother's body back to Sweden, burying it at Vadstena, in the convent of the Order of the Holy Saviour, which Bridget had founded.

Catherine was then appointed superior of the order, and worked tirelessly to have her mother officially recognized as a saint. She achieved this in 1381 and died that same year.

St Catherine de Vigri *Feast day: 9 March. Born in Bologna, Italy, 1413; died in 1463. Canonized in 1712 by Pope Clement XI.* Patron of artists. Catherine was the daughter of a diplomatic agent of the Marquis of Ferrara. She was appointed maid of honour to the daughter of the Marquis at the age of 11, but left the court to follow the religious life. She entered a Franciscan order when she was 14. Her Community eventually became part of the Poor Clares.

She experienced visions of both Christ and Satan and wrote about them; in a short time she was appointed prioress of a new convent in Bologna.

A persuasive speaker before popes, and an effective trainer of novices, Catherine was also known for her special artistic talents, particularly in calligraphy and miniature painting.

St Cecilia *Feast day: 22 November. Born in Rome in the third century.* Cecilia was a devout and humble Christian who wore sackcloth next to her skin, fasted, and prayed to the saints, beseeching them to guard her virginity.

She was given in marriage to a pagan youth named Valerian, but after she explained her faith to her new husband, he too became a believer and was baptized by **Pope Urban** (223-230). The marriage was never consummated.

Tibertius, Valerian's brother, was also baptized, and the two brothers devoted themselves to burying the martyrs slain daily in Rome. When this was discovered they were arrested and questioned. When they refused to sacrifice to the gods they were executed with the sword, after which Cecilia took charge of the bodies of the two men and arranged their burial.

Her preaching converted 400 people, and after sending them to Pope Urban to be baptized she was arrested. She too refused to sacrifice to the gods, an act which converted her persecutors. Cecilia was condemned to death by suffocation in the baths but though the fires were heaped up as high as they could be, she did not even break out in perspiration.

When the governor heard this, he sent an executioner to cut off her head in the bath. The man struck three times without being able to sever the head completely and he left her still bleeding. She survived a further three days, praying and preaching to the visiting Christian folk who flocked to her side. She then died and was buried by Pope Urban and his deacons.

Cecilia was also associated with music and the organ since at her wedding she sang her vows, in her heart, to the Lord.

St Cedd *Feast day: 26 October. Born in Northumbria, England; died at Lastingham in Yorkshire, 664.* St Cedd and his three brothers **St Chad**, Cynebill, and Cælin all became monks. He was a disciple of **St Aidan of Lindisfarne**, ordained in 653, and a year later, when the East Anglian king Sigbert converted to Christianity, he was sent as a missionary to Essex. **St Finnian** of Lindisfarne made him a bishop because of his success in this work and Cedd founded several monasteries, including those at Tilbury and Lastingham. Cedd served as an interpreter at the Synod of Whitby in 664 and was one of the bishops who accepted the decisions of that Synod with respect to the adoption of Roman customs for their own dioceses. He died of the plague later that year.

St Celestine I *Feast day: 6 April. Born in Campania, Italy; died in Rome, 432.* Celestine was a strong and effective defender of the Christian faith. He served as a deacon under Pope Innocent I before being elected pope in 422. Although he confirmed the appointment of Nestorius to the See of Constantinople, he chose to support **St Cyril of Alexandria** in the conflict that arose between the two patriarchs.

In 431 Celestine appointed Cyril to be president of the Council of Ephesus at which Nestoriansm* was finally condemned. Later that same year, he sent St Palladius to be the first Bishop of Ireland.

Celestine was buried in the cemetery of Priscilla in Rome, and his tomb was decorated with paintings commemorating the council of Ephesus.

St Celsus *Feast day: 7 April. Born in Armagh, 1079; died at Ardpatrick, Munster, 1129.* Celsus was a layman who succeeded to the Bishopric of Armagh when only 26 years old. Church discipline in the diocese had grown extremely lax and he set about the difficult task of restoring it with wisdom and skill. He was a gifted mediator and was able to make many reforms. He carried out the last of these on his deathbed by appointing his friend **St Malachy** to be the next bishop, thus ending the custom of hereditary succession.

St Ceolfrid *Feast day: 25 September. Born in Northumbria, England, 642; died in 716.* Ceolfrid was born into a noble family and became a monk at Ripon and was eventually named prior of Wearmouth, by **St**

Benedict Biscop. Though a most learned individual he proved too much of a disciplinarian for them, and was forced to leave. He returned to the monastery at Ripon where his immense practical skills were recognized and appreciated and he was appointed baker.

Ceolfrid accompanied St Benedict to Rome in 678 and became the deputy abbot of St Paul's monastery at Wearmouth, in 685 and abbot of the newly formed daughter monastery at Jarrow soon after. The early days saw a dramatic reduction in the number of monks for a variety of reasons, and the monastery ended up with only himself and one other young man who was to become famous as **St Bede**. Ceolfrid played a major role in his training and Bede was later to gain so great a reputation for his scholarly work that he was given the title 'the Venerable'.

Ceolfrid developed the twin monasteries into cultural centres and arranged for the writing of three copies of the Bible in Latin. One of these, known as the *Codex Amatianus*, is the oldest surviving copy of the Vulgate Bible in one volume.

In 716, Ceolfrid retired and left for Rome. He died en route in Burgundy, and was buried at Langres.

St Chad *Feast day: 2 March. Born in Ireland; died in 673.* Chad and his brother **St Cedd** were both trained by **St Aidan** in Lindisfarne in England. Chad spent time with **St Egbert** in Ireland, but was later called back to take over as abbot of Lastingham Monastery.

Within a year of his return Chad had allowed King Oswy to appoint him Bishop of York. However the king's son, King Alcfrid, had already appointed **St Wilfrid** to the same See and Wilfrid, unhappy with what he viewed as schismatic tendencies in some of the northern bishops, had gone to Gaul in order to seek valid consecration.

Chad approached Bishop Wine of Dorchester and two other bishops and requested to be consecrated. He was disciplined for this in 669 by **St Theodore**, the newly arrived Archbishop of Canterbury, and Wilfrid was restored to York.

Theodore was amazed by the humility with which Chad received this rebuke and soon after regularized his consecration, appointing him as Bishop of Mercia.

Chad always travelled on foot until at the insistence of Archbishop Theodore, he began to ride a horse. After only three years of unremitting hard work in his new post Chad's strength simply wore out.

As Chad lay dying, his prayer room was filled with the sound of music. A peasant in the fields nearby first heard it, drew near in wonder, and then ran to tell others. A crowd gathered outside Chad's room, and when they asked about the music Chad told them that it meant his time to die was near and the angels were calling him home. He was so well loved that on his death immediate moves were made to declare him a saint.

St Charbel *Feast day: 24 December. Born in Beqa-Kafra, Lebanon, 1828; died in1898. Canonized in 1977 by Pope Paul VI.* Charbel was the son of a mule driver who entered a monastery at an early age. He longed to imitate the desert fathers, and exhibited a great longing for Church unity. Withdrawing to a tiny four-roomed hermitage which he shared with three others, he found the same unsought-for attention from those seeking prayer and guidance, as had the desert monks of earlier times. Charbel refused to touch money and lived a very austere life, eating one meal of vegetables a day and using a plank of wood for a pillow. His peasant community had a strong faith, were devout and regular in worship and had a great devotion to the Mother of God.

Charbel exhibited the unusual phenomenon of sweating blood, which was investigated by the Roman Catholic Church twice in the last century, without any adequate conclusion being reached, as to its origin.

St Charles Borromeo *Feast day: 4 November. Born in Arona, Lake Maggiore, Italy, 1538; died in 1584. Canonized in 1610 by Pope Paul V.* Patron of learning and the arts. The son of a count, Charles was educated at the Benedictine abbey in Arona.

In 1559, his mother's brother was elected Pope Pius IV and the next year, even though he was still a layman and only 22 years old, Charles was made a cardinal and administrator of the See of Milan.

In 1562, he was instrumental in having Pius reconvene the Council of Trent, which had been suspended for ten years and he played a leading role in writing the decrees of the closing sessions.

He was ordained as a priest in 1563, and consecrated Bishop of Milan that same year. As bishop he instituted radical reforms with great effect, combating widespread ignorance and laxity in Church practise. The dignity of public worship was restored and he put in place measures to improve the morals and manners of both the clergy and the laity, establishing Sunday schools, seminaries and arranging help for the poor and needy.

Charles virtuous life and his desire to make Christ a reality meant that his influence was felt far and wide. He founded a society of secular priests known as the Oblates of **St Ambrose** (now Oblates of St Charles) in 1578.

Charles was one of the leading figures of the Catholic Reformation.

The Venerable Charles de Foucauld *Feast day: 1 December. Born in 1858; died in Algeria, 1916.* Orphaned at the age of six, Charles and his sister were brought up by their wealthy grandfather. In 1878, his grandfather died and he began to live a reckless and riotous life, but thanks to the influence of his deeply spiritual cousin, Marie de Bondy, who lived nearby, he underwent a gradual conversion.

Charles became a Trappist monk, but soon asked to be released from his temporary vows in order to spend time with the Poor Clare nuns in the Holy Land. He discovered his vocation to the priesthood there. Finishing his studies in 1901, he left for Algeria to live as a desert hermit, planning to establish two religious orders patterned on the life of Jesus of Nazareth. His open hermitage had a wall so low that it could easily be stepped over by visitors and despite his best efforts, no one came to join him and his venture appeared to be an abject failure.

In 1916, Charles de Foucauld was murdered by two Arab soldiers who were suspicious of his behaviour, and his hopes of founding a new society appeared to be over. However, following the discovery of his notebooks, three societies were formed which drew their inspiration from his life and teaching; namely the Little Brothers of Jesus, Little Sisters of the Sacred Heart, and Little Sisters of Jesus. By the end of the twentieth century the number and influence of small groups living out the principles that were discovered in the notebooks had expanded exponentially.

St Charles Garnier *Feast day: 19 October. Born in Paris, France, 1606; died in 1649. Canonized in 1930 by Pope Pius XI.* Charles was the son of the treasurer of Normandy. He joined the Society of Jesus in Paris when he was 18 and went on to teach at the Jesuit College at Eu for three years. He was ordained in 1635.

The following year, he was one of four priests sent to Quebec, Canada, as missionaries to the Huron Indians. Badly wounded at the village of Etarita while helping the Huron escape an attack from their traditional enemies the Iroquois, he tried to reach one of his flock who was dying to give him absolution but was killed by a tomahawk blow to the head. His superior wrote of him, 'His very laugh spoke of goodness.'

St Christina *Feast day: 24 July. Born in Bolsena in Tuscany, Italy in the fourth century.* Christina was the Christian daughter of a rich and powerful pagan magistrate who owned a number of golden idols. She broke these and gave the pieces away to the poor.

Furious at this, her father had her whipped with rods and then thrown into a dungeon. She remained unrepentant so he gave the order for her to be torn by iron hooks then tied to a rack and held over a blazing fire. She survived all these tortures and even when she was tied to a heavy stone and thrown into the lake of Bolsena, she did not die. In the end, she outlived her father, who died in a fit of anger, rage and spite.

Sometime later the judge who succeeded her father continued the persecution, and had her thrown into a burning furnace, where she remained, unhurt, for five days. She then overcame the serpents among which she was thrown, had her tongue cut out, and was eventually killed by being pierced with arrows. Her relics now lie in Palermo in Sicily.

St Christina the Astonishing *Feast day: 15 December. Born in Brusthem, Belgium, 1150; died in Saint-Trond, Belgium, 224.* Christina was orphaned when she was three years old and died at the young age of 21. During the requiem mass her body suddenly soared out of the coffin and rose to the roof of the Church. When the priest ordered her to come down, she did so, and related that she had been to Heaven, Hell, and Purgatory. Christina went on to say that she had been called to return to earth to pray for suffering souls.

She loved solitude and would take extreme steps to escape human contact such as climbing high up trees or even hiding in an oven. Christina was considered by many to be insane, but those who knew her well esteemed her highly for her holiness of life. She lived in poverty and spent her last three years living in St Catherine's convent at Saint-Trond.

St Christopher *Feast day: 25 July. Born in Canaan in the third century.* Patron of travellers and motorists. Christopher was a man of great strength and ferocity, with a passion to find a king stronger than himself who would be worth serving. He finally decided to try following Christ, and a hermit suggested that he should use his strength and knowledge to live in a way that only he could: by helping people to cross over a local swift-flowing river.

One day a young boy asked Christopher to carry him across. When Christopher put the child on his shoulders, he found him to be unbelievably heavy. On enquiring how that could be, his passenger, who was Christ in the form of a child, explained that he had been carrying a weight equivalent to that of the whole world and its sins.

The name Christopher means Christ-bearer and is usually associated with a Christopher who died as a martyr during the reign of Emperor Decius.

St Christopher Magallenes *Feast day: 15 July. Born in Mexico, 1868; died in 1927. Canonized in 2000 by Pope John Paul II.* Christopher Magallenes entered the seminary at Guadalahara, was ordained in 1899 and became the parish priest of Totalic in 1909. Though dedicated to non-violent protest, Magallenes became caught up in a battle between rebel and government forces. He was arrested, charged with being a traitor and sent for trial without any proper legal representation. When false accusations went unchecked, he was found guilty and taken out to be shot four days later.

In 2000, Pope John Paul II canonized him, along with 25 others from Mexico who were executed in similar circumstances.

St Clare *Feast day: 11 August Born in Assisi, Italy, 1194; died in 1253. Canonized in 1255 by Pope Alexander IV.* Clare was a beautiful Italian noblewoman who was greatly inspired by the preaching of **St Francis of Assisi**. At the age of 18 she left home secretly and in a little chapel outside Assisi, St Francis cut off her hair and she adopted the rough brown habit and plain waist cord of his order.

Francis put her in the care of the Benedictine nuns at Bastia, and though her parents tried every way they could to get her to return, she refused. Other young women joined her including her sister, **St Agnes** and later their widowed mother. Their first community house was near the newly restored church of San Damiano. In 1215 St Francis drew up a rule of life for them, and much against her will appointed Clare as the first abbess.

When an army led by Frederick II and the Saracens came to attack Assisi, St Clare, though sick at the time, asked to be carried to the convent wall where she placed the Blessed Sacrament in full view of the enemy. This caused the attackers to turn and run.

St Clare suffered illness for many years, but did so without complaint.

St Claudia *Feast day: 7 August. Born in England in the first century.* Claudia was the daughter of the British King Caractacus. Following her father's defeat by Aulus Plautius she was sent to Rome in chains along with other members of her family.

The family was later freed by the Emperor Claudius, but one of Caractacus' daughters, who took the name Claudia, remained in Rome, was baptized, and is mentioned in St Paul's second letter to Timothy (4:21). She was the mother of Linus, who became the second pope.

St Clement I *Feast day: 23 November. Born in Rome; died in 100.* Patron of marble workers. Clement was a disciple of both Sts Peter and Paul.

St Paul praised him as a faithful fellow-worker, whose name was written in the Book of Life (Philippians 4:3), and he is recorded as the third Bishop of Rome.

In order to limit the effectiveness of his preaching Clement was exiled to Caesarea and condemned to work in the marble quarries where he found there to be many other Christian believers amongst his fellow-convicts. Water was scarce in that place, the only spring being six miles away, but one day Clement saw a lamb scraping at the soil and taking this as a sign, he dug down in the same spot and found a spring.

Clement succeeded in converting so many people that 75 churches were built. News of this spread to the prefect, Aufidianus, who ordered him to be drowned in the Black Sea with an old anchor attached to his neck.

St Clement of Okhrida *Feast day: 17 July. Born in Southern Macedonia, died in 916.* He became a bishop in the reign of Khan Simeon, was the first Slav to become a bishop and also founded a monastery at Okhrida, near Velitsa, Bulgaria. His missionary work had such widespread effect that he is listed among the Seven Apostles of the region.

St Clotilde *Feast day: 3 June. Born in Lyon, France, 474; died in 545.* In 492, Clotilde married King Clovis, the founder of the Merovingian dynasty, which ruled the Franks for over 200 years. Their first son died soon after being baptized, and when their second son was also taken ill soon after his baptism service, King Clovis began to have doubts as to whether his children should have been baptized, but his second son soon recovered and Clotilde went on to bear him two more sons and a daughter.

In 498, while preparing for a battle, Clovis prayed to 'the God of Clotilde' for success and when it was forthcoming he sought baptism, thus becoming the first Christian King of the Franks.

When Clotilde's eldest son Clodomir died, her other two sons assassinated two of his heirs and the third, **St Cloud,** gave up all claim to the throne, her daughter also died soon after. She retired to Tours where she continued a life of prayer and service and several churches in the region owe their origins to her. She died at the tomb of **St Martin of Tours**.

St Cloud *Feast day: 7 September. Born in France/Germany, 524; died in 560*. Cloud was the youngest of three grandsons to whom King Clovis and **St Clotilde** left a share of their dominions. When he was only eight years old, his uncle Childebert devised a plan to get rid of the boys and steal their inheritance. Cloud alone escaped, and when he came of age, made no attempt to recover his kingdom but instead became a monk, later being ordained a priest.

He put himself under the discipline of St Severinus, a recluse who lived near Paris.

After a period of withdrawal in Provence, he returned to Paris and went to live in Nogent on the Seine, becoming abbot-founder of a monastery there. The town of Saint-Cloud near Versailles developed around that monastery.

He was known for his quiet perseverance and good works.

St Colette *Feast day: 7 February. Born in Corbie, Picardy, France, 1381; died in 1447. Canonized in 1807 by Pope Pius VII*. Colette was the daughter of a carpenter who was employed at Corbie Abbey in Picardy, France. She was orphaned at 17 and entered the Franciscans, becoming well known for her holiness and wisdom. In 1406, in response to a dream directing her to reform the Poor Clares, she visited Peter de Luna, whom the French recognized as pope, and, impressed by her sanctity and fervour, he gave her permission to do so.

She was met by strong opposition but persisted in her efforts, eventually founding 17 new convents and reforming several older ones. She was renowned for her prayerfulness, tenacity, visions and prophecies; she even prophesied her own death in her convent at Ghent, Belgium. This reformed branch of the Poor Clares is known as the Collettines in memory of her work.

St Colman of Dromore *Feast day 7 June. Born in Dalriada in 450*. Colman was one of the earliest disciples of **St Patrick** and a friend of **St Macanisius**.

St Colman spent some time at the great monastic school of Emly around 475 but eventually he returned to the monastery on Mahee Island, where he had been trained, to act as assistant in the school there. St Macinasius, his friend and advisor, predicted that he would one day found a monastery on the Coba plain by the river Lagan, which he eventually did.

He became the first Bishop of Dromore in 514.

St Colman of Lindisfarne *Feast day: 18 February. Born in Connaught, Ireland; died in 676.* Colman was an Irish Bishop of Lindisfarne, and a disciple of **St Columba**. At the Synod of Whitby, he was the main spokesman for the Celtic Church practices, and opposed St Eilfrid and St Agilbert.

Neither side was decisive in their arguments, so the king went with the view that was most widely held in the rest of the known world and favoured the Roman rites. Colman felt unable to accept this decision and left, along with all his Irish and 30 of his English monks to form a monastery on the Isle of Innishboffin, near Connaught.

A difference of opinion arose between the Irish and English monks over the allocation of labour during the summer months and the problem was eventually solved by moving the English monks to a separate monastery in Mayo.

Colman lived simply and frugally and his commitment to faithful discipleship was highly praised by **St Bede**.

St Columba *(Latin: Columbcille, dove) Feast day: 9 June. Born in Gartan, Donegal, in 521; died in 597.* Columba was trained from an early age by **St Finnian** and went on to be ordained as a priest. During his 15 years of active missionary work in Ireland he was known as a powerful and persuasive speaker who founded several monasteries.

Religious documents were highly valued in those days and great prestige was attached to the few monasteries that possessed copies. When Columba's request to make a copy of a manuscript of the Psalms was refused, he decided to do so anyway in secret, making a copy in the middle of the night by candlelight. St Finnian discovered this ploy just when the work was almost completed, and in a rage he brought Columba before the High King of Ireland.

After hearing the case, the king pronounced 'to each cow her calf', in other words ruling that the copy belonged to the holder of the original document and had to be handed over.

Columba was furious; a proud and independent man, and a prince of the O'Neills, he went home, raised an army against the king and entered into a bitter civil war in which many thousands died.

When he had calmed down, and in deep penitence, Columba and a group of 12 companions left their homeland to sail across the Irish Sea. Columba vowed to convert as many souls for Christ as there had been needless deaths because of his actions. A self-imposed exile of this kind is known as white martyrdom.

They founded a monastery on Iona, the first island he reached from which he could no longer see his beloved homeland. This was to become the monastic capital of Scotland and the centre of Christianity for northern Britain. The life was hard and primitive, especially for Columba, who slept on the bare earth with a rock for a pillow for over 30 years.

The lives of these monks were typified by a missionary zeal, which included a deep respect for nature and a poetic view of life. Along with fervent preaching and loosely knitted organizational structures, these aspects were to become the hallmarks of Celtic Christianity.

Columba and his brother monks' primary interest was in converting the Gaelic people of Scotland, though he is credited with the conversion of the Pictish King Brude.

Widely known as a wonder-worker, one of the most amazing miracles accredited to him by his biographer **St Adamnan** was an encounter with a water monster on the banks of Loch Ness. Columba ordered the creature to go back into the water and stop terrorizing the local community whereupon it obeyed him and immediately retreated.

Columba's rapport with nature and the animal world in particular continued to the very end of his life. On what was to prove to be his last ever trip to the Abbey, Columba sat down to rest awhile by the side of the road. His great white horse came up to him, and leaned his head upon the saint's chest. It is said that it was as if the faithful companion knew that this was the last time it would see his master, and was saying a last goodbye in preparation for the great mourning that was to follow.

Columba died before the altar of Iona cathedral just before Morning Prayer that very day.

St Columba of Cordova *Feast day: 17 September. Born in Cordova, Spain; died c.853*. Columba was still a young girl when she became a nun at Tabanos, in a community organized by some of her relatives. When the community was dispersed during the Moorish persecution of Christians, which began in 852, Columba went to the Moorish magistrate in Cordova, openly criticized him and affirmed her faith in Christ. She was beheaded, and her body thrown into the River Guadalquivir. This was later recovered and given a proper burial by her friends.

St Columban *Feast day: 23 November. Born in Leinster, Ireland, in 543; died in 615*. Columban was educated in Bangor by Sinell, the Abbot of Cluaininis in Lough Erne. He later left Ireland with 12 other monks and established a monastery in the ancient Roman castle at Annegray at the invitation of King Childebert, the son of Clovis of Burgundy, before going on to found similar centres at Luxeuil and Fountaine.

He was accused of keeping Easter according to the out-of-favour Celtic tradition, although the real problem seemed to be much deeper and related to his criticism of the lax morals of the Burgundian Church and court. Columban finally appealed to **St Gregory the Great**, and was exonerated.

His refusal to bless the illegitimate sons of Theuderic II involved him in controversy once again and Columban left Burgundy to preach to the Allemani of Switzerland. He later moved again to northern Italy, where he established a monastery at Bobbio in 613.

His monasteries were known for their strict discipline, the monks being expected to work until they were totally exhausted. Columban led by example, always taking part in physical labour even into his late 60s.

In addition to his rule for monks, Columban wrote studies on the Psalms and poems and had a real appreciation of nature and solitude.

St Comgall *Feast day: 10 May. Born in Ulster, Ireland, in 516; died in 601.* Educated by **St Fintan**, Comgall chose to live as a hermit. He went on to found a monastery in Bangor where he was the abbot of 8,000 monks. His monastic rule was strict, holy and constant.

Comgall visited **St Columba** on Iona and accompanied him on a mission to Inverness, Scotland. With the help of another companion **St Canice** they converted the Chieftain Brude, laying great stress on the importance of soul friends. One of his sayings was 'a man without a soul friend is a head without a body.' He was the abbot and teacher of **St Columban** and monks from his foundation went out from Bangor to evangelize all over France and central Europe.

St Cornelius *Feast day: 2 February. Born in the first century.* Cornelius was a centurion in the Italian cohort of the Roman legion Caesarea, Palestine, and became the first bishop of that town. Cornelius had a vision instructing him to send for **St Peter**, who came to his home and baptized him. A detailed account of this is given in the New Testament book the Acts of the Apostles.

St Cornelius *Feast day: 16 September. Born in Rome, Italy; died c.253.* Cornelius was elected pope to succeed Fabian after a 12-month vacancy, due in part to the severity of the Decian persecution of the Christian Church. Cornelius bravely accepted the post of pope, but found that the main issue of his short pontificate was not related to the persecution of the Church by the ruling authorities but rather to the question of how Christians who had fallen away during earlier persecution should be treated.

Cornelius, who was supported by **St Cyprian**, then Bishop of Carthage, held that the Church should forgive those who repented and that they could be readmitted to the sacraments after due penance. This point of view was strongly opposed by Novitian, a Roman priest, who declared that the Church could not pardon those who had committed such apostasy. Novitian declared himself pope, becoming the first anti-pope to gain some degree of popular support.

A synod of Western bishops in Rome in 251 upheld Cornelius, condemned the teachings of Novitian, and excommunicated him. When persecutions of the Christians began again in 253 under Emperor Gallus, Cornelius was exiled and died of the hardships he suffered during his imprisonment. His body was returned to Rome for burial.

Sts Cosmas and Damian *Feast day: 27 September. Born in Arabia; died c.283.* Cosmas and Damian were twin brothers from Syria who studied the sciences and went on to become skilled medical practitioners. They lived at Aegaea in Cilicia, where they were well-thought of by all. Being Christians, they regarded their work as part of their duty of care for others and never took money for their services.

They were arrested during the persecution by Emperor Diocletian and underwent various tortures before finally being martyred. Their bodies were then taken to Syria by faithful friends and buried at Cyrrhus.

In the Middle Ages, the name Cosmas became synonymous with disinterest in money.

Sts Crispin and Crispinian *Feast day: 25 October. Born in Rome in the third century.* Crispin and Crispinian were noble brothers who accompanied St Quintinus to Gaul to preach the Gospel. They settled at Soissons, and spent their days spreading the Gospel and making converts, while working as shoemakers by night in order to maintain to provide themselves with a living.

Their work was brought to the notice of Emperor Maximian, and he handed them over to Rictiovarus, who greatly detested Christians. They were subjected to a variety of tortures, but when Rictiovarus finally tried to kill them, he failed, panicked and committed suicide. Maximian then ordered that the two brothers be beheaded, which was duly done.

They are known chiefly from Henry V's famous speech on the eve of Agincourt in Shakespeare's *Henry V* (Act iv scene 3).

St Crispin of Viterbo (Peter Fioretti) *Feast day: 19 May. Born in Viterbo near Rome, Italy, 1668; died in 1750. Canonized 1982 by Pope John Paul II.* Peter, a shoemaker by trade, joined the Franciscan Capuchins at the age of 25 and took the name Crispin. He served as a gardener and a cook, and proved himself to be a great encourager and tireless worker. He disliked any acknowledgement of what he regarded as simply his duty of service and asked to be known as 'the little beast of burden'.

During one epidemic, Crispin brought about many miraculous cures. He was venerated for his holiness, prophecies and spiritual wisdom.

St Cuthbert *Feast day: 20 March. Born in northern Britain, 634; died in 687.* Cuthbert was orphaned as a young child, and became a shepherd. Feeling the call to the religious life, he entered Melrose Abbey in 651 and was made prior ten years later. Many short missionary trips followed over the next three years. When the Council of Whitby decided to accept Roman liturgical practices, **St Colman** refused to do so and emigrated to Ireland with most of the monks of Lindisfarne. Cuthbert was then appointed bishop and prior in his place by **St Eata**.

Cuthbert continued his missionary activities, attracting large and responsive crowds. He eventually felt the need to retreat from this active ministry, and with his abbot's permission he moved to one of the Farne Islands near Bamborough to live as a hermit.

He was reluctantly elected Bishop of Hexham in 685, but arranged with St Eata to swap Sees, so that he could become the Bishop of Lindisfarne, although he stopped short of accepting responsibility for the monastery there.

He spent the last years of his life caring for the sick, and working numerous miracles of healing, exercising the gift of prophecy, and administering his diocese.

St Cuthman *Feast day: 8 February. Born in Chidham, Bosham, England in the eighth century.* Cuthman was a shepherd who lived near the centre of missionary work in Sussex. When his father died, he took over the care of his paralyzed mother so that when he felt called to become a wandering hermit, Cuthman constructed a wheelbarrow couch for her. With the help of a rope over his shoulders, he wheeled her everywhere with him. Finally, the rope snapped when they were near Steyning in West Sussex and he took this as a sign from God that this was the place where they were to settle. He constructed a hut for them both, and with the help of local people, he went on to build a church nearby. Cuthman is generally known for his miracles.

St Cyprian *Feast Day: 9 December. Died in 586.* Cyprian was a monk at Périgueux in France. In later life he moved away from the community to adopt a solitary life on the banks of the Dordogne and ended his days as a hermit. St Gregory of Tours wrote the *Life of St Cyprian*.

St Cyprian of Carthage *Feast day: 6 September. Born in Carthage, 200; died at Curubis, 258.* Cyprian was a barrister and teacher of oratory till his conversion at the age of 45. He was made bishop within three years, but was persuaded to flee during the Decian persecution, continuing to encourage his flock through letter writing.

When persecution ceased, the question arose as to whether there was a need for those who had fallen away to be rebaptized. Pope Stephen II felt that this was unnecessary while, Cyprian and the other African bishops insisted upon it.

Under the Valerian persecution, he was exiled to Curubis for refusing to sacrifice to the pagan gods, and after a second hearing, when he explained he could not change his faith, he was beheaded.

Cyprian is sometimes referred to as 'the African Pope'.

St Cyril of Alexandria *Feast day: 27 June. Born in Alexandria, Egypt, 376; died in 444.* Cyril was the nephew of Theophilus, the then patriarch of Alexandria, and was ordained to the priesthood by him.

He was present at the Synod of the Oak in 403 when John Chrysostom, whom he believed guilty of heresy, was deposed. He succeeded his uncle as Patriarch of Alexandria in 412, but only after a riot between his supporters and those of his rival.

Cyril was severe and authoritarian and unafraid of conflict. He once began a series of attacks against all those he saw as enemies of true faith.

In 430 Cyril became embroiled in a long-running struggle with Nestorius, Patriarch of Constantinople. Emperor Theodosius II had both Cyril and Nestorius arrested but released Cyril, declaring him innocent of all charges. Two years later Nestorius was forced into exile.

Cyril, who was an outstanding theologian, produced many papers and sermons against heretical teaching and a series of commentaries on books of the Bible.

St Cyril of Jerusalem *Feast day: 18 March. Born in Jerusalem in 315; died in 386.* Cyril is best remembered for his opposition and defeat of the false teaching of Arius. He was a member of a community of men who lived in their own houses in the holy city but practised a common rule of life. After being ordained a priest, his bishop **St Maximus** put him in charge of the instruction of new converts.

On the death of Maximus, Cyril was consecrated Bishop of Jerusalem.

When a famine affected the city, the new bishop sold some of the goods of the churches to feed the poor, saving many lives. Rumours spread that some of the vestments had been misused, and though this was later shown to be untrue, Cyril was banished.

He was allowed to return some time later, but found the city in such a sad state, physically and spiritually, that he was never able to restore it completely. He attended the Council at Constantinople in 381 where the Nicene Creed and orthodoxy triumphed and the supporters of Arius* were finally condemned while Cyril was commended for his perseverance and courage.

Methodius did just this, eventually translating almost the entire Bible and the works of the Fathers of the Church into Slavonic. However within two decades of his death the use of local languages in liturgy was banned.

Sts Cyril and Methodius *Feast day: 14 February. Cyril was born in Thessalonica, 826; died in Rome, 869. Methodius was born in Thessolonica, 815; died, 885.* Constantine (Cyril) and Methodius were brothers, born into a prominent Christian family who travelled as missionaries to the Ukraine.

Their concern that the liturgy should be fully expressed in people's native language encouraged them to devise a new alphabet, which is the origin of Cyrillic script and is so named in honour of their work.

The German hierarchy that held power over Moravia at that time strongly objected to this development, fearful that such a move might eventually lead to a weakening of their authority.

After much debate the brothers finally won the argument, but were left much weakened by the protracted discussions. Constantine died in Rome after assuming the monastic robes and the name Cyril. His dying wish was that his brother should return to continue missionary work in the local language.

D

St Damasus *Feast day: 11 December. Born in Rome in 304; died in 384.*
Damasus was the son of a priest of Spanish extraction. In 366, he succeeded Liberius as pope, but the supporters of a rival named Ursinus, who had also laid claim to the title of bishop of Rome, violently opposed his appointment. Over 100 people were killed in the ensuing riots. This caused the Emperor Valentinian to intervene in support of Damasus; the opposition was treated with considerable cruelty, and swiftly defeated.

Damasus greatly increased the popularity of Rome as a pilgrimage centre, and was widely known for his poems and epitaphs, which he composed for the tombs of the martyrs. He vigorously opposed the heresies of Arianism*, and Donatism*

When **St Jerome** came to Rome, Damasus, who was a very learned man himself, quickly recognized his abilities and appointed him as his secretary. The Latin text of the Bible was written in many different forms at that time and Damasus instructed Jerome to combine these into one 'vulgate' version.

Damasus was commended for his purity of faith, innocence, humility, compassion for the poor and his learning. His last request was to be laid to rest with his mother and sister at a small church on the Via Ardeatina, as he did not consider himself worthy to be buried in the 'papal crypt'.

St Daniel *Feast day: 16 February. Born in Egypt; died in 309.* During Maximus' persecution, Daniel and four companions, Elias, Isaias, Jeremy and Samuel, visited the Christians who worked in the mines of Cicilia, in order to bring them some comfort. On their return journey home, they were arrested at the gates of Caesarea, Palestine, charged with being Christians, tortured and then beheaded.

Porphyry, a young servant of St Pamphilus, demanded that the bodies be properly buried; was arrested and tortured, and when it was discovered that he was a Christian, Porphyry was burned to death. A bystander named Seleucus, who witnessed his martyrdom, applauded his constancy in the face of such cruelty. He too was arrested and brought before the governor who gave the order that he be beheaded.

St Daniel the Stylite *Feast day: 11 December. Born in Maratha, Syria, 409; died in 493.* Daniel was a priest who became a monk in the region of the Upper Euphrates. He visited **St Simeon Stylites** the Elder, who was living on a pillar in Antioch, on at least two occasions. At the age of 42, Daniel felt called to emulate Simeon and become a stylite (from the Greek *stylos*, meaning pillar). Emperor Leo I had two pillars constructed for him. They were connected by a railed platform which supported a shelter. Daniel became a great attraction and from his pillar he gave spiritual advice, preached, healed the sick and celebrated the Eucharist.

The only time in 33 years that he came down from his pillars was to visit the Emperor Baliscus to stop him being misled by the heresy of Monophysitism*. He is the best-known stylite after St Simeon.

St David I *Feast day: 24 May. Born in Scotland, 1084; died in Carlisle, 1153.* David was the youngest of six sons born to King Malcolm Canmore and **St Margaret of Scotland**. He was sent to the English Norman court at the age of nine, and subsequently married Matilda, the widow of the Earl of Northampton, and, in 1113, became an English baron.

David succeeded his brother, Alexander I, as the King of Scotland in 1124. He greatly relied upon the advice of his close friend **St Aelred of Rievaulx**. On the death of Henry I David had been encouraged to try to push the Scottish border further south, but in 1138, at the Battle of the Standard near Northallerton, he did not follow up an attack by the Scottish knights

After some time of unrest, a peace agreement was finally reached in 1139.

In retrospect, David expressed genuine regret for having failed to control the merciless excesses of his invading troops during these skirmishes.

David founded monasteries in Scotland, instituted Norman law, and was known for his many charitable works. Aware that death was near, he used his last day to pray and prepare himself by 'thinking about the things of God'.

St David Lewis *Feast day: 27 August. Born at Abergavenny, Monmouthshire, Wales, 1616; died at Usk, 1679. Canonized in 1970 by Pope Paul VI. One of the Forty Martyrs of England and Wales.* David was the son of a Protestant schoolteacher and a Catholic mother and was the only one of the nine siblings to have been raised as a Protestant. After studying law at the Middle Temple in London, he accompanied a nobleman's son to the continent as his tutor, and while visiting Paris, converted to Catholicism. He went on to study for the priesthood in Rome and two years after his ordination, he joined the Jesuits.

In 1648 David was sent to Wales where he used a farmhouse at Cwm as his headquarters for the next 31 years. During the Papal Plot persecution of Catholics David was captured, imprisoned and sent to London to be examined by Titus Oates, the man responsible for fabricating a Catholic plot to overthrow the Charles II. Although no evidence could be found to link David Lewis to any such conspiracy, he was convicted of being a Catholic priest and sent back to Usk where he was hanged, drawn, and quartered.

St David of Wales *Feast day: 1 March. Born in south Wales; died in Menevia, 569.* Patron of Wales. Canonized in 1123 by Pope Calixtus II. David was the son of King Sant of south Wales and **St Non**. He was ordained a priest and later studied under St Paulinus. He founded the monastery at Menevia in south west Wales. The monks drank only water, worked hard and studied intensely. Around the year 550, David attended a synod at Brevi in Cardiganshire. His insightful contributions and obvious sanctity were appreciated by all present and this resulted in his being elected primate of the Cambrian Church. He was consecrated archbishop by the patriarch of Jerusalem while on a visit to the Holy Land.

St Declan *Feast day: 24 July. Born in Lismore in the early fifth century.* Declan was baptized by **St Colman of Dromore**, and studied both at home and abroad. He was one of those who preached and taught in Ireland before the arrival of **St Patrick**, and he it was who confirmed Declan as the first bishop of the See of Ardmore. Many miracles are ascribed to him.

Sts Denis, Rusticus, and Eleutherius *Feast day: 9 October. Born in Italy; died in 258.* Patron of France. Denis was raised in Italy and was sent with others as a missionary to France in 250, by Pope St Clement. Travelling to Paris, he chose an island in the Seine to be their missionary centre. They preached with great passion until Denis and two of his companions were arrested and beheaded, their bodies being thrown into the river. His converts later retrieved Denis' body from the Seine and buried him. A chapel was built over his tomb, which is on the site of the present abbey of Saint-Denis.

Denis is pictured as he was martyred, headless (with a vine growing over the neck) and carrying his own mitred head. He was the first bishop and saint of Paris.

St Derfel-Gadarn *Feast day: 5 April. Born in the sixth century.* Derfel-Gadarn was a Welsh soldier who took part in the battle of Camblan in 537, during which King Arthur was killed. He lived as a solitary hermit before becoming a monk at Lianderfel, in Gwynedd, Wales.

A carved-wood statue depicting Derfel-Gadarn as a mounted soldier was highly venerated in Wales. It was said that anyone who made an offering to this saint would be delivered from hell. Amid much protest, the statue was removed by order of Thomas Cromwell and brought to London where it was used to burn Blessed John Forest at Smithfield in 1538. This fulfilled an ancient Welsh prophecy that 'this image should set a whole forest afire', as it did indeed set Friar Forest on fire and consumed him to nothing.

St Desiderius *Feast day: 23 May. Born in Autun, France; died in Vienne, France, 607.* Desiderius was a strong and fearless bishop during a period of much corruption in the Church. His uncompromising opposition made him many enemies, the chief of whom was Queen Brunhildis whose grandsons, Theodebert and Thoedoric, were kings of Austria and Burgundy respectively.

The learned bishop was accused of being too worldly because he read the great Latin classics and he gave lessons in grammar. **St Gregory the**

Great was asked to examine the charges, and completely exonerated him. However Brunhildis proceeded to have him expelled for a further four years on a series of fictitious charges.

Following his recall, Desiderius strongly condemned King Theodoric's lifestyle to the court. The king, angry at what he perceived as Desiderius' presumption, ordered three of his hired men to give him a severe beating on his journey home. These men carried out their orders with such ferocity, that Desiderius died as a result of their extreme violence.

St Dionysios *Feast day: 17 December. Born on the Greek island of Zakynthos, 1546; died in 1624.* Dionysios was born into the royal household of the Venetians, but refused to use his lofty position to personal advantage. He was highly intelligent and by the age of 21 he had mastered several languages. When his parents died, Dionysios entered the monastery of Strophades and was ordained priest in 1577.

He was known not only for his piety but also for his wisdom and beneficence.

In 1572 Dionysios planned a mission to the Holy Land but he stopped over in Piracus, Greece and never completed his journey. Nikanor of Athens encouraged him to accept the appointment of Bishop of the Island of Aegina. His reputation for miracles and holy wisdom spread quickly, attracting pilgrims from far and wide so that he was soon overwhelmed by his great popularity. He asked for and was given permission to return to his native island.

He died peacefully at the age of 75, and a tomb was built for him in the church of Dionysios on the Island of Zakynthos. The cover is removed from time to time, to permit worshippers to see his body 'perfectly preserved and aromatic'.

St Disibod *Feast day: 8 September. Born in Ireland in the seventh century.* Discouraged by his lack of success as a missionary in Ireland, Disibod, an Irish bishop, underwent a voluntary self-exile, or white martyrdom similar to that endured by Columba. He travelled to Germany, where he met with much greater success, and founded a monastery on a hill near Bingen, which was later to become the home monastery of **St Hildegard**.

St Dismas *Feast day: 25 March. Died in Jerusalem, 33.* Dismas was the name of the good thief who was crucified with Christ on Calvary. In response to his plea that he should remember him when he came into his kingdom, Jesus Christ responded, 'Today you will be with me in paradise' (Luke 23: 39–43). The name Dismas comes from the Greek word *dysme*, which means dying.

One legend tells of how the two thieves, the other being known as Gestas, held up and detained the Holy Family on their way to Egypt; Dismas bought off Gestas with 40 drachmas to leave them unmolested, whereupon the infant predicted that they would be crucified with Him in Jerusalem, and that Dismas would accompany Him to Paradise.

St Dominic *Feast day: 4 August. Born in Calaruega, Spain, 1170; died in 1221.* Patron of astronomers. Canonized in 1234 by Gregory IX. Dominic was the youngest of four children of a town warden. He was a keen student, and also made time to care for the poor, on one occasion selling his books in order to give money to the poor. He was appointed Canon at Osma at the age of 26, and soon became prior superior of the chapter, a community which was noted for its strict adherence to the rule of **St Augustine of Hippo**.

In 1203 the Bishop of Osma chose Dominic to be his companion on a special mission to a heretical group which had become firmly established at Languedoc. They were known as the Albigensians*, and previous attempts to restore the group to orthodox faith had failed. The group had been unimpressed by the formality and arrogance of previous official Church representatives, but in contrast, Bishop Diego and Dominic decided to prepare meticulously for a careful, reasoned discussion. This respectful approach, coupled with their obvious sincerity and simple lifestyle, proved most effective.

Dominic founded an institute for women at Prouille in Albigensian territory in 1206, and attached several preaching friars to it, but disaster struck their carefully planned mission work when, in the same year that Bishop Diego died, the papal legate was murdered by the Albigensians. Pope Innocent III launched a crusade against them, which lasted five years, but all through this time, Dominic continued with his attempts to win the heretics back to the faith by persuasive preaching, and argument.

In 1214 Dominic was given a castle at Casseneuil, and along with six followers he founded an order devoted to the conversion of the Albigensians. Through his willingness to preach everywhere and anywhere, the Order of Preachers (the Dominicans) came into being, and was formally approved by Rome in 1216.

Dominic spent the last years of this life travelling all over Western Europe, setting up new houses and centres for preaching. His early disciples held together the spiritual and intellectual aspects of faith, alongside simple tasks of everyday living.

Dominic was a compassionate man, who had as his constant reading material, the gospel of Matthew, Paul's letters and the works of John Cassian. He cared deeply about preaching the Gospel and missionary work right up to the end of his life. Dominic was the founder of the order of preachers known as the black friars, and died in Bologna after illness forced him to return there while on a preaching tour in Hungary.

Note: The Inquisition was an institution within the Catholic Church responsible for wiping out heresy. Those whose beliefs or practices deviated markedly from the orthodoxy of the councils of the Church became the target of efforts to bring them back. It came to be that resistance was seen as rebellion, which often led to active persecution. Many of Dominic's followers (the black friars) became actively involved in this, and thus, the move from a simple and humble approach to win the hearts and minds of the heretics imperceptibly moved to become the active and powerful imposition of orthodox faith.

Dominic was known for his involvement in the Inquisition, which in his day was a neutral term meaning the enquiry into what is believed. He was given the title 'Inquisitor General'.

St Dominic of Silos *Feast day: 20 December. Born in Canas, Navarre, Spain, 1000; died in 1073.* Dominic's early years were spent as a shepherd boy, looking after his father's flocks, on the Spanish side of the Pyrenees. He entered the Benedictine order at San Millan de la Cogolla, eventually becoming abbot of that monastery. King Garcia III of Navarre exiled him because of his refusal to surrender part of the Benedictine lands to the crown.

Dominic and some other monks then asked King Ferdinand I of Castile and Leon for help, and the king appointed him abbot of the struggling and rundown St Sebastian Abbey, at Silos near Burgos. Only six monks were left, but, using the rules of monastic life which had been recently developed by the monks at Cluny in France, Dominic transformed the place. He added cloisters, and a room for copying and illuminating manuscripts and as his reputation for holiness spread throughout the region, more and more people came to visit.

The monastery became a centre of learning and liturgy in that part of Spain and by the time he died, it had developed into be a healthy and growing community of over 40 monks.

Dominic is one of Spain's best-loved saints, who was noted for his miracles. Until 1931 it was the custom for the Abbot of Silos to bring the staff of Dominic of Silos to the Spanish royal palace whenever the queen was in labour. It would be left by her side until the child had been safely delivered.

St Donald *Feast day: 15 July. Born in Ogilvy in Forfarshire, Scotland in the eighth century.* Donald's wife bore him nine daughters who, on the death of their mother, embarked on a life within a religious community under his direction and care. Many places, wells, and hills, have been named the 'Nine Maidens' in their memory. The nine daughters all entered a monastery at Abernethy, which had been founded, by St Darlugdach and **St Brigid** at Abernethyn.

St Donan *Feast day: 17 April. Born in Ireland; died in 618.* Donan left for Scotland and visited **St Columba** on Iona to ask if he would be his spiritual advisor or 'soul friend'. Columba declined, and Donan set off for the Isle of Eigg where he formed a large monastic community, which was to suffer the greatest recorded martyrdom of the early Celtic Church.

Christian missions in Celtic lands seldom experienced violent opposition in the early days, but there were occasional exceptions. A raiding party, whether of early Vikings or pirates paid to carry out an attack resulting of some perceived wrong done by the community broke in just as Donan was celebrating communion. Surprisingly they agreed to his request to let them finish the service. Donan then led the monks across to the refectory, which the raiders set on fire. Any who survived the fire were killed later by the sword. Fifty-two monks in all were martyred that day.

St Dorothy *Feast day: 6 February. Born in Caesarea, Cappadocia; died in 304.* During Emperor Diocletian's persecution of the Christians, Dorothy was one of the many Christian believers who refused to sacrifice to the gods. The governor tortured her and ordered that she be executed. On the way to the place of execution, a young lawyer called Theophilus mockingly suggested that she should send him fruits from 'the garden' of Paradise where, she had joyously announced, she would soon be.

Dorothy prayed that this might happen, and just before she was executed an angel appeared to Theophilus bearing a basket of three roses and three apples. The angel also carried a message from her, saying that she would meet him in the garden. Theophilus was converted soon afterwards and martyred in the same period of persecution.

St Drithelm *Feast day: 17 August. Born in Northumbria, England; died in 700.* Drithelm was a wealthy man, whose experience of conversion was as unusual as it was traumatic. **St Bede** records that he died, experienced a powerful vision of heaven, hell, and purgatory, and then found himself alive again whereupon he felt compelled to tell others of his experience.

As a result of this, he divided his possessions among his wife and children, made some gifts to the poor, and became a monk at Melrose Abbey. He lived there in great austerity for the rest of his life.

St Drostan *Feast day: 11 July. Born in Ireland; died in 610.* Drostan was a member of the royal Cosgrach family of Ireland, and a disciple of **St Columba**. He was named the first Abbot of Deer in the heart of rural Aberdeenshire, Scotland. Drostan ended his days near Glenesk, Angus, and there are many place names associated with him all over northeast Scotland including a well at Aberdour.

St Dunchad *Feast day: 24 May. Born in Ireland; died in 717.* Dunchad was born into the family of the Irish king, Conall Gulban. He became a monk and an abbot. For the last decade of his life he was Abbot of Iona, in Scotland. During this time he was persuaded that the Roman liturgical customs, which had been so divisive for the Church since the Synod of Whitby, should be adopted on Iona.

St Dunstan *Feast day: 19 May. Born near Glastonbury England, 909; died in 988.* Dunstan was born into a noble family and educated by Irish monks. From an early age he was interested in the creative arts and he became a Benedictine monk, when he was 25 years old. He was ordained by his uncle **St Alphege** and appointed abbot of Glastonbury Abbey in 943, which became a great centre of learning under his leadership. He also made time to encourage other nearby monastic institutions.

Dunstan was a skilled musician who played the harp well and composed several hymns. He was also skilled at metal work, and a writer of manuscripts.

When civil war broke out, Dunstan became deeply involved in politics, which angered those who regarded this as unwarranted interference. He openly criticized several influential people for immorality and his proposals that a peace agreement with the Danes would be a good option was not well received by the authorities.

The country was reunited in 957 under King Edgar and Dunstan was appointed Archbishop of Canterbury. A thorough reform of Church and state was initiated, with the restoration of Church discipline as a central aim. Clergy were once again expected to live in accordance to their vows. They were also encouraged to learn a handicraft and to play their full part in the rebuilding of the monasteries which had been destroyed by the Danish invaders.

Dunstan served as Edgar's chief advisor for 16 years and was unafraid to correct him when he felt it necessary. In old age he retired but continued to teach at the cathedral school until his death.

St Dymphna *Feast day: 15 May. Born in Ireland in the seventh century.*
Patron of those suffering from nervous and mental afflictions. Dymphna was only a child when her mother, whom she resembled greatly, died. Her grieving father King Damon, who was afflicted with a mental illness, fell in love with her. In order to escape her father's incestuous desires, Dymphna fled to Europe with her confessor St Gerebran. Damon followed in hot pursuit, caught up with them in Belgium, and ordered that the priest's head be cut off. He tried to persuade his daughter to return to Ireland with him, but when she refused he had her beheaded also.

Many miracles have taken place at Dymphna's shrine, which was constructed on the spot where her body was buried at Gheel in Belgium.

E

St Eata *Feast day: 26 October. Born in England; died in Hexham, 686.* St Eata was educated by **St Aidan** at Lindisfarne where he became a monk and a priest. At **St Colman**'s request, he was made abbot there, and then Abbot of Melrose. He founded the monastery at Ripon in Yorkshire, but Eata was obliged to leave his post because he refused to celebrate Easter on the date observed by the Roman tradition. This lack of compliance was the outward sign of a much deeper disagreement between the Celtic and Roman styles of Christian Church, both in government and practice.

After the Synod of Whitby had decided in favour of the Roman practices, Eata, a man of peace and conciliation, finally agreed to adopt them. He was appointed Bishop of Bernicia in 678 but traded sees with **St Cuthbert** at the latter's request. Eata briefly became the Bishop of Hexham before dying of dysentery.

St Ebbe *Feast day: 25 August. Born in Northumbria, England; died Berwickshire c. 683.* Ebbe was the sister of St Oswald the King of Northumbria and, assisted by the generosity of her other brother Oswi, founded a nunnery on the Derwent at Ebbchester in the See of Durham.

She also established a double monastery (one each for monks and nuns) at Coldingham near Berwick, and she governed the house of nuns herself until she died. The site is still known as St Abb's Head.

Ebbe was a holy and dedicated woman, but proved to be a weak leader and following her death the nunnery fell into lax behaviour before eventually being destroyed by fire.

St Ebbe the Younger *Feast day: 22 June. Born in Northumbria, England; died at Coldingham, England, 874.* Ebbe the younger was Abbess of Coldingham Abbey in the border region between Scotland and England. At that time the abbey was the largest monastery in the area, and had been founded by another **St Ebbe**, 200 years earlier, hence her title 'the Younger'.

During one Danish invasion, the nunnery was attacked and Ebbe disfigured her face by mutilating it, cutting her lips and nose, in order to discourage the Danish raiders from raping her. The rest of her community followed her example and when the raiders encountered the disfigured nuns they were so disgusted that they kept their distance. However the invaders returned soon after and burnt the abbey to the ground, killing everyone in it.

St Edbert *Feast day: 6 May. Born in northern England; died in 698.* Edbert was a monk who was widely respected for his Bible knowledge and great learning. He was also famed for his generosity, as he regularly tithed everything he possessed. When he was appointed Bishop of Lindesfarne, he replaced the wooden church roof with one of lead. He followed the custom of his predecessor **St Cuthbert** and withdrew to a nearby island during the 40 days of Lent.

Edbert instructed his monks to open the tomb of **St Cuthbert** who had died nine years earlier, and examine the body. They found that it had not suffered corruption and Edbert ordered a new tomb be constructed for the saint's body, asking that, when he died, he should be buried in the old tomb. Before the year was out, he was dead and his monks did as he had requested.

St Edburga *Feast day: 12 December. Born in Wessex, England; died in 751.* Edburga was a princess of Wessex who became a Benedictine nun and a disciple of **St Mildred** whom she succeeded as Abbess of Minster-in-Thanet. She generously endowed several missionary projects and built a church for her convent.

She met **St Boniface** while on a pilgrimage to Rome, and subsequently entered into a long correspondence with him. Most of what is known about her has been gleaned from these letters. Skilled at calligraphy, she copied several religious books at Boniface's request. St Lull, who was one of Boniface's companions, sent her a present of a silver stylus and some spices to aid her in her work. Edburga lived a long and fruitful life, marked by prayerful tranquillity.

St Edgar *Feast day: 8 July. Born in Wessex, 935; died in 975.* Edgar, the son of Edmund king of Wessex, was educated by **St Dunstan** and **St Ethelwold**. He became king of all England when he was only 16. His early life was wild and unruly, and he fathered a child, **St Edith**, by seducing a nun named Wulfthryth.

In later life he reformed and made a positive and effective contribution to Church life, going on to help in the foundation of 30 monasteries. These revived monastic foundations became thriving centres for education and the arts.

Edgar married twice: his first wife gave him a son, **St Edward the Martyr;** and his second wife bore him a second son, who became known as Ethelred the Unready. Edgar was buried at Glastonbury.

St Edith of Wilton *Feast day: 16 September. Born in Kensing, England, 961; died in 984.* Edith was the daughter of King Edgar of England and Wulfthryth who was a novice at Wilton. Her mother, who later became a nun at Wilton Abbey, had placed her there as a very young child. Edith became a nun at the age of 15 and graciously declined her father's offers of positions in charge of other convents. When her half-brother **St Edward the Martyr** was murdered Edith steadfastly refused all attempts to persuade her to leave her order to become queen.

St Edmund Arrowsmith *Feast day: 28 August. Born in Haydock, England, 1585; died at Lancaster, 1628. Canonized in 1970 by Pope Paul VI.* Edmund was the son of a farmer named Robert Arrowsmith. He was constantly harried for his adherence to Catholicism and left England for France in order to study for the priesthood. Following his ordination in 1612, he was sent on a mission to England. He was allowed to minister without hindrance in Lancashire until 1622 when he was arrested and questioned by the Protestant Bishop of Chester. Under the instruction of King James, all arrested priests were set free two years later, and upon his release Edmund joined the Jesuits.

In 1628 he was rearrested on false charges when a young man he had censured for an incestuous marriage betrayed him. Edmund was convicted of the crime of being a Catholic priest, and was sentenced to death.

He was hanged, drawn and quartered at Lancaster that same year.

St Edward the Confessor *Feast day: 13 October. Born in Islip, England, 1003; died in 1066.* Patron of kings, difficult marriages and separated spouses. Canonized in 1191 by Pope Alexander III. Edward was the son of King Ethelred the Unready and when the Danes invaded England in 1013 he and his mother Emma were sent to Normandy for safety. Following Ethelred's death in 1016, Canute became King of England and took Emma, who had returned to England by this time, as his wife. Edward remained in Normandy until he was invited to return to be crowned King of England in 1042. He married Edith, daughter of the Earl of Godwin in 1045 although the marriage was never consummated.

He proved to be a gentle, peaceful and non-confrontational monarch who was generally well appreciated even though he favoured the Normans in the early years of his reign.

Edward was responsible for building and endowing St Peter's Abbey at Westminster, the site of the present Abbey. One day, Edward gave one of his rings to a beggar in the vicinity of the new building. Two years later some pilgrims from England visited the Holy Land and met an old man who told them that he was **St John the Divine**, gave them the ring and asked that it be returned to the king. They were also asked to warn him of his impending death, and within the year he was buried in the Abbey at Westminster.

Edward's devotion to the Christian faith, his willingness to be available to his subjects and concern for the poor earned him the title 'the Confessor'.

St Edward the Martyr *Feast day: 18 March. Born in England, 962; died in 979.* Edward was the eldest son of King Edgar of England and his first wife Ethelfleda who died shortly after her son's birth. **St Dunstan** baptized him. On his father's death in 975 he became king with Dunstan's support but against the wishes of his stepmother, Queen Elfrida, who had intended that her own son Ethelred should succeed to the throne.

Edward was cruelly murdered in 979 while hunting in the forest. Elfrida bore some responsibility for this, but following the event, she was filled with remorse and withdrew from society, later providing the means to build monasteries at Amesbury and Wherwell.

Many miracles were reported at Edward's tomb in the years following his death.

St Edwin *Feast day: 12 October. Born in Yorkshire, England, 584; died at Hatfield Chase, England, in 633.* A prince of Deira, Edwin spent many of his early years in exile, before becoming king of the whole kingdom of Northumbria. He gradually gained lordship over the other English kings and married Ethelburga, daughter of the King of Kent, after promising to allow her to practise her Christian religion. **St Paulinus of York** was chaplain to the queen, and acted as bishop for new converts. When Queen Ethelburga gave birth to a daughter Eanfleda, she was baptized along with 12 others, thus becoming the first indigenous Northumbrians to become Christians.

Edwin, though thoughtful and wise, had a melancholic disposition and took time to decide which religion he should follow. All the while Paulinus gently instructed him and prayed for his conversion. He finally sought baptism at Eastertide in 627, in the wooden church of St Peter which stood on the site of the present York Minster.

When an alliance between the Welsh army of Cadwalon and the Penda of Mercia threatened his kingdom, Edwin went out to oppose them at Hatfield Chase and was killed in the ensuing battle. Pope Gregory XIII gave permission for him to be represented among the English martyrs on the walls of the chapel of the English College at Rome.

St Egbert *Feast day: 24 April. Born in Northumbria, England; died in 729.* Egbert was of noble birth, and became a monk at Lindisfarne. While studying in Ireland, his companion died during an outbreak of the plague and Egbert, while seriously ill, vowed that if he was spared he would never return home.

Egbert was a peacemaker by nature and tried unsuccessfully to persuade King Egfrith not to invade Ireland. He inspired **St Wilfrid** and several other Anglo-Saxon missionaries to go and work on the continent though he himself was prevented from going with them. He travelled instead as a peace emissary to the island of Iona where Abbot **Adamnan** had failed to persuade the monks to accept the Roman customs following the Synod of Whitby. Egbert's calm and measured approach succeeded in convincing them to do so, and on the very day he died, monks on Iona celebrated Easter on the Roman date for the first time.

St Egilo *Feast day: 28 June. Born in Germany; died in 875.* Egilo was Abbot of Prum, near Trier, Germany. It was here that he admitted St Humphrey to the novitiate. In 860 he was directed by Emperor Charles the Bald to restore Flavigny Abbey at Dijon, and he went on to found the Abbey of Corbigny in the Burgundy region of France.

St Egwin *Feast day: 30 December. Born in Mercia, England; died in 717.* A relative of Ethelred, who was King of Mercia, Egwin became the Bishop of Worcester, England in 692. He was accused of being overly strict by his clergy, and deposed. Egwin went to Rome to clear himself, locking his feet in chains before setting out on his journey. When he arrived he bought a fish in the market and on opening its mouth found a key, which fitted the padlock. The pope vindicated him of the vague charges that had been brought against him and he returned to England to be reinstated.

He was subsequently prompted by a vision of Mary to found Evesham Monastery with the aid of the kingdom of Mercia. In 709, Egwin made a second pilgrimage to Rome, this time accompanied by King Cenred of Mercia and King Offa of the East Saxons. On this occasion he was granted special privileges for the Abbey at Evesham by Pope Constantine.

St Eleanora *Feast day: 21 February. Born in Provence, France, 1226; died in 1276.* Eleanora was the daughter of Count Raymond IV of Provence. She married King Henry III of England when she was ten. After 37 years of marriage her husband died and she became a Benedictine nun. She was well known for her holy and pious life.

St Elfleda *Feast day: 8 February. Born in Northumbria, 653; died in 714.* Elfleda was the sister of King Oswy of Northumbria, England. She had been placed in the convent of Hartlepool at a young age. When the abbess, **St Hilda**, moved to Whitby, she took Elfleda with her, and on Hilda's death Elfleda succeeded her as abbess there.

She proved to be extremely influential as a mediator in theological disputes and with her help **Sts Wilfrid** and **Theodore** resolved their differences. She was also highly thought of by **St Cuthbert**.

St Elizabeth of Hungary *Feast day: 19 November. Born in Hungary, 1207; died in Marburg, 1231. Canonized in 1235 by Pope Gregory IX.* Elizabeth was the daughter of Alexander II, King of Hungary. A pious child, her spirituality blossomed and matured in adolescence.

In 1221 she married Louis of Thuringia but continued to lead an austerely simple and disciplined life, practising penance regularly, and showing great generosity to the poor and needy.

Her husband Louis greatly admired her faith and encouraged her in it. He was killed while fighting with the Crusaders, and following his death Elizabeth made arrangements for the care of her three children, left the court, and in 1228 entered the Franciscan order.

She organized the building of a Franciscan hospital at Marburg, and devoted herself to the care of the sick until her death at the age of 24.

St Elizabeth of Portugal *Feast day: 4 July. Born in Spain, 1271; died in 1336. Canonized in 1625 by Pope Urban VIII.* Elizabeth was a Spanish princess who, at the age of 12, was given in marriage to King Denis of Portugal. She was very beautiful and devout, and though she proved to be a holy and devoted wife, and Denis a fair ruler, his personal life caused a great scandal. A servant lied to the king about Elizabeth's pages, and the king in a jealous rage ordered the one he believed to be guilty, to be sent to a lime-burner who had been given secret orders to throw the young man into the furnace on arrival. However, Elizabeth's page stopped to attend communion, as was his daily custom, and having missed the early service, remained for the later one.

Meanwhile, the king sent the wicked page to the lime-burner to find out if the order had been carried out. Seeing this page approaching, the lime-burner grabbed him, believing he was obeying the king's command, and threw him into the furnace.

When the king learned the truth of the matter, he made a public apology to his wife and from then on showed her even greater respect. Elizabeth was constantly at his side during his last long illness, and she lived a further 11 years, doing works of charity. She was a model of kindness toward the poor and a successful peacemaker between friends, family and even nations.

St Elizabeth Seton *Feast day: 4 January. Born in New York, 1774; died in 1821.* Elizabeth was born into a prominent family and married a professor of anatomy.

They had four children together but her husband died when she was only 29. Two years later, she founded a religious community for children of the poor, and this developed into the American Sisters of Charity. Though often tempted to discouragement and surrounded by many difficulties, she never took the easy way out by returning to her privileged upper-middle-class life. Her faithful perseverance stands as a testimony to her disciplined holiness.

St Eloi *Feast day: 25 June. Born in Chaptelet, Haute Vienne, 588; died in 660.* Eloi was a goldsmith, famous for his skill as a designer and also for his economical use of materials. He was ordained priest and proved so effective as a preacher that he was chosen to be Bishop of Noyon. He was fervent and hardworking in his new appointment and went on to found a number of monasteries.

One of his surviving sermons warns against relying on fortune-tellers and omens, arguing that Christians should arm themselves with the sign of the cross as the only safe defence against harm.

Late in life he became counsellor to **St Bathildis**, and together they helped influence the Council of Chalon to pass motions that restricted the sale of slaves and safeguard Sunday as a day of rest for them.

In spite of his heavy Episcopal responsibilities Eloi continued to be an expert goldsmith and fine craftsman.

St Emily de Vialar *Feast day: 17 June. Born in 1797 at Gaillac, Languedoc, France; died in 1856. Canonized in 1951 by Pope Pius XII.* Emily was the eldest child and only daughter of Baron James Augustine de Vialar and his wife Antoinette. At the age of 15 she was removed from school in Paris to become companion to her widowed father, but this proved to be an uneasy relationship. Known as the good angel of Gaillac, she devoted herself to caring for the poor, especially those children who had been neglected by their parents.

In 1832, her maternal grandfather Baron de Portal, who was physician to Louis XVIII and Charles X of France, died, leaving her a considerable fortune. She used this to buy a large house at Gaillac in which she set up a religious community with herself as abbess. She clothed the 12 postulants with the religious habit, marking the beginning of the Congregation of Sisters of St Joseph of the Apparition.

In the course of 22 years the Congregation expanded to more than 40 houses, many founded in person by St Emily.

From her youth she was troubled by a hernia, contracted while doing a deed of charity. Her last message to her congregation was 'Love one another.'

St Emma *Feast day: 27 June. Born in Austria in the early eleventh century; died in Gurk, Austria, 1045.* Emma was a relative of Emperor St Henry II, and was raised at Henry's court by St Cunegund. She was happily married to William Landgrave of Friesach, and their two sons oversaw the family mining interests. They found the miners difficult to control, and attempted to enforce their authority by imposing strict new disciplines on the workforce. This caused so much resentment that a riot ensued during which the brothers were murdered.

Though overcome by grief, William managed to show restraint in his response to the incident and set off on a pilgrimage to Rome. Sadly he died on the way back, and Emma then made the decision to devote her life to God. She was generous to the poor, founded several religious houses and a double monastery at Gurk in Austria.

St Emmeramus *Feast day: 22 September. Born in Poitiers, France; died at Feldkirchen, near Munich, Germany, 690.* Emmeramus preached for several years in France before travelling to Germany to preach to the pagan population and then on to Bavaria. He became a Benedictine monk, Abbot of Regensburg Monastery and subsequently bishop of that same city. After three years Emmeramus decided to make a pilgrimage to Rome, much to the displeasure of Duke Theodo who tried everything he could think of to persuade him to stay and minister to his subjects.

Emmeramus was attacked and badly beaten by hired assassins at Kleinhelfendorf, near Munich, Germany, and although he managed to reach Feldkirchen, he died of his injuries there. Duke Theodo appears to have had some involvement in the attack on Emmeramus.

St Enda *Feast day: 21 March. Born in Ireland; died 530.* Enda was noted for his military feats but had agreed to leave the army due to his forthcoming marriage. Tragically, on his return from war, he found his fiancée dead, and after a time of mourning and reflection he decided to become a monk.

Enda set out on a pilgrimage to Rome and was ordained there. On his return to Ireland, he established churches at Drogheda, and then, with the help of **St Ailbhe**, he secured the Aran Islands from his brother-in-law King Aengus of Munster, where he built the monastery of Killeaney. Ten other foundations eventually developed, and Enda is renowned as one of the founders of monasticism in Ireland.

St Ephraem *Feast day: 9 June. Born in Nisibis, Mesopotamia, 306; died in 373.* Ephraem was born into a Christian family, although he was not baptized until he was an adult, which was common practice at the time. Ephraem served as a teacher and permanent deacon under four successive bishops in Nisibis.

Heretical ideas were the subject of popular ditties in his day and in order to counteract these, Ephraem made up his own hymns. Their originality and imagery captured the hearts of the Christians so well that Ephraem is given credit for awakening the Church to the importance of music and poetry in spreading the faith.

During the siege of Nisibis in 350, Shapur II, the King of Persia, instructed his engineers to divert a river in order to flood the city. However, when he tried to invade, his army found that their diversion had made the waters too high to cross, and this gave the citizens, including Ephraem, time to ambush and defeat the invaders. Later, in 363, Nisibis was captured, the Christians were forced out and Ephraem became a solitary ascetic on Mount Edessa.

During the famine that hit Edessa in 372 Ephraem learned that some citizens were hoarding food. When told that they couldn't find a fair way to distribute the daily food, he volunteered to organize this and, with the help of some hand-picked assistants, accomplished this to everybody's satisfaction.

The famine ended with a year of abundant harvest, and the following year Ephraem died. He left hundreds of hymns and poems that strengthened and inspired the whole Church. For example 'Give me as provision for my journey your prayers, yours psalms and your sacrifices.'

St Erastus of Corinth *Feast day: 26 July. Born in Corinth in the first century.* Erastus was the treasurer of the city of Corinth (Romans 16:23) and was converted by the ministry of **St Paul** and became one of his helpers. Paul sent **St Timothy** and Erastus on ahead from Ephesus to Macedonia (Acts 19:22), while he stayed a little longer there.

Erastus is especially well known to the early Church as an effective follower of the way and was given permission by Paul to stay in Corinth (2 Timothy 4:20) and work there. He went on to become Bishop of Philippi in Macedonia and was later martyred for his faith.

St Eric IX *Feast day: 18 May. Born in Vastergotland, Sweden; died in Uppsala, Sweden, 1161.* Patron of Sweden. Eric was brought up in a noble family and married into the royal family, becoming King in 1150. A devout Christian, he spread the faith throughout his own nation and campaigned to both convert and conquer Finland. He persuaded the English Bishop Henry of Uppsala to remain in missionary service there.

Eric was slain by Swedish nobles who were allies of Prince Magnus of Denmark. They beheaded him near Uppsala Cathedral as the Danish army led by Magnus entered the region.

He was author of the *Code of Uppland* or *King Eric's Law*.

St Ethbin *Feast day: 19 October. Born in Britain; died in Ireland in 600.* Ethbin was entrusted to **St Samson**'s care when he was 15, and he later became a monk at Taurac, Brittany. His mentor and teacher, St Winwaloe, came upon a leper one day when Ethbin was with him. When asked what they should do, Ethbin replied, 'Do what the apostles of Christ did. Bid him rise up and walk.' Emboldened by the faith of his young disciple, Winwaloe had faith to do just that, and the leper was healed.

The monastery was destroyed in a raid by the Franks in 556, and Ethbin fled to Ireland. He became a hermit in a wood in Kildare and lived there for the last 20 years of his life.

St Ethelbert *Feast day: 20 May. Born in East Anglia, England, 770; died at Sutton Walls, Herefordshire, 794.* Ethelbert was the son and heir of Ethelred, King of East Anglia who went to Mercia to ask for the hand of King Offa's daughter Alfreda. Although Ethelbert was received with outward courtesy, after a few days he was murdered on the instructions of the queen. His body was roughly treated and his head cut off and buried in a shallow grave. Later the remains of his body were buried in Hereford and the severed head was buried in Westminster Abbey.

St Ethelburga *Feast day: 11 October. Born in Stallington in Linsey, Kent, England; died in Essex, 675.* Ethelburga was the daughter of a wealthy king of the East Angles. She was determined to become a nun, and her sister St Erkennwald founded a convent for her at Barking, in Essex, England.

In order to ensure her proper training, an abbess, St Hildelitha, was brought from France to instruct her. There was some rivalry between the two as they endeavoured to outdo one another in extreme austerity.

When the convent of Barking was hit by a plague epidemic and several of the nuns died, Ethelburga and her sisters experienced reassuring visions of eternal life.

St Ethelreda *Feast day: 23 June. Born in Exing, Suffolk, 640; died in 679.* Ethelreda (who was also known as Audrey) was an English princess whose marriage at an early age was never consummated. She was widowed after three years, and though she had taken a perpetual vow of virginity, she married again, this time for political reasons.

Her young husband however, soon grew dissatisfied, and urged her to become his wife in more than name. **St Wilfrid of York** helped Ethelreda escape, and she fled south with her husband chasing her all the way to Colbert's Head, where a miraculous seven-day high tide keep the two apart. Eventually her husband left, and he later married someone else, while Ethelreda became a nun and founded the great abbey of Ely.

An enormous tumour developed on her neck, which she bore gladly, regarding it as divine punishment for all the necklaces she had worn in her early years. Seventeen years after her death, Audrey's body was moved to a stone sarcophagus in Grantchester and she became one of the most popular of the Anglo-Saxon woman saints.

A festival, known as 'St Audrey's Fair', was held at Ely on her feast day. The cheap jewellery sold then was called 'tawdry' (a corruption of Audrey) as a reminder of her experience.

St Ethelwold *Feast day: 1 August. Born in Winchester, England, 912; died in 984.* Ethelwold was ordained by **St Alphege the Bald**, and in 943 he joined the Benedictines at Glastonbury under **St Dunstan**. He became Abbot of Abingdon in 955 and bishop in 963. Ethelwold worked with **Sts Dunstan** and **Oswald** of York in bringing about a monastic revival after the Danish invasions. He founded several abbeys and wrote a monastic community rule based on that of **St Benedict**. His school of illumination at Winchester was widely respected, and because of his spiritual wisdom he was known as 'the Father of Monks'.

St Eugene de Mazenod *Feast day: 21 May. Born in Aix-en-Provence, 1782; died in 1841. Canonized in 1995 by Pope John Paul II.* Eugene grew up in the days following the French Revolution and though these were dangerous times for priests, decided to enter the seminary, and accepted ordination, ministering mainly to the poorest of the poor. Others soon joined him, and they formed themselves into a religious community with special care for the destitute, adopting the name the Missionaries of Provence. Eugene became Bishop of Marseilles and worked to strengthen and advance the work of the diocese by constructing churches, caring for the clergy, and giving sound teaching. He also founded an order called the Oblates of Mary Immaculate, which specialized in the difficult task of mission outreach to the most remote parts of the known world.

St Eulalia of Merida *Feast day: 10 December. Born in Spain, 290; died in 304.* Eulalia was an enthusiastic young believer who was just 12 when the persecutions of Decian began. Her mother, afraid that her outspokenness might get her into trouble, took her into the country at the first sign of trouble. She escaped, returned to the town, and presented herself before the local judge, Dacian of Merida.

She questioned him about the unfair treatment of Christians, who were being forced to worship false gods. Initially amused by her apparent precociousness but latterly angered by her stubborn resistance, Dacian ordered that she be torn by iron hooks, and a lighted torch was applied to her wounds. Her hair caught fire and she was suffocated by the smoke.

St Eulogius of Cordova *Feast day: 11 March. Born in Cordova, Spain; died in 859.* Eulogius was born into a land-owning family during a period when this part of Spain was under Islamic rule. Christians were obliged to pay increased taxes and any attempt to convert followers of Mohammed was punishable by death.

He was ordained priest and proved himself to be devout, restrained and kindly. A respected theologian, he worked to support the Christian community, and during the times of persecution in the 850s, he wrote extensively about the sufferings and torture that had been carried out and of the faithfulness of the Christian martyrs.

Eulogius was named Archbishop of Toledo, but he was never actually consecrated. When it was discovered that he had been hiding a young Moorish woman named Leocritia, who had converted to Christianity, in his house, both Eulogius and Leocritia were arrested. At the trial Eulogius spoke bravely on behalf of the Gospel, refusing all efforts to make him change his mind, and consequently both he and Leocritia were found guilty and beheaded.

St Euphemia *Feast day: 16 September. Born in Chalcedon; died in 303.* Euphemia was a Christian virgin who refused to attend a pagan ceremony in honour of the god Ares. She was tortured by being beaten in the mouth with a mallet and then slain by a wild bear. A church was erected in her honour in the fifth century.

St Euphrosyne of Polotsk *Feast day: 23 May. Born at Polotsk; died in Jerusalem, 1173. Canonized in 1984 by Pope John Paul II.* Euphrosyne was the daughter of Prince Svyatoslav; at the age of 12 she became a nun and withdrew from society. She was gifted in calligraphy and used the money she raised by copying manuscripts to provide help for the poor. She travelled widely, and also founded a convent at Seltse. Her final days were spent in the Holy Land and Euphrosyne died in Jerusalem, Israel. Following her death, her body was returned to Kiev for burial.

St Eusebius of Vercelli *Feast day: 2 August. Born in Sardinia, Italy, 315; died in 371.* Eusebius' father died as a martyr in Sardinia, and he grew up in Rome where he was ordained a lector and then bishop by popular acclaim. Gifted in conflict resolution, the pope sent him to the Emperor Constantius to try to resolve the troubles between the Arians* and Catholics, and as a result a council was held in Milan in 355.

Eusebius refused to condemn **St Athanasius**, and because of this the emperor exiled him to Scythopolis in the Holy Land. Once there his troubles continued; local Arians stripped him half naked and dragged him through the streets to a tiny cell, where they kept him for four days without food. Later they broke into his home, stole all his belongings, and imprisoned him again.

Emperor Constantius' successor Julian finally allowed Eusebius and other exiled bishops to return home in 361. He worked with Athanasius and participated in various Church councils, travelling widely to strengthen and support Christian communities.

St Eustace *Feast day: 20 September. Born in Rome, date unknown.* Eustace, who was originally named Placidas, rose to be a general in the Roman army, under Trajan. He was out hunting in the woods one day when he encountered a stag with the crucifix between its antlers. This unusual sight was enough to bring about his instant conversion. Taking the name Eustace, he was baptized along with his entire family. Due to a series of unfortunate incidents he was parted from his family, and his formerly prosperous life was destroyed.

In a time of national trouble, Eustace was recalled to command an army, and he and his family were miraculously reunited as a result. After achieving a famous victory, Eustace refused to sacrifice to the gods and he and his family were finally martyred by being roasted inside a brass bull.

St Eustochium Calafato *Feast day: 20 January. Born in Messina, Sicily, 1435; died in 1468. Canonized in 1988 by Pope John Paul II.* Eustochium was the daughter of Bernard, a rich merchant, and Countess Matilda, from Messina, Sicily. On the death of her father in 1446, she sought baptism and was christened Smeralda (Emerald).

Following a vision of the crucified Christ, she joined the Poor Clares at the convent of Bascio and devoted herself to penance and charitable activities. Finding the community too lax in some of their practices, Eustochium sought and received authorization to begin a new community nearby with stricter observances. This community, which eventually came to include both her mother and sister, transferred to the Monte Vergine Convent and Eustochium took over as abbess in 1462.

St Everild *Feast day: 9 July. Born in Wessex in the seventh century.* Everild was of noble birth. She travelled north in the company of **Sts Bega** and Wulfreda to become a Benedictine nun. **St Wilfrid** received her and gave her a place called 'the Bishop's Farm', where Everild founded a religious house of which she became the first abbess. This quickly grew to be a thriving community of over 80 nuns.

St Exuperius *Feast day: 2 May. Born in Pamphylia; died in 127.* Exuperius was one of a family of slaves of the Roman pagan Catulus. He and his wife Zoe were born into Christian families, and although they had been negligent in their religious observance, they brought up their two sons, Cyriacus and Theodolus, as Christians.

Shamed out of their lukewarm faith by the fervent devotion of their children, the parents refused to sacrifice to idols. This resulted in the whole family making a bold confession, before being roasted to death in a furnace on the order of Catulus.

F

St Fabian *Feast day: 20 January. Born in Italy; died in 250.* Fabian was a layman, who out of curiosity travelled to Rome after Pope Anteros died in 236 to find out who the new pope would be. In the middle of the discussion, a dove flew down and settled on Fabian's head. As far as the waiting crowd was concerned this was a clear sign that the Holy Spirit had made its choice and Fabian was proclaimed pope by popular acclaim.

Under Emperor Philip, Fabian divided the city of Rome into seven districts, appointing a deacon to care for each one and was most active in collecting and collating the acts of the martyrs. He was gifted in administration and initiated a restoration programme for Church property.

On Philip's death his successor Decius, ordered all Christians to offer incense to idols. Many Christians complied but Fabian courageously refused to do so. He died a martyr in 250 and was buried in the Cemetery of Calixtus, a cemetery that he had helped to restore. A stone slab with his name on it can be found to this day.

St Fabiola *Feast day: 27 December. Born in Rome; died in 399.* Fabiola was born into a wealthy and famous family. Strong-willed and passionate, she understandably divorced her first husband because of his refusal to leave his riotous lifestyle, but her remarriage was against Church rules, causing a scandal in Church circles. Both her first and second husbands died shortly after this and after due penance she returned to the Church, devoting herself to doing good and giving financial support to various churches and communities.

She visited **St Jerome** at Bethlehem in 395, and gave him great support and encouragement in his controversy with Patriarch John of Jerusalem. She firmly resisted an underhand attempt to gain her sympathy by the bishop's supporters. It was decided that she was too extrovert to belong happily to the community of nuns there and that her talents and lifework lay elsewhere. Fabiola returned to Rome and continued her charitable work, and with St Pammachius opened a hospice for poor pilgrims at the coastal town of Porto.

St Fara *Feast day: 3 April. Born in France; died in 657.* Fara was the daughter of Count Agneric and served in the court of King Theodebert II. She resisted her father's demands to marry, and she managed to convince him to build a convent of which she became abbess. Fara was responsible for the running of this community for 37 years. After her death the convent was renamed after her, and this in time became the famous Benedictine Abbey of Faremoutiers.

Sts Faustinus and Jovita *Feast day: 15 February. Born and died in Brescia. Date uncertain.* Faustinus and Jovita were brothers of noble birth who preached fearlessly during a time of persecution, while their bishop lay in hiding. They were captured and paraded around the north of Italy, but continued to preach and baptize at every opportunity, causing a furious response from the pagan population. Neither threats nor torments could shake their convictions and the Emperor Hadrian, who happened to be passing through Brescia at that time, ordered that they be killed. Calocerus, one of Hadrian's court officials, was present in the amphitheatre when the two brothers were led in. Their shining faith, coupled with the refusal of the wild beasts to touch them, brought about his conversion and Bishop Apollonius baptized him.

Calocerus was arrested, tortured and imprisoned before being taken to Albanga in Liguria and beheaded on the seashore.

St Faustus *Feast day: 28 September. Born in Brittany, France 400; died in 490.* Faustus was a lawyer by training. He served as a monk on the island monastery of Lérins, and then as abbot. He was highly thought of as a Christian writer, but was driven into exile by the Visigoth King Euric, and only returned after the king had died. Faustus was Bishop of Riez, France, from 459. Though a strong supporter of the teachings of **St Cassian**, which at that time was thought to be on the very edge of orthodoxy, he proved to be an articulate and influential opponent of both the Arian* and Pelagian* heresies. When he died he was deeply mourned and a large church was built in his honour.

Sts Felix and Audactus *Feast day: 24 October. Born in Rome; died in 303* Felix was a priest who suffered under the persecutions of Diocletian. As he was being led away to the place of his execution, a stranger in the crowd, learning that he was being killed for being a Christian, called out that he too was a believer.

The man, who never disclosed his name, was known simply as Audactus (the added one), and was immediately arrested and martyred alongside Felix. Their tomb is in a cemetery on the Ossian Way and later a church was built over the site.

Sts Felix and Augebert *Feast day: 6 September. Born in England in the seventh century.* Felix and Augebert were captured in England and sold into slavery in France. Pope **St Gregory I** arranged for them to be ransomed and subsequently Felix became a priest and Augebert a deacon. While preparing to return to England as missionaries, they were slain by pagans in Champagne, France.

St Felix of Nola *Feast day: 14 January. Born in Nola near Naples, Italy in the 3rd century.* Felix's father, Hermias, was born in Syria, had served in the Roman army and retired to an estate in Italy. On his father's death Felix gave away his inheritance and was ordained by Bishop St Maximus of Nola. During the persecution of Christians in 250, the bishop took refuge in the desert and so the soldiers arrested Felix instead and threw him into jail. He was released by an angel, who led him to the ailing Maximus. He entreated the bishop to return to his post and, having convinced him, they travelled back to Nola together.

Felix kept well hidden until the persecution ended and when Maximus died he was unanimously elected bishop but declined the post in favour of a senior priest named Quintus. For the remainder of his life Felix retreated to live on a small piece of land which provided for his needs and he shared all that he had with the poor and needy.

St Ferdinand III of Castile *Feast day: 30 May. Born in Salamanca, Spain, in 1199; died in 1252. Canonized in 1671 by Pope Clement X.* Patron of engineers. Ferdinand was the son of Alfonso IX, King of Leon, and Berengaria, daughter of Alfonso III, King of Castile (Spain). He was declared king of Castile at the age of 18 and his mother advised him during the early years of his reign. He married Princess Beatrice of Germany and they had seven sons and three daughters.

The King of Leon turned against his son and tried to take control of his throne but they were later reconciled and fought successfully together against Islamic invaders. Ferdinand prepared for battle by praying and fasting and proved successful in seizing the city of Cordova from the Moors. He also captured Seville in 1236, and shortly after this his wife died. He founded the Cathedral of Burgos and the University of Salamanca; he later remarried.

During his lifetime Ferdinand compiled and reformed a code of laws which stood the test of time for many centuries. He was a just ruler who frequently pardoned former offenders and political rivals. Ferdinand regarded war as a painful necessity to rescue Christian people from the infidels, and even then it was only justified when all else had failed.

Ferdinand died after a prolonged illness and was buried in Seville cathedral, dressed not in royal robes but in the habit of his secular Franciscan Order.

St Fergus *Feast day: 27 November. Born in Ireland; died in the eighth century.* Fergus was known as 'the Pict' in his homeland. He was made a bishop before leaving Ireland to evangelize Scotland. He settled in Strathearn in Perthshire. He preached in the north and east of the country, especially Caithness, Buchan and Forfarshire founding a church at Glamis. He assisted Pope St Gregory II, at the Roman Council of 721.

St Fiacre *Feast day: 12 October. Born in Ireland; died in 670.* Fiacre was an Irish monk who willingly left his homeland to live as a recluse in Europe. When he reached Meaux in France the bishop St Faro gave him some land for a hermitage. He became renowned for his gardening skills and also gained a reputation for misogyny because he never allowed a woman to enter the enclosure of his hermitage or even his chapel. He gave special care and concern to those who suffered from venereal disease.

His name is also remembered in the hackney carriages that used to be hired out from the hotel in Paris, which was named after him. This is also the likely derivation of the French word *Fiacre* which is used to describe taxicabs.

St Fillan *Feast day: 19 January. Born in Ireland in the early eighth century.* Fillan was the son of Feriach and St Kentigerna. He became a monk in his youth and came to Scotland and lived for many years as a hermit near the monastery of St Andrew's, finally being elected abbot. He later resigned and resumed his eremitical life at Glendochart, Perthshire, where he built a church and was known for his miracles and his powerful and effective prayer.

According to legend, an ox, which Fillan was using to drag materials to the site of the church he was building, was killed by a wolf. He immediately commanded the wolf to take the ox's place and the animal meekly complied.

St Finbar *Feast day: 25 September. Born in Connaught, Ireland in 560; died in 610.* Finbar was the son a lady of the Irish royal court. He was educated at Kilmacahil, Kilkenny, where the monks named him Fionnbharr (white head) because of his light-coloured hair. He went on pilgrimage to Rome with some other monks from his community and visited **St David** in Wales on their return journey. On another visit to Rome the pope, who had wanted to consecrate Finbar a bishop, had a vision that God had different plans for the holy monk.

He preached in Scotland and in southern Ireland, lived as a hermit on a small island on the river Lee, and gathered a small group of followers around him They founded a monastery, which was to form the basis for the city of Cork, and of which he was the first bishop.

His monastery continued to attract numerous disciples, and many miracles were attributed to him. It was said that the sun did not set for two weeks after he died at Cloyne.

St Finnian *Feast day: 17 February. Born in Ireland; died in 661.* Finnian was an Irish monk on Iona, Scotland, and a close friend of King Oswy of Northumbria, England. He baptized King Penda of Mercia and King Sigebert of the East Saxons. As an evangelist in southern England, he worked with **St Cedd**, and succeeded **St Aidan** as Bishop at Lindisfarne. At the Synod of Whitby, Finnian was one of those who favoured the retention of the Celtic practises over those of the Roman tradition.

St Fintan *Feast day: 17 February. Born in Leinster, Ireland; died in 603.* Fintan was educated by St Colum of Terryglass and became a hermit in Clonenagh, Leix, Ireland. Disciples gathered around his hermitage and he eventually became their abbot. Fintan lived a very austere life but was always compassionate and understanding, even allowing his followers less strict dietary rules than he allowed himself.

When soldiers arrived bearing the severed heads of their enemies, Fintan buried these in the monks own graveyard in the hope that they might benefit from the prayers of the monks. He was a wonder worker, and also known for the accuracy of his prophecies. He was also disciple of **St Columba**.

St Flavian of Acquapendente *Feast day: 22 December. Died in 362.* Flavian was a former prefect of Rome and the father of **St Bibiana**. Julian the Apostate had him branded on the forehead as a slave and exiled him to the small village of Acquapendente in Tuscany. He died while at prayer.

St Flavian of Constantinople *Feast day: 18 February. Died in 449.* Flavian succeeded St Proclus as Patriarch of Constantinople in 446. The Emperor Theodosius II expected some favours from Flavian for making him patriarch and when they were not forthcoming, treated him with great hostility.

Flavian also opposed Eutyches, who began the heresy of Monophysitism*. This led to his being deposed and exiled at the so-called 'Robber Synod' (*Latrocinium*) at Ephesus in 449, when Pope Leo I's (also known as Leo the Great) representatives were not even permitted to read his letters. When he appealed to the Pope, Flavian was beaten so mercilessly that he was mortally wounded and died three days later in exile.

The Council of Chalcedon proclaimed him a saint and martyr only two years after his death in 451.

St Frances of Rome *Feast day: 9 March. Born in Rome, 1384; died, 1440. Canonized in 1608 by Pope Paul V.* Patron of cars and drivers. Frances was born into a wealthy, noble family and though she believed that she had a vocation to be a nun at a very early age, her father had already promised her in marriage to the son of another wealthy family.

Out of obedience to her father, she married Lorenzo Ponziani, a good person who loved her deeply. However, her mother-in-law's expectation that she should enter into a full and active social life proved too much for Frances and, within a few months, she collapsed from emotional exhaustion. Close to death, and unable to eat, move or speak, she had a vision of **St Alexis** in which she believed God wanted her to recover, and she did so with great rapidity.

She became close friends with her brother-in-law's wife Vannozza. They developed a simple rule of spiritual disciplines for themselves, visiting prisons and hospitals and praying together in an abandoned tower.

Following a flood, there was famine in Rome and Frances and Vannozza began giving away the household supply of corn, wine, and oil. Their father-in-law was furious and proceeded to sell off everything that was surplus to the family household requirements before the women could give it away. Frances was so desperate for food to give away that she scraped the floor of the storehouse for the few remaining corn seeds.

Some time later her husband discovered that the previously empty granary had miraculously been filled to overflowing with corn. About the same time the wine casks were found to be empty, and Frances was rightly accused of giving wine away. However when she he turned the tap of an empty cask, the wine flowed abundantly. These miracles, along with the faithfulness of the two women, brought about the conversion of both Lorenzo and Frances' father-in-law. She sold her jewels, gave the money away, and from that point on wore only a simple green dress.

In a time of war, some drunken soldiers broke into her home and tore it apart, smashing everything. Rather than give up in despair, Frances cleared out the wreckage and created a makeshift hospital and shelter for the homeless.

Lorenzo had returned from the war a sick and broken man, but with his support and respect, Frances started a lay order called the Oblates of Mary. These were women who lived in the world but were attached to the Benedictines. When Lorenzo died, Frances, now aged 52 moved into the community house with the other Oblates and was appointed their superior. She died four years later.

St Frances Xavier Cabrini *Feast day: 13 November. Born in Italy, 1850; died in 1917. Canonized in 1946 by Pope Pius XII.* Patron of immigrants. Of peasant stock, Frances worked on a farm with her brothers and sisters.

Poor health prevented her from becoming a nun, but she became a teacher in a girls' school and stayed for six years before going on to found the Missionary Sisters of the Sacred Heart. At Pope Leo XIII's request, Frances and a small band of supporters (six nuns) travelled to the United States in 1889 to work among the Italian immigrants.

Though not fluent in English and somewhat disdainful of the protestant culture with which she was unfamiliar, her deep trust in God, her administrative gifts and dogged determination helped her to overcome many barriers.

She founded schools, hospitals, and orphanages for Italian immigrants and children. Her work spread to England, France, Spain, and South America. In 1946, she became the first American citizen to be officially recognized as a saint. She died in Chicago, Illinois on 22 December, 1917.

St Francis of Assisi *Feast day: 4 October. Born in Umbria, Assisi, 1181; died in 1226. Canonized in 1228 by Pope Gregory IX.* Patron of animals, merchants and ecology. Francis was the son of a successful cloth merchant and was well provided for in his early years. He was happy, charming, well-liked, and a natural leader. A lover of music and pleasure, Francis, surrounded by a group of young people of similar age, led the casual and frivolous lifestyle of a French troubadour.

Through the bravado of youth he became involved in a local war, but found himself easily captured and was imprisoned for a year in a dungeon until the ransom was paid for his release.

Francis set out on the Fourth Crusade, fully arrayed in new, shining white armour but he had completed only one day of the journey before turning back on account of a dream. He was ridiculed as a coward and a spoilt young brat, but from that time on he began to remove himself at every opportunity to pray secretly for forgiveness for his former lifestyle.

More and more moved by the love of God, he approached a leper whom he came across in the street and kissed the man's hand. When the leper returned the holy kiss, Francis experienced a great sense of joy and on turning round to look again at the leper, found that he had vanished.

While praying in the church at San Damiano, Francis heard the figure on the crucifix say, 'Build my Church.' Assuming that the message referred to the decaying church buildings of his hometown, Francis enthusiastically set about fixing them with the help of a team that he had gathered for the purpose.

Much to his father's anger, he sold some of the cloth from the family business to get money for the repairs. Following his discovery of the missing goods Francis' father brought his son before the bishop and furiously demanded that he be recompensed. The bishop advised that the money should be returned, and Francis obliged immediately, also taking off all of his clothes as a sign that he renounced all connection with his earthly father.

Wearing nothing but the rough brown cloth that had been given him to cover his nakedness, Francis went to live in the woods, and from then on had no possessions.

He begged for stones and with the help of a few others, rebuilt the church of San Damiano. Slowly he became aware that the call was not simply to build structures, but also faithful congregations and leaders. People from all walks of life came to join him and adopted his lifestyle of sleeping rough, begging for food and showing forth God's Love. He based his 'rule' on the call to poverty as expressed in the Sermon on the Mount (Matt 5–7). Though he never wanted to found a religious order people continued to join him, and the brotherhood could be said to have brought itself into being.

Francis believed that all of God's creatures were part of his brotherhood and he preached to hundreds of birds about being thankful. Another famous story tells of how he fearlessly 'told off' a wolf that had been killing and eating people, but also criticized the villagers for not providing food for their fellow creatures.

His brothers were passionate missionaries and would go out in pairs to preach, encouraged by what they referred to as the constant joy of holy poverty.

He told his brothers to treat coins as if they were pebbles in the road; for Francis, to possess something was to bring about the death of love. He was a man of action who acted passionately from the heart.

Francis felt called to go to Syria to convert the Muslims while the Fifth Crusade was being fought, going straight to the sultan who was won over by his passionate preaching. He said to Francis, 'I would convert to your religion – but both of us would be murdered.'

Returning to Italy, he found that the brotherhood had grown to 5,000 in ten years. When his dream of radical poverty and simplicity was severely challenged, he handed over his role of authority to become just another brother, as he had always wanted.

Suffering and humiliation marked Francis' last years and his harsh living caught up with him as he found that he was also losing his sight. The pope ordered the best of treatments for him, which at that time involved cauterizing his face with a hot iron. During the treatment Francis spoke to 'Brother Fire' and reported that his Brother Fire had been so kind that he felt nothing at all. In later years, he also received the stigmata (the marks of the wounds of Christ).

St Francis Borgia *Feast day: 10 October. Born in Ganadia, Valencia, Spain, 1510; died in 1572. Canonized in 1670 by Pope Clement X.* Francis was a duke at the Spanish court who, on the death of his wife, became a Jesuit priest. A descendant of the Borgias – his great-grandfather had been the notorious Pope Alexander VI – he did much to restore the good name to his family.

St Ignatius of Loyola appointed him to oversee the Society of Jesus in Spain and Portugal, which he did with great success through powerful preaching and the establishment of many houses and colleges. He was made Superior General of the Jesuits in 1561, and was responsible for sending Jesuit missionaries all over the world.

Francis Borgia, who has been called the second founder of the Jesuits, remained completely humble to the end of his life and his self-effacing, determined yet winning ways were recognized by people of all social classes.

Blessed Francis Pacheco *Feast day: 20 June. Born in Ponte da Lima, Portugal; died in 1626.* Francis Pacheco entered the Society of Jesus in 1584 and was subsequently sent to Macao where he was ordained. He travelled to Japan with Bishop Louis Cerquiera as vicar general to the recently constituted diocese, of which Cerquiera was head. The bishop died in 1614 and Pacheco was forced to leave Japan following the formal expulsion of all foreign clergy. He took the risk of returning to Japan in disguise and managed to serve the people for a short time as an Episcopal administrator. He was soon discovered, however, and arrested, along with eight other Christians. All nine of them were burned alive at Nagasaki.

St Francis of Paola *Feast day: 2 April. Born in Paola, Italy, 1436; died in 1507. Canonized in 1512 by Pope Julius II.* Francis was educated at the Franciscan friary of San Marco and became a hermit near Paola. The community he began with two others developed to become known as the Hermits of St Francis of Assisi, also called the Minim Friars. Their rule emphasized penance, charity, and humility, and added to the three monastic vows another relating to fasting.

Francis had the spiritual gifts of miracles, prophecy and discernment. His giftings were so widely known that Pope Sixtus II ordered him to France in response to a request from King Louis XI, who was dying and believed that Francis could heal him.

He established bases in southern Italy and Sicily before spending the rest of his life at the monastery of Plessis, France.

St Francis de Sales *Feast day: 24 January. Born in Thorens, France, 1567; died in 1622. Canonized 1665 by Pope Alexander VII.* Patron of journalists. Following his father's wish, Francis became a soldier. He then studied in Paris, and went on to receive a doctorate in law in Padua, before being ordained.

His first mission was to the Cablais district in Switzerland, which was Calvinist territory. His father refused to give him any aid for this plan to convert the 60,000 Calvinists back to Catholicism, and the diocese was too poor to support him.

By the time he left, his expedition consisted of himself and one of his cousins. After three years, he had not made one convert, and even his cousin had left him. Finding people unwilling to listen, he copied out his sermons by hand and slipped them under people's doors, thus Francis was the first to use religious tracts to communicate the Gospel. He showed great love in all his actions, and slowly, as he began to talk with people, especially to the children, his message began to get through. In four years most of the population had reconverted to Catholicism.

In 1602, he was made Bishop of the Diocese of Geneva, which was in the centre of Calvinist territory, though he only visited the city of Geneva twice. He encouraged a movement toward holiness and mystical union with God.

A widow from Dijon called **Jane Frances de Chantal**, sensing the call to become a mystic, asked Francis for spiritual direction. This encounter helped to clarify his own beliefs about mysticism and after three years of working with Jane, he finally decided to form a new religious order, but they were unsure where they might find a convent for their contemplative Visitation nuns. Francis told Jane, 'God will be with us, if he approves.' In due course a man who had known nothing of their plans felt guided to offer them a place for use by pious women.

Though Francis was often ill and tired out with preaching, visiting, and instruction, he never lost his inner peace. He directed many people by correspondence, and a selection of his letters for ordinary people was collected into a book entitled *Introduction to the Devout Life*. This became an instant success all over Europe, although some tore it up because he tolerated dancing and jokes. For Francis, the love of God was the key and the test of prayer was a person's actions.

Francis wanted to be a hermit but he was more in demand than ever. He was systematic and simple in his approach to letter writing. He wrote, 'I have more than fifty letters to answer. If I tried to hurry over it all, I would be lost so I intend neither to hurry nor to worry. This evening, I shall answer as many as I can. Tomorrow I shall do the same and so I shall go on until I have finished.' His last word of advice: 'Humility'.

St Francis Xavier *Feast day: 3 December. Born in Pamplona in the Basque area, Spain, 1506; died in 1552. Canonized in 1622 by Pope Gregory XV.* Francis was sent to the University of Paris to study and came under the influence of **St Ignatius of Loyola** during his time in that city, becoming one of the band of seven who in 1534 founded the Society of Jesus at Montmartre.

In 1536, he left Paris for Venice to join Ignatius, and was ordained there in 1537. Soon after, when the pope had formally recognized the Society, Francis was ordered, along with Fr Simon Rodriguez, as Jesuit missionaries to the Far East.

After six months in Mozambique spent preaching and giving aid to the sick they travelled to Goa, India with two companions. In 1542, India and the East were set up as a separate province, and Ignatius made Francis its first monastic superior.

He began preaching to the people of India, but also attempted to reform his fellow Europeans, living among the local people and adopting their customs on his travels. Though Francis had no gift for foreign languages, during the next decade he converted tens of thousands to Christianity.

His missionary zeal was undiminished, even though he was working with inadequate funds, and often met open resistance from officials. In 1552 he set out for China, landed on the island of Sancian within sight of his goal, but died before he reached the mainland.

St Frideswide *Feast day: 19 October. Born in Eynsham, Mercia, 680; died in 735.* Patron of Oxford University. Frideswide was the daughter of Prince Didan of the Upper Thames region of England. A prince named Algar from a neighbouring kingdom was smitten by her beauty and pursued her, seeking her hand in marriage. She ran away to Thomwry Wood in Birnsey, and hid there for three years, using a former pigsty as her monastic cell. On hearing that her suitor had become temporarily blind and had given up the pursuit, she interceded for him and his sight was restored.

Frideswide then became a hermitess and founded the St Mary's Convent in Oxford. She is patron of the university of that city, and in liturgical art is depicted as a Benedictine nun, sometimes with an ox for companion.

St Fridolin *Feast day: 6 March. Born in Ireland; died in 540.* Fridolin travelled to France and settled in Poitiers, rebuilding the monastery of St Hilary, which had been destroyed by Vandals. He then became a hermit, living on an island on the Rhine, becoming known as 'the Wanderer' because of his many evangelizing journeys. He built the abbey of Sackingen, and was remembered as 'the Apostle of the Upper Rhine'.

St Fructuosus *Feast day: 21 January. Died in 259.* Fructuosus was martyred along with two of his deacons, Augurius and Eulogius, in Tarragona, Spain. He was the Bishop of Tarragona, and all three were arrested just as they were preparing for a church service. They were tried by the Roman governor Emilian a few days later, and when they refused to deny their faith, were sentenced to be burned at the stake in the local arena.

Fructuosus even refused drugged wine to lessen the pain of the ordeal, reminding the kindly person who offered it that it was a Wednesday and therefore a day of fasting. As they died they continued to pray and worship the triune God. **St Augustine** admired these martyrs greatly.

St Frumentius of Ethiopia *Feast day: 27 October. Born in Tyre; died in 380.* Frumentius and Aedesius were young Christian brothers who studied philosophy in Tyre under Meropius. In the year 330 their teacher decided that he would like to take a voyage along the coasts of Arabia. To the young men's overwhelming delight, he offered to take them along with him.

On their return journey the sailors got involved in a fight with the local populace at Adulis, Abyssinia (Ethiopia) which led directly to the murder of Meropius and everyone on ship except the boys. They had been studying under a tree some way from the ship and were forced into slavery in the royal court at Aksum.

The king was greatly impressed by their learning and Frumentius was soon made the king's chief secretary and Aedesius his cup-bearer. They gained permission to try to convert the people and for churches to be opened in Ethiopia. When the king died, the two men were given their freedom, but at the queen's request they remained for a time to help ensure a safe transition of the monarchy.

Aedesius then returned to Tyre, while Frumentius went on to Alexandria to visit St Athanasius to ask for a bishop to be sent to Aksum. Athanasius decided Frumentius would be the ideal candidate and ordained him bishop and sent him back to plant the Christian Church in Ethiopia.

St Fursey *Feast day: 16 January. Born on the island of Inisguia, Lough Carri, Ireland; died in 648.* Of noble birth and brother of Sts Foillan and Ulan, he left his native land and became a pilgrim for Christ in 630. Fursey and his friends went to East Anglia, England, and founded a monastery near Ugremouth on land donated by King Sigebert. In his later years Fursey went to France and built another monastery at Lagny, near Paris, again on land donated to him, this time by Erichonald, mayor of Neiustria.

Fursey is especially remembered for his visions and religious imagination, and was known to enter into long trance-like meditations on the reality of wickedness breaking in on the world. He died in Mezérolles and was buried in Picardy.

St Fulk *Feast day: 22 May. Born in Italy; died in 600.* Patron of Castrofuli. Fulk was on a pilgrimage to Rome, when he came into the vicinity of Castrofuli in Italy. On hearing of an outbreak of plague in the city he chose not to bypass it, but rather went and stayed there in order to help care for those who had been infected.

Eventually he became infected also, and died among the people he had so selflessly gone to serve.

G

St Gabriel the Archangel *Feast day: 29 September.* Patron of soldiers, postal and telephone workers. Gabriel's name is Hebrew for 'man of God'. He was the angel who announced to Daniel (9:21) the time of the coming of the Messiah, who appeared to Zachariah to announce the birth of **St John the Baptist** and who appeared to the **Virgin Mary** to announce that she would bear a son who would be conceived of the Holy Spirit. He is also referred to in the revelation of **St John** as the captain of the heavenly host and is thus seen as the protector of Christians in general.

The feast day of 29 September is now associated with all angels and is celebrated under the collective commemoration of **St Michael** and All Angels.

St Gaius of Korea *Feast day: 15 November. Born in Korea; died in 1627.* Gaius was a former Buddhist monk from Korea, who travelled to Nagasaki, Japan. He began training for the Dominican order, but was arrested and charged with harbouring missionaries. He was found guilty as charged and executed.

St Gall *Feast day: 1 July. Born in Ireland; died in 645.* Gall was trained by **Sts Columban and Comgall**, and was one of the 12 men who accompanied **St Columban** to France.

A well-respected scholar, he helped found the monastery of Luxeuil, but when St Columban was exiled in 610, Gall followed him to Switzerland and then to Italy. They built themselves cells near Bregenz, converted many idolaters and following one of his sermons, Gall broke some pagan idols and threw them into the lake. This action made them as many enemies as it did converts. They stayed there for two years, made gardens and Gall spent his spare time making nets and fishing on the lake. A disagreement arose between them because Columban thought Gall was malingering, and imposed a penance on him, forbidding him to say Mass, which he obediently observed.

He remained in Switzerland and became a hermit refusing promotion three times before he died in Arbon. The monastery of St Gall, though not founded by him, was erected on the site of his hermitage.

St Galla *Feast day: 5 October. Born in Rome in the sixth century.* Galla was the daughter of Symmachus the Younger, a Roman scholar known for his holiness. The Emperor Theodoric condemned him to death in 525 on false charges.

When Galla's husband died within months of their marriage she chose to enter a convent and founded a convent and hospital near St Peter's in Rome. She spent the remainder of her days in works of mercy and the pursuit of holiness and ended her life there.

St Gelasius I *Feast day: 21 November. Born in Rome; died in 496.* Of African descent, Gelasius was born in Rome and served as an archdeacon before being elected pope in 492. He was the first pope to be called the Vicar of Christ.

He remained on good terms with the temporal powers, but was not under their thumb. Gelasius was always ready to stand against heresy by whatever means. He burnt several Manichaen books and openly opposed the celebration of pagan feasts.

While he recognized that both spiritual and temporal powers are separate trusts from God, he did not regard them as equal, affirming the spiritual as superior. On his death, he was buried in St Peter's, but it is now impossible to determine which of the tombs is his.

St Geminian *Feast day: 31 January. Died in 348.* Geminian is remembered chiefly for his kindness to **St Athanasius** who had to pass through Modena on his way into exile in France. Geminian was Bishop of Modena and received him hospitably as he did **St John Chrysostom**. Geminian was firm and unbending in his opposition to heresy.

St Genesius *Feast day: 25 August. Date unknown.* Patron of actors. During a stage entertainment before Emperor Diocletian in Rome, Genesius had been chosen to act the part of a catechumen who was about to be baptized in a play that ridiculed the Christian sacrament. During the performance, he was suddenly struck by the power of the Christian gospel and was converted to Christianity there and then.

When he was presented to the emperor after the entertainment, he could not contain his excitement and declared his newfound faith to everyone. This enraged Diocletian who had him handed over to be tortured in an effort to force him to recant and sacrifice to the pagan gods. When Genesius continued to refuse, he was beheaded.

St Genevieve *Feast day: 3 January. Born in Nanterre near Paris, 422; died in 512.* Patron of Paris. When Genevieve was seven years old, **St Germanus of Auxerre** passed through her village on his way to Britain. He recognized her gifts and encouraged her in her pursuit of holiness. At the age of 15, her bishop consecrated her to God with the symbolic veil of a virgin and after her parents died, she moved to live with her grandmother in Paris. Although she led a life of prayer and service to the poor, she experienced opposition and criticism, even when Germanus spoke out on her behalf.

When Attila the Hun was reported to be marching on Paris, the inhabitants of the city prepared to evacuate, but Genevieve persuaded them to avert the scourge by fasting and prayer, assuring them of the protection of heaven. In the event the invading army suddenly and unexpectedly changed the course of their march and thus avoided the city. Genevieve also helped the city when the Franks blockaded it by leading out a group to procure provisions from the town of Troyes. They returned with several boats laden with corn. She bravely and successfully appealed to both Childeric and King Clovis on behalf of prisoners of war.

The life of Genevieve was one of great self-discipline, prayer and service. One of the symbols of this saint is a loaf of bread, a symbol of her generosity to those in need.

St George *Feast day: 23 April. Born in Cappadocia in the third century.* Patron of England and Catalonia. George was a brave knight who rescued a maiden princess from a dragon at Silene in Libya. The dragon was a local pest that had been kept at bay with a daily offering of two sheep, but when the situation failed to improve they became extremely apprehensive, a human victim was chosen by lot as an offering of appeasement. Eventually the lot fell to the king's daughter who was dressed as a bride and sent to her fate. George intervened by piercing the dragon with his lance and then leading it captive as if it were a pet, assuring the people that it would be harmless from now on if they were willing to put their faith in Jesus and be baptized. The people agreed, and 15,000 were baptized, including the king. George asked for no reward other than that the churches be maintained, their priests properly supported, and the poor cared for.

Later, he became a soldier in the Roman army and was one of the Emperor Diocletian's favourite soldiers, even though the emperor was a bitter enemy of Christianity. George directly criticized the emperor's cruel and selfish ways and then resigned his post in the army. He was arrested, tortured and finally beheaded.

George's story tells in graphic terms the triumph of good over evil. The Eastern Orthodox Church greatly values the image of St George and the dragon and it is a common iconic image, giving, as they see it, a perfect example of theology in line and colour.

St Gerald of Aurillac *Feast day: 13 October. Born in Aurallic, France, 855; died at Cézenac in Quercy, 909.* Gerald was born into a noble family and became the Count of Aurillac upon the death of his father. He rejected the trappings of wealth, gave away a large part of his inheritance and always dressed very simply. He rose at 2 a.m. every morning to say the first part of the divine office.

At one time he sought to enter the monastic life but Bishop Gausbert of Cahors persuaded him not to do so. The bishop explained that he would be able to exercise much more influence for good if he were to remain in his present position, as a count. In the last seven years of his life he was afflicted with blindness.

St Gerard *Feast day: 3 October. Born in Namur in Belgium; died in 959.* Gerard, who was born into a noble family, had a gentleness and holiness of life which was apparent to all from an early age. Though he first entered the army he never lost his simple piety.

Gerard first encountered the Benedictine monks of St Denis in Paris while on a diplomatic mission to the court of France. He went home, settled his affairs, and returned at the first opportunity to join the monastic community, living there for 11 years before being ordained priest. In 931 he was sent to found an abbey upon his home estate at Brogne, near Namur. He became a Benedictine abbot general and helped 18 other abbeys with their monastic disciplines.

After 20 years he retired to his cell at the Abbey of Brogne.

St Gerard Majella *Feast day: 16 October. Born in Muro Lucano, Italy, 1725; died in 1755. Canonized in 1904 by Pope Pius X.* Patron of expectant mothers. Son of a tailor and servant to the Bishop of Lacedogna, Gerard Majella was noted for his generosity and the long hours that he spent in prayer. At the age of 23 he felt called to enter the monastic life but was turned down by his first choice, the Capuchins, because of his weak health. He joined the Redemptorist order, becoming a lay brother in 1752, and served as a gardener, porter, and tailor. No matter which task he was given, he exhibited great piety, and the gift of supernatural knowledge.

He also experienced bi-location, the ability to appear in two different places at the same time, and was said to have asked for the gift of invisibility so that he might be left to pray undisturbed by those who might come looking for him. Such gifts are associated with mystics of an extreme depth of spirituality. His service, generosity and abounding humility made him the perfect model to lay brothers.

Gerard is known as the most famous wonder worker of the eighteenth century, and helped many women in labour with his prayers. He died of consumption at the age of 29.

Sts Gerard Miles and Francis Dickenson *Feast day: 30 April. Born in Lancashire, England; died in 1590.* Gerard and Francis left England and went to the Douai College at Rheims in order to train for the priesthood, and were ordained in 1583. Six years later they were sent back to England but when the ship they was travelling on was wrecked off the Kent coast, they were arrested on suspicion of being traitors. They were put on trial, found guilty and condemned to death. Both of them were hanged, drawn, and quartered at Rochester on the last day of April 1590.

St Gerasimus *Feast day: 5 March. Born in Lycia, Asia Minor; died in 475.* Gerasimus was a merchant and a follower of St Euthymius in Asia Minor. He decided to visit the hermits in Egypt and upon his return he founded a large ascetic community, in Jericho, Israel.

Gerasimus was a miracle worker who was famous for his austerity; his monks lived in almost complete silence on a diet of bread, dates and water. Their beds were simple rush mats and they had no fires or doors in their cells.

On one occasion, a lame lion approached him on the banks of the river Jordan and Gerasimus removed a thorn from its paw, after which the animal became his devoted pet. When Arab traders stole a donkey, the lion was suspected of having eaten it and Gerasimus ordered that, as a penance, the lion should take over the donkey's job of fetching water. The lion obediently submitted to this, but when he saw the Arab trader who had stolen the donkey approaching, he scared the thief away and led the donkey by its bridle back to Gerasimus. Gerasimus was very contrite for having prejudged the poor lion, and named him Jordan.

St Germaine of Pibrac *Feast day: 15 June. Born in Pibrac, 1579; died in 1601. Canonized in 1867 by Pope Pius IX.* Patron of victims of child abuse. Germaine's mother died when she was still a baby and she was brought up by her father and step-mother Hortense. She was treated very badly as a child, her basic needs went uncared for and she was forced to sleep outside in the barn. Germaine became a shepherdess, began to attend church and was known for her generosity.

On one occasion, seeing her apron folded up and knowing that a beggar had just been to the door, her step-mother thought she had stolen bread to feed him and, screaming at the top of her voice, she began to beat her, whereupon Germaine's apron fell open and a bundle of bright spring flowers tumbled out.

As time passed, Hortense's feelings towards Germaine began to soften, and she even invited her back into the house to sleep, but Germaine preferred her straw bed and continued to sleep outside. She died at the age of 22, overcome by a life of suffering.

When her body was exhumed 40 years later, it was found to be incorruptible. Her simple life of devotion to God and her neighbourly love were the marks of her holiness.

St Germanus of Auxerre *Feast day: 31 July. Born in Auxerre, in 378; died at Ravenna, in 448.* Germanus was trained as a lawyer, became governor of the Armorican border province, and was chosen to succeed **Amator** as Bishop of Auxerre. He renounced all wealth and founded a monastery near the cathedral, becoming a champion of the people in negotiations on tax with the Roman authorities.

Popes Celestine I and Leo I sent him to England along with St Lupis, Bishop of Troyes, to combat the rise of the heresy of Pelagianism* which was rife there at the time. A conference was called at Verulamium to discuss these matters, and the result was greatly encouraging in affirming the traditional point of view. A deacon called Palladius, who was the first recorded missionary to Ireland, accompanied them on their first missionary visit to England.

On his second trip, Germanus led the Britons in the defeat of an Irish and Pictish marauding party without anyone being killed. This happened at Eastertide, and he instructed British soldiers to use the war cry 'Alleluia' as they charged at the enemy. The ensuing battle is known as the 'Alleluia Victory'.

Germanus realized the importance of teaching and established schools. He was highly respected across Celtic Britain and **St Patrick** was under his tutelage for 12 years. On his death his body was taken back to

Auxerre cathedral for burial, and his shrine became a famous pilgrimage centre.

St Gertrude *Feast day: 16 November. Born in Eisleben, Saxony; died in 1302.* Patron of the West Indies. At the age of five Gertrude was placed in the care of the Benedictine nuns at Rodalsdorf and later became a nun in the same convent. She had an excellent education, and was able to write and compose in Latin prose. After her conversion she made use of these skills in her theological studies and she wrote several books, the most famous of which was entitled *The Herald of God's Loving Kindness.* Her life was filled with great mental activity, and as a mystic she explored the life hidden with Christ in God.

Sts Gervase and Protase *Feast day: 19 June. Died in Milan, date unknown.* Gervase and his twin brother Protase were the sons of the martyrs Vitalis and Valeria, and they were both martyred also. Gervase was beaten to death with a lead-tipped whip and Protase was beheaded. They are considered the first martyrs of Milan and **St Ambrose**, guided by a vision, unearthed their headless remains in the city.

St Gilbert of Sempringham *Feast day: 16 February. Born at Sempringham, England, 1103; died in 1189. Canonized in 1202 by Pope Innocent III.* Gilbert was the son of Jocelin, a wealthy Norman knight. He was born with a physical deformity, and was sent to France to study for the ministry. He was still not ordained when he returned to England to take charge of the parishes of Sempringham and Tirington, which had been granted him by his father. In due course Gilbert was ordained and when his father died in 1131 he also became Lord of the manor.

A group of seven young women lived under his spiritual direction in a house near Sempringham Church. Other new foundations followed, and Gilbert went to Citeaux, in France in 1148 to ask the Cistercians to take over the Community, but they declined. Instead, **St Bernard of Clairvaux** helped him draw up a rule for the lay brothers and sisters to follow. Pope Eugene III approved Gilbert's continuing role of oversight and the community became known as the Gilbertine Order.

Gilbert encouraged manual work of all sorts including the manufacture of furniture and the copying of manuscripts. This was the only English religious order to originate in the medieval period and it continued until King Henry VIII suppressed all the monasteries in England.

Gilbert imposed a strict rule on his Order and some lay brothers complained to the pope of too much work and too little food. Following this appeal, he received these brothers back without anger, and devised 'better conditions' for them from then on.

Gilbert was imprisoned in 1165 for aiding Thomas of Canterbury during the latter's exile, but was later exonerated. He faced a revolt by some lay brothers when he was in his 80s, but received great support from Pope Alexander III. Gilbert resigned his office late in life because of blindness, and died at Sempringham.

St Gildas *Feast day: 29 January. Born in Scotland, 500; died in the Isle of Houat, France, 570.* Gildas became a monk at Llanilltud in south Wales. **St Illtyd** helped to train him, and St Finnian became his disciple. He later made a pilgrimage to Ireland to consult with other religious communities and had considerable influence on the development of the Irish Church.

Gildas attributed the success of the Anglo-Saxon invasion to the moral laxity and general permissiveness of Britain's rulers and clerics, and used a wide range of scriptural references to back up his argument.

During a period spent as a hermit on Flatholm Island in the Bristol Channel, Gildas copied a missal for **St Cadoc**. He made a pilgrimage to Rome and on his return founded a monastery on an island near Rhuys in Brittany.

St Godric *Feast day: 21 May. Born in Walpole, Norfolk, England, 1069; died in 1170.* A peddler by profession, Godric made many pilgrimages: to Rome three times; to Jerusalem twice; to St Gilles in Provence; and to Compostela in Spain.

In 1105 he sold all he had and became a hermit, finally settling at Eskdaleside near Whitby. Godric lived on roots and berries until he was able to establish a small food garden, constructing a rough wooden hut to act as his cell. He filled his days with prayers of repentance and confession for his past sins and his evident holiness and gift of foreseeing the future drew many to him. Always eager to listen and slow to speak, he was both sympathetic and serious. He cared much for creation in general and for animals in particular. In the coldest winters he would bring rabbits and mice into his hut, warm them by the fire and set them free. Once a hunted stag came into his hut, and when the huntsmen arrived asking if he had seen it, he replied, 'God knows where it is.' He thus avoided telling a lie but also protected the animal.

Godric was a both a musician and verse writer, and some of his work still survives today. Following a long illness, during which monks from Durham nursed him, he died peacefully.

St Gregory III *Feast day: 10 December. Born in Syria; died in 741.* Gregory was known for his holiness, and following the funeral of Pope Gregory II, he was carried off by popular acclaim to be made the next Bishop of Rome. Being well educated in the scriptures, and fluent in Latin and Greek, he proved to be an excellent choice.

When the Emperor Leo II condemned the veneration of holy images, and ordered that all of them should be destroyed, Gregory strongly resisted this. He called a synod which approved specific measures that were to be taken against anyone who attempted to tear down sacred images. The controversy escalated to the point where Leo sent a fleet to Rome in an attempt to kidnap Gregory and bring him to Constantinople. However a storm wrecked several of Leo's ships and all they were able to do was to capture a few papal lands in Sardinia. Gregory fully backed **St Boniface**'s missionary work and that of **St Egbert** of York.

St Gregory VII *(Hildebrand) Feast day: 25 May. Born in Soano, Tuscany, 1020; died in Salerno, 1085.* Hildebrand was educated in Rome, became chaplain to Gregory VI, and went into exile with him. He entered a monastery where he remained until Leo IX called him to Rome to serve as Church treasurer. On being elected pope in 1073, Hildebrand took the name Gregory in honour of **St Gregory the Great** and instituted reforms against simony, clerical marriage, unchastity, and lay investiture.

He issued the *Dictatus Papa*, which proclaimed the supremacy of the pope, stating that the pope inherited the personal sanctity of **St Peter**. This led to conflict with Emperor Henry IV, who deposed Gregory at the Synod of Worms in 1076. Gregory responded promptly by excommunicating Henry. The two were reconciled in 1077 when Henry came to the castle gate at Canossa begging forgiveness. He was left standing in the snow for three days before receiving absolution from Gregory.

A further dispute arose three years later when Henry failed to keep his word and was excommunicated once again. His response this time was to set up William of Ravenna as a rival pope (anti-pope), and in 1084, following a siege of more than two years, Henry's forces captured Rome. Robert Guiscard and a band of Norman soldiers rescued the pope, who later fled to Monte Cassino to escape a popular rebellion.

St Gregory the Enlightener *Feast day: 30 September. Born in Cappadocia; died in 326.* Gregory was smuggled out of Armenia to Caesarea as an infant in order to escape violent threats against his life as a result of his father's involvement in the murder of the king. He was baptized, married, and had two sons in this enforced exile, but when Tiridates became king, Gregory returned home.

It was not long before he incurred the king's wrath with his zealous missionary efforts and this resulted in a time of persecution for believers. Eventually, Tiridates himself was converted, and Christianity became the official religion of Armenia.

Gregory was consecrated Bishop of Ashtishat, and set about building up the Church communities there through local language teaching by Armenian lay missionaries which centred on the scriptures and on Christian morality.

He consecrated his son Aristakes as his successor, and retired to a hermitage on Mount Manyea in Taron. The following year, Gregory was found dead by a wandering shepherd and was buried nearby. Several family members also followed his son as bishop until the year 438, when Isaac I decreed that the office of bishop be restricted to unmarried clergy only.

Many legends and miracles are associated with Gregory and these are connected with special Armenian Feast days. He is known as the apostle of Armenia.

St Gregory the Great *Feast day: 3 September. Born in Rome in 540; died in 604.* Patron of choirboys, educators, England and gout. Gregory was the son of a wealthy Roman senator, St Gordian and St Silvia, a nephew of St Emiliana and St Tarsilla, and a great-grandson of Pope St Felix III. He was educated by the finest teachers in Rome, and became the Prefect of Rome for a year before deciding to sell all his possessions. He gave the proceeds to the poor, turned his home into a Benedictine monastery, and used his money to build six monasteries in Sicily and one in Rome. After seeing English children being sold in the Roman Forum, he decided to become a missionary to England.

He was elected pope by unanimous acclamation in 590, and was the first monk ever to be appointed to this high office. He sent **St Augustine of Canterbury** and a company of monks to evangelize England, and other missionaries to France, Spain, and Africa.

Gregory is considered one of the four great Doctors of the Latin Church. He loved music and collected the melodies for liturgy and worship. The plainchant hymns he gathered became known as 'Gregorian Chants', because of his close association with their popularization.

St Gregory of Nazianzus *Feast day: 2 January. Born in Nazianzus at Arianzus, Cappadocia, 329; died in 390.* Gregory was the son of a bishop and received a broad education in Christian writings, and Greek philosophy. He spent ten years studying in Athens and among his fellow students was the future Emperor Julian, to whom he took a great dislike. He also met **St Basil** at this time and they formed a close friendship. They spent two years together in a lonely spot in Pontus on the river Iris, assembling an anthology of the works of the theologian Origen.

Gregory resisted ordination to the priesthood and his mother, Nonna, encouraged him toward the ascetic life, however his father's strong and persistent influence meant that he finally agreed to be ordained. Still unsure of his future, he ran away more than once to a monastery.

From 379–381 he was appointed Bishop of Constantinople, but due to the aggressive opposition of the local governor, he never took up the post. St Basil was greatly disappointed in his friend and their friendship was permanently affected by what he regarded as Gregory's lack of proper regard for his ecclesiastical responsibilities.

Gregory's skill and defence of the orthodox faith earned him the title, 'The Theologian', and was one of the greatest orators of his time, but he also loved privacy and retired to tend his garden.

St Gregory of Nyssa *Feast day: 9 March. Born at Caesarea, in 330; died in 395.* Gregory was the younger sibling in a famous Christian family, which included **Sts Macrina the Elder** and **Younger**. He received an excellent education in Athens, married a woman called Theosebeia, and became a leader in the Church, but was led to accept a wholly secular post as professor of rhetoric. When his wife died, he entered the monastery of his brother, **Basil the Great** and in his early 40s, became the Bishop of Nyssa.

He was deposed as bishop in 376, having been accused of embezzlement by the Arians*, only to be reinstated two years later by the Emperor Gratian.

Gregory was well known for his Trinitarian theology, and his support of decisions made at the Council of Nicea. He attended the first Council of Constantinople in 381, after which he travelled in Transjordan (Arabia) preaching, teaching and settling Church disputes. He was a man of extraordinary intellect and is best known for his writings on the life of Moses and for his sermons on the Song of Songs.

St Gregory Palamas *Feast day: 14 November. Born in Constantinople, 1296; died 1359. Canonized in 1368 by Pope Urban V.* Gregory was a clever and hardworking young man. His father died when he was quite young and the emperor, Andronicus II Paleologos, took a special interest in his education, hoping that he would enter his administration, but at the age of 20 Gregory withdrew to become a novice monk on Mount Athos. After a decade or so, Gregory moved to a small cell where he sought to practise unceasing prayer.

In 1326, fearing a Turkish invasion, Gregory and some others withdrew to Thessalonica. He was ordained and lived as a priest/hermit, spending the week in silence and prayer, while preaching sermons and doing priestly duties on Sundays.

In the year 1330, a teaching monk named Barlaam who was a skilled orator arrived in Constantinople from Italy. He ridiculed mental prayer, claiming it was an heretical error, and Gregory was asked by his fellow monks to put together a response to Barlaam's attacks. As a result the Constantinople Council of 1341 was called and this found in favour of Gregory.

Barlaam's disciples did not readily accept the decision and accused Gregory of being a disruptive influence, which resulted in him being imprisoned for four years.

He was eventually freed in 1347, and made Archbishop of Thessalonica in 1351.

Gregory was later captured when the ship he was travelling on was attacked, but he used the opportunity to preach both to the Christian prisoners and his Muslim captors. He was severely beaten for this, but his captors stopped short of killing him, hoping that they could obtain a ransom. This was arranged a year later, and Gregory was returned to Thessalonica.

In the three years before his death Gregory performed many miracles and healings, and on his last evening on earth **St John Chrysostom** appeared to him in a vision with the words, 'To the heights! To the heights!'

St Gregory the Sinaite *Feast day: 8 August. Born in Asia Minor in the late 13th century.* Gregory was captured by Turks as a young man, was ransomed and then travelled to Cyprus. He was later professed as a monk and received the monk's tonsure on Mount Sinai before travelling to Crete to become a disciple of Arsenios, from whom he learned the practice of continuous prayer. Sts John Climacus and **Symeon the New Theologian** also had great influence on Gregory's spiritual development.

Around the year 1300, Gregory moved to Mount Athos and he and his contemporary, **Gregory Palamas,** helped to establish Athos as a centre of mystical spirituality based on the prayer of the heart.

When the Turks began to raid Athos in 1325, Gregory sought refuge in Bulgaria, where he established a monastery. Gregory saw prayer as a continuation of the work of the Holy Spirit that was begun at baptism.

St Gregory Thaumaturgus *Feast day: 17 November. Born in Neocaesarea, Pontus; died in 268.* Gregory studied law before travelling to Caesarea, Palestine intending to continue on to Beirut to study law. Instead, he met Origen and entered his theological school at Caesarea where he was converted to Christianity. Gregory returned to Neocaesarea, intending to practice law, but found himself elected bishop by the 17 Christians in that city.

He was an eloquent preacher who brought in many converts, built a church, and soon was so renowned for his miracles that he was surnamed Thaumaturgus ('wonder worker'). A wise and much-sought-after counsellor, he advised his flock to go into hiding during the Decius persecution of 250, and fled to the desert with his deacon. On his return, he continued to minister to his flock during an outbreak of plague and also when the Goths devastated Pontus, 252–254.

At his death at Neocaesarea, only 17 unbelievers were left in the city. He stopped the flooding Lycus, and on another occasion he moved a mountain. According to **St Gregory of Nyssa**, Gregory Thaumaturgus experienced a vision of Our Lady, the first such recorded vision. He wrote a treatise on the Creed, and a dissertation addressed to Theopompus.

St Gundisalvus Garcia *Feast day: 6 February. Born in East Indies, 1556; died in 1597. Canonized in 1862 by Pope Pius IX.* Of Portuguese descent, Gundisalvus was a catechist with the Jesuits in Japan before going into business. He joined the Franciscans in Manila in the Philippines as a lay brother in 1591 and then returned to Japan with St Peter Baptist. He was one of the Japanese martyrs crucified at Nagasaki.

St Guthlac *Feast day: 11 April. Born in Mercia, England, 675; died in 714.* Guthlac belonged to the tribe of Guthlacingas and was a relative of the royal house of Mercia. He served in the army of Ethelred of Mercia for nine years before becoming a monk at Repton. On taking his monastic vows, he restored a third of his war spoils to his victims.

In 701, after two years in the monastery, Guthlac became an anchorite, making his cell on an island in the marshes of Lincolnshire. He was attacked by Britons and experienced many temptations by demons but with the help of **St Bartholomew**, to whom he had a special devotion, he was able to remain faithful.

St Guthlac had a special affinity with birds and fishes. The site of his hermitage became the monastery of Crowland, which was a frequent place of pilgrimage until the Reformation.

St Guy of Anderlecht *Feast day: 12 September. Born in Anderlecht near Brussels; died in 1012.* Guy was born into a poor family and had no formal education. He gave away the little he had in order to lead a more austere life. Guy undertook a seven-year pilgrimage on foot to Jerusalem and Rome and died soon after returning to his home city. Miracles were reported at Guy's grave. He was known as the 'poor man of Anderlecht'.

St Gyavire *Feast day: 13 June. Born in Uganda; died in 1886. Canonized in 1964 by Pope Paul VI.* Gyavire was a page to the notorious king Mwanga of Uganda. He was known as 'the good runner of messages' and was martyred by being thrown into a fire with 22 others for his faith, and for refusing to make himself available to fulfil the king's sexual demands.

H

St Hallvard *Feast day: 15 May. Born in Norway; died in 1043.* Patron of Oslo. Hallvard was of noble birth. He was the son of Vebjorn of Husaby, who was a Viking 'trader' in the Baltic Islands. On one occasion, while preparing to cross the Drammenfiord a woman, who had been falsely accused of theft, approached him and begged for help. The accusers refused to listen to his reasoned arguments, and even though he offered to reimburse them fully for whatever they claimed had been stolen, they killed with arrows both Hallvard and the poor woman. Attaching a stone to his dead body they threw it into the sea, and were amazed to find it that it floated to the surface. He became revered as a martyr because of his selfless defence of an innocent person.

St Hedda *Feast day: 7 July. Born in England; died in 705.* Hedda was educated in Whitby and ordained priest there. He travelled to London to be consecrated as the first Bishop of the West Saxons by **St Theodore**. He was a wise and prudent leader and respected for his holiness. Following his death the place of his burial at Winchester became well known as a site of miraculous healing. The belief in the holiness of this place became so strong that visitors would carry off small quantities of earth to mix as healing balm. The Venerable Bede records that in time this resulted in a large hole being excavated on the site.

St Hedwig *Feast day: 16 October. Born in Andechs, Bavaria, Germany, 1174; died in 1243. Canonized in 1266 by Pope Clement IV.* Patron of Silesia region of Eastern Europe. Hedwig was the daughter of the Duke of Croatia and Dalmatia and aunt of **St Elizabeth of Hungary**. She was married, at the age of 12, to Duke Henry of Silesia, the head of the Polish Royal family. They had a happy marriage and their union produced seven children, who unfortunately did not get on well together. Hedwig founded several hospitals and monasteries including a Cistercian convent at Trebnitz, which was built by convict labour. When her husband Henry died in battle, Hedwig became a Cistercian nun at Trebnitz where she restored the sight of a blind nun by giving her a blessing.

A skilled and patient peacemaker, Hedwig was forced to leave the convent on a few occasions to help sort out political and family disputes. She befriended a poor old woman who was very slow at learning, deciding to teacher her to say the Lord's Prayer. This took over ten weeks and involved taking the woman into her own room to sleep so that every spare moment they could go through it together. In the end the woman could both understand it and repeat it perfectly.

St Hedwig *Feast day: 28 February. Born in Buda, Hungary, 1374; died in 1399. Canonized in 1997 by Pope John Paul II.* Hedwig was the daughter of King Louis I of Hungary, and was chosen to be Queen of Poland at the tender age of ten. Her marriage was the subject of much political intrigue but it was finally decided by her advisors that she should marry Jagiello of Lithuania, but only after he became a Christian. The couple then actively promoted Christianity in Lithuania and established strong links with Poland and other neighbouring countries. Hedwig acted as a moderating force on her husband who had a genuine deep affection for her.

The Hapsburgs claimed that she and her husband were usurpers and also that she was an adulteress, but Pope Boniface IX stood firm by the couple, giving them his full support and even offering to be godfather to their first child. Hedwig died during childbirth and her daughter a few days later.

St Helena *Feast day: 18 August. Born in Drepanum, Bithynia, 250; died in 330.* Helena was an innkeeper's daughter who married the Roman general Constantius Chlorus who later divorced her when he was made emperor. Their son, who was later to become the Emperor Constantine, greatly respected and honoured her and when he became ruler he gave her the title Augusta, meaning empress.

She became a Christian late in life, when she was 62 but was so fully and enthusiastically committed to the faith that she gave the impression of having never known any other way of life. She dressed soberly, and made several pilgrimages to the Holy Land in order to conduct searches for the sites of the New Testament events. **St Ambrose** believed that, as a result of these research trips, Helena was helping to find the original cross on which Jesus was crucified. In liturgical art Helena is depicted as an empress, holding a cross.

Helena had an immense passion for the Holy Land and spent most of her later life there. She arranged for the construction of churches at the Grotto of the Nativity at Bethlehem and on the Mount of the Ascension near Jerusalem.

St Helen of Skovde *Feast day: 31 July. Born in Våastergütland, Sweden; died in 1160. Canonized in 1164 by Pope Alexander III.* Helen was a noble woman whose husband died while she was still young. She gave away her possessions and devoted herself to prayer and the care of the poor. Helen made a pilgrimage to Rome, but upon her return found herself in deep trouble because during her absence, her son-in-law had been murdered and some relatives falsely accused her of being been responsible for his death. It was later established that others had been responsible and Helen was totally exonerated. Following her death miracles were reported at Helen's tomb.

St Helier *Feast day: 16 July. Born in Tongres, Belgium in the sixth century.* Helier was orphaned and brought up by a priest; later, he spent time with St Marculf at Nanteuil. He came to the Channel Islands to be a hermit and took up residence in a cave on the isle of Jersey above the town that now bears his name. Helier was tragically murdered by a group of pagans whom he had been attempting to evangelize.

St Heliodorus *Feast day: 6 May. Born at Altino, Persia; died in 400.* Heliodorus was a soldier; he met **St Jerome** in 372 and became his disciple. He refused Jerome's invitation to join him as a desert monk, and returned home instead. Soon after he was made Bishop of Aquileia, and proved to be an excellent choice. Jerome was full of admiration for his former disciple and never lost his affection for him. Heliodorus in turn gave financial and practical support to Jerome in his great project of translating the Bible into Latin.

St Henry *Feast day: 13 July. Born in Bavaria, 972; died in 1024.* Patron of the childless, of Dukes, of the handicapped and those rejected by religious orders. Henry's father was the Duke of Bavaria and his mother was Gisella, daughter of Conrad, King of Burgundy. He received an excellent education at Hildesheim under the care of **St Wolfgang**, Bishop of Ratisbon. On marrying, he and his wife agreed to live as a celibate couple. In his early twenties Henry succeeded his father as Duke of Bavaria, and six years later was elected emperor. He was watchful over the welfare of the Church and the state and carefully maintained the balance between the two.

He gained several military victories, but he was extremely gracious in victory, and received the imperial crown from Pope Benedict VIII, in 1014.

Henry possessed a rare humility and sensitivity of spirit. On one occasion, casting himself at the feet of Herebert, Bishop of Cologne, he begged forgiveness for having wrongly judged him.

On his return from an expedition against the Greeks Henry was taken ill at Monto Cassino. He was miraculously cured by **St Benedict**'s prayers, but was left with a permanent limp. Henry wished to abdicate and retire into a monastery, but yielded to the advice of the Abbot of Verdun not to do so

He gave liberally to Christian institutions and was a supporter of the monastic movement reform which originated at Cluny Abbey in France. He was also responsible for the building of Bamberg Cathedral.

St Henry of Sweden *Feast day: 19 January. Born in England; died in 1156. Canonized in 1158 by Adrian IV.* Patron saint of Finland. Henry was an Englishman who accompanied Cardinal Nicholas Breakspear to Sweden and Norway in 1151. He was made Bishop of Uppsala, in Sweden a year later and accompanied King **St Eric** of Sweden on a military campaign to Finland in response to the war-like invasions of the Finns into Sweden. The Swedish army won the ensuing battle. Many of the defeated people were baptized by Henry, who stayed on to do missionary work, in the Spring of Kuppis near Turku.

Some years later a Finn called Lalli was found guilty of the murder of a Swedish soldier and Henry excommunicated him. Furious at this Lalli lay in wait for Henry, attacked him with an axe and killed him.

St Herbert *Feast day: 20 March. Born in England: died in 687.* Herbert was a Saxon hermit and friend of **St Cuthbert**. He lived as a recluse priest on an island in Lake Derwentwater, England. He used to visit Cuthbert at Lindisfarne every year. In the year before his death the two met in Carlisle and Cuthbert had a vision that they would both die on the same day within a few months. This came to pass on 20 March 687. The island he lived on was named St Herbert's in his honour.

St Heron *Feast day: 14 December. Born in Egypt; died in 250.* Heron was arrested along with Arseinus, Dioscorus and Isidore because of their Christian convictions. Heron, who was a young boy at the time, was scourged and then set free. The others were burned at the stake in Alexandria, Egypt.

St Hervé *Feast day: 17 June. Born in Wales; died in 575.* Patron of Brittany, France. Son of the bard Hyvarnion, Hervé was born blind. His mother was a hermit and so his uncles raised him. One day, as Hervé was working in the fields a wolf came and devoured the ass which was drawing the plough; a young child who was acting as his guide cried out in fear, but in answer to Hervé's prayers the wolf passed his head into the ass's collar and finished the work.

Hervé was later taken to Brittany where he built an abbey at Lanhourneau. He was venerated as a miracle worker and popular bard and is invoked against eye trouble.

St Hilarion *Feast day: 21 October. Born in Tabatha, Palestine, 291; died in 371.* Hilarion was educated in Alexandria, Egypt. He stayed in the desert with **St Antony of Egypt** before becoming a hermit at Majuma, near Gaza, Israel. In 356 Hilarion returned to Antony in the Egyptian desert in an attempt to escape the increased interest he had provoked as a spiritual guide, only to find that his fame had spread there too. He fled to Sicily to escape further attention, but Hesychius, who was to become his disciple, traced him there. The two went to Dalmatia, Croatia, and then to Cyprus where he died. Hilarion was widely known as a worker of miracles, and crowds flocked to him whenever the word spread that he was in the vicinity.

St Hilary of Arles *Feast day: 5 May. Born in Lorraine, France, 400; died in 449.* Hilary was born into a noble family, and developed a close friendship with his relative **St Honoratus**. He gave up a successful secular career to join Honoratus at Lerins Abbey. Honoratus died in 429, shortly after being named Bishop of Arles, and Hilary was chosen to be the new bishop by popular acclaim. He was a great orator and could readily adapt his message to be acceptable to audiences of all kinds. He was also known for his holy and austere life, care for the poor, and concern for captives.

He became involved in controversy with Pope St Leo I the Great who accused him of being fanatical and overbearing in manner, but the pope quickly realized that the Church needed his Episcopal gifts and they were reconciled. Hilary wrote a discourse on the life of Honoratus, which still survives to this day.

St Hilary of Poitiers *Feast day: 13 January. Born in Poitiers in France, 315; died in 368.* Patron against snake bites. Proclaimed a doctor of the Church in 1851. Hilary was born into a highly cultivated and well-known family. He was greatly troubled by the question of the meaning of life, and was drawn to explore the subject deeply, quickly coming to the conclusion that there was only one God who must be eternal and unchangeable. This led him to study the New Testament and to become a committed Christian. He was elected Bishop of Poitiers by the laity and clergy, soon after his baptism. He was already married by this time and had one daughter named Apra.

The Arians* had gained the support of the Emperor Constantius, and this resulted in a general persecution of orthodox believers, and when Hilary refused to support the Arian condemnation of **St Athanasius** he was exiled from Poitiers to Phrygia in the East as a result of the direct command of the emperor. He accepted this banishment willingly and with a light heart.

Before this period Hilary knew very little of the finer details of the Arian controversy but now, released from the cares of office, he used his time to study the background theology. He wrote responses and questions to the Arian leaders at very regular intervals and his books spread the orthodox message of the Christian faith with great clarity. Amongst the most famous of these were writings on the Trinity, and commentaries on Matthew's gospel and the Psalms. **St Jerome** described him as a 'fair cedar transplanted out of this world into the church'.

After three years the emperor, tired of Hilary's troublemaking, sent him back to Poitiers. However no instructions were given as to which route he should take. Hilary decided to undertake a long and leisurely route home, travelling through Greece and Italy and preaching against the Arians wherever he went, earning the title the 'Athanasius of the West'.

During his period of exile in the East he had also become familiar with the unscriptural hymns and chants that the Arians used as propaganda. In response, Hilary started writing positive, scripture-based hymns as a way to counter these false teachings and to spread the Trinitarian faith in the one God. These hymns are the first in the West to be identifiable with a known writer.

Hilary did not regard the dispute as an argument about words or ideas but rather as a spiritual battle for the eternal life of the souls of all those who might hear the Arians and stop believing in the Son of God.

The death of Constantius in 361 ended the persecution of the orthodox Christians and Hilary was permitted to go about his work without any further hindrance.

St Hilda *Feast day: 17 November. Born in Northumbria, 614; died in 680.* Hilda was the daughter of a king of Northumbria, England, and was baptized by **St Paulinus of York** when she was 13. At age 33 Hilda entered Chelles Monastery in France, where her sister was already a nun. She returned to Northumbria at **St Aidan**'s request and became the Benedictine Abbess of Hartlepool. Later she began her own foundation of the double monastery of Streaneschalch, at Whitby.

She trained five bishops and greatly encouraged the poet Caedmon. She also convened the Council of Whitby, openly supporting the Celtic tradition. All who knew her called her mother because of her gentle holiness and graceful concern for others.

St Hildegard of Bingen *Feast day: 17 September. Born in Bockelheim, Germany, 1098; died in 1179.* Hildegard was a sickly child who had been given to an aunt, Jutta, who was a well-known recluse living near Speyer. In 1147 Hilda founded Rupertberg Convent near Bingen on Benedictine principles and became first abbess there. A mystic, a poet, and prophetess, Hildegard recounted her mystical experiences in music and poetry. While thought by some to be a saint, others suspected that her spiritual experiences must be feigned. Hildegard's best-known work is *Scivias*, written between 1141 and 1151, and giving the account of 26 of her visions.

Hildegard also devised a new language and invented an alphabet for the language using a mixture of Latin and German. She was known as 'the Sybil of the Rhine'.

St Hippolytus *Feast day: 13 August. Born in Rome; died in 235.* Hippolytus was a well-educated and strong-minded man who criticized Pope **St Zepheryinus** for failing to detect and denounce heresy. On the appointment of his successor Pope **St Callistus** I, he broke communion with him and allowed himself to be set up as a rival pope, or anti-pope, the first in the history of the Church. During the persecution of Maximinus, Hippolytus was banished to do hard labour in the quarries of Sardinia. He died there as a result of hard treatment, but was reconciled to the Church before he finally expired.

Hippolytus was a scholar and was familiar with the Greek language. His writings were important, including *A Refutation of All Heresies* and *The Apostolic Tradition*.

The Holy Innocents *Feast day: 28 December. Born in the first century.* Herod the son of Antipater ruled the Holy Land for almost 50 years, and towards the end of his reign Jesus Christ was born in Bethlehem. As a result of the unusual sighting of a star, wise men from the East came to Herod's palace seeking to worship the new born king. Knowing of no recent births in his own lineage and fearful for his own position, Herod ordered that every male child under two years old in Bethlehem and its surrounding region should be killed (Matt 2:16–18). These children became known as 'the holy innocents'.

Joseph was warned in a dream that this would happen and fled to Egypt, taking with him his wife Mary and the baby Jesus (Matt 2:13–15).

St Honoratus *Feast day: 16 January. Born in Lorraine, 350; died in 429.* Honoratus was born into a Roman consular family. After he converted to Christianity, Honoratus studied monasticism in Greece with his brother Venantius and St Caprosius. Returning to France, he founded Lerins Abbey in about 400 and in 426 was forced to become Archbishop of Arles, France. He died three years later.

St Hope *Feast day: 1 August. Born in Rome.* Hope was the daughter of Wisdom, a widow in Rome and the sister of Faith and Charity. The daughters suffered martyrdom during Hadrian's persecution of Christians. Faith, who was 12 at the time, was scourged and went unharmed when boiling pitch was poured on her, she was then beheaded; Hope, who was ten at the time, and Charity, a year younger, were also beheaded after emerging unscathed from a furnace. Their mother Wisdom died three days later while praying at their graves.

St Hubert *Feast day: 3 November. Born in Belgium; died in 727.* Hubert was a courtier serving Pepin of Heristal, France. He was out hunting one Good Friday and having found a fine stag was about to kill it, but was prevented from doing when he had a remarkable vision of a crucifix suspended between the horns of the stag. He became a famous missionary though out the Ardennes district of Belgium. On the death of his wife he entered Stavelot Monastery, Belgium, and was ordained by St Lambert at Maastricht succeeding the latter as bishop in 705.

St Hugh the Great *Feast day: 29 April. Born in Semur, France, 1024; died in 1109. Canonized in 1120 by Pope Callistus II.* Hugh entered Cluny Abbey, France, at the age of 15, was ordained at 20, and succeeded **St Odilo** as abbot when he was 25. He attended the Council of Rheims, and strongly supported Pope **St Leo IX**'s efforts at reform. In 1057 he was appointed a papal legate and negotiated a peace treaty between King Henry IV and King Andrew I of Hungary. Hugh also mediated in the feud between the Holy See and King Henry IV.

Cluny was at this time the largest church in Christendom. Hugh also founded a hospital for lepers and preached for those going out on the First Crusade to the Holy Land. He died at Cluny, having been abbot for six decades.

St Hugh of Grenoble *Feast day: 1 April. Born in the Dauphin region of France, 1053; died in 1132. Canonized in 1134 by Pope Innocent II.* Hugh was handsome but very reserved in manner. He was ordained, made a canon of the Cathedral of Valence and in 1080, much to his surprise, appointed Bishop of Grenoble, during a session of a Synod in Avignon.

Hugh courageously set to the task of reforming the diocese, which had fallen into corruption and moral decay. Even though he met many discouragements and repeatedly tried to resign, Pope **St Gregory VII** ordered him to continue.

Hugh gave **St Bruno** the land on which the monastery known as 'the Grande Chartreuse' was founded, thus playing a key role in the founding of the Carthusian order. Even his own father became a Carthusian monk.

During the last weeks of his life Hugh forgot almost everything except the psalms and the Lord's Prayer, and he died surrounded by his fellow monks.

St Hugh of Lincoln *Feast day: 17 November. Born in Avalon, Grenoble, Burgundy; died in 1200. Canonized in 1220 by Pope Honorius III.* Hugh was the son of William, Lord of Avalon, and was ordained a deacon at the age of 19, and in due course he became prior of the monastery at Saint-Maxim. He became a Carthusian monk and was ordained there. In 1175 he became abbot of the first Carthusian monastery in England, which was built by King Henry II as part of his penance for the murder of Thomas Becket.

Hugh was respected as a holy and upright man. He criticized Henry for deliberately failing to appoint bishops quickly, being fully aware that the proceeds of their dioceses would continue to be at the crown's disposal during the vacancies. When Hugh was nominated as Bishop of Lincoln in 1186, he only accepted after he was ordered to do so by his former prior. He quickly restored clerical discipline, revived schools, and helped to rebuild the cathedral with his own hands.

He denounced the persecution of the Jews, repeatedly forcing armed mobs to release their victims, and was unafraid to correct both Henry II and King Richard the Lionheart whenever he felt the occasion demanded; even so they never lost their respect for him.

A swan used to follow him everywhere and, if he was praying or requiring to be left alone, it would hiss at any who tried to disturb him.

He returned from a diplomatic mission to France in 1199, having visited the Grande Chartreuse, Cluny, and Citeaux, in poor health, and died a few months later.

St Hyacinth *Feast day: 17 August. Born in Oppeln, Poland, 1185; died in 1257. Canonized in 1594 by Pope Clement VIII.* Hyacinth was an adventurous traveller and missionary. He received the Dominican habit in Rome in 1217 from **St Dominic** himself. His preaching ministry took him to many countries including Denmark, Lithuania, Sweden, Norway, and Russia and all over his native Poland. The Mongols had destroyed many Dominican missions when they crossed the Volga in 1238, and Hyacinth was instrumental in restoring these. Just before his death in Cracow, Poland he exhorted his brothers to 'esteem poverty as men who had renounced all earthy things'. He is known as 'the Apostle of Poland'.

St Hypatius *Feast day: 17 June. Born in Phrygia; died in 446.* Hypatius was educated by his own father who was a great scholar and a strict disciplinarian. At the age of 18, having been cruelly beaten by his father, he ran away to Thrace and took a job as a shepherd. Some years later, a priest who overheard him singing to his flock taught him to chant the psalms. Hypatius went to join the hermit Jonas, an ex-soldier, who lived nearby, and joined in the extreme austerities he had taken upon himself. His father finally discovered him there and they were reconciled.

Hypatius and Jonas made their way to Constantinople and when Jonas chose to stay there Hypatius journeyed on into Asia Minor, reviving an old Rufinian monastery there. He and his fellow monks were stalwarts of orthodoxy, and when the proposal to reintroduce the Olympic Games at Chalcedon had met with no opposition from the Bishop Eulalius, Hypatius took up the case and defeated the project with strong and dedicated protest; he insisted that he and his monks would rather die than allow such pagan practices to be reintroduced.

He died at the age of 80, and was known as a 'scholar of Christ' due to his depth of knowledge and the clarity of his teaching on doctrinal matters.

Sts Hypatius and Andrew *Feast day: 29 August, Born in Lydia; died in 735.* Hypatius was a bishop and Andrew one of his priests. They died martyrs' deaths in Constantinople while they were defending sacred images whose destruction had been ordered by Emperor Leo III.

I

St Ia *Feast day: 4 August. Born in Greece; died in Persia, 360.* Ia was a Greek slave who lived in Persia. She was so successful in converting the Persian women amongst whom she lived that an order was issued for her arrest. King Shapur II's forces tortured her by stretching her limbs and severely beating her. Ia was then imprisoned for several months in the hope that she would deny her faith. When she continued to refuse to do so, she was tied up by the hands and lashed to death, her flesh being cut through to the bone. The soldiers then severed her head and threw the body away.

St Ibar *Feast day: 23 April. Born in Ireland in the fifth century.* Ibar was a missionary along with Sts Kiaran, **Ailbhe**, and **Declan** who evangelized the regions of Leinster and Meath. He was a disciple of **St Patrick** and became one of the most successful early missionaries among the Irish. As a result of a dispute that Ibar had with Patrick, he was expelled from Ireland. He went on to found Beggary Monastery and a famous monastic school that was based at the monastery, on the island which he had named Beg-Eire, making it his personal 'little Ireland' ('Beg' meaning little, and 'Eire', Ireland).

St Ignatius of Antioch *Feast day: 1 February. Born in Antioch; died in 107.* Ignatius was appointed Bishop of Antioch, where he governed for 40 years. In the year 107 he was arrested and since he refused to deny Christ, he was taken in chains to Rome to face the wild beasts. During this journey he was able to be visited by the faithful of Smyrna, Troas, and other places along the way. As he arrived in Rome, the faithful of the city came out to meet him. The amphitheatre was just about to close but he was immediately rushed into the arena, where two fierce lions devoured him. He described himself as 'the wheat of Christ' because he longed to make himself agreeable bread to the Lord. During his last journey, he wrote seven epistles to the various congregations he visited. Ignatius was a disciple of **St John the Evangelist**.

St Ignatius of Loyola *Feast day: 31 July. Born in Azpeitia, Guipúzcoa, Spain, 1491; died in Rome, 1566. Canonized 1622 by Pope Gregory XV. Founder of the Jesuits.* Ignatius was the youngest of 13 children. He entered the army and fought against the French in northern Castile but in 1521 his military career was ended at the siege of Pampeluna when a cannon ball broke his right shin and tore open his left calf. His broken leg was badly set and had to be rebroken, and as a result he was left with a permanent limp.

Among the limited reading matter available to him during his long recovery was a book on the lives of the saints and their stories encouraged Ignatius to explore the Christian faith more fully.

He not only experienced inspiring visions but also anxieties, which brought on a form of spiritual depression. He used these early experiences as the basis for his famous 'Spiritual Exercises' that he began writing at Manresa, and which were first published with papal approval in 1548.

In 1523 he travelled to Jerusalem intending to stay, but instead he returned to Barcelona and began a course of study in different schools, finishing in Paris.

He attracted several followers at the university, including **St Francis Xavier**, and soon began his order called The Society of Jesus, or Jesuits, which pledged complete obedience to the pope. In 1541 Ignatius was elected first General of the Jesuits and immediately appointed himself as cook.

The main mission of the Society was, in the words of the Apostle Paul in his first letter to the Corinthians (1:23), to 'preach Jesus Christ and Him crucified'; that is they refused to dilute the Gospel message that Jesus freely gave his life for others. They also emphasized care for the poor.

In the 15 years that he directed his order, Ignatius saw it grow from ten members to 1,000, in nine countries including India, Brazil, China and the Congo. Though Ignatius suffered a series of illnesses in later life, when death came it was sudden and unexpected.

St Illtyd *Feast day: 6 November. Died in Brittany, 535.* Illtyd studied with St Dudricius and founded the great abbey of Llanilltud Fawr in Glamorgan, Wales. He was a disciple of **St Cadoc**. According to one Welsh legend, Illtyd was one of the three Knights of the Holy Grail.

St Ingrid of Sweden *Feast day: 2 September. Born in Skänninge, Sweden; died in 1282.* Ingrid was the first Dominican nun in Sweden. Her spiritual director was the Dominican priest, Peter of Daci. She founded the first Dominican cloister of St Martin's in Skänninge and died the following year. She was renowned for her miraculous powers.

St Irenaeus *Feast day: 28 June. Born in Smyrna, Asia Minor, 125; died in 202.* Irenaeus was directly linked to the apostles through his teacher **St Polycarp**, Bishop of Smyrna, and described how he could recall every detail of his mentor's voice, mannerisms and appearance as Polycarp recounted conversations with the apostle John.

Irenaeus travelled to Lyon to serve as a priest under its first bishop, St Pothinus, and was one of several Asian priests and missionaries of that time who brought the Gospel to the pagan Gauls.

Having been summoned to Rome, he was absent during the persecutions in Lyon when St Pothinus was martyred, but when the persecution ended, he returned to Lyon as bishop and began his lifelong battle against heresy. He produced a five-book study exposing the errors of various sects, and his careful arguments succeeded in exposing the dangers and errors of Gnosticism*, which meant that it ceased to present a serious challenge to the Church.

Irenaeus was buried in a crypt under the altar of what was then called the church of St John, in Lyon, but later the name was changed to St Irenaeus in honour of the saint himself. His shrine was destroyed by Calvinists in 1562.

St Irene *Feast day: 26 February. Born in 470: died in 490.* Irene was raised a pagan, but when she was 14 years old she came to the rescue of St Porphyrius when she saw a mob violently abusing him because of his faith. Surprised and shamed by her bravery the pagan attackers left him alone. Porphyrius recovered and brought her to Christianity.

St Isaac the Great *Feast day: 9 September. Born in Armenia, in 347; died at Ashtishat, in 438.* Isaac was the son of **St Nerses** I of Armenia and studied at Constantinople, where he married. Following the untimely death of his young wife, he became a monk.

He was called to rule the Armenian Church and this ended its long dependence on the Church of Caesarea in Cappodocia. Isaac ended the practice of married bishops, enforced Byzantine canon law, encouraged monasticism, built churches and schools, and fought Persian paganism. He supported **St Mesrop** in his creation of an Armenian alphabet and helped to promote the translation of the Bible into Armenian. He also established a national liturgy, but when the Persians conquered part of his territory he retired. He was later invited to return and take charge of his former See at Ashtishat, which he did with some reluctance.

Sts Isaac Jogues and Rene Goupil *Feast day: 19 October. Born in Orléans; died in Canada, 1642. Canonized in 1930 by Pope Pius XI.* Isaac entered the Jesuit order at the age of 17. After ordination he was assigned to missionary work in Canada, arriving there with a team of fellow Jesuits in 1636. Work amongst the Native American population at first proved very difficult, but a slow trickle of baptisms had begun by 1640.

In 1642, during a time of severe food shortage, Isaac led an expedition from the Huron country to Quebec for vital supplies for the mission. On the return journey the Iroquois, who were the fiercest tribe in the region, ambushed their party.

Isaac and his assistant Rene Goupil were beaten to the ground with knotted sticks. The Christian converts with them were cruelly abused; their hair, beards and nails were torn off and their forefingers bitten through. The first to die was Rene Goupil who was killed with a toma-hawk for having made the Sign of the Cross on the brow of some children. Goupil had been through the novitiate in the Society of Jesus, but had to give up because of poor health. He turned to the study of medicine and emigrated to Canada where he offered his services to the missionaries whom he met there. Isaac Jogues and Rene Goupil were but two of the North American martyrs who died at the hands of the Native Americans between the years 1642–49.

St Isadore the Farmer *Feast day: 15 May. Born in Madrid, Spain; died in 1130. Canonized in 1622 by Pope Gregory XV.* Isadore was born into a poor, pious family. He became a farm labourer and adopted a holy and simple lifestyle, rising early to pray in church before going out to work and then spending the day communing with God as he went about his various tasks.

Isadore experienced visions and miracles and others reported that they had seen angels helping him with his work in the fields.

One snowy day when Isadore was carrying a sack of corn to be ground at the mill, he noticed some small birds perched on the bare branches, obviously hungry. Taking no notice of his companions' taunts, Isadore emptied out half his sack. When he arrived at the mill, the sack was found to be full to the brim of corn, and when ground it produced double the amount of flour.

St Isadore of Seville *Feast day: 4 April. Born in Spain; died in 636. Canonized in 1622 by Pope Gregory XV.* Patron of the Internet. In 1947 he was proclaimed the patron of the National Rural Life Conference in the United States. Isadore was born into a family of saints: his brothers Leander and Fulgentius became bishops and one of his sisters, Florentina, was an abbess.

Leander took over Isadore's education and treated his little brother extremely harshly, punishing him severely when he made mistakes. Though intelligent and hardworking, Isadore ran away as a result of his brother's overly-strict regime.

Lonely and dejected, he stopped to rest by a small stream and noticed how the persistent dripping of water in one place on the rock had, over time, worn deep holes.

Isadore saw this as a visual parable for his life, and came to understand that through disciplined study seemingly small efforts could eventually build up into great learning. He returned home, and was confined by his brother until he had completed all that he had missed by running off.

Eventually Isadore's love of learning caused him to become the most learned man of his age and monastic institutions from all over Spain asked him to establish a code of rules to be taught in the seminaries. He didn't limit his own studies to one area of expertise but happily drew on all branches of knowledge including the arts and medicine, and went on to become a famous writer.

His encyclopaedia of knowledge known as *The Etymologies* was a popular textbook for nine centuries. He also wrote books on grammar, astronomy, geography, history, and biography as well as theology. Isadore's creative approach reintroduced the work of the philosopher Aristotle to students and aided his efforts in converting the Barbarian Visigoths from Arianism* to Christianity.

He lived until he was almost 80 years old. As he was dying, his house was filled with crowds of poor and his last act was to give away all his possessions.

St Ita *Feast day: 15 January. Born in Decies, Waterford, Ireland; died in 570.* Ita was of royal lineage and after securing her father's permission to live a virginal life; she moved to Killeedy, Limerick and founded a community of women. Ita also founded a school for young boys, and one of her pupils was **St Brendan**.

A miracle worker, Ita reunited the head and body of a man who had been beheaded, and on one occasion she lived entirely on food from heaven. She is widely venerated in Ireland because of her reputation for holiness and saintly behaviour.

St Ivo of Brittany *Feast day: 19 May. Born in Kermatin, Brittany, France in 1235; died in 1303.* Patron of lawyers and judges. Canonized 1347 by Pope Clement VI. Ivo's father sent him to study law in Paris, and following his training he was appointed as a legal official to the Church courts, first by the Archdeacon of Rennes and then by the Bishop of Tréguier, who had become aware of Ivo's talents and appointed him as a judge.

He gained a reputation for being totally impartial, and possessed a remarkable gift for conciliation. Ivo often persuaded those about to seek his ruling as a judge to come to an agreement and settle out of court, and thus save everyone concerned both time and money.

He was ordained a priest in 1284 and appointed to the parish of Tredrez, subsequently moving to Lovannec. Being fluent in Latin, French and Breton he was in great demand as a preacher and arbiter in disputes of all kinds. He died after a long illness.

J

St Jambert *Feast day: 12 August. Born in Kent; died in 792.* Jambert was a Benedictine monk who succeeded St Bregwin as Archbishop of Canterbury in 766. As a result of a long-running dispute, King Offa convinced the pope to reduce the size of Jambert's province. In due course the land was restored, thanks to Jambert's persistent protests. He was especially known for his support of monasteries and of the poor.

St James the Less *Feast day: 3 May. Born in Galilee, the Holy Land in the first century.* Patron of hat makers. James, the son of Alphaeus of Cleophas, was also known by the titles 'the Just' and 'the brother of the Lord'.

He was a witness to the resurrection of Christ and one of the 'pillars' of the early Christian Church in Jerusalem. He was first bishop there, attended the Council of Jerusalem in 50, and was later martyred in 62.

He wrote an epistle addressed to the 'twelve tribes that are in the Dispersion', which forms part of the New Testament.

St James of the Marches *Feast day: 28 November. Born in Montebrandone, in the March of Ancona, Italy, 1394; died in Naples, 1476. Canonized in 1726 by Pope Benedict XIII.* Prior to joining the Franciscans at Assisi in 1416, James Gangala was initially trained as a civil lawyer. He went on to study theology under **St Bernardino of Siena** and, following his ordination, became a forceful and effective preacher. James practised strict self-discipline and permitted himself only three hours' sleep a night.

He travelled widely on preaching missions from Sweden to Bosnia. His great zeal led him to oppose heresy wherever he found it and he strongly opposed a group in Italy known as the Fraticelli*. He ordered the destruction of 36 Fraticelli houses, but the severity of the attacks resulted in some of the Fraticelli being burned at the stake, which caused great controversy.

James was not a great success at resolving differences and in 1460, wisely rejected the opportunity to become the Bishop of Milan. In 1462 he experienced the effects of the inquisition when he expressed the opinion that the blood of Jesus shed during the Passion was not united with the Divinity of Christ during the three days of His burial. When James failed to respond to his accusers, the case was referred to the pope, and the result was that three years later, with the issues still unresolved, the pope imposed silence upon both parties. James retired to Naples where he died a few years later.

St James of Nisibis *Feast day: 15 July. Born in Syria; died in Nisibis, 338.* James was renowned for his exceptional holiness, learning and miracles and **St Ephraem** was one of his pupils. He was named first Bishop of Nisibis, in Mesopotamia in 308 and took part in the Council of Nicea, proving to be an ardent opponent of Arianism*, even being credited with praying for the death of Arius. He built a basilica and founded the theological school of Nisibis.

St Jane Frances de Chantal *Feast day: 21 August. Born in France, 1572; died in 1641.* Jane Frances was orphaned at an early age and despite early financial worries, she refused a marriage of convenience. Jane eventually married Baron de Chantal and they had four children. When the baron was killed in a hunting accident, Jane continued to serve as humbly as she could despite the added responsibilities, ill treatment from servants and constant demands from others that she should remarry.

In 1609 Jane Frances took leave of her family; her son, then aged 15, begged his mother not to leave and laid himself across the doorway of the room. In great anguish and distress she stepped over his body, asked her aged father for his blessing and left for a new life of prayer, service and contemplation.

Her bishop and spiritual director **St Francis de Sales** was impressed by her practical spirituality and with his support, Jane Frances founded an order for women who were rejected by other orders because of poor health or age.

St Jan Sarkander *Feast day: 17 March. Born at Skotschau in Austria; died in 1620. Canonized in 1995by Pope John Paul II.* Jan was educated by Jesuits in Prague and was ordained priest in 1607. He served in various parishes, and had notable success in restoring lapsed members and in defending the faith against the followers of John Huss known as the Hussites.

In 1618, at the start of the Thirty Years' War, Jan took temporary refuge in Poland. He returned two years later only to be arrested as a spy, put on trial and found guilty. Since he was known to be the confessor of Baron Lobkowitz, one of the Catholic barons, he was tortured in an attempt to gain confidential information. After being racked and burned, he was finally tortured to death.

When it was proposed that Jan be canonized in 1995, the local Church leaders expressed deep concern that this might re-ignite old rivalries. However, when it was explained that the process was intended to lay to rest old injustices and hatreds and to seek mutual pardon, Pope John Paul was able to proceed, visiting the Czech Church that same year.

St Januarius *Feast day 19 September. Born in Italy; died in 305.* Januarius was the bishop of Benevento during Emperor Diocletian's persecution. He was arrested as a result of jealous rumours about him and when two fellow believers Desiderius and Festus visited him in prison, they too were arrested and imprisoned.

They were thrown to the wild beasts, but the animals refused to attack them, lying down at their feet instead. All three were then beheaded.

A phial of Januarius' blood is kept in Naples as a relic. It is taken out and exposed to view by the priests at designated intervals in the cathedral, and is seen on occasion to liquefy and effervesce. No plausible scientific explanation for this phenomenon has so far been proposed.

St Jeanne de Lestonnac *Feast day: 2 February. Born in Bordeaux, France, 1556: died there February 2, 1640. Canonized in 1949 by Pope Pius XII.* Jeanne was born into a distinguished family. Her mother continually tried to undermine Jeanne's faith and, when her attempts failed, she would abuse her child and treat her harshly, but this only served to strengthen Jeanne's beliefs.

When she was 17, Jeanne married Gaston de Montferrant and they had eight children together. Though three died young, the others grew up to be healthy and strong. In 1597, after 24 years of marriage Gaston died and five years later Jeanne decided to enter the Cistercian monastery at Toulouse.

She became seriously ill and her superiors advised her to form her own order and live outside the convent. Jeanne recovered quickly as soon as she left the monastery and she gathered a band of young girls on her estate, La Mothe in Périgord, spending two quiet years there. On returning to Bordeaux, her group served as nurses during a savage plague that had afflicted the city.

Jeanne's new order, the Company of Mary, was approved by Pope Paul V in 1607, and in 1610 she became the mother superior of their first house in Bordeaux.

The sisters, who lived an extremely simple life, founded schools for girls throughout the region.

Resenting the success of this new order, the Archbishop of Bordeaux all too readily believed lies spread about Jeanne, and ordered that she be dismissed as superior. Her chief antagonist was appointed in her place.

After three years of rejection, which she bore with great patience, her former accuser confessed that she had lied and the two were reconciled. Jeanne did not return to the role of abbess, but regained the high respect of all who knew of her faithful fortitude.

From 1625 to 1631 Jeanne visited each of the other 26 houses that had grown up.

She returned to Bordeaux to find that two of her daughters and at least one of her granddaughters had joined the Company of Mary. Revised rules and constitutions for the order were drawn up in 1638. Meanwhile, Jeanne's health began to fail and she died soon after these had been completed. Miracles were reported at her tomb in Bordeaux.

St Jerome *Feast day: 30 September. Born in Stridonius, at the head of the Adriatic, 331; died in 420.* Patron of librarians. Jerome's father, who was a Christian, sent him to study in Rome where he became a skilled orator, fluent in both Latin and Greek. He loved books, Cicero being his favourite author, and proved himself to be a skilled copyist. Pope Liberius baptized Jerome in 360 and, after three years travelling, he eventually settled in Aquileia, dedicating himself wholly to God.

He travelled to Antioch in 373 to study under Apollinaris, the Bishop of Laodicea, and then spent four years in the desert of Chalcis. Jerome continued to read the pagan classics for pleasure until a vivid and disturbing dream caused him to stop. He took up the study of Hebrew to keep himself from troubling sensual thoughts.

When a doctrinal dispute arose in the Antiochian Church, Jerome supported the Bishop Paulinus and consented to be ordained by him on the understanding that he would not be given any specific ministerial responsibilities. In 382, they both attended a council in Rome which Pope Damasus held to deal with the dispute. Jerome impressed the pope so much, that he kept him there as his personal secretary. The Latin version of the New Testament that was commonly in use had been badly corrupted by poor copying and careless editing and Pope Damasus asked Jerome to prepare a revised version, based on the original Greek version, which he did.

Pope Damasus died in 384 and Jerome began to experience open criticism. Many people had been upset by his biting sarcasm and unbending nature and now with the pope no longer there to protect him, his reputation, appearance and even the way he walked were openly ridiculed. Distressed by all this, Jerome left Rome for the Holy Land and made a home for himself in a large cave near Bethlehem. A group of holy women from Rome, led by **St Paula**, travelled with him and set up a convent nearby. They helped him to found a school and a hospice for pilgrims. Jerome found great contentment in this simple life and he translated most of the books of the Old Testament directly from Hebrew at this time.

Jerome was involved in a dispute with Rufinus, in which **St Augustine** became unwillingly involved. Jerome also strongly opposed Pelagianism and as a result of his outspoken comments, his institutions were attacked and set on fire, causing him to go into hiding for a time. The aged Jerome soon fell ill and died two years later. He was buried under the Church of the Nativity at Bethlehem.

St Joan of Arc *Feast day: 30 May. Born at Domrémy, Champagne, France, 1412; died at Rouen, France, 1431. Canonized in 1920 by Pope Benedict XV.* Joan's father, Jacques d'Arc, was a well-respected peasant farmer. Joan never learned to read or write. She had the first of her several visions and messages from saints at the age of 13. In 1428, they instructed her to go to the commander of the king's armies at nearby Vaucouleurs. He simply laughed at her but her visions continued and, as Joan had predicted, the French were defeated at the Battle of Herrings near Orléans in 1429. She was then taken more seriously and was sent to the king, travelling in men's clothes for her own protection

When they first met at Chinon, Charles, the Dauphin, disguised himself but Joan picked him out and managed to convince him of the divine origin of her mission.

She asked to be given a troop of soldiers that she could lead to Orleans, and after three weeks of examination by a panel, Charles was advised to make use of her services.

Wearing white armour, Joan led the soldiers to the city of Orleans. The English forts surrounding the town were soon captured due to her presence and courage, though she was wounded in the breast by an arrow during the fight. Joan joined in a further successful campaign with the Duke of Alençon, and she finally persuaded the dauphin to accept his responsibilities and to be crowned King Charles VII in 1429.

Military defeats followed, and further wounding. She was taken prisoner in 1430 after she had led a sortie out from the gates of a besieged castle and a drawbridge was closed too soon, leaving her stranded.

King Charles made no efforts for her release and, as she had predicted, she was sold to the English leaders. They arranged to have her sentenced as a sorceress and heretic. In 1431 she appeared before a tribunal which was led by the politically motivated Bishop of Beauvais. She was questioned about the 'voices' that she heard and about her wearing of male clothing. Joan was told that if she refused to retract, she would be handed over to the secular court as a heretic. When she was brought before a huge crowd for formal sentencing, she appeared to recant, but after being led back to prison, she reassumed the male dress that she had agreed to give up. Joan then regained her courage and asserted that all she had said during her testimony was true. She was taken to the marketplace of Rouen and burned at the stake. Her ashes were thrown into the Seine.

St John-Baptist de la Salle *Feast day: 7 April. Born in Rheims, France, 1651; died in 1719. Canonized 1900 by Pope Leo XIII.* John-Baptist de la Salle was born into a noble family, tonsured at an early age, he became a canon of Rheims at 16, was ordained priest in 1678, and founded the Institution of Christian Brothers in 1686. He liquidated his considerable personal fortune and used it to buy food for the hungry during the great famine in Champagne in 1683–84.

He began schools for boys too poor to pay for instruction otherwise, and an internal conflict arose during John-Baptist's lifetime with some of the order claiming that the poor should only be taught manual skills but the Christian Brothers persevered with their broad approach and became widely known for their educational achievements with the poor, their training of teachers and the rehabilitation of delinquents.

St John Bosco *Feast day: 31 January. Born in Piedmont, Italy, 1815; died in Turin, 1888; Canonized in 1934 by Pope Pius XI.* John was born of peasant stock. His father died when he was two and he was raised by his mother in extreme poverty. He decided to become a priest and devote his life to children at the age of nine. With this in mind, he diligently practised circus skills, giving performances at every opportunity and always ending with a sermon.

John had a charismatic personality, a fine memory and a good sense of humour, but he was also somewhat impetuous. Throughout the strict teaching of his seminary, he managed to retain his spirit of joyfulness, and was ordained in 1841. John Bosco then began his work with boys from the slums in Turin, and while others considered the children wild and unruly, he never found the need for formal punishment.

Well-meaning friends, concerned for his mental health at this time, tried to have him committed to an asylum. Two priests were sent as an escort but John simply followed them to the carriage, politely allowed them to enter first, slammed the door, and called out to the driver, 'To the asylum'.

A few months after beginning this work, he became totally exhausted and contracted pneumonia. On his recovery, his mother became house-keeper for the boarding house which he had opened for 40 destitute boys in the Valdocco area.

John used to take the boys into the country and encourage them to experience the joys of the natural world, at the same time giving them spiritual instruction.

In 1859, John opened a religious seminary and in 1874 this group received the approval of the pope. He wrote several books including a biography of St Dominic Savio, who was one of his own pupils.

In later life John Bosco's health once again began to give way under the many demands made upon him. Following his death, a large propor-tion of the population of Milan followed the funeral and over 40,000 people visited his body as it lay in state.

St John Cassian *Feast day: 23 July. Born in Romania, 360; died in 433.* John Cassian became a monk in Bethlehem and then travelled to Egypt to learn first-hand from his observation of the lives of holy monks. The teaching of Evagrius Ponticus greatly affected him and on his return to Constantinople he was made a deacon and became a fervent supporter of **St John Chrysostom**. When that saint was deposed John Cassian trav-elled to Rome to plead for his reinstatement, and then continued on to Marseilles where he was ordained priest. Many refugees who had been displaced from their own countries by Barbarian invasions had chosen to settle in that region.

The monastic movement had fallen into disrepute, and so, with his per-sonal experience of Eastern monasticism, Cassian set about the work of reform.

He wrote two major works: one, *The Institutes* outlined the principles of community living; and *The Conferences*, which was based on sermons given by the Egyptian monks. His writing and teaching was highly respected by **St Benedict**.

Cassian's view on grace earned him the reputation of being the founder of a heresy known as Semi-Pelagianism*. He also proposed a four-fold reading of Scripture, which suggested that literal, allegorical, analogical and metaphorical approaches were all of value in Christian spirituality.

St John Chrysostom *Feast day: 14 September. Born in Antioch in 347; died in 407.* Chrysostom's father, an officer of high rank in the Syrian army, died soon after John was born and he was brought up by his mother. He became a brilliant classical scholar, and spent six years as a monk in the mountains south of Antioch before being ordained deacon in 381.

The name 'Chrysostom' (meaning golden-tongued) was given to John because of the outstanding gift he had for preaching. **St Jerome** already recognized this as early as 392.

In 398, following a dispute over the succession at the See of Constantinople, John was hurried to the capital, and ordained bishop. He immediately acted to bring about reconciliation and reform.

Chrysostom began to simplify and reduce expenses wherever possible; he sold off some expensive ornaments and furniture in the bishop's residence and in his first year built a hospital with the money raised. Many clergy and monks had been living undisciplined lives and Chrysostom, after putting measures in place to stop this, turned his attention to his flock. He frequently preached against extravagance and laxity, and though his forthrightness made him unpopular in the Imperial court, congregations showed their appreciation by applauding his sermons.

However, Chrysostum's irritability and obstinacy caused him increasing difficulty and from the beginning of the year 401 the court and empress were alienated and the clergy had become increasingly keen to get rid him. A long list of false charges was drawn up against Chrysostom and he was deposed, although the empress ordered his immediate recall.

Less than a year later he was sent into exile a second time to Armenia, and in the summer of 407 the order was given to carry him to Pithyus, a place at the extreme boundary of the empire, near the Caucasus. He was forced to make a long march there, exposed to all the elements and his body, already weakened by several severe illnesses, finally broke down and Chrysostom died.

His last words were: 'Glory be to God for all things.' He is recognized as one of the four great doctors (Teacher/theologians) of the Eastern Church, the other three being **St Athanasius**, **St Basil** and **St Gregory of Nazianzus**.

St John of the Cross *Feast day: 24 November. Born in Fontiveros, Spain, in 1542; died in 1591. Canonized 1726 by Pope Benedict XIII.* John followed his father's trade as a silk weaver in Toledo, Spain, for seven years before going to study at the University of Salamanca. He became a Carmelite in 1563, and was ordained in 1567. A year later he founded the first Carmelite reformed monastery at Duruelo, which marked the beginning of the Discalced (shoeless) Carmelites. He aim was to return the order to the simplicity and purity of its origins and to avoid what he regarded as the excesses of 'comfortable living' that had crept in over the passage of time. At **St Teresa**'s request, John served as spiritual director to her Convent of the Incarnation at Avila for five years.

In 1577 he was imprisoned for nine months in Toledo for refusing the order of the provincial of Seville to return to Medina. During his imprisonment, John experienced visions and began his spiritual writings. In his greatest work, *The Dark Night of the Soul*, he describes how a mystic must lose all earthly attachments and pass through a personal experience of the Passion of Christ in order to be in communion with God.

His reforming efforts finally met with success and the Discalced Carmelites received formal recognition. When he was appointed prior at Los Martires near Granada, he insisted upon choosing the worst room in the monastery for his cell.

John enjoyed the beauties of nature and often led the monks out into the open countryside. Although he was outwardly severe in appearance, John cared deeply for any of the brothers who fell ill.

When the Discalced Carmelites formed a permanent committee to run the order, John resisted this and supported the moderate party under Jerome Gratian. The other side prevailed and again John found himself at odds with the authorities of his order. He was eventually reconciled and was appointed Vicar Provincial of Andalusia in 1585. Three years later he was made prior at Segovia and several new monasteries were established in the years that followed.

In the last year of John's life, a dispute broke out again amongst the Spanish Carmelites and, having been threatened by expulsion from the very order he had established at great personal cost, he withdrew to complete solitude and died alone.

St John the Divine *Feast day: 26 September. Born in Galilee, c.6; died c. 104.* John was the son of Zebedee and Salome and the younger brother of James the Great. They worked as fishermen on Lake Galilee until they were called by Jesus to be fishers of men. Christ gave James and John the surname of 'Boagernes' (which means, 'the Sons of Thunder').

John was one of the disciples closest to Jesus, being present at the Transfiguration, the raising of Jairus's daughter from the dead, the events of the Passion of Christ and on the day of Pentecost when the Holy Spirit was poured out miraculously. **St Paul** referred to John, Peter, and James as the 'leaders' and 'pillars' of the Church in Jerusalem.

John was known as the 'beloved disciple' and is the author of the Book of Revelation, the last book of the New Testament which was written during his exile on the island of Patmos off the coast of modern Turkey.

St John of Egypt *Feast day: 27 March. Born in Egypt, 304; died in 394.* At the age of 25, John went into the desert to live as a hermit as a disciple of a famous hermit. Ten years later he spent four years in several monasteries, and finally found himself a roomy cave high in the rocks.

Many people came to seek his advice and brought him gifts of food. Even Emperor Theodosius I asked his advice twice, in 388 and in 392. John was also known by **St Augustine** and **St Jerome** who both referred to his holy example.

Though John never founded a community, some of his supporters built a hospice for visitors near to his cave. Known for his humility and wisdom, John was famous for gifts of prophecy and healing. He never ate before sunset and never ate meat or cooked or warm food. John died peacefully at the age of 90.

St John Fisher *Feast day: 22 June. Born in Beverley, Humberside, 1469; died in 1535. Canonized in 1935 by Pope Pius XI.* John Fisher was the chancellor of Cambridge and Bishop of Rochester. He was a great scholar, was renounced for his holiness, and became confessor to Henry VIII's wife Catherine of Aragon.

Fisher was condemned to perpetual imprisonment and had all his property seized because he protested against King Henry's taking the title 'supreme head of the Church'. Though this sentence was later commuted to a fine, he never gained the king's trust. He was a friend **Thomas More** and wrote a book on prayer during his time of imprisonment in the Tower of London. On hearing that Fisher had been elected Cardinal, Henry VIII said that even if he were sent a red hat, he would have no head to put it on, and ordered his execution.

On the scaffold John pardoned his executioner as was the custom, and recited the *Te Deum* and a psalm, before being beheaded. His head was displayed for two weeks on London Bridge and then thrown into the river.

St John Ogilvie *Feast day: 10 March. Born in Banffshire, Scotland, 1579; died in Glasgow, 1615. Canonized by Pope Paul VI in 1976.* John Ogilvie was brought up as a Calvinist but during his education at Louvain in France, he decided to become a Roman Catholic. John continued his studies at Regensburg, and in 1600, he joined the Society of Jesus at Brunn, working in Austria, mainly at Graz and Vienna, for ten years before being ordained in Paris in 1610 after which he was stationed in Rouen.

In 1613 he received permission to go to Scotland to minister to the persecuted Catholics there. Owing to the penal laws he disguised himself as John Watson, a horse trader and/or a soldier, and found that most of the Scottish Catholic noblemen had conformed and were unwilling to help. Finding progress all but impossible, he went back to Paris only to be clearly told to go back to Scotland, which he did. Ogilvie eventually was successful in winning back a number of converts to the Church and soon attracted the attention of Archbishop Spottiswoode.

He was entrapped by a man named Adam Boyd who pretended to be a potential convert and then betrayed him. John was imprisoned, tortured, had his hair torn out, and deprived of sleep in an effort to make him reveal the names of other Catholics. He wouldn't comply and was found guilty of high treason for refusing to acknowledge the supremacy of the king in spiritual matters. John wrote an account of his trials in prison that was smuggled out by visitors. Following the trial, John Ogilvie was hanged in Glasgow.

St Josémaria Escriva de Balageur *Feast day: 26 June. Born in Barbastro, Huesca, Spain, 1902; died in 1975. Canonized in 2002 by Pope John Paul II.* Josémaria was the son of a textile merchant, who entered a seminary at the age of 16. After ordination he worked as chaplain to the nuns who cared for the poor and sick, but during a retreat in

1928 he received a vision for a secular institute, known as Opus Dei ('the work of God'). His followers, all men, lived a common life, which encouraged strict ascetic practices; they did so without formal rules or distinctive dress and in total obedience to their founder.

During the civil war of 1936 when General Franco rose to power, many hundreds of monasteries and churches were burned and thousands of priests and nuns were killed. Opus Dei prospered in these circumstances because it was not a formal institution, and within a short space of time its members became prominent in educational circles. The organization was given official recognition in 1943, permitted to train their own priests, and encouraged to become an international movement.

However, with its strong political and financial base and with a degree of independence from local bishops, this movement still had to deal with severe criticism from several quarters for its supposed excessive secrecy. This has led to the order being negatively portrayed in one of the world's bestselling novels of the early twenty-first century, *The Da Vinci Code* by Dan Brown. The subsequent publicity has provided ample opportunity for members to explain their faith and practice to a worldwide audience.

St Joseph *Feast day: 19 March. Born in Bethlehem, Palestine in the first century before the birth of Jesus Christ.* Joseph was a carpenter in Nazareth who was betrothed to **St Mary** and became the guardian of the child Jesus. He is referred to as a 'just man'.

His faith in his spouse was greatly tested when it was revealed that she was expecting a baby. He had decided to leave her without making any trouble until an angel explained that this was God's doing. After the birth, Joseph took Mary and the child Jesus to safety in Egypt.

Following a trip to Jerusalem, Joseph and Mary went looking for Jesus, then aged 12, finally finding him in the temple in Jerusalem debating with the wise scholars. There is no further reference made to Joseph in the New Testament and it is likely that he died before Jesus began his earthly ministry at the age of 30.

St Joseph Calasanz *Feast day; 25 August. Born in Peralta de la Sal, Spain, 1550; died in 1648. Canonized in 1767 by Pope Clement XIII.* Joseph was the son of a nobleman of Valencia and after being ordained priest he was quickly promoted and appointed vicar general. He was sent to deal with problems of Church discipline in Andorra, but feeling himself called to work in the inner city, he gave up a promising career in the Church and travelled to Rome in 1592.

His first work was ministering to those who were sick and dying as a result of a great plague, but soon Calasanz began to provide education for the poor of the inner city. In 1597, he and three friends began a school, which proved immensely successful, and within 14 years it had grown to 1,200 pupils and received full papal approval.

Other schools soon opened, and the institute known as the Clerks Regular of Christian Schools, expanded greatly and became recognized officially as a religious congregation, with Calasanz the founder.

Mario Sozzi, a jealous and devious priest appointed to overlook the work of the Institute in Tuscany, reported Calasanz to the pope's advisors on some serious but fictitious charges and suggested that he was going senile. Suspended pending investigation, Calasanz was publicly paraded through the streets like a common criminal.

The charges were shown to be false, but the sordid tale of intrigue continued well into the last years of Calasanz's life. When he died, aged 90, the congregation had still not been fully reinstated, but within a couple of decades of his death his movement had been made into a full religious order called the **Piarists**, which went on to flourish in Spain, Italy and South America.

St Joseph of Copertino *Feast day: 18 September. Born in Copertino, Puglia, 1603; died in Osimo, 1663. Canonized in 1767 by Pope Clement XIII.* Patron of aviators, flying and studying. Joseph's father, a carpenter, fell into financial difficulties and had to sell the family home to pay off his debts. His wife Franceschina gave birth to their son Joseph in a shed in which they lived at that time. His father soon died and his mother brought him up on her own, surrounding him with much resentment and criticism. Joseph became enthralled with spiritual things while still very young but was thought to be slow-witted and absent-minded, due to his habit of wandering around with his mouth wide open. He earned the nickname, 'the gaper'.

When he was 19, Joseph was admitted to the Capuchins as a lay brother, but after eight months he was asked to leave because of his clumsiness and forgetfulness. He applied to the nearby Grotella Convent near Copertino and undertook the worst jobs, such as cleaning out the stables, and spent many hours in prayer.

Joseph was ordained a priest even though he lacked any intellectual gifts. The examining bishop asked Joseph to expound the only text about which he had something to say, and during the oral examination the first few candidates performed so well that all the rest, including Joseph, were passed without further questioning.

His ecstatic prayer frequently caused him to levitate, and this began to attract large crowds. Those who were envious of his popularity made complaints to the pope and Joseph underwent three trials, and on each occasion he went into ecstasies while defending himself, and levitated into the air. Terrified, the judges refused to condemn him. When Joseph met Pope Urban VIII, he again went into ecstasy and flew high over the heads of the Vatican Court in Rome, and on seeing this marvel with their own eyes, everyone present affirmed his gift of holiness.

Joseph stayed in Assisi for 14 years before being sent to an isolated convent in the Monti di Carpegna, then later to a convent in Fossombrone and, in 1656, to Osimo in the Province of Ancona, where he spent the last six years of his life. His health had badly deteriorated by this time but he never complained about these ailments of old age and died peacefully.

St Joseph Cottolongo *Feast day: 29 April. Born in Bra, Peidmont, Italy, 1786; died in 1842. Canonized in 1934 by Pope Pius XI.* Joseph was educated at Turin and ordained priest in 1811. Inspired by **St Vincent de Paul**, he spent his life caring for the poor. He began by founding a small hospital of five beds for the slum dwellers, and several other homes were soon built nearby to care for a whole variety of illnesses, and also a hospice. This became known as Turin's street of charities.

Joseph's habit of keeping no accounts and spending all monies on arrival earned him the reputation in some quarters of being imprudent. Others however held the view that he was simply doing right by trusting in Providence. 'In the Little House,' he used to say, 'we progress as long as we possess nothing.'

St Joseph Tommasi *Feast day: 1 January. Born in Alicati in Sicily, 1649; died in Rome, 1713. Canonized 1986 by Pope John Paul II.* Joseph was the son of a duke. Both of his parents and four of his sisters later entered the religious life, and Joseph himself entered the Theatine novitiate at Palermo at the age of 15.

Joseph went on to study scripture, Hebrew and Greek philosophy in Rome and later wrote learned works on the Psalms and on liturgy. In 1697 Pope Innocent XII called him to the Vatican where he worked for reforms among religious orders while continuing his interest in theology and music, which he combined with a deep concern for the poor and destitute. He was a careful, scholarly man with a gentle temperament.

Joseph was the confessor of Cardinal Albani who, upon being elected pope was ordered by Joseph to accept the papacy as a matter of holy obedience. He became Clement XI. The new pope responded in kind by insisting that Joseph, in obedience, accept appointment as a cardinal.

In late 1712 he prophesied his own death and let others know the exact spot in which he wanted to be buried.

St Joseph of Volokolamsk *Feast day: 9 September. Born in Lithuania, 1439; died 1515. Canonized in the Orthodox Church in 1578.* Joseph Sanin became Abbot of Borovsk in 1477. He had a strong personality and was gifted with great intelligence, but found his brother monks lacking in fervour and unwilling to change. Because of this, Joseph felt obliged to leave and found a new community near Volokolamsk. He saw an important role for his monastery's particular regime, which differed radically from the conventions of his time and from other reformers such as St Nilus. Joseph believed in a close association between Church and state and defended monastic land rights, while Nilus argued for monastic poverty, separation from the state, and a more conciliar approach to heretics.

Joseph encouraged his monks to support the social work in the area, and to do this under the direction of the local secular authorities. During a Church council in Moscow in 1503, Joseph's vision for monastic life triumphed over that of Nilus. Both men are now recognized as saints in the Orthodox Church.

St Julian of Norwich *Feast day: 13 May. Born in England,1342; died in 1416.* Julian had a vision in 1373 during a serious illness and wrote a brief account of it. This vision continued to dominate her spiritual life for many years till, in 1394, she became an anchorite and took up residence in a cell attached to the parish church of St Julian in Norwich, from which her name is derived. She lived there till her death in 1416.

Julian wrote *Showings*, which is the first book written in English by a woman. She was known for her positive attitude in times of trial, her most often quoted saying being, 'But all will be well, all will be well, and all manner of things will be well.'

St Justin Martyr *Feast day: 1 June. Born in Nablus, Samaria, 100; died in 165.* Justin was a layman and the first Christian philosopher to write books of any sizable length. His parents were pagans of Greek origin and he was given a liberal education moving on to the study of philosophy. He was inspired to learn about Christianity by a study of the Scriptures, and was greatly influenced by reading about and observing the heroism of martyrs. He became a Christian at the age of 30, after which he travelled widely and debated with non-Christian thinkers, always attempting to demonstrate that the faith he held was entirely compatible with rational thought.

Though Justin wrote two Apologies (defences) of Christianity, he did not believe that everything he had learned before his conversion was irrelevant. He travelled to Rome and opened a Christian school there, but was arrested soon after he conducted a public dispute with a Cynic named Crescens. He openly shared his beliefs at his trial before Rusticus, the prefect of Rome, and when asked to sacrifice to idols, Justin replied, 'No right-minded man forsakes truth for falsehood.' He was found guilty, scourged and then beheaded.

K

Blessed Kateri Tekakwitha *Feast day: 14 July. Born in Auriesville, New York, 1656; died in 1680. Beatified in 1980; work is currently underway to have her canonized.* Patron of the environment and ecology. Kateri was the daughter of a Mohawk warrior. Her mother died of smallpox when she was very young and Kateri's skin was also permanently marked. She was brought up by her two aunts and an uncle, and was converted and baptized as a teenager. Her tribe were very hostile to this and Kateri went to a new Christian colony of Canadian Indians. Here she lived a prayerful, penitent life while caring for the sick and aged. She died aged 24, and is known as the 'Lily of the Mohawks'.

St Katherine Drexel *Feast day: 3 March. Born in Philadelphia, 1858; died in 1955. Canonized in 2000 by Pope John Paul II.* Katherine was born into an extremely wealthy family of Austrian origin who were great philanthropists. After nursing her mother through a long terminal illness, Katherine developed an interest in missionary work. The seeds of a vocation to the religious life were sewn during a visit to Europe in 1883. Having been granted an audience with Pope Leo XIII, she asked him to send more missionaries to Wyoming. He immediately suggested that she be one of them.

After her father died in 1885, she inherited the family fortune and began to organize aid to the existing Native American missions. Rather than give all the money away, she spent it constructively over the years in support of missions, and in building schools and hospitals. This continued until she had finally exhausted all her inheritance.

After serving her novitiate and gathering postulants to join her in the work, she was eventually given permission to found a new order called the 'Sisters of the Blessed Sacrament for Indians and Colored People', now know as the Sisters of the Blessed Sacrament.

By 1942 she had a system of black Christian schools, mission centres, and universities across 13 states of the U.S.A.

St Kenelm *Feast day: 17 July. Born in Mercia; died in 821.* Kenelm was the son of King Kenulf, and came to the throne at the age of seven. His sister bribed some men to murder him, and he is buried at Winchcombe Abbey, in Gloucestershire. Miracles took place at the site of his grave. Geoffrey Chaucer mentions Kenelm in *The Canterbury Tales*.

St Kentigern (Mungo) *Feast day: 14 January. Born in Scotland; died in 612.* Patron of Glasgow. Kentigern was the son of a British princess, and his nickname, Mungo, means 'dear one'. He was raised by **St Serf** in the Irish tradition and was consecrated as a bishop in 540. Soon after this Kentigern was driven south into exile for 13 years. He spent some of this time with **St David** in Wales and on his return to resume his Episcopal role he brought many Welsh disciples with him.

On one occasion, the queen approached Kentigern for help as she had foolishly given her husband's ring to her lover. When the king discovered this, he threw the ring into the sea and told her to find it within three days or she would die. When Kentigern heard what she had to say, he was able to return the ring to her and save her life. One of his monks had found the ring in the mouth of a salmon, which he had caught earlier that same day. The coat of arms of the city of Glasgow includes a salmon with a ring in its mouth as a reminder of this story.

St Kessag *Feast day: 10 March. Born in Cashel, Ireland; died in 560.* Kessag was the son of the King of Munster. He became a Christian, travelled to Scotland where he served as a monk and then a missionary bishop. The centre of his activities was Monk's Island in Loch Lomond. He was killed by assassins at Bantry, where a cairn was built in his memory. During a road-building project in the eighteenth century, some of the cairn stones were removed, and a statue of the saint was discovered. Kessag performed amazing miracles from his childhood onwards.

St Kevin *Feast day: 3 June. Born in Leinster, Ireland, 498; died in 618.* Kevin was of royal descent. He was baptized by St Cronan, educated by **St Petroc** and went on to become a hermit in a cave by the upper Lake in Glendalough. After seven years, he had attracted so many disciples that he had to move to a new site beside the lower lake where he founded a monastery. He made a pilgrimage to Rome and returned with a collection of relics for the monastery.

Kevin's communion with nature was legendary. On one occasion he fed his entire community on the salmon brought to him by an otter, and on another he was so still in prayer that a blackbird laid its egg in his hand.

St Keyna *Feast day: 18 October. Born in Wales in the fifth century.* Keyna was one of the 24 children of St Brychan, Chieftain of Brecknock, Wales. She became a hermitess in Somerset, but her nephew **St Cadoc**, convinced her to return to Wales. She went on to found churches there and in Cornwall, England.

St Kiernan *Feast day: 22 March. Born in Ossory, Cork, Ireland in the fifth century.* Kiernan went to Europe as a young man and was baptized and ordained there before returning home to found a monastery. He is known for his love of nature and influence over wild animals. The story is told of a wolf, a badger and a fox that worked with the monks, helping them to gather wood. The fox stole Kiernan's shoes and fled to its set but, on learning of this, the monk instructed the badger and the wolf to bring him back. The badger returned, presenting the fox tightly bound and Kiernan rebuked the animal thief, gave a penance, as if he were a monk, and then welcomed him back into the community.

Kiernan's hermitage was on the island of Cape Clear, Ireland.

St Kilian *Feast day: 8 July. Born in Mullagh, Ireland; died in 689.*
Kilian was an Irish monk who became a bishop. He and a group of companions travelled to Rome in 686 and on their way, they met with and converted Gosbert, Duke of Wurzburg. On the return journey, Kilian and two of his companions visited the duke again and he told them of his marriage to Geilana, his brother's widow. Kilian informed him that this marriage was forbidden by the Church. Gosbert left on a military expedition soon after this, and as soon as he had gone, Geilana had the three missionaries beheaded.

St Kunegunda *Feast day: 24 June. Born in Poland, 1224; died in 1292.*
Kunegunda was the daughter of King Bela IV and the niece of **St Elizabeth of Hungary**. She married King Boleslaus V of Poland at the age of 16. When her husband died in 1284, she entered the order of Poor Clares in a convent which she herself had founded at Sandeck. She was known for her care of the sick and poor, and for paying a ransom in order to free Christians who had been captured by the Turks.

L

St Lanfranc *Feast day: 24 May. Born in Pavia, Italy, 1005; died in 1089.* Lanfranc studied law in Pavia before going for further training in France in 1035, and was known as a scholar and teacher. He became a monk at Bec at the age of 37 and three years later he was made abbot.

After initially opposing Duke William's marriage to Matilda of Flanders in 1059 on the grounds that they were distant cousins, he eventually managed to negotiate a papal dispensation for this and was appointed prior of a new monastery at Caen four years later.

In 1070, at King William's request, Lanfranc was consecrated Archbishop of Canterbury. The ceremony took place in the burnt shell of the cathedral. He initiated a rebuilding programme for the cathedral and introduced Norman practices into Church life. On occasion the weight of responsibility caused Lanfranc to suffer deep depression. His friend **St Anselm** succeeded him as archbishop.

St Laserian *Feast day: 18 April. Born in Ireland; died in 639.* Laserian became a monk on Iona, Scotland, before travelling to Rome to be ordained by Pope **St Gregory the Great**.

On his return to Ireland he supported Roman practices and became embroiled in various disputes with those who followed the ancient Celtic liturgical traditions.

He made a second trip to Rome, this time accompanied by a small delegation. Soon after their return once again to Ireland, and as a result of their consultations with the pope, all of Ireland, except for Columba's monasteries, adopted the new date for Easter. This was 30 years before the Council of Whitby came to a similar decision.

Laserian was made a bishop and Papal Legate to Ireland and, in 637, he succeeded his brother, St Goban, as Abbot of Leighlin. A cave hermitage on Holy Island, off the isle of Arran, Scotland, bears his name.

St Lawrence *Feast day: 14 November. Born at Castledermot, Kildare, Ireland, 1128; died at Eu, Normandy, France, 1180. Canonized in 1225 by Pope Honorius III.* Lawrence was a member of the O'Toole clan. When he was only ten years old, his father handed him over as a hostage to the King of Leinster. He was cruelly treated and eventually given into the care of the Bishop of Glendalough, County Wicklow. Lawrence was well known for his holiness and was elected bishop in 1150. He carried out his responsibilities well and 11 years later was unanimously chosen to be Archbishop of Dublin.

In 1171 he travelled to England to visit King Henry II, who was then at Canterbury, and the Benedictine monks received him with the greatest respect. The next day, on his way to the altar to officiate, he was attacked by a madman who, believing that such a holy person should have the same end as **St Thomas**, struck him violently on the head. Lawrence appeared to have been fatally wounded, but he asked for some water, blessed it, and washed his wound with it. The bleeding ceased and he went on with the service.

In 1175 Lawrence travelled to England once again, in an effort to bring reconciliation between King Henry II and Roderic, King of Ireland.

Henry became so convinced of Lawrence's holiness and prudence that he entrusted him with all details of the negotiation. In later years Henry grew less friendly towards Lawrence and banned him from entering the country. Lawrence followed the king to Normandy seeking reconciliation, but was taken ill and died before he could meet him. He is buried in the church of the abbey at Eu.

St Lawrence of Brindisi *Feast day: 21 July. Born in Brindisi, Naples, Italy, 1559; died in Lisbon, Portugal, 1619. Canonized in 1881 by Pope Leo XIII.* Caesare de Rossi was educated by the Franciscans and by his uncle at St Mark's College in Venice. He proved himself to be both a brilliant military tactician and a peacemaker.

He joined the Capuchins at Verona, taking the name Lawrence, and studied theology, philosophy, the Bible and languages at the University of Padua.

Following ordination he became an effective preacher in northern Italy, and was became Definitor General of his Order in Rome in 1596. He was commissioned to evangelize the Jews, later being sent to Germany with Benedict of Urbino to combat Lutheranism. He founded friaries at Prague, Vienna, and Gorizia, and Emperor Rudolf II asked Lawrence to help him to unite the German rulers to fight against the Turks, who were threatening an attack. He became chaplain and military strategist to the army, which soon won a decisive victory.

In 1602 he was elected Vicar General of the Capuchins, but refused re-election in 1605. He went on to serve as an effective and trusted conciliator in several royal disputes. In 1618 he retired to the friary at Caserta, but was recalled to travel to Spain in order to intercede with King Philip on behalf of the rulers of Naples. He managed to avert an uprising but the trip totally exhausted him and he died a few days later.

St Lawrence of Canterbury *Feast day: 2 February. Born in Rome; died in Canterbury, in 619.* Lawrence accompanied **St Augustine** to Canterbury in 597 and succeeded him as Archbishop in 604. He went back to Rome to tell **St Gregory the Great** about the first conversions in Kent and to seek his advice on how to proceed. He followed the work of Augustine in bringing together the Churches in southeast Britain.

When things grew especially difficult, Lawrence made plans to return to France, but following a vivid dream in which he saw himself being beaten by **St Peter** for abandoning his flock, he decided to remain. He lived long enough to see King Edbald converted to the faith, and died while still in post.

St Lawrence (martyr) *Feast day: 10 August. Born in Rome; died in 258.* Lawrence was one of seven deacons who were in charge of almsgiving when a persecution broke out in Rome, and Pope St Sixtus was condemned to death.

The prefect of the city was convinced that the Church had a great fortune hidden away, and ordered Lawrence to bring the Church's treasure to him. Lawrence agreed to do this in three days' time. After selling the expensive vessels and giving away to the poor any remaining funds, he gathered together the poor and sick people who had been supported by the Church and brought them to the Prefect, saying, 'Here is the Church's treasure!'

The prefect was furious and condemned Lawrence to be tied on top of an iron grill over a slow fire and roasted slowly until he was dead.

St Lawrence Ruiz *Feast day: 28 September. Born in Manila, the Philippines; died in 1630. Canonized 1987 by Pope John Paul II.* Lawrence was a martyr of Japan with Michael Aozaraza, Antony Gonzales, William Cowtet, Vincent Shiwozuka, and Lazarus. He and his companions were tortured and slain on Okinawa.

St Lebuin *Feast day: 11 November. Born in England; died in 773.* Lebuin became a monk at **St Wilfrid**'s monastery at Ripon, and was sent to the eastern Netherlands in 754 to work with St Marchelm among the Frisians.

Lebuin risked his life by going to the annual pagan gathering at Marklo clothed in his full priestly vestments. His boldness and courage won the respect of the Westphalian Saxons, and he was given permission to preach to the assembly. From then on he was allowed to travel and preach wherever he pleased. Lebuin return to Deventer and built a church there. It was later burnt down but, undaunted, he simply rebuilt it, and it was there when he died.

St Leger *Feast day: 2 October. Born in, Poitiers, France, 616; died near Artois, 679.* Leger was raised at the court of King Clotaire II, and educated by his uncle Didon. He became a deacon at the age of 20 and, once ordained in 651, he was appointed Abbot of Maxentius Abbey, where he introduced the Rule of **St Benedict**.

He served Queen Regent **St Bathildis** and helped her govern when Clovis II died in 656. He was named Bishop of Autun in 663. At this time Autun was in a state of complete disorder. There had been no bishop for two years and before then there were two rivals for the see, one of whom had been murdered and the other exiled because of corruption. Leger began by physically restoring the town, and the situation greatly improved through his gift of mediation.

On the death of Clotaire III, he supported young Childeric II for King against his brother Thierry, but in 675 Leger denounced the marriage of Childeric to his uncle's daughter. Furious, the king interrupted the Autun cathedral Easter service in a drunken state and ordered that the bishop be arrested and banished him to Luxeuil.

Following the murder of Childeric in 675, his successor, Theodoric III, restored Leger to his see, but when the Duke of Champagne and his allies attacked Autun, Leger surrendered himself in order to save the town from destruction. He was blinded, had his lips cut off and his tongue pulled out.

Ebroin, who had been deposed earlier by Leger's supporters, was reinstalled as mayor. Erboin convinced the King that Leger and his brother Gerinus had murdered Childeric. As a result Gerinus was stoned to death, while Leger was imprisoned at Fécamp Monastery in Normandy and regularly tortured. Two years later he was finally executed at Sarcing, Artois, still protesting his innocence.

St Leo III *Feast day: 12 June. Boren in Rome, Italy: died 816. Canonized 1673 by Pope Urban VIII.* Leo was elected pope in 795 on the day his predecessor, Hadrian I, was buried. Hadrian's nephew, who had hoped to succeed his uncle, sent a gang of young nobles to attack Leo with the aim of badly maiming him and forcing his resignation. They dragged him from his horse, tried to cut out his tongue and blind him, and left him unconscious. Leo was taken to the Monastery of St Erasmus where he made a miraculously quick recovery. After a few months in refuge with the Frankish king Charlemagne at Paderborn, Leo returned to Rome, entering the city to joyous acclaim.

In 800, in a further attempt to remove him, Leo's enemies accused him of perjury and adultery but Charlemagne came to Rome and appointed commissioners to examine the charges. The accusations were found to be false. Leo also took an oath that he was innocent of any of the charges before the assembled bishops.

On Christmas Day that same year Leo crowned Charlemagne Holy Roman Emperor in St Peter's Basilica. Leo and the new emperor worked closely to resolve disputes throughout the empire and to combat the spread of Islam. There was general agreement on most issues, and with Charlemagne's advice and support, Leo created a fleet to combat the Saracens. They recovered some of the Church's land in Gaeta, and captured a large amount of treasure. Charlemagne's support allowed Leo to restore many churches, and he encouraged him to give help to the destitute and needy.

Following the death of Charlemagne in 814 Leo's enemies once more began to conspire against him. He successfully combated all their plots but died within two years of his great ally.

St Leo IX *Feast day: 19 April. Born in Alsace, France, 1002: died in Rome, 1054. Canonized in 1087 by Pope Victor III.* Pope Leo IX, who had been baptized Bruno, was a deacon when his cousin, Emperor Conrad II, invaded Italy. Despite his calling, Bruno readily joined his cousin's army and fought valiantly, and he was still both a deacon and a soldier when he was chosen to be bishop of Toul in 1026.

He was a stern disciplinarian who chided lax priests and insisted upon the restoration of proper order in the monasteries of his diocese. When he was elected pope in 1048, he attempted to apply this same approach across the whole Church. He set about eradicating simony and enforcing celibacy among the clergy. He also encouraged the development of chanting and liturgy, and worked tirelessly to prevent the schism between the Eastern and Western Churches.

Leo travelled extensively throughout Western Europe, putting into effect his reforms and encouraging his fellow clergy, earning himself the name 'the pilgrim pope'.

Unfortunately Leo IX's attempt to add parts of southern Italy to the papal territories, proved disastrous. After the Normans invaded these new territories, the soldier pope was much criticized when he himself led an army in their defence. The Normans prevailed in the battle and Pope Leo IX was captured at Civitella and imprisoned at Benevento for several months.

Leo used his time in prison to learn Greek with the aim of gaining a better understanding of the Eastern Orthodox Church, which had recently split from Rome. However by this time his health had begun to fail and he died soon after his release.

St Leocritia of Cordova *Feast day: 15 March. Born in Cordova, Spain; died in 859.* Leocritia's parents were wealthy Moors who followed the teachings of Islam. Even though conversion to the Christian faith was punishable by death in those days, Leocritia secretly did so. When her parents discovered this they disowned her and threw her out of the house. She went to **St Eulogius** who took care of her. Eulogius was put on trial for harbouring her and when questioned he explained that it was his Christian duty to provide shelter and help for those who were destitute, and that he would do the same for the judge if he were in the same situation.

Eulogius was found guilty scourged and beheaded and Leocritia met the same fate.

St Leo the Great *Feast day: 10 November. Born in Tuscany, Italy; died in Rome, 461.* Leo was a man of noble character and great ability. While still only a deacon, the Emperor Valentinian III sent him to Gaul to mediate between two of his generals.

He was appointed pope in 440 and during his reign persuaded Emperor Valentinian to recognize the primacy of the Bishop of Rome. Leo wrote extensively in defence of the Christian faith against the many heresies present at this time, and was widely respected for his diplomatic skills and eloquence. For example, he came out to meet Attila the Hun, at the very gates of Rome and persuaded him to turn back, rather than sack the city.

He was less successful when the Vandals came to Rome, but after two weeks he managed to persuade the invaders to stop pillaging the city and killing its inhabitants. After the Vandals left Leo ministered to the spiritual and practical needs of the people, and sent priests to Africa with money to ransom the captives the Vandals had carried off with them.

St Leonard of Port Maurice *Feast day: 20 December. Born at Porto Maurizio, Liguria, Italy, 1676; died in Rome, 1751. Canonized in 1867 Pope Pius IX.* Patron of parish missions. Leonard was baptized Paul Jerome and was the eldest son of Captain Dominic Casanuova, a master mariner. When he was 13, his father, a good Christian man, sent him to stay with his wealthy uncle in Rome so that he could study at the Jesuit College there. Paul Jerome went on to study medicine, but when he refused to become a doctor his uncle disowned him.

In 1697 he joined the Franciscans of the Strict Observance at Ponticelli, and took the name Leonard. He was ordained in Rome in 1703.

For five years, Leonard had to stop preaching because of illness and vowed that if ever he were healed, he would devote his entire life to the conversion of sinners.

Following his recovery in 1709, he went to the San Francesco del Monte monastery in Florence and began to preach all over Tuscany, with tremendous results, for the next 44 years.

In 1730 Leonard was appointed Guardian of St Bonaventure's in Rome and spent the next six years conducting missions, preaching to soldiers, sailors, convicts, and galley-slaves as well as leading many parochial missions. In 1736, he was released from this position as Guardian so that he could continue his calling to evangelization in Umbria, Genoa, and the Marches of Ancona. His missions were often held in the open air and attracted huge crowds.

In 1744, Pope Benedict XIV sent Leonard on a preaching mission to Corsica in the hope of restoring peace. Unfortunately the people of that island regarded him as a political tool rather than a missionary, and he was forced to leave after only six months. He returned to Rome in 1749 and preached for two weeks in the Piazza Navona, which had once been the hippodrome of Emperor Domitian.

Leonard was taken ill while preaching at a mission in the pope's native city of Bologna in 1751, and had a premonition that he would soon die. Conscious of a promise he had made to Pope Benedict that he would die in Rome, he set out immediately for that city. He arrived worn out and exhausted from his arduous work and severe mortifications and died that same night.

Leonard was a prolific writer and his printed works, mostly letters and sermons, fill 13 volumes.

St Leonides of Alexandria *Feast day: 22 April. Born in Alexandria; died in 202.* Leonides was a distinguished and well-respected philosopher and the father of seven children. One of his sons was Origen, who was to become a leading theologian in the Egyptian Church of the third century.

When it was discovered that Leonides was a Christian, he was imprisoned and had all his property confiscated. He was later beheaded during the reign of Septimus Severus when Laetus was Governor of Egypt. Origen's mother was forced to hide her son's clothes in order to prevent him from accompanying his father to his martyrdom.

St Longinus the Centurion *Feast day: 15 March. Born in Caesarea, Cappadocia in the first century.* Longinus was the centurion at the Crucifixion who acknowledged Christ as, 'the Son of God' (Matt 27:54; Mark 15:39; Luke 23:47). He left the army and converted to Christianity undergoing instruction from the Apostles, themselves. Longinus then returned to his homeland, and became a hermit in Caesarea, Cappadocia. He was later arrested and tortured in an attempt to make him deny his faith. He refused to sacrifice to the gods but instead smashed the idols with a nearby axe. The governor who was trying him went mad and blind with rage. Before Longinus was killed his teeth were smashed and his tongue plucked out.

St Lucy of Syracuse *Feast day: 13 December. Born in Syracuse, Sicily; died in 304.* Lucy was the daughter of wealthy well-connected parents and was brought up as a Christian. During the persecutions under Diocletian, her mother pressed her to marry a pagan, but Lucy refused. The man whom she was to have married became frustrated and denounced her to the governor as a Christian. Lucy refused to deny her faith and the judge ordered that she be placed in a brothel, however the guards were miraculously prevented from taking her there. Attempts to burn her also failed and she was finally killed by a sword being thrust into her throat.

Lucy is represented in art as a maiden with her eyes in a dish, or on a book. They were reputedly torn out by a discouraged suitor who had admired them, and were later miraculously restored and were even more beautiful then before.

St Ludan *Feast day: 12 February. Born in Scotland; died in 1202.* Ludan was the son of a Scottish prince. When his father died he devoted his inheritance to the building of a large hospice for pilgrims and those in physical need, and then set off on pilgrimage to Jerusalem.

On his return journey he grew weary while passing near the town of Northheim, Alsace, fell asleep under an elm tree and received a vision of his impending death.

He died not long after this and a boy found in the wallet he carried on his body a small scroll on which was written: 'My name is Ludan: I am the son of the noble Scottish prince Hiltebold. For the honour of God I have become a pilgrim.'

St Luke *Feast day: 14 October. Born in Antioch; died at Boeotia, Greece in the first century.* Patron of doctors, artists, lace makers and bulls. Luke was Greek by birth and a physician by profession. He is the author of one of the Gospels and of the Acts of the Apostles. In his Gospel, Luke is careful to note any dealings with those of Gentile origins and emphasizes

Jesus' special concern for outcasts and the poor. He pays particular attention to the women who followed and assisted Jesus in His ministry, and
he learned much about Jesus from **St Mary** herself

Certain passages of the Acts of the Apostles that clearly describe the
voyage he made to Italy with **St Paul,** are in the first person plural. The
ship they were travelling in was wrecked off the coast of Malta, and Luke
was also with Paul during some of his imprisonment. In his letters, Paul
describes him as his only companion. When Paul appealed to Caesar,
Luke went with him and didn't leave his side until his martyrdom in 67.

Luke died, unmarried and 'full of the Holy Spirit', at the age of 84.

M

St Macanisius *Feast day: 3 September. Born in Ireland; died in 514.* Macanisius was a disciple of **St Patrick** who baptized him as an infant and then later consecrated him as bishop of his own clan. He made a pilgrimage to the Holy Land and after returning via Rome he became a hermit in the vicinity of Kells Monastery. Macanisius had great respect for the Holy Scriptures, so much so that he refused to follow the custom of his fellow monks, who would carry the gospels in a leather satchel. He would carry the precious manuscripts on his back, moving on all fours, or he would cradle them perched upon his hunched up shoulders.

St Macarius of Jerusalem *Feast day: 10 March. Born in Jerusalem; died in 335.* Macarius became Bishop of Jerusalem in 314 and was a noted opponent of the Arian* heresy that supported Orthodoxy at the Council of Nicea. **St Helena** asked Bishop Macarius for help in identifying some wood which she believed had come from the cross used to crucify Jesus as she was unsure which of several pieces were authentic. He suggested that a seriously ill woman be touched by each of the pieces in turn. The woman was instantly cured when touched by one of the pieces, giving rise to the belief that this was indeed the true cross. Macarius built a church over Christ's sepulchre in response to a command from the Emperor Constantine and this was later consecrated as a basilica.

St Machar *Feast day: 12 November. Born in Ireland in the sixth century.* Machar was baptized by **St Colman** and later joined **St Columba** on Iona. He evangelized the island of Mull, was consecrated a bishop, and became the Apostle to the Picts in the northeast region of Scotland. Machar was the founder of the city of Aberdeen.

St Macrina the Elder *Feast day: 14 January. Born in Neocaesarea; died in 340.* During a time of persecution, which had been instituted by Emperors Galerius and Maximinus, Macrina and her husband had to flee to Pontus and lived in great hardship for many years on the shores of the Black Sea.

Macrina was the grandmother of **St Basil the Great**, **St Gregory of Nyssa** and **Macrina the Younger**, and was an avid student of the teaching of **St Gregory Thaumaturgus**.

St Macrina the Younger *Feast day: 19 July. Born in Caesarea in Cappadocia, 327; died in 379.* Macrina the Younger was the granddaughter of **St Macrina the Elder** and elder sister of **St Basil, St Gregory of Nyssa**, and St Peter of Sebastea. She was educated in the Christian faith from an early age.

Macrina was engaged to be married when she was only 12 years old, but her fiancé died and she dedicated the rest of her life to God, beginning by pouring all her energies into the education and care of her brothers.

When her father died, she and her mother withdrew to Pontus and then to an island on the river Isis. There, others joined them to form a religious community centred on prayer and contemplation. Macrina became head of the group when her mother died and continued to live there until her own death at the age of 50.

St Madeleine Sophie *Feast day: 25 May. Born in Joigny, France, 1779; died in 1865. Canonized in 1925 by Pope Pius XI.* Madeleine was the daughter of a cooper, and educated by her brother who was 11 years her elder. She worked extremely hard at her studies, but her young teacher rewarded her with more work, rather than with praise or encouragement.

In 1793 the reign of terror that existed during the French Revolution caused all religious schools to be closed, but when the situation became more stable, a group of young priests of the Sacred Heart Fathers, led by Jean Vadin, began to make provision for the education of children. He invited Madeleine to become a teacher at a convent school at Amiens and she was soon appointed as leader of the small community of postulants who had become teachers alongside her. She was only 23 years old at the time, and held the position for the next 63 years. Madeleine went on to help in the foundation of many other community houses of the Sacred Heart for the education of girls. These were to become among the most efficient educational institutions in the Roman Catholic Church.

Madeleine's success was in large part due to her great perseverance and humility, which she combined with a highly developed insight and wisdom.

St Maelruain *Feast day: 7 July. Born in Ireland; died in 792.* In 774 Maelruain founded the monastery of Tallaght in County Wicklow on land gifted by Cellach mac Dunchada, King of Leinster. He made it his mission to re-establish ascetic practices and disciplines in the Irish monasteries, many of which had fallen into lax behaviour.

Maelruain was the key motivator in the Culdee reform movement, which insisted on celibacy, strict observance of the Sabbath and abstinence from alcohol.

The Culdees laid great stress on disciplined prayer, manual work and study and Maelruain led by example in all three.

St Magnus of Orkney *Feast day: 16 April. Born in Orkney; died in 1116.* In the early 11th century two brothers called Paul and Erling jointly ruled the Orkney Islands. Erling had two sons, Magnus and Erland and Paul had one son, an ambitious and quarrelsome young man called Haakon who had been sent to the Norwegian court to keep him out of trouble. Haakon persuaded King Magnus Barefoot to invade the Scottish islands and coast. They subdued the Orkney Islands and forced Erling's son Magnus to go with them on a raiding party down the west coast of Scotland. When a skirmish began, he refused to join in, was dubbed a coward and consigned to the hold of the ship where he comforted himself by reading his Psalter.

Soon after this incident, Magnus escaped by jumping into the sea and swimming ashore where he sought refuge with King Malcolm III of Scotland.

On the death of King Magnus Barefoot, Magnus returned to Orkney only to find that his cousin Haakon had taken over the throne. Magnus attempted to reclaim the throne and was invited to a meeting by Haakon on the isle of Egilsay, where he was overpowered and slain without making any attempt to resist. His body was eventually taken to Kirkwall for burial in the cathedral which now bears his name.

St Maharsapor *Feast day: 10 October. Born in Persia: died in 421.* Maharsapor was a zealous Christian of noble birth who lived during the reign of King Varahran of Persia. He was put on trial because of his faith, along with his companions Narses and Sabutake. All three were found guilty by a cruel and vengeful judge who had been recently promoted to that post from slavery. His companions were tortured and Maharsapor was left to languish in prison for three years, still refusing to deny his faith. After this time, Maharsapor was thrown into a deep pit where he was left to die of starvation. When the pit was opened, he was found to have died on his knees in prayer.

St Maieul *Feast day: 11 May. Born in Avignon, France, 906; died in 994.* Maieul was a dignified man of fine appearance and a Christian of aristocratic descent. He was forced to flee his estate when the Saracens invaded the region and moved to Lyon, where his gifts were recognized and he was given the rank of archdeacon.

Maieul later became a monk at the Benedictine Abbey of Cluny, where he served as bursar and librarian. He succeeded Abbot Aymard as head of that community and under his wise guidance Cluny prospered and a great new church, the largest in Christendom at that time, was built.

Maieul was well-thought of by the emperor, mediated in a dispute between Empress **St Adelaide** and her son, and was even proposed as pope. He retired at the age of 88 to pursue a life of prayer, but died on his way to help in the reform of St Denis Abbey near Paris.

St Malachy O'More *Feast day: 3 November. Born in Armagh, Ireland, 1095; died in 1148.* Malachy was the pious son of a teacher who accepted ordination by St Cellach in 1132, and carried out further studies under the elderly scholar bishop St Maichius of Lismore. He was appointed Abbot of Bangor, where the abbey building had fallen into a bad state of disrepair, and began by living in holy poverty, building wooden structures and gathering a group of ten others monks around him. He replaced the Celtic liturgy with the Roman one and in 1125, he was made Bishop of Connor and found much work to be done in bringing the church congregations out of lethargic and lax behaviour.

Malachy established a monastery at Iveragh, Kerry and was named Archbishop of Armagh in 1129. This latter appointment was contentious, since up to that time the Archbishopric had been a hereditary see. Even though it was **St Celsus'** dying wish that Malachy be appointed, he experienced continuous opposition, even travelling for a time with an armed bodyguard for fear of attacks from the relatives of the former archbishop.

In 1138 he reorganized the diocese and made a pilgrimage to Rome to explain and seek papal approval for his actions. Malachy visited **St Bernard** at Clairvaux, France, on the way, and they became firm friends. Malachy longed to stay there, but in obedience he returned to Ireland going on to found Mellifont Abbey along similar Cistercian lines to Clairvaux. He also served as papal legate to Ireland.

On a subsequent visit to the pope, Malachy again stopped at Clairvaux. He was warmly greeted but caught a severe fever soon after arriving and died in St Bernard's arms. Malachy is known for many miracles, including healing the son of King David I of Scotland.

St Malchus *Feast day: 27 July. Born in Nisibis, Mesopotamia; died in the fourth century.* Malchus was the only son of wealthy parents who wanted him to marry, but he ran away to join a group of Syrian Hermits in the desert region close to Khalkis. When Malchus learned that his father had died, he decided, against the advice his abbot, to return home to comfort his mother, intending to claim his inheritance and use this money to build a monastery.

The caravan he was travelling home in was attacked and he and a young woman were carried off by the Bedouin raiders. The nomads gave him a job as a goatherd and shepherd. It was suggested that he should marry his fellow captive, but since the woman already had a husband and Malchus had taken monastic vows, they privately agreed simply to live together, but give the appearance of marriage to their captors. Eventually they managed to escape, taking with them goatskins full of food and drink, which when empty they inflated and used as floats to cross the river Euphrates. Their pursuers continued to chase them hard but Malchus and his companion hid themselves close to the mouth of a cave. Their former captors, wrongly assuming that they had hidden themselves inside, rushed in and were killed by a lioness that had made a home for her cubs there. Malchus and his companion captured their pursuers' camels and used them to escape through Edessa.

Malchus returned to his fellow hermits at Khalkis and his companion, who never did find her husband again, lived nearby for many years.

St Malo *Feast day: 15 November. Born near Llancarfan in Wales, 520.* Malo became a monk under **St Brendan** and went with him to Brittany. He was a fervent missionary and would sing praise songs and recite Psalms in a loud voice while travelling the countryside on horseback.

He founded a centre at Aleth, now called Saint-Malo, but pagan opposition forced the monastic community to move to Saintes, France, where Malo became regarded as a bishop. In due course a deputation arrived from Aleth asking if Malo might help them end the extreme drought that their region had been suffering. Full of compassion for their plight, he agreed to return with them and immediately upon his arrival, the heavens opened, releasing a heavy deluge of rain. He then set out once more for Saintes but died on the journey home.

St Marcellina *Feast day: 17 July. Born in Trier, Gaul in the fourth century.* Marcellina was the daughter of the prefect of Gaul and sister of **St Ambrose**. She travelled to Rome with her family when she was quite young, and was consecrated to the religious life by Pope Liberius in 353. When Marcellina went to Milan to visit her brother, he tried to dissuade her from being too strict upon herself in her spiritual disciplines. Nevertheless, Ambrose was clearly filled with admiration for his sibling, and dedicated his treatise on virginity to her.

Sts Marcellinus and Peter *Feast day: 2 June. Born in Rome; died in 304.* Marcellinus, a priest, and Peter, an exorcist, were arrested during the persecution of Emperor Diocletian. They regarded their time in prison as an opportunity to make new converts and even managed to convert their jailer Arthemius and his family. They were secretly beheaded in a wood called the Silva Nigra, in the hope that their bodies would remain undiscovered and thus provide no proper place of remembrance for their fellow Christians. However, two women found the bodies and had them properly buried in marked graves.

Pope **St Damasus** gave an account of the imprisonment and death of Marcellinus and Peter and records that he heard the story of their martyrdom from their executioner who became a Christian soon after their deaths.

St Marcellus the Centurion *Feast day: 30 October. Died in 298.* Marcellus was a centurion who, during the birthday celebrations of the emperors Diocletian and Maximian in Tangier, removed his belt which was the equivalent of removing his uniform, and announced that he was no longer a soldier of the empire but only of Christ. He was arrested and at his trial again declared himself to be a follower of Christ. Marcellus received the sentence considered appropriate for any soldier who had broken his oath of allegiance to the emperor, and was put to death by the sword.

St Marcian of Chalcis *Feast day: 2 November. Born in Cyrrhus, Syria; died in 387.* Marcian was a member of the emperor's court who gave up a promising military career for the life in the desert of Chalcis between Antioch and the Euphrates. His cell was so narrow and low that he was unable to either stand or lie down lengthways. In spite of Marcian's best efforts he was could not stop those seeking a similar way of life from finding him. Two of the first to join him were Eusebius and Agapitus. When others followed, Marcian appointed Eusebius as abbot over the newly formed monastic community.

Marcian would not listen to requests for miraculous intercession, but those who sought help frequently found their prayers miraculously answered.

In his later years Marcian, aware that his bodily remains would be greatly sought after by those who sought to venerate him, persuaded Eusebius to have his body buried secretly. Eusebius agreed to do this and the site of Marcian's grave remained hidden for over 50 years. When his burial place was finally discovered, the relics were solemnly translated and became an object of pilgrimage.

St Marek Krizin *Feast day: 7 September. Born in Croatia; died in 1619.* Marek studied at the Germanicum in Rome but returned to Hungary after his ordination to become a canon at Esztergom. Along with two companions, he was assigned to missionary work near Kosice, Slovakia where in 1619 they were taken prisoner by invading Calvinist troops, tortured and put to death.

St Margaret of Antioch *Feast day: 20 July. No date.* Patron of childbirth. Margaret was the beautiful daughter of a pagan priest at Antioch in Pisidia. She acted as a nurse to a Christian family and subsequently converted to Christianity. She was disowned by her father as a result and became a shepherdess. When she rejected the unwanted amorous advances of Olybrius, the governor of Antioch, Margaret was charged with being a Christian, tortured and imprisoned.

During her time in captivity, the devil appeared to her in the form of a dragon and swallowed her up. However, the cross she carried in her hand so irritated the dragon's throat that he was forced to disgorge her.

The following day an attempt was made to kill Margaret by burning her to death; when this failed the soldiers attempted to drown her. She miraculously survived both ordeals and thousands who witnessed what had happened were converted on the spot. The governor ordered that all who had witnessed these miraculous deliverances were to be immediately put to death, and Margaret herself was finally killed by being beheaded.

St Joan of Arc heard the voice of Margaret of Antioch in one of her early visionary experiences.

St Margaret of Cortona *Feast day: 22 February. Born at Loviano, Tuscany in Italy, 1247; died in Cortona, 1297. Canonized in 1728 by Pope Benedict XIII.* After an unhappy home life as a result of her stepmother's lack of support, Margaret eloped with a young nobleman, bore him a son, and lived as his mistress for nine years. He was murdered in 1274 and Margaret saw this as a sign from God, publicly confessed to the affair, and took shelter with the Friars Minor at Cortona. To make herself unappealing to local young men, she once tried to mutilate herself, but a Friar named Giunta managed to dissuade her. She began caring for the sick and poor, asking for nothing in return, and joined the Franciscans in 1277.

She gathered others of like mind and formed them into companies. They founded a hospital at Cortona and were later given the status of a congregation, and called the Poverelle (Poor Ones). Margaret preached against vice and worked for all those in need. Her critics never allowed her to forget her past life and she was the target of local gossips right to the end of her life.

St Margaret of Hungary *Feast day: 26 January. Born in Turoc in Hungary, 1243; died in 1270. Canonized in 1943 by Pope Pius XII.* The daughter of King Bela IV, Margaret became a Dominican novice at the age of 12 with the full approval of her parents. A convent was specially constructed on an island in the Danube for her and the sisters of her new order.

Margaret went out of her way to perform the most menial tasks on behalf of the poor and sick and sought no special privileges because of her royal descent. She had intense sympathy for the squalid conditions in which the poor were forced to live, and adopted such conditions for herself.

When a maidservant of the convent fell down a well in the dark of night, all the sisters and the girl herself were quite certain that it was the strength and power of Margaret's prayer that kept her from drowning. Eventually, a rope was found and lowered into the well and the maid was pulled out safe and well.

Margaret used to spend the 40 days of Lent without sleep, and practised extreme fasting and prayer. Her excessive asceticism went unchecked due to the absence of a strong wise abbess, and this almost certainly contributed to her early death at the young age of 27.

St Margaret of Scotland *Feast day: 16 November. Born in England, 1046; died in 1093.* Margaret was an English princess, the daughter of Edward the Atheling who died in 1057. She was educated in Hungary and, following the Norman Conquest, she and her mother escaped to Scotland by sea.

King Malcolm of Scotland made them welcome, fell in love with the beautiful and gracious Margaret and in 1070 they were married in Dunfermline castle. Queen Margaret proved to be a good influence on both her husband and the country at large, for though Malcolm was a good ruler, he and his court were unsophisticated and uncouth. Margaret handled her husband's bad tempers well and encouraged him to practise charity with integrity. She was also a strong civilizing influence on the whole of the court. The princes developed better manners, while their ladies copied Margaret's purity and devotion.

Inspired by this example of spiritual and practical religion, Malcolm grew close the Christian faith, and even 'stole' his wife's prayer book in order to have the cover encrusted with gold and precious stones as a mark of his respect for her and her faith. He presented the bejewelled book to her on her birthday that same year. The king and queen prayed together, distributed alms to the poor with their own hands, and in every way strived to bless and serve everyone who was part of their kingdom.

Margaret brought good teachers into the land and supported the building of churches, which she beautified by personally embroidering church vestments and hangings.

Malcolm and Margaret had six sons and two daughters, whom they loved dearly. The youngest boy **St David I** became king in 1124. Margaret never lost her faith even when, during her last illness, she learned that both her husband and her son, Edward, had been killed in battle.

St Margaret Ward *Feast day: 25 October. Born in Congleton in Cheshire, England; died in 1588. Canonized in 1970 by Pope Paul VI.* Margaret served as a companion to the Wittle family in London. She smuggled a rope into the cell of priest William Watson in Bridewell Prison in order to help him make good his escape. Although William was injured in a fall from the roof, he managed to get away but the rope was traced back to Margaret Ward.

Even though she was severely tortured, she refused either to disclose the priest's hiding place or to convert to the Protestant faith. Margaret was tried at the Old Bailey and hanged, drawn, and quartered at Tyburn, together with a priest and four other laymen. She is one of the 40 martyrs of England and Wales.

St Marguerite Bourgeoys *Feast day: 12 January. Born in Troyes in France, 1620; died in Québec, 1700. Canonized in 1982 by Pope John Paul II.* Marguerite was the daughter of a candle-maker. Her vocation to the religious life led her to apply to enter the Carmelites and then the Poor Clares but both rejected her request.

In 1652 the Governor of Montreal visited Troyes and invited Marguerite to come back with him to tutor the children of the French garrison. She accepted, and travelled to Canada the following year to take up a post as a teacher and nurse. Marguerite was appointed as headmistress of the first school to be established there in 1658. She returned to France to recruit more helpers and, in 1676, with the approval of her bishop, established a missionary teaching order named the Sisters of Notre Dame.

The sisters taught throughout Canada, and continued to expand despite many privations, fires, and even massacres. Schools were established for local children and in 1689 the congregation received papal approval to begin working in the United States. Many were greatly helped as a result of Marguerite's perseverance, wisdom and goodness.

St Marguerite d'Youville *Feast day: 16 October. Born in Varennes, Quebec in Canada, 1701; died in1771. Canonized in 1990 by Pope John Paul II.* Marguerite married Francois d'Youville in 1722, and was widowed eight years later. She worked to support herself and her three children and devoted her spare time to the charitable activities of the

Confraternity of the Holy Family. In 1737 she and three of her companions founded the Grey Nuns. Marguerite was appointed Directress of the General Hospital in Montreal when it was taken over by the Grey Nuns, and in 1755 Bishop Pontbriand of Quebec confirmed her as superior of the order.

Since her death in 1771 the Grey Nuns have established schools, hospitals, and orphanages throughout Canada, the United States, Africa and South America, and are especially known for their work among the Inuit.

St Maria Crocifissa di Rosa *Feast day: 14 December. Born in Brescia in Italy, 1813; died in 1855.* Maria was educated by Visitandine nuns, but she left school early to look after her widowed father's estate. She was greatly drawn to convent life, took care of the spiritual needs of the young girls who worked in her father's mills, and was a voluntary worker in the local hospital during a cholera epidemic in 1836. She later founded a home for girls and a school for the deaf. In 1840 Maria was appointed by her superior to be in charge of a group who cared for the sick, named the Handmaids of Charity of Bescia.

She took the religious name Maria Crocifissa because of her devotion to the crucified Christ.

St Maria-Domenica Mazzarello *Feast day: 14 May. Born in Mornese in Piedmont, France, 1837; died in 1881. Canonized in 1951 by Pope Pius XII.* Maria-Domenica Mazzarello was born into a large country family. She caught typhoid fever while nursing her family and lost much of her physical strength. She began her own dress-making business as well as developing her own religious order. **St John Bosco** came to Mornese with the hope of starting a school for boys but, when this failed, he put his energy into supporting a similar venture for girls supported by nuns. He installed Maria-Domenica as first superior of the Salesian Sisters. Although she had no formal education, she shared John Bosco's infectious joy and also proved to be a fine administrator. She was later elected superior general of the mother house at Nizza Monferrato. In 1876 she was sent along with five other nuns to Argentina to begin a new work there. Maria-Domenica was taken ill in 1881 and returned to the mother house, hoping to recuperate, but died soon after her return.

St Maria Goretti *Feast day: 6 July. Born in Corinaldo in Ancona, Italy, 1890; died in 1902. Canonized in 1950 by Pope Pius XII.* Patron of youth, young women, purity, and victims of rape. Maria's father was a farm worker who died of malaria when she was very young, and her mother had to struggle to feed her children. In 1902, an 18-year-old neighbour named Alexander abducted Maria from her home and tried to rape her. She resisted, saying that she would rather die than submit and, in a fit of rage, her assailant stabbed her with a knife. Maria was fatally wounded but was able to forgive her attacker before she died.

Alexander was arrested and sentenced to 30 years in prison. Initially unrepentant, he later became a reformed character as a result of a dream in which he saw himself in a garden with Maria giving him flowers. He was released 27 years later and went directly to Maria's mother to ask for her forgiveness, which she readily gave.

Alexander was present in the crowd in St Peter's Square in Rome to join in the celebration of her canonization when she was officially declared a saint by Pope Pius XII in 1950.

St Maria Skobtsova *Feast day: 20 July. Born in Anapa in Latvia near the Black Sea, 1891; died in 1945. Canonized in 2004 Pope John Paul II.* Maria was born into a well-to-do Latvian family in 1891 and was given the name Elizaveta Pilenko. A strong and committed atheist in her younger days, she moved to St Petersburg where she became involved in radical intellectual circles and married in 1910. During this period, Maria wrote and published many poems, but 1913 saw the end of her marriage to Dimitri and she moved south.

Following the Bolshevik Revolution in 1918 she was elected mayor of Anapa in Southern Russia. Maria was tried for being a Bolshevik, acquitted and ended up marrying the judge.

Her strong will and unwavering persistence made her many enemies, and she was threatened with assassination but escaped to France in 1923. By this time she had two children and was pregnant with a third. Her son was born safely after her arrival in Paris, but her second child died of meningitis soon after. She was deeply affected by this experience and as a result became more involved in theological study and developed a growing interest in the Christian faith.

Her second marriage became increasingly strained and, with her husband's permission, she took her bishop's advice and became a nun, taking the name Maria. She lived in a rented house in Paris which served as a convent, and this also became a shelter for refugees. Maria and some friends formed the Orthodox Action group with the aim of making active connections between Christian worship and service.

During the German occupation of Paris in 1940, Maria did all she could to assist the persecuted Jewish population of Paris and, in 1942, when thousands of Jews had been herded into a Paris sports stadium, she courageously gained access and helped to smuggle Jewish children out in garbage bags.

In 1943 Maria was arrested by the Gestapo and sent to Ravensbrück concentration camp. In captivity she would trade food for needles and thread in order to embroider holy images, which gave her strength. Maria survived almost to the war's end but, on Good Friday, 1945, she volunteered to take the place of a Jewish prisoner who was to be sent to the gas chamber.

St Maria Soledad *Feast day: 11 October. Born in Spain, 1826; died in 1887. Canonized in 1970 by Pope Paul VI.* Maria was the second of five children of a dairyman, and always longed for the contemplative life.

Father Michael, a pastor of one of the poorer suburbs of Madrid, who had learned of her desire to serve God in the religious life, invited her to be part of a new nursing order for the poor. These sisters lived in extreme poverty and often struggled to have enough to eat. Father Michael appointed Maria superior general of the community and she lived to see it receive full papal approval in 1876. She died at the mother house from chronic pneumonia in 1887 and in 1893, when her remains were exhumed from the sisters' plot at the cemetery and transferred to the mother house, her body was found to be intact.

St Marinus *Feast day: 3 March. Born in Caesarea; died in 260.* Born into a wealthy and successful Christian family, Marinus made a fine career in the Roman army. He was appointed to a senior post at a young age but a jealous rival denounced him to the authorities as untrustworthy because of his Christian faith.

The magistrate questioned Marinus closely and asked him to show his allegiance to the emperor by sacrificing to the gods. When he refused to do this he was given three hours to consider his position.

He went to seek the advice of Bishop Thoetecnus of Caesarea. The bishop pointed at Marinus' sword and then to a copy of the Gospels, asking him which he preferred. Marinus pointed to the Gospel book straight away, and the bishop then advised him to hold fast to God. Marinus returned to the magistrate reaffirming his belief with even greater certainty, and was taken out and executed.

St Astyrius, a Roman Senator, was present at the martyrdom. Taking off his cloak, he wrapped up the body of Marinus, carried it away on his shoulders and buried it with great honour.

St Mark *Feast day 25 April. Born in Jerusalem in the first century.* Patron of notaries. John Mark lived with his mother in Jerusalem where their home was a gathering place for Christians. He was a close friend of the disciples and has been identified with the young man who ran away from the Garden of Gethsemane on the night of the arrest of Jesus Christ, leaving his cloak behind (Mark 14:51–2).

He was with his cousin **St Barnabas** and **St Paul** on one of their missionary journeys and later accompanied St Barnabas alone. Mark was also in Rome with **St Peter** and Paul and, following a request from some Roman Christians that the teaching of St Peter be recorded, he wrote what has become the second Gospel in the New Testament. Mark went on to found the church in Alexandria and he is regarded as its first bishop.

Sts Mark and Marcellian *Feast day: 18 June. Died in Rome in 287.* Mark and Marcellian were twin brothers of high birth, both of whom had become Christians in their youth. Soon after Diocletian became emperor, they were arrested, thrown into prison and condemned to be beheaded by Chromatius, a lieutenant to the Prefect of Rome.

Their friends managed to have the execution delayed for 30 days in order to give them time to change their minds and make the obligatory sacrifices to the gods. Their families begged them to change their minds but **St Sebastian**, who was at that time an officer in the army, visited them daily and encouraged them not to give in.

The outcome of this period of discussion was that all their family members, who had previously been unbelievers, converted to Christianity. Even the Roman Lieutenant Chromatius was moved to set the prisoners free, resign his post and retire to the country.

Mark and Marcellian were soon recaptured by Chromatius' successor Fabian, who quickly arranged for their execution to be carried out. They were bound to two wooden pillars to which their feet were nailed. Their bodies were then pierced with lances until they were dead.

St Maro *Feast day: 14 February. Born in Cyrrhus in Syria in the fourth century.* Maro was a hermit who lived as a solitary mainly in the open air although he would use a small hut covered with goatskins as a shelter in emergency. He found the ruins of a heathen temple, dedicated it to God, and made it a house of prayer. **St John Chrysostom** wrote to him while in exile at Cucusus, coveting his prayers. Maro was also a disciple of St Zebinus. He would spend days and nights standing in prayer without showing any signs of weariness, though in extreme old age he was known to support himself with a staff during such vigils. Maro was renowned for his spiritual wisdom, as a monastic teacher, and for the three monasteries which he founded.

St Martha *Feast day: 28 July. Born in Bethany in the first century.* Patron of cooks. Martha was the sister of Mary and Lazarus and Jesus was a frequent guest at their home in Bethany near Jerusalem (Luke 10:38–42).

Jesus stayed with the family for the last week of his earthly life. Martha served Jesus faithfully in many practical ways, though it was her sister Mary who was commended for knowing how to be still and listen at the right time (John 12:1–11).

St Martin de Aguirre *Feast day: 6 February. Born in Vergara (near modern Pamplona) in Spain; died in 1597. Canonized in 1862 by Pope Pius IX.* Martin joined the Franciscan Order in 1586, was ordained, and volunteered for overseas missions. He was sent to Mexico, then to Manila in the Philippines, before going on to Japan. Christianity was tolerated at this time in that country and Martin was able to preach and give instruction to a steadily growing number of Japanese converts.

Several members of the Japanese government, however, counselled opposition to the Christian faith, which they believed to be a prelude to a European invasion. Not long after Martin's arrival, the Emperor Toyotomi Hideyoshi became convinced that Christianity was indeed a threat to Japanese culture and independence and issued edicts which greatly inhibited all foreign influence, and a severe persecution of Christians followed.

A price was put on the heads of priests, and thousands of native Japanese who refused to deny their faith were killed. While in Roman times the person accused of being a Christian could escape punishment by sacrificing to the gods, in Japan anyone accused of being a Christian and wishing to deny their faith could show they had recanted by trampling on boards bearing holy images related to the Christian faith.

Martin was arrested along with 25 of his companions. They were marched to Nagasaki, tied to crosses and killed.

St Martin of Braga *Feast day: 20 March. Born in Pannonia (Hungary), 520; died at Dumium monastery in Spain, 579.* Martin made a pilgrimage to the Holy Land and became a monk before founding a monastery in Spain. He converted a tribe known as the Suevi, which had settled in Galicia and had become supporters of Arianism*.

Martin wrote effectively about the virtuous life and made a collection of the writings of the Desert Fathers for his fellow monks. **St Gregory of Tours** regarded him as one of the finest scholars of the age. His writings included valuable information on how to correct many superstitious customs and he followed the model of persuasion and instruction rather than coercion, which was a characteristic of the Celtic approach to missions. In this he owed much to the influence of his forebear in the faith, **St Martin of Tours**.

Noting that most of the growth in the Church had, up to this time, been in the towns and cities, Martin made it his aim to communicate the Gospel to the largely pagan rural population. Martin built Dumium Monastery, and then became Bishop of Braga and metropolitan of Galicia.

St Martinian *Feast day: 13 February. Born in Caesarea in the Holy Land; died in Athens, 422.* Martinian became a hermit at the age of 18 and chose to make his cell on a site known as the Place of the Ark. A woman of evil reputation named Zoe tried to seduce him but Martinian resisted her by walking barefoot into a fire and standing there. His faithful patience and steadfast obedience eventually led her to the point of conversion and she became a nun in Bethlehem. In the last years of his life, Martinian took to wandering from place to place and he finally died at a great age in Greece.

St Martin de Porres *Feast day: 3 November. Born in Lima in Peru, 1579; died in 1639. Canonized in 1873 Pope Pius IX.* Patron of barbers and race relations. Martin was the illegitimate son of the Spanish knight Juan de Porres, and Anna Velasquez, a black freed-woman from Panama. At the age of 15 he became a lay brother at the Dominican Friary at Lima but, because of his dark skin, he was socially spurned, and spent his life there as a barber, farm labourer, almoner and hospital worker. He longed to be involved in foreign missions but, when this proved impossible, he threw himself into strict disciplines of daily service to the poor and sick, and long sessions of nightly prayer. He devoted himself to ceaseless and severe penances and God endowed him with grace, wisdom and the gift of miracles. He also exhibited such wondrous gifts as aerial flights and bilocation.

St Martin set up an animal hospital in his sister's house, where he showed equal concern for all animals including vermin. He also possessed spiritual wisdom, perceptively advising his sister on her marriage problems, and managed to raise a dowry for his niece in three days.

St Martin of Tours *Feast day: 11 November. Born in Pannonia, (Hungary), 316; died in 397.* Patron of soldiers. Martin, the son of a pagan Roman army officer, became a catechumen at the age of ten, however he was still unbaptized when he was forced to join the army at 15. The law required sons of veterans of the Roman army to serve in the military and even though Martin was so reluctant to do this that he had to be held in chains before taking the oath, he finally felt obliged to obey. He was assigned to the emperor's ceremonial cavalry unit and thus was far removed from combat, until he was eventually assigned to garrison duty in Gaul.

Riding home one day, Martin saw a beggar who was practically naked and shivering with the cold. He took off his cloak, slashed it in two with his sword and gave half to the poor man. That night Martin had a dream in which he saw Jesus wearing the half of the cloak that he had given to the beggar. Martin's disciple and biographer Sulpicius Severus states that as a consequence of this vision Martin 'flew to be baptized'.

Martin became convinced that he was to leave the army and follow Christ but his unit had just been transferred to the dangerous Rhineland area where they were confronted by a Saxon army, and some suspected his 'conversion' might simply be the result of cowardice. In order to counter this and to disprove his accusers, although he continued to be adamant that he could not fight, Martin offered to stand in front of the army without weapons or armour. The next morning he went out ready to do as he had said only to find that the Saxons had broken camp and fled in the night.

Martin sought guidance from **St Hilary of Poitiers** who suggested that he should be ordained priest but he refused, agreeing instead to be ordained as an exorcist. When Martin began to publicly denounce the Arian* heresy, he was whipped and driven out of his hometown. Discovering that Hilary had been exiled for the same reason, Martin went to an island near Milan to live as a hermit. When Hilary returned to Poitiers, Martin was there to meet him, and in order to fulfil Martin's call to solitude, Hilary gave him a wilderness retreat. Disciples flocked to him for spiritual direction, and he founded the monastery of Ligug for them, the first of its kind in Gaul.

Following Hilary's death, Martin was chosen as his successor by popular consent. He made his first home as bishop in a cell attached to a church in the hope of being able to maintain his lifestyle as a monk. However he soon found this to be impossible and withdrew to live outside the city in a cabin made of branches. Disciples flocked to him and he founded the monastery of Marmoutiers at that place.

Martin's evangelistic strategy was to visit an area, house by house, taking every opportunity to speak to people about God, then gather those who embraced the Christian faith into communities and place these under the direction of a priest or monk. He would make regular return visits to these fledgling communities to encourage and guide their development.

Martin replaced many pagan temples with churches and on one occasion he persuaded one group to cut down a tree that had been regarded as sacred. They agreed but only if Martin were prepared to sit under it. He agreed to do so and the tree fell away from him, leaving him unharmed.

He showed great compassion for those in need and once, when a father brought his mute daughter to him, he healed her by asking her to say her father's name. His compassion and mercy led him to intervene on behalf of the heretic Priscillian. While agreeing that the heretics should be excommunicated, he strongly opposed plans to execute them. Having talked with the Emperor Maximus, he left believing that he had won the argument and was therefore shocked to find out later that Priscillian and others had been tortured and executed. Martin returned immediately, hoping to put a stop to a wholesale massacre, but refused to take communion with the bishops who had murdered the people, thus showing his complete disapproval of their actions. When Martin was assured, however, that if he did share communion the prisoners would be released, he changed his mind. However, later, on calm reflection, he felt that he had given in, and suffered deep guilt and remorse. He refused to attend any more assemblies of bishops.

Martin was over 80 years old when he died. At his request, he was buried, in the Cemetery of the Poor.

St Mary *Feast day: 8 December. Born in Nazareth in the first century.* Mary was the virgin mother of Jesus, and the wife of **St Joseph**. The principal events of her life are celebrated as liturgical feasts of the universal Church. She was the daughter of Sts Joachim and Anne and betrothed to St Joseph. The Archangel Gabriel visited Mary and announced to her that she would have a child by the power of the Holy Spirit. Following this, she visited her cousin Elizabeth who was carrying a child who was to become known as **St John the Baptist**. The baby leapt in Elizabeth's womb and she recognized Mary as the Mother of God. Mary and Joseph travelled to Bethlehem, which was the town of Joseph's ancestors, for a census, and Mary gave birth to Jesus there.

Mary and Joseph presented Jesus in the Temple, where St Simeon and St Anna were overjoyed to see him and Mary received word of the sorrows to come. The family escaped to Egypt and remained there until King Herod died, following which they returned to Nazareth.

Mary was present at the first recorded miracle of Jesus, turning water into wine at a wedding in Cana, at the Crucifixion in Jerusalem, and was also with the disciples in the days preceding Pentecost. She spent her last years in Ephesus, where she died.

St Mary of Egypt *Feast day: 2 April. Born in Egypt; died in 437.* Mary moved to Alexandria at the age of 12, became an actress and later a prostitute. She decided, out of curiosity, to join a group of pilgrims who planned to visit Jerusalem to see the Holy Cross. On arrival, the rest of the party went inside the church but Mary found it impossible to enter. She soon became aware that she would be unable to enter until she had confessed her sins, which she did readily. Mary was then able to go inside and experienced such a powerful conversion that she immediately withdrew into the desert beyond Jordan.

A hermit called Zosimas discovered her there 47 years later. Mary told him her life's story and asked if he would give her Holy Communion, which he did. When he returned a year later, he found that Mary had died, probably soon after he had left her the year before.

St Mary Magdalene *Feast day: 22 July. Born in Magdale, Northern Galilee in the Holy Land in the first century.* Though Mary was Jewish, her cultural background and manners were those of a Gentile. When Jesus was at supper at the home of a rich man named Simon, Mary came to weep at his feet and then wiped his feet dry with her long hair, anointing them with expensive perfume. Some were surprised that Jesus had allowed her to touch him but he explained to them that love was increased in those who were forgiven much. **St Luke** records that Christ cast out seven devils from her.

Mary Magdalene was present at the Crucifixion and was the first to see the risen Christ at the tomb on Easter morning; her name was the first word spoken by the risen Christ.

Fourteen years after the resurrection, St Mary was put in a boat, without sails or oars, along with Sts. Lazarus and **Martha**. They were sent drifting out to sea and landed on the shores of southern France, where St Mary spent the rest of her life in solitary prayer in a cave known as Sainte-Baume.

St Mary Magdalene de Pazzi *Feast day: 25 May. Born in Florence, 1566; died in 1607. Canonized in 1669 by Pope Clement IX.* Mary Magdalene de Pazzi was taught to pray at an early age at the request of her mother. She regularly practised half an hour of meditation and experienced her first spiritual ecstasy at the age of 12 when she was contemplating a sunrise and was left trembling and speechless.

Mary was very beautiful and her family was most distressed when, at the age of 18, she decided to become a novice in the Carmelite order. A year later, she entered a long period of spiritual dryness and desolation during which she experienced great temptations, and was sometimes close to suicide.

When Mary believed that God had commanded her to go barefoot, she cut the soles out of her shoes so that no one would be aware of her self-imposed discipline. Mary Magdalene could be extremely forthright in her spiritual direction, and was also so physically sensitive that, at times, she could not be touched without feeling pain. Her last three years were particularly difficult but on her deathbed she was able to encourage her fellow sisters to love Jesus alone and to trust him implicitly.

St Mary the Slave *Feast day: 1 November. Died in 300.* Mary, born and raised a Christian, was the slave of a Roman official named Tertullus. When persecution broke out, Tertullus, fearful of being found to have knowingly employed a Christian, handed her over to the local governor. Mary suffered unspeakable public torture but, thanks to the efforts of her master and the compassion of onlookers, was released into the custody of a soldier who aided her escape. Mary died a natural death but is venerated as a martyr because of the intensity of her sufferings.

St Matilda *Feast day: 14 March. Born in Westphalia, Denmark; died in 968.* Patron of parents of large families. Matilda was the daughter of Count Dietrich of Westphalia and Reinhild of Denmark and was raised by her grandmother, the Abbess of Eufurt convent. In 909 she married Henry the Fowler, son of Duke Otto of Saxony.

She was noted for her piety and charitable works but, after her husband died in 936, both of her sons, Otto (the Great) and Henry, severely criticized her seemingly extravagant charity. She then handed over the family fortune to her sons and retired to her country home. When Henry revolted in 941, Otto put down the insurrection with great cruelty. Matilda censured Henry for beginning another revolt against Otto in 953, and for his ruthlessness in suppressing a revolt by his own subjects, and subsequently prophesied his imminent death. Henry died in 955, after many disputes with his brother.

Matilda built three convents and a monastery, and was again left in charge of the kingdom when Otto went to Rome in 962 to be crowned Emperor (of the Holy Roman Empire).

She spent most of her declining years at the convent at Nordhausen which she had built, and died at the monastery at Quedlinburg.

St Matthew *Feast day: 21 September. Born in Capernaum in the first century.* Patron of bankers. Matthew, the son of Alpheus, was of Jewish origin and was called to be a disciple from his seat as a tax collector at Capernaum. **St Mark** and **St Luke** in their Gospels also know him as Levi. Matthew wrote the first of the four Gospels in Aramaic in a style suitable for liturgical reading and full of references which would be familiar to a Jewish audience. His Gospel was written before the Romans destroyed the temple in Jerusalem in AD 70.

After the resurrection of Christ, Matthew left his homeland for missionary work abroad and little is known of his later life and death.

St Matthias *Feast day: 14 May. Born in Palestine in the first century.* Following the Ascension of Jesus the Apostles set about finding a replacement for Judas. It was decided that the replacement was to be someone who was a witness to Jesus' resurrection and a follower of Jesus from his baptism to the time of his Ascension. Two men fitted this description, Matthias and Joseph (called Barsabbas). Matthias was chosen by lot to become one of the 12.

He accepted enthusiastically all that his new appointment implied, evangelizing, enduring persecution and even death in service to the Lord. **St Clement of Alexandria** explains in his writings that Matthias, like all the other apostles, was not chosen by Jesus for what he already was, but for what Jesus foresaw he would become.

His emblem in Christian art is an axe, which is taken to be a sign that he suffered a martyr's death.

St Maurice *Feast day: 22 September. Died in 287.* Emperor Maximian sent an army to quell the rebellion of the Bagaudae in Gaul, instructing that sacrifices be made to the gods to ensure victory over the rebels.

Maurice was an officer in the Theban Legion, which consisted of 6,000 men, and was composed entirely of Christians from Upper Egypt. He and his fellow soldiers repeatedly refused orders to sacrifice and withdrew from the army encamped at Octodurum (Martigny) near Lake Geneva to Agaunum (St Maurice-en-Valais).

Maximian refused to compromise and insisted that all who continued to disobey his orders should be executed. Maurice encouraged the men to remain faithful to the end and was the first to be executed.

St Maurus *Feast day: 25 January. Born in Italy in the sixth century.* Maurus, son of a Roman noble, became **St Benedict**'s assistant at the age of 12 and succeeded him as abbot of Subiaco Abbey in 525.

In obedience to Benedict's instructions, he saved a boy named Placid from drowning by walking on water without realizing it. The young lad had gone to collect water at a nearby lake, fallen in, and been carried away as far as a bowshot from the bank. Maurus grabbed him by the hair and pulled him out.

St Maximilian *Feast day: 14 August. Born in 274; died in Algeria in 295.* In 295, the proconsul Dion was sent to Tebessa, Algeria to recruit soldiers for the third Augustinian legion, which was stationed in that region. Centurion Fabius Victor duly presented his son Maximilian, then 21, to serve as the law required.

When asked to give his name, Maximilian declined, simply explaining that he was a Christian. No amount of threats of torture or even death was able to shake his resolve. His father Victor respected his son's views and did not even try to persuade him. The proconsul explained that some of the Emperor Diocletian's personal bodyguard were Christian centurions and that they saw no conflict between their faith and serving in the army.

Maximilian replied that he could not answer for them but only for himself and he knew that it would be wrong to agree to serve in this way. When news came that he was to die because of his refusal, Maximilian said, 'God lives.' As he was led out to be beheaded, he asked his father to give the new cloak that had been prepared for him to wear as a solider to his executioner.

St Maximilian Kolbe *Feast day: 14 August. Born in Poland, in 1894; died in 1941. Canonized in 1982 by Pope John Paul II.* Patron of journalists, families, prisoners, the pro-life movement and the chemically addicted.

After joining the Franciscans in 1910, Maximilian was sent to study in Rome and was ordained there in 1918. He returned to Poland in 1919 and began spreading his Militia of the Immaculata movement of Marian consecration (whose members are also called MIs), which he founded on 16 October 1917.

In 1927 he established a centre for evangelization near Warsaw, and in 1930 he established a community in Nagasaki, Japan. By 1938 the community in Warsaw had become the largest Catholic religious house in the world, with over 650 monks. The friars used modern printing and business techniques, which allowed a monthly magazine with a circulation of over one million to be regularly produced. Maximilian also started a shortwave radio station and began planning a studio for film production.

In 1941 Maximilian Kolbe was arrested in Poland and imprisoned in Auschwitz concentration camp. There was an escape from the camp in July 1941, and ten men were selected to be killed in retribution. One of those chosen was a married man with young children; out of compassion Maximilian volunteered to take his place. He was condemned to a slow death in a starvation bunker. After three weeks Maximilian was one of the few found to be still alive and his impatient captors ended his life with a lethal carbonic acid injection. His body was burned in the ovens of Auschwitz.

When Pope John Paul II canonized Maximilian Kolbe in 1982, the man who had been allowed to live as a result of his selfless example was present in the crowds in St Peter's Square in Rome.

St Maximus *Feast day: 10 June. Born in Asia; died in 250.* Maximus was a merchant who was called before the consul Optimus in the time of the persecution under the Emperor Decius. When questioned he provided his name, profession and identity as a Christian. A decree had been issued demanding the veneration of the bust of the Emperor under pain of torture and death, but when Optimus ordered Maximus either to sacrifice and save his life or die in torment he replied, 'I have always wished it; it is in order to pass out of this short and miserable life to the life eternal that I have declared my faith.'

Maximus was tortured on the rack and beaten with rods. When he still refused to recant Optimus ordered that he be taken outside the city walls and stoned to death.

St Maximus the Confessor *Feast day: 13 August. Born in Constantinople, 580: died at Skhemaris (on the Black Sea), 662.* Born to a noble family in Constantinople Maximus served for a time as principal secretary to Emperor Heraclius. He resigned to become a monk and in due course became abbot at Chrysopolis, Turkey. He was known for his detailed theological writings.

When Emperor Constans II favoured Monothelitism*, Maximus opposed him and defended the memory and teaching of Pope Honorius. He then attended the Lateran Council in 649, which Pope St Martin I had convened. Pope Martin I was taken prisoner, charged with treason and sent into exile in the Chersonese, where he was bullied and starved to death. Maximus was also arrested and spent six years at Perberis before being brought back to Constantinople with two companions who were both named Anastasius. They were tortured and mutilated by having their tongues and hands cut off to prevent them speaking or writing. They were then sent to Skhemaris on the Black Sea, where Maximus died. Maximus was sometimes known as 'The Theologian'.

St Maximus of Jerusalem *Feast day: 5 May. Born in Jerusalem; died in 350.* Maximus was tortured for his faith and left permanently crippled. He followed **St Macarius** as Bishop of Jerusalem around 335 and, while he had originally been critical of **St Athanasius**, he later became his ardent supporter and a staunch opponent of the followers of Arius*. Nevertheless, because of his earlier stance, Maximus was always treated with some suspicion during his own lifetime.

St Mel *Feast day: 6 February. Died in 488.* Mel was the nephew and disciple of **St Patrick** who travelled with his uncle to Ireland to help with the evangelization of that country. St Patrick himself built the church at Ardagh and appointed Mel to it. He willingly took up the work, supporting himself by the work of his hands, and giving away as much as he was able to the poor.

Mel lived with his aunt Lupait but gossip spread about their relationship and Patrick came to investigate the situation for himself. Mel was ploughing when Patrick arrived and in order to show himself innocent of the charge, he miraculously pulled out a live fish from the newly broken earth. Lupait established her innocence by carrying glowing coals in her bare hands without burning either herself or her clothing.

Satisfied that all was well, Patrick advised them that for the sake of propriety, they should live and pray apart. He also suggested that his nephew should, in future, do his fishing in the water and his ploughing on the land.

St Mellitus of Canterbury *Feast day: 24 April. Born in Rome; died in 624.* In 601, Mellitus was sent from St Andrew's Monastery in Rome to England by Pope **St Gregory I the Great** and he spent three years there aiding **St Augustine**. Mellitus had brought fresh instructions from Gregory regarding the destruction of the temples of the Saxons, which modified the previous orders given to Augustine. Mellitus was asked to tell Augustine simply to destroy the idols, convert the buildings into churches, and the feasts to Christian purposes and themes. This approach has proved to be of great significance in Christian world mission.

Mellitus became the first Bishop of London in 604, and was responsible for converting Narberth, King of the East Saxons. When the king died in 616, Mellitus was exiled but returned to England in 619 to be named Archbishop of Canterbury, in succession to **St Lawrence**. His faithful prayers helped the city of Canterbury survive a disastrous fire.

St Mennas *Feast day: 10 December. Born in Athens in Greece; died in Alexandria, 312.* Mennas, called 'of the beautiful voice', was sent to Alexandria on an imperial commission by Emperor Galerius. When he had successfully completed his work, he announced that he and his assistant, Eugraphus, were Christians. They were taken before Hermogenes, a judge, where Mennas used his beautiful voice to give a four-hour defence of Christianity. Although this made a great impression, it was ordered that his eyes should be gouged out and his tongue cut off. The next day, however, he was found to have fully recovered, a miraculous event which caused Hermogenes and many others to be converted.

Mennas was martyred with Eugraphus and Hermogenes, all three being beheaded.

St Mercurius of Caesarea *Feast day: 25 November. Born in Caesarea, Cappadocia; died in 250.* Mercurius was the son of a Scythian officer in the Roman army. He also joined the army and led his men to a famous victory during a Barbarian attack on Rome, to the great delight of the Emperor Decius.

However when Mercurius failed to make the usual thanksgiving sacrifice to the gods after the victory, Decius questioned him closely and Mercurius openly professed his faith in Christ. After further questioning under torture Decius sent Mercurius home to Caesarea in Cappadocia, where he was tortured further and finally beheaded.

Mercurius was widely venerated as a warrior saint and active protector of Christians from the sixth century onwards. It is recorded that he appeared to fight alongside St Demetrius at Antioch during the First Crusade.

St Mesrop *Feast day: 19 February. Born in Armenia, 361; died in 441.* Mesrop was a civil servant who retired to live a solitary life. He was ordained priest and set about a serious study of the Greek, Syriac and Persian languages. When he began his mission work amongst his own people he decided, in co-operation with **St Isaac the Great**, to construct an Armenian alphabet. Mesrop was personally responsible for the books of the New Testament.

St Michael the Archangel *Feast day: 29 September.* Patron of grocers, mariners, paratroopers, police and sickness. The name Michael means 'Who is like to God?' and was the war cry of the good angels in the battle fought in heaven against Satan and his followers. St Michael is described in the book of the prophet Daniel (10:13 ff and 12:1) as 'one of the chief princes', and in the book of Revelation as leader of the forces of heaven in their triumph over the powers of the dragon (or devil) Rev 12:7–9.

He has been especially honoured as patron and protector of the Church from the time of the Apostles. He is referred to as 'the Archangel' and the Greek Fathers, among others, regard him as chief of all the angels and Prince of the Seraphim.

St Michael Ghebre *Feast day: 1 September. Born in Ethiopia; died in 1855.* Michael Ghebre was converted by the Vincentians in 1844, and soon after joined the religious order and was ordained priest in 1851. During the persecution of Negus Theodore II he was arrested along with four others because of their Christian faith. He was roughly treated and dragged from place to place, before being imprisoned where he died as a result of further harsh treatment.

St Miguel Cordero de la Salle *Feast day: 9 February. Born in Cuenca in Ecuador, 1854; died in 1910. Canonized 1984 by Pope John Paul II.* Miguel was the son of a political leader and a devout Christian mother. He joined the de la Salle brothers at the age of 14 and proved to be a gifted teacher. When he was only 20 he wrote his first book, a Spanish grammar which received wide acclamation. He translated John Baptist de la Salle's life and writings into Spanish, and later moved to Europe to make further translations from French into Spanish. Miguel was caught up in the general strike and anti-clerical riots of 1909 and along with other brothers was evacuated by gunboat. This experience badly affected his fragile health.

He was meticulous and passionate in his spiritual observance, and was known and respected for his love of God and of the brothers, which was evident to all.

St Mildred *Feast day: 14 July. Died in 700.* Mildred was the daughter of Merewald, an Anglian ruler of the seventh century. Her mother was St Ermenburga, a Kentish princess. Mildred was educated at the convent school in Chelles, near Paris but, following her stay in France, she was pursued by a young man who wanted to marry her. Mildred rejected his advances and sought refuge in a monastery her mother had founded on the Isle of Thanet. **St Theodore of Canterbury** received her into the community, of which she eventually became abbess.

Mildred had a reputation for great holiness, generosity and compassion for the poor. She rejected what could have been a titled life of ease for the discipline of the religious life, and her detachment from this world's riches led her to a firm commitment to Jesus and the poor.

St Miltiades *Feast day: 10 December. Died in 314.* The first pope to govern the Church after the various edicts of toleration, Miltiades was a Roman of African descent, and a priest at the time of his election in 311. Emperor Constantine gave Miltiades a building called the Lateran as a gift to serve as church and centre of the Christian Church. In 313 a council which condemned the Donatists* was convened there. Miltiades died the following year.

St Mirin of Benchor *Feast day: 15 September. Born in Ireland; died in 620.* Mirin, a contemporary of **St Columba**, was a disciple of **St Comgall** at Bangor in County Down, Ireland. He went on to found an abbey at Paisley in Strathclyde, Scotland, where he became abbot, and on his death he was buried there. His shrine became a pilgrimage centre and there is a chapel dedicated to him among the ruins of Inch Murryn, the largest island in Loch Lomond. He is patron of the football club of his native town which is named after him.

St Modwenna *Feast day: 5 July. Born in Ireland; died in 695.* Modwenna was involved in missionary work in her homeland and was known for her great spiritual gift of healing. She travelled to southwest Scotland and founded churches at Prestwick, Dundonald, Stirling and Edinburgh.

St Monica *Feast day: 27 August. Born in Tagaste or Carthage, 331; died at Ostia in Italy, 387.* Patron of wives and abuse victims. Monica was married by arrangement to Patricius, a pagan official in North Africa who was much older than she who, although generous, had a violent temper. His equally difficult mother lived with them, which proved a constant challenge to St Monica. She had three children named Augustine, Navigius and Perpetua. Through her patience and prayers, she was able to draw both her husband and his mother to the Christian faith, and Particius was baptized a year before he died in 371.

Perpetua and Navigius entered the religious life but Augustine proved much more of a challenge to her gentle, prayerful persuasion. Monica had to pray for him for 17 years, begging the prayers of priests who, for a time, tried to avoid her because of her persistence at this seemingly hopeless endeavour. One priest did console her by saying, 'It is not possible that the son of so many tears should perish.' This thought, coupled with a reassuring vision, strengthened her and **St Ambrose** eventually baptized **St Augustine of Hippo** in 387. St Monica died later that same year on the way back to Africa from Rome in the Italian town of Ostia.

St Moses the Ethiopian *Feast day: 28 August. Born in Egypt, 330; died in 405.* Moses was an Abyssinian slave known for his strength and ferocity. He was released because his violent nature made him impossible to control and he became the leader of a gang of thieves. He was known to have been able to swim the width of the Nile with a stolen sheep on his shoulders.

On one occasion, while being chased by folk from whom he had stolen, Moses sought refuge at Sketis where he was converted to Christianity. From that time on he became renowned for his supernatural gifts. Some of his wise sayings are included in the sayings of the Desert Fathers, and Theophilus of Alexandria ordained him to the priesthood. When Bedouins attacked and killed Moses he offered no resistance and was buried at Dair al-Baramus, the Monastery of the Romans, in the Valley of Natron. His relics are now in the Church of Al Adra the Virgin.

N

St Narcissus *Feast day: 29 October. Born in Jerusalem in 97; died in 215.*
Narcissus was almost 80 years old when he was appointed to be the 30th
Bishop of Jerusalem. In 195 Narcissus, along with Theophilus, Bishop of
Caesarea, presided in a council which decided that Easter should always
be celebrated on a Sunday.

He was later falsely accused of a serious crime, which never seems to
have been specified. He was found to be completely innocent but still felt
the need to withdraw for a time. Narcissus spent several years of contentment in a secret retreat.

When Narcissus reappeared the whole Church was overjoyed and
asked him to resume his role as bishop. He agreed, and continued to serve
his flock, and even other churches, with assiduous prayers and earnest
exhortations to unity and obedience. In later years he required the
assistance of **St Alexander**. He was well over 116 years old when he
died.

St Nathalan *Feast day: 19 January. Born in Aberdeenshire in Scotland;
died in 678.* Born to a noble family near Aberdeen, Nathalan became
aware that the cultivation of the soil offered him an ideal opportunity for
contemplation. During a famine he distributed all his grain to the starving
people, including all that he had saved for the next year's sowing. When
spring came he had a divine revelation to sow the land with beach sand
and in the autumn a fine crop was ready for harvest. But a thunderstorm
threatened to destroy the whole crop and Nathalan got angry with God.
The rain suddenly stopped and he felt so guilty about his lack of faith that
he padlocked his right hand to his leg and threw the key into the river
Dee. He vowed never to attempt to unlock it until he had made a pilgrimage of penance to Rome. When he at last arrived in Rome, he met a
half-naked boy in the street carrying a small fish for sale. Nathalan
bought the fish and by divine power he found the key that he had thrown
into the river in its stomach, as good as new, and with it he undid the
padlock.

The pope learned of this miraculous happening and summoned
Nathalan to meet him. He was soon chosen to be a bishop, and was consecrated by the Holy Father. He returned to Tullicht, where he built
churches, conducted missionary activities, and continued to perform
miracles.

St Nectan *Feast day: 17 June. Born in Wales in the sixth century.* Patron
of Hartland, Devonshire.

Nectan was the eldest son of St Brychan and lived as a hermit in the
forests of Devonshire, going on to found churches there and in Cornwall.
Nectan is the patron saint of Hartland in Devonshire, and was much venerated during the Middle Ages. Following the theft of some his livestock
he tracked down and confronted the culprits. They beheaded him.

St Nectarius *Feast day: 11 October. Born in Tarsus, Cilicia; died in 397.* Nectarius was the son of a senator of Constantinople who succeeded **St Gregory Nazianzus** when the latter resigned. His name had been added to the list of possible candidates submitted to the emperor, and Nectarius was selected despite the fact that he was married and had not yet been baptized.

Once installed, he showed himself to be a most able and discerning leader. He fought against Arianism* and forbade public penance, going on to serve as Bishop of Constantinople for 16 years.

St Nektarios of Pentapolis *Feast day: 9 November. Born at Silyvria in Asia Minor, 1846; died in Aegina, 1920. Canonized in the Orthodox Church in 1961.* Nektarios was brought up in a Christian home, and at the age of 14 he went to Constantinople, to work as a shop assistant. He regularly studied the Scriptures and the writings of the Church fathers. In 1866 he was appointed to be a teacher on the island of Chios, and in 1886 he was ordained to the priesthood. His energy and zeal led to his being ordained as the Metropolitan of Pentapolis in Egypt where he was greatly loved and admired, but certain high officials plotted to have him removed from office and in 1890 they succeeded.

He returned to Greece to become a preaching monk and to continue his writing, and in 1894 he became Director of the Rizarios Ecclesiastical School. At the age of 62, Nektarios withdrew to a convent in Aegina where he acted as spiritual guide. He was known as a great wonder worker, and many flocked to him for healing.

St Nerses *Feast day: 20 November. Born in Persia; died in 343.* Nerses was arrested with a group of ten or twelve disciples, one of whom was a eunuch from the royal palace, during the persecution of Christians under King Shapur II of Persia. Dragged before the king, they were offered the choice of worshipping the sun or being executed. When they refused to worship, a priest named Verdan who had rejected the faith put them all to death. Nerses was Bishop of Sahgerd when he died.

St Nerses the Great *Feast day: 19 November. Born in Caesarea, Cappodocia in the fourth century.* Nerses studied in Cappadocia and married a princess who gave birth to a son who was to become known as **St Isaac the Great**. After the death of his wife, Nerses became an official in the court of King Arshak of Armenia. He received holy orders in 353 and was made Bishop of the Armenians in 363.

He was a strong reformer in the Armenian Church, establishing new hospitals and monasteries, and convening a synod in 365 based on the principles he had studied under **St Basil** at Caesarea.

In spite of all his good work, he was exiled as a result of his condemnation of King Arshak's murder of his wife. Following Arshak's death in battle, he returned but would not tolerate the loose living of the new Armenian ruler, Pap, and refused him admission into church. In response

Pap invited Nerses to a royal banquet at Khakh on the Euphrates River and had him poisoned.

St Nicasius of Rheims *Feast day: 14 December. Born in France; died in 451.* Nicasius was the Bishop of Rheims, during a time when Barbarian hoards were launching raids on Gaul. He had a premonition of the fall of the city and urged his flock to be penitent and pray that this might be averted. When the army arrived at the gates of the city, he walked the streets encouraging the people to be patient and faithful and to pray for their enemies. He placed himself outside the church in order to try to protect some of his flock, but was struck down by the invaders and beheaded along with his deacon, St Florentius, and St Jucundus his lector. His sister St Eutropia was spared and, fearing that she would be raped, attacked her brother's murderer, scratching and kicking him until he killed her with his sword.

St Nicephorus *Feast day: 13 March. Born in Constantinople; died in 828.* Nicephorus was the son of the secretary of Emperor Constantine V and was raised as an opponent of the Iconoclasts* (icon breakers) in the imperial capital. He was a respected and valued teacher who was known for his intellect and eloquence, receiving in time the post of imperial commissioner. After founding a monastery near the Black Sea, he was chosen, while still a layman, to succeed **St Tarasius** as Patriarch of Constantinople in 806. **St Theodore of Studites** opposed Nicephorus' decision to forgive a priest who married Emperor Constantine VI to Theodota since Constantine's wife, Mary, was still alive.

When Nicephorus challenged the Iconoclast policies of Emperor Leo V the Armenian, he was removed from office and although he survived several assassination attempts, he was finally exiled to the monastery which he had founded on the Black Sea. He brought in various reforms which inspired the lay people, and wrote works on the history of orthodoxy.

St Nicetas *Feast day: 22 June. Born in Dacia (Romania); died in 414.* Nicetas was the bishop of Remesiana in Dacia (modern Romania and Yugoslavia) and was noted for his successful missionary activities, especially amongst a marauding tribe known as the Bessi.

Nicetas wrote several books on faith, the creed, the Trinity and liturgical singing, and composed the famous praise hymn of the early Church, the 'Te Deum'. **St Jerome** also speaks very appreciatively of his work in converting the people of Dacia, and he was also a close associate of **St Paulinus of Nola**.

St Nicetius *Feast day: 5 December. Born in Auvergne in France; died in 561.* Nicetius was a monk at Limoges, and later became abbot there. Having been ordained in 532, he was named Bishop of Trier thanks to the intervention of King Theodoric I.

Nicetius was a strong and fervent preacher who was unafraid to oppose those in power if he believed that they were in the wrong. On his way to his new diocese, the soldiers accompanying him turned their horses loose into the local peasants' fields; when Nicetius ordered them to be removed the soldiers simply laughed at him. Nicetius threatened them with excommunication and drove the horses out himself.

He preached to his monks on the text that a man can fall in three ways: by thought, by word and by deed. He urged Queen Clodesinde to convert her husband from the errors of Arianism*, endured the oppression of several Frankish kings, and was exiled by King Clotaire after he excommunicated the monarch. The king's son Sigebert reinstated Nicetius as soon as his father had died.

He brought in Italian craftsmen to rebuild the cathedral, and fearlessly faced up to corruption wherever he met it. He also founded a school for clerics.

St Nicholas *Feast day: 6 December. Born in Patara in Lycia (in Modern Turkey); died at Myra in the fourth century.* Patron of Russia, Greece, Apulia, bakers, pawnbrokers, sailors and children.

Nicholas' pious parents died when he was still a young man and, being left in a very comfortable financial position, he took the decision to use his inheritance to help others.

When Nicholas heard that a merchant of Patara had lost all his money, thus depriving his three daughters of any prospect of marriage, he went at night with a bag of gold coins and lobbed it through their window. This provided enough for the eldest girl's dowry and she was duly married. Nicholas repeated this action with the second daughter and, when he attempted to secretly provide for the third in the same way, his generosity was discovered by her father who overwhelmed him with grateful thanks.

Nicholas arrived in the city of Myra just when the clergy and people of the province were in session to elect a new bishop, and God indicated to them all that he was the man. The persecution of Christians was underway in that area and Nicholas, as chief pastor, was seized, tortured and thrown into prison. He was released when Constantine became emperor.

Nicholas was a strong supporter of orthodoxy and when he met the heretic Arius*, he slapped his face. As a result, he was temporarily deprived of his Episcopal position and imprisoned. He was tireless and took strong measures against paganism and had a temple of Artemis destroyed.

At one time he discovered that Governor Eustathius had taken a bribe to condemn to death three innocent men. Nicholas publicly intervened at the execution site, and forced Eustathius to admit his crime and plead for forgiveness. Three imperial officers who were on their way to serve a tour of duty in Phrygiall witnessed this. When they returned to Constantinople, they found themselves condemned to death on false charges and, recalling the incident, they prayed for St Nicholas to intervene. That night, St Nicholas appeared in a dream to Constantine and instructed him to release the three innocent men. In the morning the emperor shared this experience with the prefect Ablavius, only to find that he had had an identical dream. The condemned men were sent for and questioned and, on hearing that they had called on Nicholas of Myra for help, they were released immediately.

When St Nicholas died, he was buried in the city of Myra and a basilica was built in his honour in Constantinople. In Byzantine art, the image of St Nicholas usually has a very large forehead to signify sanctity and wisdom.

St Nicholas I *Feast day: 13 November. Born in Rome, 820; died in 867.* Nicholas was the son of a Roman official, and a deacon in the Church. Following the death of Benedict III in 858, he was elected pope, and proved to be a strong leader unafraid to exercise control. Nicholas held that the emperor possessed temporal power only and should not have any influence over the Church but, because the pope's spiritual authority affected all of life, he was duty bound to comment on matters of state.

Nicholas excommunicated and deposed Archbishop John of Ravenna because of his independent attitude, and also the Patriarch Photios of Constantinople for deposing the previous patriarch Ignatius. In return, Photios excommunicated Nicholas.

St Nicholas Cabasilas *Feast day: 20 June. Born in 1320; died in Constantinople, 1391.* Nicholas was a Byzantine layman who studied under his mother's uncle Archbishop Neilos of Thessalonica, before going on to Constantinople where he studied theology, rhetoric, astronomy and law. Nicholas was an intensely spiritual man with poetic gifts, and endeavoured to practise constant prayer. He also had a deep concern for the practical implications of his beliefs, refusing to stay neutral when civil war broke out. His writings on usury show a genuine concern for social issues.

Nicholas was the author of several books on lay theology in the Eastern Church.

St Nicholas Pieck *Feast day: 9 July. Born in Holland; died at Briel, 1572. Canonized in1867 by Pope Pius IX.* Nicholas served as a guardian of the Franciscan friary at Gorkum near Dordecht, and he devoted himself to converting Calvinists to the Catholic faith. He was taken prisoner along with 18 others by Calvinist forces known as the *Watergeuzen* or Sea-Beggars, who treated their captives with extreme cruelty. Even though many appealed for their release, including William of Orange, the martyrs were hanged from two wooden beams in a secluded turf barn in the disused monastery of Ruggen. They were left there till dawn, when their bodies were cut down and mutilated by their captors.

St Nicholas Studites *Feast day: 4 February. Born in Sydonia, Crete, in the ninth century.* Nicholas studied at the Studius Monastery in Constantinople, and became a monk there at the age of 18. He opposed the Iconoclasts* and assisted his fellow monks who were subjected to persecution by the imperial government. He continued his opposition after his own election as abbot. In 858 Emperor Michael III exiled St Ignatius and installed Photius as Patriarch of Constantinople. Nicholas refused to acknowledge this new appointment and went into voluntary exile. When the new emperor Basil I was appointed, Nicholas considered himself too old to return to his former post but continued as a monk until his death.

St Nicholas of Tolentino *Feast day: 10 September. Born in Saint Angelo, near Tolentino in Italy, 1245; died in 1305. Canonized in 1446 by Pope Eugene IV.* Nicholas' middle-aged parents prayed to have a child at the shrine of St Nicholas of Myra, after whom he is named. He became a monk at 18, was ordained a priest at 25 and gained a reputation for being a gifted preacher and a skilled confessor. Sent to Tolentino in1274 at a time when the town was in the grip of civil strife between the Guelphs, who supported the pope, and the Ghibellines, who sided with the emperor, Nicholas ministered productively and with great compassion to the poor, sick and notorious criminals.

He was widely known as a worker of miracles and is usually represented with a basket of bread, which is known as St Nicholas' bread and represents the bread that he once gave to a woman in labour. Nicholas had said a healing prayer over it, explaining that it would strengthen her for a safe delivery.

St Nicholas von Flue *Feast day: 21 March. Born near Sachseln, in the Canton Obwalden, Switzerland, 1417; died in 1486. Canonized in 1947 by Pope Pius XII.* Patron of Switzerland. Nicholas was the son of a peasant couple who was named after the Flueli River near his birthplace. He married, had ten children, and fought heroically in the forces of the canton against Zurich in 1439.

He served as a magistrate and councillor, but refused to be considered for the post of governor on several occasions. At the age of 50, he gave up all political activity and, with the approval of his wife, became a hermit, living in a tiny mountain cottage at Ranft, near his home. He became known as Brother Klaus and prayed from midnight to noon each day. Many seeking spiritual and practical advice visited him and the belief arose that he neither ate nor drank during this period of his life.

He helped to prevent a potentially disastrous civil war by arranging for Fribourg and Soleure to be included in the Swiss Confederation in 1481.

St Nicodemus of the Holy Mountain *Feast day: 14 July. Born on the Island of Naxos, Greece, 1749; died in 1809.* Nicodemus was born to pious parents, and his mother eventually entered a convent. He was a brilliant and attentive scholar who from an early age was gifted with a photographic memory. He studied at the Evangelical School at Smyrna, learning Greek, Italian and French and was quickly recognized as a diligent and brilliant student.

Nicodemus became greatly impressed by Orthodox monastic spirituality and travelled to the island of Hydra to meet St Macarios of Corinth, who was to become his lifelong friend. Nicodemus became the librarian at the Mount Athos monastery and was joined there by Macarios. They began work on compiling *The Philokalia*, a massive compendium of monastic life and Orthodox spirituality. Nicodemus was a prolific author, writing over a hundred original books and also making translations of a variety of Western spiritual writings. He compiled an extensive and fully annotated hagiography.

His lifestyle was that of a simple ascetic, ever ready to expound the Scriptures, always closing by tilting his head to the left and secretly praying the Jesus prayer. Nicodemus died after suffering a stroke while at the monastery of Skourtaioi.

St Nikon *Feast day: 26 November. Born in Pontus, on the Black Sea, Asia Minor; died in Peloponnesus, 998.* Nikon entered a monastery at Khrysopetro and after 12 years of prayerful ascetic preparation he was sent to preach in Crete. He enjoyed considerable success in reconverting the lapsed and those who had gone over to Islam, before travelling back to his homeland of Armenia and then on to Greece. He was given the title Metanoeite (a term based on the Greek word for repentance) because he began every sermon with the word 'Repent'. He was widely known as a miracle worker.

St Nilus the Elder *Feast day: 12 November. Born in Constantinople; died in 430.* Nilus was a member of the imperial court at Constantinople when he felt a strong call to the monastic life and, with the agreement of his family and the companionship of his son Theodulus, entered the monastery on Mount Sinai.

Arab raiders kidnapped Theodulus, and Nilus set out to find him. They were reunited at Eleusa, south of Beersheba, where the local bishop had ransomed Theodulus. He ordained both father and son, and following this, they returned to Sinai. Nilus became the Bishop of Ancyra and was the author of several ascetical treatises, including one on prayer, and many letters which advised on spiritual matters. He was a friend of **St John Chrysostom**.

St Nilus the Younger *Feast day: 26 September. Born in Calabria in southern Italy, 910; died in 1004.* Nilus' parents were of Greek extraction. He spent his early years in wild undisciplined living, but when he was about 30 years old, all this changed. His mistress and their child both died and Nilus decided to enter the Basilian order of monks in southern Italy. After living as a hermit for a time, he stayed in several communities and finally was elected the Abbot of San Demetrio Corone.

When marauding Saracens threatened southern Italy in 981, Nilus fled with his monks to Monte Cassino and spent 15 years in the monastery of Vallelucio, before founding a new community at Serpero. Later Count

Gregory of Tusculum granted him more land and, under Nilus' disciple **St Bartholomew** this became the Monastery of Grottaferrata.

St Nina *Feast day: 14 January. Born in Cappadocia in the late third century.* Nina was a relative of **St George**, and was freed from slavery before travelling to Iberia (Georgia) with the firm intention of converting the people to Christianity.

Her quiet piety and preaching did indeed have a powerful effect and Queen Nana was converted after Nina had healed her of a seemingly incurable disease. Following this King Mirian also became a Christian, and sent to Constantinople for bishops and priests for his kingdom, while Nina continued to preach throughout Georgia until her death at Bodke.

St Ninian *Feast day: 16 September. Born in south west Scotland in the fifth century.* Ninian was the son of a converted chieftain of the Cumbrian Britons, who went to study in Rome before being ordained and then consecrated as a missionary bishop. Ninian returned to evangelize his native land, via Tours in France. He took with him a team of stonemasons from St Martin's Monastery to help with the building of a stone church at Whithorn in Scotland, known as *Candida Casa* (the white house), which served as their missionary centre. Ninian and his monks evangelized neighbouring Britons and the Picts of Valentia, establishing churches wherever they went.

Ninian was known for his miracles, which often had evangelical significance. On one occasion he cured a chieftain of his blindness, and this single event led to the conversion of many people.

St Noel Chabanel *Feast day: 26 December. Born in Saugues, France, 1913; died in 1641. Canonized in 1930 by Pope Pius XI.* Noel Chabanel was a Jesuit missionary in Canada in the seventeenth century.

Being unable to learn the local language, and finding both the culture and food of the Native Americans distasteful, Chabanel found his missionary calling a real challenge.

He suffered from a spiritual dryness during the whole of his stay in Canada, but in spite of this he made a solemn vow to stay, whatever might happen to him in this mission.

Noel Chabanel was not present when his missionary companion Charles Garnier was killed by a hatchet blow to the head by Iroquois warriors, but one day later he too was killed by a rebellious member of a Christian family who blamed Chabanel for misfortunes that had befallen him.

Chabanel and his colleagues saw little positive results from their work but within a few years of their martyrdom, nearly every tribe in the region had accepted the Christian faith.

The martyrs of North America were Sts John de Brebeuf, **Isaac Jogues**, Antony Daniel, Gabrial Lalemant, **Charles Garnier**, Noel Chabanel, **Rene Goupil** and John Lalande.

St Non *Feast day: 3 March. Born in Dyfed, Wales in the fifth century.* Non was of noble descent, and the mother of **St David of Wales**. Two versions of her life exist: in the first she is described as a nun who was seduced by a local chieftain named Sant; and in the other she became a nun after her husband's death. Both stories agree that the couple were the parents of St David, and that Non travelled to Cornwall and from there went on to Brittany where she died.

St Norbert *Feast day: 6 June. Born in Xanten in the Rhineland, 1080; died in 1134. Canonized in 1582 by Pope Gregory XIII.* Norbert lived the life of a worldly and pleasure-seeking youth. To ensure his success at court and in order to obtain financial benefit he accepted holy orders and an appointment as a canon, although he refused to accept ordination as a priest.

While out riding in a thunderstorm one day a sudden flash of lightning caused Norbert's horse to bolt, throwing him to the ground. For almost an hour he lay unconscious in the storm, and when he awoke his first words were the same that Saul spoke on the road to Damascus: 'Lord, what do you want me to do?' Norbert sensed in his heart that the answer was: 'Turn from evil and do good. Seek peace and pursue it.'

He immediately returned to his birthplace, Xanten, and devoted himself to prayer and penance. He then began his studies for the priesthood and was ordained in 1115. Norbert gave away everything he owned to the poor and went to visit the pope to ask for permission to preach. This was granted and he became an itinerant preacher, travelling throughout Europe with two companions. In a reaction against his former lifestyle, he chose to walk barefoot in the middle of winter through snow and ice, and though his health was unaffected by this extreme behaviour, his two companions died from exposure at Valenciennes.

Norbert began his community with 13 others in a lonely valley known as Prémontré in the forest of Coucy. He attracted so many disciples that eight abbeys and two convents were needed to house them. Even the canons who originally rejected him asked to be part of the reform. In Norbert's community, lay affiliation with a religious order was permitted.

Norbert was chosen by Emperor Lothair as Bishop of Magdebourg but the porter refused to let him into his new residence, thinking he was a beggar.

Norbert's reforming work in his new diocese made him many enemies who were so fervent that they even tried to assassinate him. Distressed by the continuing lax and rebellious behaviour of many of his clergy, Norbert left the city but was soon called back by the citizens who feared retribution from the emperor.

When two rival popes were elected after the death of Honorius II, Norbert tried to bring about reconciliation by encouraging the emperor to support Innocent II, who had been elected first. At the end of his life he was made an archbishop but died soon after his consecration.

St Notburga *Feast day: 14 September. Born in Rattenberg in the Tyrol; died in 1313.* Notburga was the daughter of peasants, and became a servant in the household of Count Henry of Rattenberg but was dismissed by Count Henry's wife Ottilia for giving food away to the poor. She became a servant to a farmer at Eben.

One Saturday evening during harvest time the bell for Vespers sounded, indicating that Sunday had begun. Notburga made to lay down her sickle when the farmer ordered her to continue. Notburga refused and when he persisted she said, 'Let this settle it.' Taking up the sickle she threw it into the air and there it remained suspended, looking like the first quarter of the harvest moon against the evening sky.

Count Henry suffered a series of unfortunate occurrences and as soon as his wife died, he reinstated Notburga. She remained his housekeeper for the rest of her life, and was widely known for her miracles and care for the poor.

St Numidicus *Feast day: 9 August. Born in Africa, in the third century.* Numidicus was one of a group of Christians who were burned at the stake in Carthage during the persecution of the Church under Emperor Trajanus Decius. After being dragged from the ashes at the site of his execution, he was found to be alive. He made a full recovery and was later ordained by **St Cyprian of Carthage**.

O

St Odilo *Feast day: 1 January. Born in France, 962; died in 1049.* Odilo was born into the aristocracy. He felt called to the monastic life at an early age and by 994 was named abbot of Cluny Abbey in central France. He practised great personal austerities, and cared deeply for those in need, even selling Church treasures to feed the poor during a famine in 1006. Odilo greatly increased the number of subsidiary institutions dependent on Cluny and exercised great influence over rulers and leaders, many of whom sought him out for spiritual advice.

Massacres and pillage were common in those days, owing to the right claimed by every lord to avenge his own injuries by private wars, but under the terms of an agreement known as 'The Truce of God' Odilo succeeded in having fighting limited during Lent and established the rule which guaranteed sanctuary to those who sought refuge in a church building. He inaugurated the annual commemoration of the departed faithful, known as All Souls' Day.

The last five years of his life were clouded by illness but he still continued to travel, and he died while on a visitation to his monasteries, at a priory in Souvigny. He had been a monk at Cluny for 54 years.

St Odo *Feast day: 18 November. Born in Le Mans, France; died in Tours, France, 945.* Odo, who was raised in the households of Count Fulk II of Anjou and Duke William of Aquitaine, entered holy orders at 19, and received a canonry at St Martin's in Tours. He then studied music in Paris for several years.

Odo became a monk at Baume-les-Messieurs near Besançon in 909, and was named director of the Baume Monastery school. In 924 he was chosen as Abbot of Baume, and following St Berno's death in 927, he became the second Abbot of Cluny.

In 931 Pope John XI authorized him to help to reform the monasteries of northern France and Italy. In 936 Odo helped to arrange a temporary peace between Alberic of Rome and Hugh of Provence after the latter had laid siege to the city, by brokering a marriage between Hugh's daughter and Alberic. Odo returned twice in the next six years in order to maintain good relations.

Under Odo's direction the reforming influence of Cluny Abbey spread to monasteries all over Europe. He persuaded secular rulers to relinquish their illegal control of monasteries, sometimes experiencing severe opposition in the process. He wrote extensively and widely; hymns, treatises on morality, an epic poem on redemption, and a life of **St Gerald of Aurillac** were amongst his most popular works.

St Olaf of Norway *Feast day: 29 July. Born in Norway, 995; died in 1030. Canonized in 1164 by Pope Alexander III.* Patron of Norway. Olaf was the son of King Harald Grenske of Norway, and as a youth took part in many Norse raids and acts of piracy. He was baptized at Rouen by

Archbishop Robert at the age of 15, and thereafter sought to bring those who were conquered into the Christian Church. He went to stay in England in 1013 and fought for King Ethelred against Danish intruders during his time there. He became King of Norway in 1016 and sought to free his country from the domination of the Danes and the Swedes.

Olaf asked English missionaries to come to Norway, but he had no hesitation in using force and bribery to achieve his ends in his over-enthusiasm for the conversion of his subjects. In 1029 the Norwegian nobles rebelled, aided by King Canute of Denmark, overthrew him and sent him into exile in Russia.

In 1030 Olaf attempted to regain his throne with the help of a small army of Swedish troops but was killed in the ensuing battle at Stiklestad, Norway.

After Olaf's death healing miracles were reported at his tomb, and he became greatly respected as a champion of Norwegian independence. His burial place became the foundation of the cathedral of Trondheim, and was a popular place of pilgrimage during the Middle Ages.

St Olaf of Sweden *Feast day: 30 July. Born in Sweden, king from 993; died in 1024.* Olaf was the son of Eric the Conqueror who was converted to Christianity by St Sigfrid. He became king of Sweden in 993, and defeated King Olaf I Tryggvason of Norway at Svolder in 1000 with the aid of King Sweyn of Denmark and Eric, Jarl of Lade. His attempts to introduce Christianity to Sweden met with strong opposition and after he refused to sacrifice to pagan idols, he was martyred at Stockholm by rebel forces.

St Olga *Feast day: 11 July. Born in Russia, in 879; died in 969.* Olga married Prince Igor of Kiev in Russia in 903. She was a cruel and bar-barous woman and when Prince Igor was murdered in 945 she had those responsible scalded to death. She also pursued and murdered hundreds of their followers.

Olga changed completely after her baptism at Constantinople in 957 and requested Emperor Otto I to send missionaries to Kiev. This resulted in a mission that was led by St Adalbert of Magdeburg, but even though the queen made every effort to support him, his mission ended in abject failure. Olga also longed to convert her son Svyatoslav, but failed in this also, since he is recorded as saying, 'My men would laugh at me if I took up this strange religion.' It was to be her grandson **St Vladimir** who was finally successful in introducing Christianity to Russia.

Olga is a popular saint of the Eastern Orthodox Church and recognized as the first baptized female saint.

St Oliver Plunkett *Feast day: 11 July. Born in Loughcrew in County Meath, Ireland, 1625; died at Tyburn, England in 1681. Canonized in 1975 by Pope Paul VI.* In 1647 Oliver went to study for the priesthood in the Irish College in Rome, and was ordained a priest 1654. He taught in Rome until 1669 when he was appointed Archbishop of Armagh and

Primate of Ireland. Oliver was a man of great religious fervour and peaceful disposition whose faithful visiting resulted in him confirming thousands and establishing several schools.

In 1673 bishops were banned by edict and Oliver, determined not to abandon his people, went into hiding. He suffered a great deal from cold, hunger and other privations. Though the persecution eased a little after a time and Oliver was able to move more openly among his people, he was finally arrested in 1679 and falsely charged with treason. At his trial in Dundalk he was found not guilty but he was put on trial again in London where, with the help of perjured witnesses, he was sentenced to be hanged, drawn and quartered at Tyburn. Oliver calmly refuted the charges, and refused offers of clemency in return for giving false evidence against his brother bishops. Before his execution he publicly forgave all those who were responsible for his death.

St Olympias *Feast day: 17 December. Born in Constantinople, 361; died in 408.* Olympias was born into a wealthy family, but was orphaned as a child and was given into the care of the prefect Procopius. She married the prefect Nebridius but was soon widowed and refused all further offers of marriage. Emperor Theodosius had her fortune put in trust until she was 30 when she also refused his choice of a husband for her. He restored her estate in 391 and she was consecrated deaconess and founded a community of women.

St John Chrysostom was a good friend, and remonstrated with her when he became Patriarch of Constantinople in 398 for her over-lavish almsgiving, after which he took her under his direction.

A firm supporter of Chrysostom when he was expelled in 404, Olympias firmly rejected the claims of the usurper Arsacius as Patriarch of Constantinople. The prefect, Optatus, fined her for this and Atticus, Arsacius' successor, disbanded her community and ended her charitable works. Her final years were beset by illness and persecution but she was greatly comforted by the exiled Chrysostom, and died in exile in Nicomedia a year after his death.

St Omer *Feast day: 9 September. Born in Constance in France, 595; died in 670.* When his parents died, Omer entered the monastery of Luxeuil under **St Eustace**. He was named Bishop of Therouanne in 637, and set about reforming the diocese, especially in the area of pastoral care for the poor.

The monks from Luxeuil helped him in this and founded the monastery of Sithiu, which became one of the most significant religious centres of its time. The town of Saint-Omer developed around this monastery.

St Osmund *Feast day: 4 December. Born in Normandy, France; died in 1099. Canonized in 1457 by Pope Callistus III.* Osmund was a member of the Norman nobility, the son of Count Henry of Seez and Isabella, who was the half-sister of King William the Conqueror of England. He took part in the Norman Conquest and served as chancellor to King William.

In 1078 he was appointed Bishop of Salisbury and completed the building of the cathedral there, and also founded a school for clerics.

Osmund also assisted in assembling the massive census of the nation known as the Domesday Book. He initially sided with King William II against **St Anselm** of Canterbury in the dispute between the two, but later admitted that he had made a mistake, expressed his contrition, and sought forgiveness.

Osmund loved collecting manuscripts, and was a skilled bookbinder and copyist. He wrote a life of **St Aldhelm** who had been Bishop of Sherborne 300 years earlier, and who was responsible for drawing up the books on liturgical matters known as *Sarum Use*. This was an English version of the Roman rite used in medieval times.

Osmund was buried in his own cathedral at Old Sarum, and 27 years later his body was transferred to the newly completed Salisbury Cathedral.

St Oswald *Feast day: 4 August. Born in Denmark; died in 992.* Oswald studied under his uncle, Archbishop Odo of Fleury in France, and was ordained there. He returned to England in 959 and was consecrated Bishop of Worcester by **St Dunstan** three years later. In 972 he became Archbishop of York while still continuing as Bishop of Worcester. This dual role, which was partly due to Oswald's close co-operation with king Edgar, enabled him to promote monastic communities in both the north and south of England, the largest of which was founded by Aethelwine outside his diocese at Ramsey. Even so, despite all his best efforts, it was not until long after Oswald's death that the monastic movement was firmly established again north of the Humber.

He tried to improve the morals and spiritual life of his clergy and their theological knowledge. Oswald remained bishop of both dioceses until his death and his passion for the monastic life never diminished.

St Otto of Bamberg *Feast day: 2 July. Born in Swabia, in 1062; died in 1139. Canonized in 1189 by Pope Clement III.* Otto was a member of the nobility and he served for a time as chancellor to Emperor Henry IV. He was appointed Bishop of Bamberg in 1103 by edict of the emperor but he refused to be consecrated until approval from Pope Paschal II had been received. This arrived in 1106, thus aiding the process of reconciliation between the pope and Emperor Henry V.

King Boleslav III of Poland asked Otto to lead a mission to Pomerania that proved so successful that Otto is widely referred to as the Apostle of Pomerania.

St Ouen *Feast day: 24 August. Born in Sancy near Soissons, France, 600; died at Clichy near Paris, in 684.* Ouen was the son of St Authaire and educated at St Medard's Abbey. He served at the courts of King Clovis II and King Dagobert I. The latter made him his chancellor and though Ouen had been persuaded not to enter religious orders himself, he continued to be extremely active in combating simony and promoting the Christian faith.

In 636 Ouen built a monastery at Rebais. He was eventually ordained and was consecrated Archbishop of Rouen in 641. Ouen was famous for his personal austerities, gracious charity and his support for missionary activities, especially the founding of new monasteries for the promotion of study and learning. He was instrumental in negotiating a peace settlement between Neustria and Austrasia in Cologne.

P

St Pabo *Feast day: 9 November. Born in Scotland; died in 510.* Pabo was the son of a Scottish or Pictish chieftain and was known for his war-like demeanour. He became a disciple of Christ and gave up his life of fighting to become a warrior in the spiritual realm. He founded a monastery on the island of Anglesey.

St Pachomius *Feast day: 9 May. Born in Upper Thebaid in Egypt, 292; died in 346.* Pachomius entered the emperor's army at the age of 20. After his discharge he recalled the great kindness of the Christians at Thebes towards the soldiers, and further exploration of the Christian faith led to his conversion. After being baptized, he became a disciple of an anchorite, **St Palemon**.

Later, Pachomius felt called to build a monastery on the banks of the Nile at Tabennisi, and in 318, with Palemon's help, he built a cell there. In a short time some 100 others had joined him in the monastic life. Pachomius organized them on principles of community living, dividing the monks into different houses according to the crafts which they practised; these included market gardening, baking and tailoring. By drawing on his experience of the army Pachomius organized the monks into groups and wrote a rule of life for them. He would transfer the monks from one house to another depending on where the need was most acute, much as a good general would do.

Other monasteries for men and two nunneries for women soon followed and by the time Pachomius died in 346, the Order was several thousand monks strong. Pachomius' rule was simple and austere, though not as extreme as some of his contemporaries'. He emphasized the importance of meditation on the Scriptures and memorization of the Psalms. Both **St Basil** and **St Benedict** drew from his rule when writing their own versions.

While **St Antony** is the founder of Christian monasticism, it was St Pachomius who instituted the form of organized monastic community that was to become widely accepted in the Western Church.

St Palemon *Feast day: 11 January. Born in Egypt; died in 325.* Palemon was an anchorite who lived deep in the desert. **St Pachomius** was his disciple for some time and helped him to set up the first organized monastery in the Egyptian desert. These desert communities formed the basis for the later development of monasticism. Palemon died at Tabennisi, which had grown to be a large and thriving monastic centre.

St Palladius *Feast day: 7 July. Born in Britain; died in 432.* Palladius was of British descent and a deacon in Auxerre, France. He convinced Pope Celestine I to send **St Germanus**, Bishop of Auxerre, to England with the aim of combating the growing influence of the Pelagian* heresy.

Palladius was consecrated by the pope as the first Bishop of Ireland and he was sent there to preach and deal with the same heresy in that country. He was the immediate predecessor to **St Patrick**, and founded at least three churches in Leinster, but was not generally well received by the local population. He left and sailed for Scotland and began to preach among the Picts, but a short time after arriving he was taken ill and died at Fordun in Aberdeenshire.

St Pancras *Feast day: 12 May. Born in Rome, 290; died in 304.* When he was still a young child, Pancras' parents died and he was brought to Rome by a kindly uncle. Both he and his uncle became Christians, and were arrested during Diocletian's persecution in 304. Even though Pancras was only 14 years old he was beheaded along with his uncle. He is especially remembered in England because **St Augustine**, the Archbishop of Canterbury, dedicated his first church to him. His relics were presented as a gift to the King of Northumberland.

St Pantaenus *Feast day: 7 July. Born in Sicily in the late second century.* Pantaenus was a stoic philosopher who became head of the catechetical school at Alexandria in Egypt. He built this up to become a leading centre of learning. St Clement had been searching for a teacher who could reveal to him the profound mysteries of life, and eventually found him in St Pantaenus. Clement succeeded him as head of this centre of study.

Pantaenus had been a missionary in Ethiopia. He had met Christians in that land who claimed to have received **St Matthew**'s Gospel in Hebrew from **St Bartholomew**.

St Pantaleon *Feast day: 27 July. Born in Nicomedia near the Black Sea; died in 305.* Pantaleon had a pagan father and a Christian mother. He was trained in medicine and became physician to the emperor. Under the influence of the corrupt pagan court Pantaleon abandoned the Christian faith entirely, but with the help of a priest named Hermolaos repented of his apostasy and rejoined the Church. In grateful thanks for what Pantaleon saw as the free grace of forgiveness, he began to take care of the poor and sick without charge.

When the Emperor Diocletian began his persecution, Pantaleon was soon arrested for being a Christian, and given the choice of worshipping the gods or being put to death. Pantaleon refused to deny his faith and survived six different attempts to kill him: by burning; liquid lead; drowning; wild beasts; the wheel; and the sword. All of these failed, and he was eventually killed by being beheaded.

In the East Church he is known as a 'Great Martyr and a Wonder Worker'.

St Panteleimon the All-Merciful *Feast day: 27 July. Born in Nicomedia in 284; died in 304.* Panteleimon was born to a pagan father and a devout Christian mother who brought him up in the faith. He was handsome and humble and radiated deep happiness and peace. Panteleimon had an interest in healing from his earliest days and, immediately after being baptized by the bishop, he cured a man of his blindness. Panteleimon gave away all his wealth to the needy, and cured all who came to him.

Other physicians became very envious and told Emperor Maximian that Panteleimon was healing Christians and converting idolaters, and Panteleimon was ordered to appear before the emperor. He was charged with malpractice and ordered to sacrifice to the gods, but he refused.

Maximian ordered him to be tortured, but even though his skin was cut with iron claws and burned with torches, and he was tied to a boulder and thrown into the sea, he would not change his mind. He was kept safe, even when placed in the stadium with the wild beasts, tied to a wheel and then rolled down a hill. When finally an attempt was made to finish him off, the executioner's sword melted.

Many were converted through this time of miraculous deliverance from tortures. Eventually Panteleimon instructed the soldiers to behead him so that he could receive the crown of martyrdom. After kissing the holy man and seeking his forgiveness, the soldiers reluctantly carried out his instructions and beheaded him.

St Paschal Baylon *Feast day: 17 May. Born in Aragon in Spain, 1540; died Villareal, Spain, 1592; Canonized in 1690 by Pope Alexander VIII.* Patron of shepherds, Paschal was the son of a peasant farmer who worked as a shepherd until the age of 24. He then joined the Franciscans and served as a doorkeeper at various friaries where he spent long hours kneeling with his clasped hands outstretched.

Paschal was sent as a messenger to France and travelled wearing his habit. He was attacked several times, and once narrowly escaped with his life after being stoned. He died on Whitsunday in church in 1592.

St Paschasius *Feast day: 26 April. Born at Soissons in France, 790; died at Corbie in France, 860.* Paschasius was found as a baby by nuns on the steps of Notre Dame of Soissons, and subsequently raised by monks. He was a wild youth but became a Benedictine monk and helped found the monastery at Corbie, France in 822.

He travelled Europe as a noted speaker and negotiator. He was unwillingly elected Abbot of Corbie in 844, but resigned in 851 following a dispute. Paschasius became a hermit in the monastery at St Riquiet at Cenula and spent the rest of his life writing on history, philosophy and theology.

St Paternus *Feast day: 15 April. Born in Poiters, France in 481; died in 564.* Paternus entered the monastery of Ansion at Poitou and then became a hermit, with St Scubilio at Scissy, near Granville, Normandy.

He attracted many others who desired to follow the same way of life and Paternus organized them into a community. They built the monastery of St Pair, and Paternus served as abbot for many years. Later, at about the age of 70, he was named Bishop of Avranches, Normandy. He died aged 83 on the same day as St Scubilio.

St Patiens *Feast day: 11 September. Born in France; died in 491.* In 450 Patiens was appointed to the See of Lyon and served for many years as an able and charitable archbishop. He devoted the resources of the diocese to those left destitute by the Gothic and Germanic invasions and to the reconstruction of churches that had been burned and looted.

Though a dedicated enemy of Arianism*, he worked hard to reconcile those who had been caught up in that particularly popular heresy. He was instrumental in having the life of **St Germanus of Auxerre** popularized by instructing Constantius, a priest of the diocese, to write an account of his life.

St Patrick *Feast day: 17 March. Born in Kilpatrick, near Dumbarton in Scotland, 387; died in 461.* Patron of Ireland. Patrick's parents were Roman officials living in Britain. As a boy of 14 he was captured during a raiding party and taken to Ireland as a slave, where he was put to work looking after sheep. He learned the language of the Druid and pagan people who held him captive, and became familiar with their customs. During his captivity he had a dream that caused him to begin to pray to God, and when he was 20 he managed to escape back to Britain to be reunited with his family.

In a further dream he experienced a call to return to Ireland. He studied for the priesthood and was ordained by **St Germanus**, the Bishop of Auxerre. Later, aged 46, Patrick was ordained a bishop and was sent to take the Gospel to Ireland. One story tells of a chieftain who wanted to kill Patrick but found it impossible to move his arm until he repented of this wicked thought. He was one of many throughout Ireland who were converted by Patrick's preaching and example of holy living.

Patrick and his disciples began building churches all over the country. He had phenomenal success, and kings, their households and even entire kingdoms converted to Christianity. Sts **Ailbhe, Asicus, Benignus, Ibar** and **Macanisius** were among his disciples.

He lived for 40 years in simplicity and with great austerity, preaching and working many miracles all over Ireland. He even found time to write his 'Confessions'.

Patrick was an inspirational preacher who had studied his culture well and made use of this knowledge as a teaching aid for the Christian faith. One example of this was his use of the shamrock as a visual aid for the Trinity. He died at Saul, where he had built the first church.

St Paul *Feast day: 29 June. Born in Tarsus; died in Rome, 67.* Paul was of Jewish origin and was brought up in Tarsus where he was educated as a Pharisee by Gamaliel. He was one of the first persecutors of Christians, actively seeking to have them arrested and imprisoned, and he approved of the death of the first Christian martyr, **St Stephen**.

Following his remarkable conversion on the road to Damascus, he was baptized and spent three years in retreat in Arabia.

On his return to Damascus, he enraged the Jews by teaching that Jesus was the Messiah in the synagogues, and had to flee for his life. Paul journeyed to Jerusalem to meet with the Church leaders there, and with encouragement from **St Barnabas** they decided to accept him as a genuine convert.

He returned to Tarsus and continued to evangelize until Barnabas invited him to do the same in Antioch. A famine occurred soon after, and Barnabas and Paul were sent to Jerusalem with alms for the Christian community there. Not long after this Paul, with Barnabus as his companion, made a missionary journey, visiting the island of Cyprus and Asia Minor, and establishing several churches.

A second missionary journey followed soon after and **Sts Silas**, **Timothy** and **Luke** all accompanied Paul for some of the time. They revisited the churches that had been established, and then passed through Galatia. Having had a vision to evangelize in Macedonia, Paul sailed for Europe and lived and preached in Philippi, Thessalonica, Beroea, Athens and Corinth before returning to Antioch by way of Ephesus and Jerusalem.

Paul visited almost the same regions on his third missionary journey, making Ephesus the centre of his missionary activity. He was then imprisoned on false charges for two years at Caesarea before being sent to Rome. He was kept for two years in chains, before being released. St Paul then travelled to Spain, before returning to Rome, where he was imprisoned and later beheaded.

St Paula *Feast day: 26 January. Born in Rome, 347; died at Bethlehem, 404.* Patron of widows. Paula was a member of the elite in Rome; she married Toxotius and had five children. When she was 32 her husband died and she renounced the world, choosing to live in great simplicity and devoting herself to helping the poor. Three years later in 382 she met **St Jerome**, who had come to Rome with St Paulinus of Antioch. Jerome gave readings from the Holy Scripture for a group of dedicated Christian women in the city among whom Paula held a position of honour, and Paula and her daughter, Eustochium, studied hard under his guidance with the aim of growing in Christian perfection.

A year after the death of Pope Damasus in 385, Paula and Eustochium left Rome for a pilgrimage to the Holy Land, via Egypt, finally ending up in Bethlehem where Jerome had made his new home.

The three began to develop monastic foundations. Two monasteries were founded, one for men, the other for women. Paula and Eustochium placed themselves under the spiritual direction of Jerome and helped him with his translation work.

Paula's generosity left her in dire need and she had many practical worries right up to the end of her life.

St Paul of Constantinople *Feast day: 7 June. Born in Constantinople; died in 350.* Paul was elected Bishop of Constantinople in 336. He was a close friend of **St Athanasius** because of his strong opposition to Arianism*, and exiled to Pontus by Emperor Constantius II in 337. Macedonius, a supporter of Arius, replaced him. In 338 Paul tried to come back but was again exiled by the Arians, who had the support of the imperial government. In 340 he returned once more only to be seized and, at the order of Emperor Constantius, exiled to Mesopotamia. Brought back in 344, he was sent yet again into exile, this time to Cucusus in Armenia where he was deliberately starved and finally strangled to death by Arian supporters.

St Paul the Hermit *Feast day: 15 January. Born in Egypt, 229; died in 342.* Paul, a Christian from an early age, was orphaned at the age of 15. Following a long period of intense persecution, he went into the desert to escape the interference of the authorities and became a hermit, living in a cave for the rest of his exceptionally long life.

St Antony used to visit the aged hermit at regular intervals, and when Paul died, Antony wrapped his body in a cloak that had been given to him by **St Athanasius** and buried him near his desert retreat. Icons of Paul and Antony frequently show two lions, which were believed to have assisted in the digging of the grave.

St Paulinus of Aquileia *Feast day: 28 January. Born in Friuli, Italy, 726; died in 802.* Paulinus was from a farming family and had been given an excellent education. He became so well known for his scholarship and eloquent speech that Charlemagne asked him to become one of his court officials.

When he was sent back to Italy in 776 he was appointed Patriarch of Aquileia.

Paul represented Charlemagne at various Church Councils and wrote against the heresy of Adoptionism*. He preached widely, was a talented poet, and wrote a treatise on Christian perfection for the Duke of Friuli.

St Paulinus of Nola *Feast day: 22 June. Born in Bordeaux, in Gaul, 354; died in 431.* Paulinus, whose father was the praetorian prefect of Gaul, studied rhetoric and poetry under the famed poet Ausonius. He became a well-known lawyer, going on to become Prefect of Rome. He married a Spanish noble lady, Therasia, and they led a pampered existence until the death of their week old son in 390.

Paulinus withdrew from the world and came to be baptized a Christian by St Delphinus in Aquitaine. Together with Therasia, they gave away all their property and vast fortune to the poor and the Church, and pursued a life of deep austerity and simplicity.

He was forcibly ordained a priest in 393 by the Bishop of Barcelona, and soon after he moved to an estate near the tomb of St Nola near Naples in Italy, where he and his wife helped to establish a community of monks. Paulinus also supported the building of a church at Fondi, a basilica near the tomb of **St Felix**, a hospital for travellers, and an aqueduct.

He brought many of the poor and sick into his own home and cared for them there.

In 409 he was elected Bishop of Nola, serving in this office with great distinction until his death. Paulinus was one of the foremost poets of his age and a great letter writer who befriended many of the leading figures of his era, including **Sts Augustine, Jerome, Ambrose, Martin of Tours**, and Pope Anastasius I. He died in church at the time of Vespers.

St Paulinus of York *Feast day: 10 October. Born in Italy, 584; died in 644.* Paulinus was a Roman monk sent by **St Gregory the Great** to England. In 625, When **St Ethelburga**, the Christian sister of the king of Kent, travelled north to marry Edwin, the pagan king of Northumbria, Paulinus went with her as chaplain.

Edwin had promised religious freedom to his new wife and had shown genuine willingness to learn more about the faith she espoused.

Within two years of their arrival, the pagan high priest Coifi had been converted to Christianity along with many nobles and King Edwin and his baby daughter had been baptized in a wooden church at York. Paulinus was appointed Bishop of York and in the five years that followed thousands of Northumbrians were converted.

When pagan Mercians killed Edwin at the Battle of Hatfield in 633, Paulinus returned to Kent accompanied by Edwin's widow Ethelburga and her two children. Paulinus became Bishop of Rochester, a post he held until he died.

St Paul Miki *Feast day: 6 February. Born in Tounucumada, Japan; died in 1590. Canonized as a Martyr of Japan in 1862 by Pope Pius IX.* Paul was born at Tounucumada, Japan, the son of a Japanese military leader. He was educated at the Jesuit college of Anziquiama and joined the Jesuits in 1580, becoming known for his eloquent preaching. He was crucified with 25 others during the persecution of Christians under Toyotomi Hideyoshi, ruler of Japan.

Among the Japanese laymen who suffered the same fate were: Francis, a carpenter who was arrested while watching the executions and then crucified; Gabriel, the 19-year-old son of the Franciscan's porter; and Leo Kinuya, a 28-year-old carpenter from Miyako.

St Paul Tong Buong *Feast day: 23 October. Born in Vietnam; died in 1833. Canonized in 1988 by Pope John Paul II.* Paul was one of the king's bodyguards who, following his conversion, began to support Christian missionary work in his homeland. He was arrested by Vietnamese authorities for being a Christian, tortured, humiliated and beheaded.

St Pelagia *Feast day: 8 October. Born in Antioch, date unknown.* Pelagia was an actress in Antioch known for her beauty, her wealth and her outrageous lifestyle. During a synod at Antioch, Pelagia rode by the church where the clergy had gathered just when Bishop St Nonnus of Edessa had begun to speak. Struck by her beauty, he pointed out to the assembly how pleasing her appearance was and with what care she had taken to make herself attractive to men. Nonnus then contrasted this with the laxity shown by Christians in the care of their immortal souls.

The following day Pelagia, having heard that the bishop had spoken about her, went to church to hear him preach. She was so moved by what she heard that she immediately asked to be baptized and gave all her belongings to Nonnus to aid the poor and left Antioch, dressed in men's clothing.

Pelagia eventually made her home in a cave on the Mount of Olivette in Jerusalem, where she lived in great austerity. She was known locally as the 'the beardless monk'. The fact that she was a woman was only discovered after her death.

St Pelagia of Antioch *Feast day: 8 June. Born in Antioch, 297; died in 311.* Pelagia, a disciple of St Lucian of Antioch, was 15 when Roman soldiers came to her house to arrest her for being a Christian. She asked for time to go upstairs and change her clothes, but instead, rather than lose her virginity to the soldiers, she went up onto the roof and hurled herself into the river. She was killed by the fall.

She was greatly admired by **St John Chrysostom**, who referred to the story of her martyrdom in one of his sermons.

St Peregrine Laziosi *Feast day: 3 May. Born in Forli in Italy, 1260; died in 1345. Canonized in 1726 by Pope Benedict XIII.* Patron of cancer patients.

Peregrine was born into a wealthy family. As a youth he was active in politics and a member of the anti-papal party. The Pope sent **St Philip Benizi** to mediate during one uprising and Peregrine struck him in the face. When Philip offered the other cheek, Peregrine was so overcome that he repented and was converted on the spot.

He joined the Servites at Siena and adopted a rule of personal austerity, which involved regular periods of silence and solitude. Not allowing himself to sit down for 30 years was but one of the severe disciplines he imposed upon himself.

Peregrine had a reputation for being a fervent preacher and a wise confessor and was later sent to Forli to found a new house of the Servite Order. When he developed cancer of the foot, amputation was decided upon, but Peregrine spent the night before the operation in prayer and the following morning the foot was totally healed.

His great energy brought many back to the church, and his reputation as a miracle worker was widespread even during his own lifetime.

Sts Perpetua and Felicity *Feast day: 7 March. Born in Carthage in north Africa, 181; died in 203.* Perpetua was a well-educated, high-spirited woman who was still nursing her baby son when, in the year 203, she became a Christian in the full knowledge of the danger involved.

The persecution under the Emperor Septimus forbade fresh conversions and Perpetua was arrested with four other catechumens including two slaves, Felicity and Revocatus. They were baptized before being taken to prison.

Two deacons who ministered to the prisoners paid the guards so that the two women would be put in a better part of the prison and Perpetua's mother and brother brought her baby to her there. When she was granted special permission for her baby to stay with her, she said, 'My prison suddenly became a palace for me.'

Her father begging her to give in, kissing her hands, and throwing himself at her feet; he also pleaded with the judge, who tried very hard to get Perpetua to change her mind, but she stood fast. She was sentenced, along with the others, to be thrown to the wild beasts in the arena.

Two days before the execution, the slave Felicity went into labour and gave birth to a healthy girl who was adopted and raised by one of the Christian women of Carthage. The officers of the prison began to help the Christians following their encounter with Perpetua and her friends and the warden began to permit regular visitors and later became a Christian himself.

The day before the games Perpetua, Felicity and their companions were paraded before the crowd who had gathered to make fun of them. The prisoners turned this all around by laughing at the crowd for being so foolish as to deny that Jesus was the son of God and exhorted them to follow their example. Perpetua walked to the arena with 'shining steps as the true wife of Christ, the darling of God', and her companions went to the arena with joy and calm, meeting the eyes of everyone along the way.

Perpetua and the others resisted attempts to dress them up as pagan gods and were allowed to keep their clothes. Bears, leopards and wild boars attacked the men, while the women were forced to face a rabid heifer. When Perpetua and Felicity were thrown into the arena, Perpetua, still thinking of others, went to help Felicity up. After being severely mauled all five martyrs stood side by side and their throats were cut. Perpetua's last words were, 'Stand fast in the faith and love one another.'

St Peter *Feast day: 29 June. Born in Bethsaida, Galilee, in the Holy Land; died in Rome, 64.* Simon Peter was the son of John and worked with his brother **St Andrew** as a fisherman on Lake Galilee. He was called to become a disciple after Andrew had introduced him to Jesus. Jesus told him that he would become a fisher of men and gave him the new name Cephas, or the rock.

Peter is always listed as the first of the Apostles in all of the New Testament accounts, and he was a member of Jesus' inner circle, with James and John.

He is the disciple most frequently referred to in the New Testament and was with Jesus at the Transfiguration, and in the Garden of Gethsemane. He played a major role in the Passion of Christ, cutting off the right ear of the high priest's slave, Malchus, during the arrest of Jesus and, later that same night, denying Christ three times.

After the resurrection, Peter went to the tomb with the 'other disciple' and rushed in first. When the risen Christ came to the disciples beside Lake Galilee, Peter alone received the instructions to 'Feed my lambs . . . Tend my sheep . . . Feed my sheep.' He became an early leader of the

Apostles, was the first to perform miracles in the name of Jesus, and he also baptized the Roman centurion Cornelius as a result of a vision he had received.

At the Council of Jerusalem Peter gave his support to those who felt it right to preach to Gentiles and to baptize them into the Christian faith, thereby permitting the new Church to become worldwide. When he was imprisoned by King Herod Agrippa, an angel helped him to escape to resume his missionary efforts and he eventually reached Rome during the reign of Emperor Nero.

When persecution broke out Peter decided it was prudent to escape, but just outside the city he met Christ going in the other direction. Peter asked, '*Quo Vadis*?' ('Where are you going?') Christ replied that he was going to be crucified again because Peter would not. At this Peter turned around, re-entered the city and handed himself over to the soldiers. When told he would have to worship the gods or die, he requested that he be crucified upside down because he declared himself unworthy to die in the same manner as the Lord. His body was buried on Vatican Hill.

In liturgical art, he is depicted as an elderly man holding a key and a book and his symbols include an inverted cross, a boat, and the cock.

St Peter of Alicante *Feast day: 13 October. Born in Estremadura in Spain, 1499; died in 1562. Canonized in 1669 by Pope Clement IX.* Peter was the son of a lawyer and was educated at Salamanca University before entering a strict order of Franciscans and being ordained a priest in 1524. Peter was an inspired preacher and his experience of the ascetic life prompted him to write a book on prayer in 1556.

He retired to Arabida near Lisbon to form a community of Franciscan hermits, known as the Alcantarines. He limited the communities he formed to a maximum of eight monks and specified that their cells were to be no longer than seven feet. Over and above all the other offices, the monks practised three hours of mental prayer a day.

Peter seldom spoke, but when he did his words had great effect. Late in life, he met **St Teresa of Avila** and explained his practices to her and encouraged her in her reform of the Carmelites. Teresa told of how he slept only an hour and a half a night, ate only once in three days, and described his body and skin as being so shrivelled that they resembled the roots and dried bark of a tree.

Peter died in prayer at his monastery at Arenas.

St Peter Canisius *Feast day: 21 December. Born in Nijmegen in Holland, 1521; died in 1597. Canonized in 1925 by Pope Pius XI.* Canisius studied canon law at Cologne University and soon after graduating joined the Society of Jesus. He became a prominent preacher and attended two sessions of the Council of Trent. He was sent to teach at the first Jesuit school at Messina and later was called to Rome to work alongside **St Ignatius of Loyola**.

In 1552 he was sent to Vienna in order to reform and revive the low morale of the local churches. Many parishes had no clergy, and there had been no ordinations for 20 years; monasteries were deserted, and most people had abandoned religious practices. Canisius' enthusiasm was infectious, and his selfless care for the sick during the time of plague won the trust and esteem of the people.

In 1556 he wrote a catechism that was translated into 15 different languages and became a standard for the reform movement within the Catholic Church.

He was put in charge of a new Jesuit province overseeing Bohemia, Austria and Bavaria, where his preaching, teaching gifts and compassion endeared him to all. He was especially effective in converting Protestants and encouraging Catholics. Though he suffered an extreme seizure in 1591, Canisius continued to write with the help of a secretary. He was always clear to distinguish between those who were set on heresy and those who had drifted into false teaching through ignorance and lack of good example.

In his discussions with the Lutherans he tried as far as possible to avoid contentious topics such as indulgences, believing that discussion of such topics served only to harden attitudes. Canisius' preference was to stress basic Christian doctrine and the common characteristics of the spiritual life.

St Peter of Canterbury *Feast day: 6 January. Born in Rome; died in 607.* Peter was a monk in the monastery of St Andrew's, Rome. He was chosen by **Pope St Gregory I the Great** to travel with **St Augustine** and others to England in 596. He became the first abbot of the Benedictine monastery of Sts Peter and Paul at Canterbury in 602, and was later drowned in the English Channel at Ambleteu, near Boulogne while on his way to a mission to France.

St Peter Celestine *Feast day: 19 May. Born in Isernia in Italy, 1210; died in 1296. Canonized in 1313 by Pope Clement V.* Peter was the eleventh child of a peasant family who became a hermit and was ordained. He reluctantly gave in to the many requests he received for leadership and guidance and formed a monastery of hermits on Mone Morone. In 1274, the order became officially approved as the Celestines.

In 1294 there was complete deadlock among the cardinals as to who the next pope should be and Peter, who was by then overseeing some 20 monasteries, sent a message strongly urging that an agreed candidate be quickly found. Much to his surprise he was chosen as the new pope and, feeling duty bound to accept, he chose the name Celestine V.

His innocence and unworldliness were exploited by the King of Naples and caused him great distress. Convinced that his resignation would be the best option for everyone, he retired to a monastery, but this did nothing to solve the political struggle. Some refused to accept his resignation and others rejected his successor.

In order to avoid a rival papacy being set up, Pope Boniface had Peter arrested and held in honourable captivity in a tightly enclosed order with some other monks at Fumome, near Anagni and Peter found contentment there, saying, 'All that I wanted in this world was a cell and that is what they gave me.' Peter died two years later.

St Peter Chrysologus *Feast day: 30 July. Born in Imola in Italy, 406; died in 450.* Peter was baptized, educated and ordained a deacon by Cornelius, Bishop of Imola. He was called 'Chrysologus' (golden-worded) because of his gift of persuasive speech. He became Bishop of Ravenna in 433 and his simple, practical and clear sermons on Gospel themes brought much hope and encouragement to his flock. Peter was a strong supporter of Pope Leo the Great and when Eutyches, who held heretical views, asked for his support he refused, advising him against creating division. He provided hospitality for **St Germanus of Auxerre** and presided at his funeral in 446. He died at Imola, four years later.

St Peter Damian *Feast day: 23 February. Born in Imola near Ravenna in Italy, 1000; died in 1072.* Peter's parents died when he was very young, and he was left in the care of an elder brother who treated him very badly. As soon as he was old enough he was sent to tend swine. However, another of his brothers took pity on him and arranged for his education. Peter proved to be an apt pupil, becoming in time a professor of great ability.

He took pleasure in serving the poor and destitute and in time Peter was called into the monastic life. He devoted considerable time to study and was the unanimous choice as abbot on the death of the community's superior in 1043. Peter governed with great wisdom and founded five other hermitages.

In 1057 Pope Stephen IX persuaded him to leave his desert retreat and become Cardinal-bishop of Ostia, but he found the office of cardinal to be extremely burdensome and constantly requested to be allowed to resign and return to the solitude. Pope Alexander II refused to countenance this for some time, but finally, out of affection for him, consented on condition that he would still make himself available as an advisor on difficult matters.

Peter Damian recommended the use of strict discipline as a substitute for long penitential fasts, but in spite of his severity, he could treat penitents with gentleness and understanding when the occasion demanded.

In 1067 Emperor Henry IV of Germany married Bertha, but two years later he sought a divorce under the pretence that the marriage had never been consummated. Pope Alexander II forbade the annulment and chose Peter Damian as his legate to preside over the synod which was called to decide this issue. Peter persuaded Henry to pay due regard to the law of God, which he eventually agreed to do. Peter then hastened back to his solitary desert life, leaving only once more to hear a dispute before he died.

Peter's preaching was eloquent and his extensive writings overflow with great graciousness and humility.

St Peter of Mount Athos *Feast day: 12 June. Born in the eighth century.* Peter was a soldier who had been captured by Saracens and held in prison. He was finally released thanks to the intervention of St Simeon. Peter then went to Rome and was granted the monastic habit by the pope himself. He became a hermit on Mount Athos, overcoming many severe trials and temptations, and remained there for half a century in absolute solitude.

Peter was the first hermit to live on Mount Athos in Greece which was to become known as 'the Holy Mountain' and the home of many generations of monastic saints.

St Peter Nolasco *Feast day: 28 January. Born in Languedoc in France, 1189: died in 1256. Canonized in 1628 by Pope Urban VIII.* Peter's father died when he was only 15, and he became the heir to the family estate. He was involved in the crusade against the Albigensians of southern France before becoming a tutor to the young King James I of Aragon and settling in Barcelona.

He made friends with **St Raymond of Pennafort**, and in 1218 they laid the foundation for the Mercedarian Order, which was devoted to the ransoming of Christian captives.

Peter and others made trips to Africa and the Moorish coast of Spain to negotiate the release of captives from Moorish jails, and managed to release almost 400 prisoners. Peter insisted that on such trips the members of the order should always travel in pairs.

He retired in 1249, and died seven years later.

St Peter of Tarantaise *Feast day: 8 May. Born near Vienne, in France, 1102; died at the Abbey of Bellevaux in 1175. Canonized in 1191 by Pope Celestine III.* At the age of 12, Peter and other family members joined the Cistercian Order at Bonnevaux. In 1132 he was appointed the first abbot of Tamie, in the Tarantaise Mountains between Geneva and Savoy, and built a hospice for travellers there. Ten years later he reluctantly accepted the role of Archbishop of Tarantaise and diligently carried out his duties of care and reform. He originated the custom of distributing bread and soup, known as 'May Bread', just before the harvest, a custom that endured throughout France until the late eighteenth century.

In 1155, Peter suddenly disappeared. He was eventually discovered serving as a lay brother in a Cistercian abbey in Switzerland, and persuaded to return. He was still a highly trusted advisor and was asked to help bring about reconciliation between King Louis VII of France and Prince Henry II of England. Even though by this time he was very elderly he set out immediately, preaching to everyone on the way. Though both parties received him graciously, reconciliation proved to be impossible.

Peter was taken ill on the way home to his diocese and collapsed and died.

St Peter of Verona *Feast day: 29 April. Born in Verona in Italy, 1205; died in 1252. Canonized in 1253 by Pope Innocent IV.* Patron of inquisitors.

Peter went to the University of Bologna, and was brought into the Dominican Order in 1221 by **St Dominic** himself. He preached with some success in Lombardy and crowds flocked to hear him, bringing their sick for healing. He was appointed Inquisitor for northern Italy in 1234 and made enemies of those who resented his skill in converting heretics back to the faith.

While passing through a wood on his way from Como to Milan, Peter was ambushed by two assassins who fatally wounded him by assaulting him with a billhook. He wrote his last message with his own blood in the dirt '*Credo in Deum*' (I believe in God).

St Petroc *Feast day: 4 June. Born in south Wales in the sixth century.* Petroc was the son of a Welsh king, who became a monk and studied for a time in Ireland before settling at Lanwethinoc (Padstow) Cornwall.

After 30 years in Cornwall he made a pilgrimage to Rome and Jerusalem, and on to the west coast of the Indian Ocean where he lived for some time as a hermit on an island. On his return to Cornwall he built a chapel at Little Petherick near Padstow, and established other monastic communities before becoming a hermit on Bodmin Moor.

Petroc continued to be in demand as a wise and respected advisor and died while travelling to visit one of his foundations. He was known for his miracles and had a great affinity with animals.

St Petronella of Rome *Feast day: 31 May. Born in the third century.* Petronella was a member of the Domitilla family; she chose to live a celibate life and steadfastly refused to marry a nobleman named Flaccus. Her intended groom wanted her killed but she died after fasting for three days.

St Phileas *Feast day: 26 November. Born in Thumis, Egypt; died in Alexandria, 307.* Phileas became a Christian in adult life, and was chosen as bishop of his native city in the Nile Delta. He was arrested soon after his consecration and during a long imprisonment he wrote a detailed and moving account of the treatment and torture of Christians

The local governor recognized his great gifts of learning and culture and sought by every means possible to persuade him to offer sacrifices to the gods. Phileas remained steadfast in the face of threat, flattery, family pressure and manipulation and was eventually beheaded.

Philoromus, who was a tribune and treasurer at Alexandria at the time, objected so strongly to the cruelties inflicted upon Phileas that he was taken to be a Christian also and was martyred along with him.

St Philemon *Feast day: 8 March. Born in Egypt; died in 305.* Philemon was a popular musician and entertainer at Antinoe in Egypt. During the persecution of Diocletian, Deacon Apollonius offered Philemon four gold pieces if he would perform the rite of eating food sacrificed to false gods in his place. Philemon agreed and dressed himself in Apollonius' clothes and his hooded cloak to hide his face. Philemon appeared before the judge who instructed him to carry out the rite, but Philemon refused, claiming to be a Christian.

Arrian the judge argued with him, still thinking that he was speaking to Apollonius, until finally the actor Philemon revealed his true identity.

The judge saw the situation as a joke but insisted that Philemon perform the rite, however Philemon, now convinced of the wrongness of such sacrifices, refused to do so. It was pointed out that the punishment for refusal was death and that he was not even baptized. Philemon prayed, and a cloud miraculously appeared and rained upon him, which he claimed was his baptism. The judge begged him to think again but he remained steadfast. Apollonius was also arrested and the two men were condemned to death for being Christians.

They were taken to Alexandria where they were wrapped in chains and hurled into the sea.

St Philibert *Feast day: 22 August. Born in Gascony in France, 608; died on Heriou Island, 685.* Philibert was educated by his father, who later became Bishop of Aire. He came under the influence of St Quen at the court of Dagobert I and became a member of the monastic community at Rebais Abbey.

Philibert was elected abbot but resigned soon after as a result of disagreements with his fellow monks. In 654, King Clovis II gave him land on which he founded the monastery of Jumieges, in Neustria, near Fontenelle, France. Because he actively opposed Ebroin, who was the mayor of the palace to the Frankish king, he was arrested, imprisoned and then exiled to Heriou Island where he founded the abbey of Noirmoutier. He also rebuilt Qincay Abbey near Poitiers, and acted as advisor to several other communities.

St Philip *Feast day: 3 May. Born in Bethsaida in the Holy Land in the first century.* Philip is one of the Apostles; he was called by Jesus himself and brought Nathanael to Christ. He was present at the miracle of the loaves and fishes and engaged in a brief dialogue with the Lord about the price of bread. Philip was one of the most accessible of the disciples and Hellenistic Jews from Bethsaida chose to approach him when they wanted to be introduced to Jesus.

At the last supper, Jesus answered Philip's query to show them the Father, and he was among the Apostles awaiting the Holy Spirit in the Upper Room.

He preached in Greece and was crucified upside down at Hierapolis during the persecution of Emperor Domitian.

St Philip Benizi *Feast day: 23 August. Born in Florence in Italy, 1233; died in Todi, Italy in 1285. Canonized in 1671 by Pope Clement X.* Philip's parents had been married for many years before he was born in answer to their fervent prayers. He was educated in Paris and Padua, where he earned a doctorate in medicine and philosophy. He practised medicine for a time, but soon joined the Servite Order in Florence and served as a lay brother until he was ordained in 1259. He was a fine preacher and was Master of novices at Siena, and then superior of several friaries. Eventually, in 1267, much against his wishes, Philip was appointed Prior General of the Servites.

His reforming zeal and patience resulted in his being named as a possible candidate to become pope. Philip was so distressed by this that he fled and hid in a cave until the election was over.

He attended the Council of Lyon, which brought about a brief reunion with the Orthodox Church, and he worked hard to bring peace between other rival groups. Philip assisted St Juliana in founding the third order of the Servites, and in 1284 he dispatched the first Servite missionaries to the Far East. He retired to a small Servite house in Todi.

St Philip Evans *Feast day: 22 July. Born in Monmouth, Wales; died in 1679.* Educated at St Omer, Evans joined the Jesuits in 1665 and was ordained ten years later. Sent to work in south Wales he was pursued and arrested when the fictitious 'papish plot' was declared by Titus Oates.

Evidence was sought to prove that he had ministered as a priest, but initially no one could be found to testify against him. After much searching, two very unreliable witnesses were persuaded to testify. On their evidence alone the court found him guilty and sentenced to death.

In the weeks preceding his execution he continued to play tennis and enjoy music, spending his last hours playing the Welsh harp. He preached movingly about his faith on the scaffold.

St Philip Neri *Feast day: 26 May. Born in Florence, Italy, 1515; died in 1595. Canonized in 1622 by Pope Gregory XV.* Patron of Rome. Philip was brought up by his stepmother, who treated him very well. At the age of 18 he began working with a relative in the family firm with a view to learning the business, but in 1533, Philip experienced a profound conversion and travelled to Rome.

He entered a period of serious study for a time but, believing that this was interfering with his prayer life, sold all his books and adopted the life of a hermit.

On the eve of Pentecost in 1544, he experienced a powerful manifestation of the love of God, which often overwhelmed him in the latter years of his life. He described it as if a globe of light had entered his mouth and moved into his heart. Philip went to work at a hospital for the terminally ill and started speaking to everyone about God, from beggars to bankers.

In 1548, he formed a confraternity to provide food and shelter for pilgrims who came to Rome, and was ordained priest in 1551. Conscious of the poor moral climate in those days and of the need for spiritual instruction, Philip and a fellow priest called Buonsignore Cacciaguerra organized afternoon classes in the Church of San Girolamo. As numbers grew, they built an extra room called the Oratory in which they held their teaching sessions.

At Carnival time Philip organized an alternative diversion; a pilgrimage to the Seven Churches. This included a lunchtime picnic, which was accompanied by instrumental music.

Philip made himself available to everyone day and night. However in 1555, the Pope's Vicar accused him of 'introducing novelties' and ordered him to stop the meetings at the Oratory. Philip was brokenhearted but obeyed, only starting again after the sudden death of his accuser.

Gossip and false accusations continued to grow, and Philip and his companions became aware of the benefits of having their own order. This came into being under the official title of the Congregation of the Oratory, and consisted of both secular priests and clerics.

Philip was known to be spontaneous, unpredictable, charming and humorous. He was always pleading for tolerance for the outcasts, and when a troublesome man came to the Oratory, Philip told the others to be patient, saying that eventually the man would come to faith, which he did.

He was not always so gentle in his approach, however. On one occasion Philip met a condemned man who refused to listen; he grabbed him by the collar and threw him to the ground. Thus, shocked into repentance, the criminal made a full confession.

Humility was the most important virtue Philip tried to teach others and to develop in his own life. Some of his lessons in humility were superficially cruel, but they were tinged with humour, like practical jokes, and were later related with gratitude by the people they helped.

For example, one priest gave a beautiful sermon and asked with some vanity how he should remain humble in view of his great gift of eloquence; Philip ordered him to keep repeating it so that people would think he only had one sermon. On another occasion he told a woman guilty of gossip to buy a chicken and walk through the streets of Rome plucking it, then when she had finished he told her to gather up all the feathers. When she replied that she could not possibly do this, he explained that neither could she ever erase all her words of gossip. Another man asked Philip if he could wear a hair shirt. Philip gave him permission, on condition that he wore it on the outside his other clothes. And once Philip commanded a member of the Oratory who wanted to preach about hell fire and damnation to teach Church history instead and 27 years later the man's talks were published as a foundational work on ecclesiastical history.

Philip wore ridiculous clothes and would walk around with half his beard shaved off. He was very serious about prayer but also aware of his own frailty and weakness, and when he was asked how to pray he replied, 'Be humble and obedient and the Holy Spirit will teach you.'

Philip died after a long illness, uttering his last words on retiring that night, 'Last of all, we must die.'

St Phocas the Gardener *Feast day: 23 July. Born in Sinope, Paphiagonia, on the Black Sea; died in 303.* Patron of sailors. Phocas was a hermit and a skilful gardener, who had been sentenced to death without trial during the persecutions of the Emperor Diocletian. A group of Roman soldiers were sent to find and execute him, and on arriving at his hermitage they asked if he knew where Phocas was.

He answered in the affirmative and suggested that he take them to him, but first offered them food and shelter for the night, and not knowing who he was, they agreed. After serving the soldiers with food and showing them where to sleep, he went out and dug his grave, using the rest of the night to prepare his soul.

In the morning he led them to his prepared grave and told them who he was. They were shocked by his revelation and hesitated to carry out their assignment, but Phocas encouraged them to do their duty and they beheaded him. He is especially venerated in the East.

St Pio of Pietrelcina (Padre Pio) *Feast day: 23 September. Born in Pietrelcina near Naples in Italy, 1887; died in 1968. Canonized in 2002 by Pope John Paul II.* Pio was the son of peasant farmers and a very devout child. He became a Capuchin novice at the age of 16 and was ordained to the priesthood in 1910, becoming known as Padre Pio.

In 1916 he was exempted from military service on the grounds of poor health and chose to serve as an orderly, but a year later his health had broken down and he was sent to the monastery of St Giovanni Rotondo where he lived for the rest of his life.

In 1918 he began to exhibit stigmata, the wounds of Christ, in his hands and feet, and side and thorn pricks appeared on his forehead. Pio tried hard not to draw attention to the miraculous wounds but word spread and many flocked to the masses he celebrated. Padre Pio predicted that these wounds would heal when he died and he was proved right; when he died in 1968 the wounds were no longer visible. The blood from the stigmata was described as having the perfume of flowers and they were strongly revered by the local populace as a sign of sanctity. Money poured into the monastery and a hospital was built.

Pio was a prayerful and wise counsellor and heard confessions for up to 12 hours per day, and his acts of charity were widely known. These acts of faithfulness were referred to in the subsequent process of beatification, rather than his receiving of the stigmata. When he died in 1968 at the age of 81, his funeral was attended by about 100,000 people, and on June 16, 2002, over 500,000 gathered in Rome for his canonization.

St Pionius *Feast day: 1 February. Born in Smyrna; died in 250.* Pionius was a priest at Smyrna who was arrested under Emperor Trajanus Decius and condemned to death along with a group of 15 companions, for refusing to sacrifice to the gods. They were arrested during a liturgical celebration on the feast of **St Polycarp**.

Pionius was known for his wisdom and preaching abilities right to the end of his life. When he was led out before the crowds for ritual humiliation, he spoke out boldly. He first addressed those of Greek origin, quoting Homer's *Odyssey*, he told them that it was not a holy thing to gloat over someone who is about to die, and then turning his attention to the Jews present he quoted from the book of Proverbs (24:17) 'Do not rejoice when your enemy falls and do not be glad when he stumbles.'

Since a leading Christian called Euctemon had been persuaded through threats to make sacrifices to the gods not too long before this, repeated efforts were made to get Pionius and his companions to do likewise. Their response was to reply in kind, encouraging their persecutors to change their minds and become believers in Jesus Christ, son of the living God.

Finally, they were put through terrible tortures before being burned at the stake.

St Pius V *Feast day: 30 April. Born in Bosco, Italy, 1504; died in 1572. Canonized in 1712 by Pope Clement XI.* Antonio Ghislieri (St Pius) worked as a shepherd boy before joining the Dominicans when he was 14. He was ordained in 1528, studied at Bologna and Genoa and went on to teach theology and philosophy and serve as prior for several Dominican houses. His great gifts were recognized and after various significant posts including that as Bishop of Nepi and Sutri he was finally named Cardinal and Grand Inquisitor in 1557.

He was unanimously elected pope in 1566, and continued to work for the reform of the Church in the wake of the Council of Trent. He insisted that bishops should reside in their diocese, and that all monastic institutions be reformed. He commissioned a new edition of the works of **St Thomas Aquinas** and a revision of the Vulgate Bible.

In 1571 Pius used the Inquisition to prevent any Protestant ideas from gaining a foothold in Italy and Spain, but his decision to excommunicate Queen Elizabeth I of England only made things worse for Roman Catholics in England.

Pius organized an alliance between Venice and Spain, in order to oppose the Turkish (Muslim) invasion into Europe. This culminated in the defeat of the Ottoman Turks in the naval battle of Lepanto.

He was wholeheartedly devoted to the religious life, though one of the negative results of his papacy was the unchecked brutal treatment of the Jews in Rome.

St Pius X *Feast day: 21 August. Born in the Province of Treviso, Venice in 1835; died in 1914. Canonized 1954 by Pope Pius XII.* Giuseppe Melchiorre Sarto (St Pius X) is remembered for the inauguration of liturgical renewal and for admitting children to their first communion at seven years old. He was born into a peasant family and had a pastor's heart from a young age. He relinquished Church property for the sake of independence from state control, asking the faithful to make considerable material sacrifices as a result. He fought against heresy and modernizing tendencies in the Church, seeking always to live a humble and holy life.

His last will and testament bears the striking sentence, 'I was born poor, I have lived in poverty, and I wish to die poor.'

St Placid *Feast day: 5 October. Born in Subiaco, Italy in the sixth century.*
Placid was placed in the care of **St Benedict** at a very young age. He was
dramatically rescued from the middle of a lake by one of Benedict's other
companions **St Maurus** as recorded in the Dialogues of Pope **St Gregory
the Great**.

Placid's father gave Benedict a gift of land on which to found the
monastery of Benedict at Monte Cassino, and Placid was part of this
community. No reliable records exist as to the day or manner of his death.

St Polycarp *Feast day: 23 February. Born in Smyrna in 69; died in 156.*
Polycarp was a disciple of **St John the Evangelist** and one of the second
generations of Church leaders and he became Bishop of Smyrna. **St
Ignatius of Antioch** positively encouraged Polycarp saying to him,
'Your mind is grounded in God as on an immovable rock.' He spoke out
courageously against the heresy of Marcion* and his followers.

In those days Easter was celebrated on different days in the Eastern and
Western Churches and Polycarp went to Rome to discuss the matter with
Pope Anicetus. Though they were unable to reach agreement on this, they
found their Christian beliefs identical and Anicetus asked Polycarp to celebrate the Eucharist in the papal chapel.

Polycarp did not chase after martyrdom as some did, but during a particularly violent time, when Christians were being rounded up and placed
in the arena to be attacked by wild animals, the crowd became so mad
that they demanded more blood by crying, 'Down with the atheists; let
Polycarp be found.' Polycarp was calm when his persecutors found him
on a nearby farm and prepared a meal for them while he prayed for an
hour. During this time, he saw a vision of his pillow turned to fire and
told his friends that this dream meant he would be burned alive.

His captors brought the 86-year-old bishop to the proconsul who
begged him to deny his faith but, observing Polycarp's lack of fear, he
ordered that he be burned alive. The proconsul wouldn't let the Christians
have the body because he was afraid they would worship Polycarp, but
after the fire had died out his followers managed to retrieve his bones.

St Praejectus *Feast day: 25 January. Born in Auvergne, France; died in
676.* Praejectus studied under Bishop Genesius and was appointed
Bishop of Clermont in 666. He was a strong supporter of monasticism,
built churches and hospitals, and aided the poor as well as being well
known for his scholarship. Praejectus was assassinated near Clermont,
along with St Amarin, abbot of a monastery in the Vosges, by a group of
soldiers who mistakenly thought he had taken part in the execution of
their leader.

St Praxedes *Feast day: 21 July. Born in Rome; died in the second century.*
Praxedes was the sister of St Pudentiana, who sought out Christians in
order to help them with money, care and comfort during the persecution
of Emperor Marcus Antoninus. She encouraged them to stand firm, and
made provision for those who were held in prison or slavery.

Finally, unable to bear the cruelties inflicted on her fellow Christians she prayed to God that, if it were possible, she might be released from beholding such sufferings and be with Him forever. Her prayer was speedily answered.

Sts Processus and Martinian *Feast day: 2 July. Born in Rome in the first century.* Processus and Martinian were warders of **St Peter** who became Christians through his ministry. They were held in the Mamertine Prison in Rome before they were executed alongside the apostle.

A spring miraculously appeared in the prison, and Peter baptized Processus and Martinian, before they were killed. Their relics are preserved in St Peter's Basilica.

St Prosper *Feast day: 7 July. Born in Aquitaine, 403; died in 460.* Prosper was a layman who lived with monks at Marseilles. He was a thoroughly committed follower of **St Augustine**, though he later took a less severe view of predestination. To strengthen his arguments, Prosper wrote to Augustine, who responded with letters that are now known as 'On the Predestination of the Saints' and 'On the Gift of Perseverance'.

Prosper, who was known as 'the best disciple of Augustine', labelled anyone who disagreed with his teacher as semi-Pelagian*, including **St John Cassian** and **St Hilary of Arles**.

In 431, the year after Augustine's death, Prosper and a friend named Hilary travelled to Rome to ask Pope Celestine I to proclaim the truth of his teachings. He later became secretary to **St Leo the Great**, and was widely known for his theological poems and his chronicle of world history which incorporated the histories of **Sts Jerome**, Sulpicius, Severus and Orosius. Prosper's history contains full records of the theological disputes of the time, and ends with the sack of Rome by the Vandals in 455.

Prosper made selections from the writings of Augustine and these were used as the basis of the decrees of the Council of Orange in 529.

St Prudentius *Feast day: 28 April. Born in Spain; died in 861.* Prudentius was elected bishop of Troyes, France in 840. He was known as an effective spiritual director, pastor and theologian. Prudentius was invited by Bishop Hincmar of Rheims to examine the case of a monk named Gottschalk who had been accused of heresy. The monk had been tortured and imprisoned but Prudentius, far from agreeing with the assessment of his fellow bishop, regarded the punishment as excessive and discerned that the fault was more with the accusers than with the accused.

He taught orthodox doctrine clearly and consistently in the disputes that followed and wrote a book to correct some of the errors. Prudentius worked hard to maintain the unity of the Church and to reform those Christians who had fallen into lax behaviour.

Q

St Quadratus *Feast day: 26 May. Died in 129.* Quadratus was a disciple of the Apostles and was appointed the Bishop of Athens. He is best known as the author of the first defence of Christianity which he wrote in the year 124 and addressed to Emperor Hadrian on the occasion of his visit to Athens for the Eleusinian games. In it Quadratus referred to the miracles of Jesus as evidence of the truth of his teaching and also to several people he had actually known who had been healed or raised to life by Jesus Christ.

St Quentin *Feast day: 31 October. Date unknown.* Quentin was a Roman who went to Gaul as a missionary accompanied by St Lucian of Beauvais. They travelled through that land together as preachers but parted company at Amiens in Picardy when Quentin felt called to settle there. He was so successful in preaching that the prefect Rictiovarus had him imprisoned.

Neither promises nor threats could win him over and the prefect ordered that he should be tortured and then taken to Augusta Veromanduorum (now known as Saint-Quentin) where, as a warning to other believers, he was tortured again and finally beheaded.

St Quintian *Feast day: 23 May. Born in North Africa; died in 430.* Quintian was the leader of a group of 19 martyrs that included Julian and Lucius who were put to death for being orthodox Christians during the Vandal invasion of North Africa, by the Arian* ruler King Hunneric.

Sts Quiricus and Julitta *Feast day: 16 June. Born in Tarsus; died in 304.* Quiricus was the three-year-old son of Julitta, a widow of Tarsus who had been arrested for being a Christian. Julitta scratched the Roman magistrate's face and he punished her by forcing her to watch her son being beaten to death before executing her.

St Quodvultdeaus *Feast day: 19 February. Born in North Africa; died in 439.* Quodvultdeaus, whose name means 'What God Wills', was Bishop of Carthage in the period after **St Augustine**, when the Vandals from Spain were invading northern Africa. The Vandals were Arians* and unleashed great hostility against the orthodox clergy, and although Quodvultdeaus encouraged his clergy to persevere, many fled from the countryside to the relative safety of the large towns, leaving their congregations unprotected. The bishop suggested that they were too keen on self-preservation and entertainments and had forgotten the example of the martyrs.

The fall of the city of Carthage in 439 saw many people killed and the bishop regarded this as retribution for their lack of faithful living. Quodvultdeaus was taken prisoner along with some of his clergy and banished. They were put on board leaky ships, without oars or sails, but managed to make landfall in Naples, where Quodvultdeaus died.

R

St Radbod of Utrecht *Feast day: 29 November. Died in 918.* Radbod was born into a noble Frankish family. His mother's brother Bishop Gunther of Cologne helped in his early education and he was ordained priest at the age of 22.

Later that same year he was unanimously chosen to be Bishop of Utrecht. Since all his predecessors had been monks, Radbod joined the Benedictine order as soon as he had been consecrated. He soon became widely respected as an abbot-bishop with a special concern for the poor and destitute.

Radbod had a special affection for **St Martin of Tours** and wrote hymns and prayers in honour of him and other favourite saints. In later life, following a Danish invasion, Radbod moved his see to Deventer where he later died.

St Rainerius Scacceri *Feast day: 17 June. Born in Pisa, Italy, in 1117; died in 1160. Canonized in by Pope Alexander III, date unknown.* Rainerius was born into a wealthy family but became a wandering minstrel. He played the fiddle and sang at festivals and gatherings all over the land, often sleeping rough. On one occasion, when performing in a castle, he met a holy man and he was so impressed that he paused in the singing of his ballads and asked him to pray for him. After further conversation, he was converted and publicly renouncing his former way of life, he threw his fiddle on the fire.

Rainerius set himself up as a trader, in the hope of earning enough money for a trip to the Holy Land. He had amassed a considerable sum, when one day on opening his purse, there was such a stench coming from it that he gave up all further thought of trade and chose a life of poverty. He eventually did make the journey to Palestine, setting out with nothing and asking for alms on the way.

In 1153, he returned home and entered the Benedictine abbey of St Andrew at Pisa. He died at the Pisan abbey of San Vito, and his fame had already grown to such an extent that he was buried in Pisa Cathedral. Rainerius was widely known as an able spiritual director with a generous winsome spirit. He performed various healing miracles during his lifetime.

St Raphael *Feast day: 29 September.* Patron of the blind, happy meetings, nurses, physicians and travellers. St Raphael is one of three archangels, the others being Gabriel and Michael. He was sent by God to help Tobit, Tobiah and Sarah. Raphael also helped Tobit's father to see the light of heaven.

Raphael's name means 'God heals' relating to Enoch's story, which claims that he healed the earth when it was defiled by the sins of the fallen angels. Raphael is also identified as the angel who stirred the waters of the healing sheep pool in Jerusalem.

St Raphael Kalinowski *Feast day: 19 November. Born in Vilnuis in Lithuania, 1835; died in 1907.* Raphael was the son of a Polish Professor of Mathematics. He graduated in Science from St Petersburg University, and was employed in planning the railway from Kiev to Odessa. When the project was delayed, he used his time productively for Christian work and set up a Sunday school.

He was arrested and sentenced to ten years hard labour in Siberia for his part in the Polish resistance against the Russian invasion of 1863. The walk to the prison camp took over nine months and many died on the way.

On his release in 1877 he decided to join the Carmelite order in Austria. He became prior in Czerna monastery and was later appointed Vicar Provincial for the Carmelite nuns. He emphasized the importance of prayer and holiness and did all he could to revive the Carmelite order in Poland.

St Raymond Nonnatus *Feast day: 31 August. Born at Portella in Catalonia, Spain, 1204; died at Cardona in Spain, 1240. Canonized in 1657 by Pope Alexander VII.*

Patron of expectant mothers and midwives because of the nature of his own birth.

His name *non natus* (not born) is derived from the fact that he was delivered by Caesarean operation; his mother died during the birth. He joined the Mercedarians under **St Peter Nolasco** at Barcelona, whom he succeeded, taking on his role of providing ransom for those who had been taken prisoner by raiders. He set off for Algiers with the gold that had been contributed by Christians and was able to arrange for the release of many prisoners before the money ran out. He then, without hesitation, offered himself in exchange for several more slaves who were still being held in prison.

During his incarceration he converted some of his guards to Christianity. This enraged the governor, who would have had him killed by impalement had not others realized that he would probably command an especially high ransom if he were kept alive. Instead, his lips were pierced and closed with a chain so that he could no longer use words to convert his jailers. After eight months of torture, Peter Nolasco himself arrived, paid his ransom, and ordered him to return to Barcelona.

He obeyed but was deeply grieved to have to leave so many others behind.

Though Pope Gregory IX made him a cardinal, Raymond continued to follow the same lifestyle as before. His simplicity offended some of his superiors who tried, unsuccessfully, to persuade him to adopt a lifestyle more suited to his position as a cardinal.

In 1240, Pope Gregory summoned Raymond to Rome. When Raymond left the monastery, people rushed to see him and do him honour but that very day he was struck with fever and died. He was 36 years old.

St Raymond of Pennafort *Feast day: 7 January. Born at Villafranca (Peñafort) in Spain, 1175; died in Barcelona, 1275; Canonized by Pope Clement VIII in 1601.* Patron of canonists.

Raymond was related to the King of Aragon. He was educated in Barcelona and made such rapid progress that by the age of 20 he had been appointed as a professor of philosophy. He did this without pay and was greatly respected. He continued his studies at Bologna, and became a famous teacher specializing both in civil and canon law, and once again he would accept no payment for his work. He was strongly attracted by the Dominican order and on a journey to Barcelona met with **St Dominic** himself.

Subsequently Raymond gave up all his honours and entered the Order of the Dominicans in 1222. He was a very humble man who was close to God and his transparent goodness and kindness won many non-believers to faith. He also co-founded the order of Our Lady of Ransom which was devoted to saving poor Christians who had been captured by the Moors.

On one occasion, Raymond was banished to an island because he disciplined King James. Even though there was no ship that would dare to defy the king and rescue him, he managed to leave the island by putting all his trust in God. He spread his cloak upon the water, tied one corner of it to a stick for a sail, made the Sign of the Cross, and stepping onto the cloak, he sailed along for six hours until he reached Barcelona. The King grew to regret his hasty response, and was soon brought to faith by the words and actions of Raymond.

St Raymond of Toulouse *Feast day: 8 July. Born in Toulouse, France, 1050; died in 1118.* Raymond was a singer and teacher who was widely known for his generosity. His wife died soon after they had married and subsequently he became a canon of St Sernin, Toulouse, helping to rebuild the church as a popular pilgrimage centre.

He is especially remembered for his care for the poor and his founding of an alms-house which could hold up to 13 people. He also helped with the construction of two city bridges.

St Raymund Palermo *Feast day: 27 July. Born in Piacenza, Italy in 1140; died in 1200.* At the age of 15, Raymund went on pilgrimage to Jerusalem with his widowed mother who died on the return trip. He returned alone carrying a pilgrim's palm branch. He became a cobbler, married and had five children, all of whom died in the same year as his wife as a result of an epidemic.

He then set out on pilgrimage to several famous places including Compostella, Pavia and Rome. On his way to Jerusalem he had a vision of Christ in which he was told to return home and look after the poor. This he did for the last 22 years of his life.

He was fervent in his mission and obtained a large building, which he transformed into a hostel and hospital for the poor and sick, begging alms in the streets for this work. He used to carry a large wooden cross, saying, 'Help us hardhearted and cruel Christians. We are dying of hunger while you live in plenty.' He aided children, orphans, pilgrims and prisoners and he received great help from the local authorities who recognized both the value of his work and his constancy.

When he died, he was buried in a magnificent tomb provided by the local authorities next to the Church of the Apostles in Piacenza.

St Realino *Feast day: 3 July. Born at Carpi in Italy, 1530; died at Lecce, Italy, 1616. Canonized in 1947 by Pope Pius XII.* Realino came from a devout family with an academic background. He studied arts, medicine and both civil and Church law, at Bologna University. After completing his studies he went into government employment, married and became superintendent of the kingdom of Naples. His wife died young and he entered the novitiate of the Jesuits, being admitted by Father Alphonso Salmeron, one of the first companions of **St Ignatius of Loyola**. He worked for ten years in Naples, doing pastoral work, preaching, cate-chizing and helping the poor, the sick and prison inmates. He became a teacher of novices at the college at Lecce, was later appointed rector, and remained there for the rest of his life.

Six years before his death he fell and suffered two wounds that would not heal. During his last illness, blood from a leg wound was collected in vials because of the great veneration in which he was held. This blood behaved in various extraordinary ways, some retaining its liquidity over a century.

His superior observed that he had never heard a single word of com-plaint about Realino, who remained a layman throughout his life.

St Reineldis *Feast day: 17 July. Born in France; died in Kontich in Belgium, 680.* Reineldis was the daughter of Count Witger and St Arnalberga, and sister of Sts Gudula and Emebert. She tried to join her father at Lobbes Abbey in France when he and her mother both decided to enter the religious life, but was refused permission to do so.

She undertook a pilgrimage to the Holy Land and on her return involved herself in a life of good works at Saintes. She was killed by Barbarian invaders.

St Remigius *Feast day: 1 October. Born at Cerny, France, c. 437; died at Rheims, 530.* As a boy Remigius excelled in learning and, in the opinion of St Apollinaris Sidonius who knew him well, he was one of the most eloquent people of his generation. He was ordained and consecrated Bishop of Rheims in spite of being only 22, and made up for lack of experience by his energetic, faithful service.

Remigius baptized King Clovis (King of the Franks from 481–511). Although the queen, **St Clotilde**, was a devout Christian, it had taken the miraculous recovery of their eldest son Clodomir from sickness and a spectacular victory over superior fighting forces, both of which Clovis attributed to Christ's intervention, to convert him to the Christian faith. In Remigius' own words, Clovis came to 'burn what he adored and adore what he had burned'.

With the encouragement and protection of King Clovis, Remigius spread the Gospel of Christ among the Franks, in which work God endowed him with an extraordinary gift of miracles. **St Gregory of Tours** referred to Remigius as 'a man of great learning, fond of rhetorical studies, and equal in his holiness to St Silvester'.

His last act was to draw up a will in which he distributed all his lands and wealth and ordered that, 'generous alms be given to the poor and that liberty be given to the serfs on his domain', concluding by asking God to bless the family of the first Christian king.

St Remigius continued to serve as a bishop for over 70 years, and died in his 'home' city of Rheims.

St Richard of Chichester *Feast day: 3 April. Born in Droitwich, England, 1197; died in 1253. Canonized in 1262 by Pope Urban IV.* Richard was orphaned at a young age and impoverished due to others' mismanagement of his family affairs but he managed to regain his fortune by patient diligence. He studied at Oxford where he became friends with St Edmund Rich, who was later to become the Archbishop of Canterbury. He then went on to earn a doctorate in law from the University of Bologna. Richard then taught at the Dominican house in Orkans, and was ordained there in 1243.

Upon going home to England, he was named chancellor to Edmund's successor, St Boniface of Savoy. King Henry III, who tried to appoint Ralph Neville to the post, opposed his appointment to the see of Chichester in 1244. In the ensuing investigation, Pope Innocent IV found in Richard's favour, but he was prevented from taking up office for two years. Henry eventually gave in when the Pope threatened him with excommunication.

The last eight years of Richard's life were spent in ministering to his flock. He denounced nepotism and simony, insisting on strict clerical discipline, and was most at home in the company of the poor and needy. He died at a house for poor priests in Dover, England, while on a preaching crusade.

St Richard Gwyn *Feast day: 17 October. Born in Montgomeryshire, Wales, in 1547; died in 1584. Canonized in 1970 by Pope Paul VI.* Richard studied at Cambridge University, England and though he was from a Protestant background, he felt called to join the Roman Catholic Church.

He returned to Wales in 1562, married, had six children, and opened a school.

Richard was accused of being a traitor because of his religion and held prisoner for four years before being hanged, drawn, and quartered at Wrexham.

He is numbered among the 40 Martyrs of England and Wales.

St Richardis *Feast day: 18 September. Born in Andlau, Alsace, 839; died in 895.* Richardis was the daughter of the Scot Kenneth I, who had become the Count of Alsace. When she was 22 years old she married Charles the Fat, and was Crowned Holy Roman Empress. After 19 years of marriage, she was accused by Emperor Charles of infidelity. She denied the charges, and was eventually 'vindicated' in a ritual trial by fire. Richardis left court to become a nun at Hohenburg. She founded a Benedictine abbey at Andlau in 887, and spent the rest of her life there.

Once, when walking in the woods near the abbey, Richardis found a mother bear pining over her dead cub. Richardis picked up the cub and it returned to life. Both mother and cub became devoted to Richardis from that day on.

St Richard Reynolds *Feast day: 4 May. Born in Devon, England, 1492; died in 1535. Canonized in 1970 by Pope Paul VI.* Richard was educated at Cambridge and in 1513 he entered the order of Brigettines at Syon Abbey, Isleworth. When King Henry VIII demanded royal oaths, Richard and others refused on religious grounds and were arrested as a result.

They were executed at Tyburn, and Richard is listed as one of the 40 Martyrs of England and Wales.

St Rita of Cascia *Feast day: 22 May. Born in Roccaporena, in Italy, 1381; died in 1457. Canonized in 1900 by Pope Leo XIII.* Patron of hopeless causes.

Rita wanted to enter holy orders from an early age, but her elderly parents insisted that she be married at the age of 12 to a man who proved to be both cruel and harsh. After 18 unhappy years, her husband was killed in a brawl and she was left with two sons to care for. When both sons also died, Rita tried to enter the Augustinians in their convent at Cascia, but was turned down because all novices were expected to be virgins. Finally, in 1413, the order relented and allowed her to join.

She became widely respected for her devotion, austerity and charity. In the midst of a chronic illness, she received visions and wounds on her forehead that resembled the crown of thorns.

Many miracles were reported in the convent at Cascia following her death.

St Robert of Molesmes *Feast day: 29 April. Born near Troyes in France, 1029; died in 1111.* Robert was born to noble parents in Champagne. He entered the Benedictine abbey of Moutier la Celle, near Troyes at the age of 15, and in 1068, he became Prior and Abbot of Saint Michael de Tonnere. His attempt to introduce extensive reforms met with such resistance that he retired in 1071. Shortly after this, a group of hermits in the forest of Collan petitioned Robert to become their head. At first he declined, but the monks persevered and, after winning papal approval for their community, Robert accepted.

In 1074 Robert moved his hermits into a monastery at Molesmes and within a few years, the community had grown in size and wealth. But along with the prosperity came laxity of discipline and Robert tried to withdraw by going to the hermitage at Or, but he was recalled. He remained for a short time before stepping down once more in the face of resistance to his style of authority.

In 1098 Robert and 21 other monks were granted permission to leave and found a new community at Citeaux. Robert's 'New Monastery', was established with the invaluable aid of the Duke of Burgundy; it soon became well known for its spiritual depth and later became the mother house of the Cistercian order.

Suitably chastened, the rebellious monks of Molesmes petitioned to have Robert returned to them, which he did without any sense of bitterness. Robert turned Molesmes into a leading centre for reform, while Citeaux became the heart of the Cistercian order.

St Robert of Newminster *Feast day: 7 June. Born in Gargrave in Yorkshire, 1100; died in 1159.* Robert was a priest from north Yorkshire who joined the Benedictine order at Whitby. He was given permission to join some monks from York who were attempting to live according to a new interpretation of the Benedictine rule at Fountains Abbey. This became a Cistercian abbey and was one of the centres of the White Monks in Northern England. Newminster Abbey in Northumberland was opened as a daughter monastery and Robert became its first abbot in 1139. He was gentle in manner and merciful in judgement.

St Roch *Feast day: 16 August. Born in Montpellier, France in the early 14th century.* Patron of invalids.

Roch was the son of a local governor. When he was 20 his father died and Roch went on pilgrimage to Rome. In the course of his journey, he came upon the victims of a plague that was ravaging Italy at that time, and gave up his pilgrimage for a time in order to devote himself to their care.

He became a victim himself at Piacenza, but recovered and went on to perform many miracles of healing. Returning to Montpellier, he was arrested on suspicion of being a spy in pilgrim's disguise. His uncle, who was governor at the time, failed to recognize him and Roch did not disclose his identity, so he was thrown into prison. He died in prison after five years and only then was he identified as the former governor's son by a birthmark in the form of a cross on his chest.

Sts Romanus and Barula *Feast day: 18 November. Born in Palestine; died in 304.* Romanus served as a deacon in both Caesarea and Antioch. He was arrested and put to death for encouraging Christian prisoners to resist the demands of the Roman authorities to sacrifice to the gods. Romanus was burned, strangled and then beheaded; seven-year-old boy, named Barula, died with him.

St Romanus the Melodist *Feast day: 1 October. Born in Emesa, Syria in the fifth century; died in 556.* Born in Syria, Romanus was of Jewish descent. He became a deacon in the church at Berytus and was ordained priest in Constantinople. One night, after having been on retreat,

Romanus had a vision in which the Virgin Mary gave him a volume of paper and said, 'Take the paper and eat it.' In his vision, he opened his mouth and swallowed the paper. In a very short time Romanus had acquired a reputation as a fine preacher and also for his wonderful poetry and brilliant musical compositions. These are similar in structure to Latin medieval hymns, or the earliest Italian religious verse, and are considered to be genuine master works of religious literature. They are based on the Church year, and include hymns to the Nativity, the Presentation in the Temple, and the Resurrection. Though only 80 of his hymns still remain, he is reputed to have written over 1,000 hymns and prayers in his lifetime and he is known as 'the Melodist' because of this. Romanus is regarded as the foremost of the Greek hymnographers.

St Romuald *Feast day: 19 June. Born in Ravenna in Italy, 956; died in 1027.* Romuald spent much of his early life totally absorbed in worldly pleasures. Painfully aware of his son's frivolous approach to life, his father, Sergius, forced him to be present at a duel he was fighting, and to watch as he slew his opponent. This made such an impression upon Romuald that he immediately went on retreat to the Benedictine monastery of St Apollinaris near Ravenna, decided to join the community and was accepted. In due course he was appointed abbot.

He went on to found several monasteries and laid the foundations of the austere order of Camaldoli which was to influence **St Bruno** and the whole Carthusian order in their hermitical lifestyle. He diligently fought spiritual battles against evil assaults that came in the form of dreams and which he conquered by vigilance and prayer.

He became the victim of calumny, which he bore with great fortitude. With increasing age, instead of lessening his severe self-disciplines, he increased them. He died alone in the monastery of Castro, which he had founded in the Marquisate of Ancona.

St Roque Gonzalez de Santa Cruz *Feast day: 17 November. Born in Asunción in Paraguay, 1576; died in 1628. Canonized in 1988 by Pope John Paul II.*

Roque was the son of noble Spanish parents, a religious youth who appeared destined to enter the priesthood. He was ordained as a young man but felt unworthy. Taking a special interest in the conversion of the Indians of Paraguay, he worked for ten years in order to get more experience, before offering himself for missionary work and joining the Society of Jesus. He played an important part in the formation of the 'reductions' of Paraguay. These were settlements of Christian Indians, which the Jesuit missionaries set up and oversaw as guardians and protectors.

Despite many discouragements, Roque threw himself into the work with wholehearted enthusiasm for nearly 20 years. He was responsible for the Reduction of St Ignatius, which was the original on which all the others were based, and spent the rest of his life establishing half a dozen other reductions, east of the Parana and Uruguay rivers.

He helped found a reduction near the Ijuhi River, but they were attacked. St Roque was about to hang up a small church bell when he was attacked from behind with a tomahawk and killed. One of his companions, St Rodriguez, came to find out what was happening and was also killed. The chapel was set on fire and the two bodies thrown onto the bonfire. Father Castillo was another member of the group who was taken prisoner and then stoned to death.

St Rose of Lima *Feast day: 30 August. Born in Lima, 1586; died in 1617. Canonized in 1671 by Pope Clement X.* Patron of Latin America and the Philippines.

Although she was baptized Isabel, she became known as Rose because she was such a beautiful baby. Afraid that her beauty might be a temptation to someone, she rubbed her face with pepper until it became red and blistered. She worked hard to support her poor parents but resisted their attempts to marry her off, because of her desire to devote her life to Christ alone.

Rose suffered many temptations and experienced times of extreme loneliness and spiritual depression. In her last long, painful sickness, this heroic young woman used to pray: 'Lord, increase my sufferings, and with them increase Your love in my heart.' Many miracles followed after her death.

S

St Sabas *Feast day: 5 December. Born in Cappadocia near Caesarea, 439; died in 532.* Sabas was the son of an army officer who was left in the care of an uncle when his father was assigned to Alexandria. Sabas was only eight years old at the time and was soon being so badly mistreated by his uncle's wife that he ran away to another uncle. A lawsuit resulted in his being returned to the first uncle but he ran away again, this time to a monastery near Mutalaska, where he was allowed to remain.

In 456 he went to Jerusalem and there entered a monastery under St Theoctistus.

Sabas was a hard worker and it is reported that he could make 50 baskets a week out of palm fronds. He became a hermit under the guidance of St Euthymius, and after this saint died, he spent four years alone in the desert near Jericho. Disciples flocked to him, despite his desire for solitude, and he was obliged to become a priest for the 150 monks who desired to be cared for by him. Sabas was ordained by Patriarch Sallust of Jerusalem in 491. He gave permission for disciples who had come from Egypt and Armenia to use their own local language liturgies. The community established several hospitals and a second monastery close to Jericho. As a result Sabas came to be regarded as one of the founders of Eastern monasticism.

He was appointed archimandrite of all hermits in Palestine and handled disputes amongst the monks with grace and charity. He was a vigorous opponent of Monophysitism*. In 531, when he was 91, he went to Constantinople and successfully pleaded with Emperor Justinian to protect the people of Jerusalem from harassment from the army following a Samaritan revolt. He fell ill soon after this and died.

St Salvatore *Feast day:18 March. Born in Santa Columba in Spain, 1520; died in 1567. Canonized in 1938 by Pope Pius XI.* Salvatore was born into a poor family and both his parents died while he was still a child. He worked as a shoemaker in Barcelona before joining the Franciscans when he was 20. He was originally employed in the kitchen but, desiring even greater humility and austerity, he moved to St Mary of the Angels at Horta, which was a house of much stricter discipline.

Eventually Salvatore returned to Barcelona where his spiritual maturity and healing gifts were quickly recognized and used to the full. He always walked barefoot, scourged himself daily, and fasted for long periods.

St Salvatore went to Sardinia at the instruction of his superiors but while he was there he developed a severe illness which was to prove fatal. He died at Cagliari at the age of 47.

St Samson *Feast day: 28 July. Born in Glamorgan, Wales; died in 565.* Samson's parents entrusted him to the safekeeping of **St Illtyd** at the monastery of Lianwit in south Glamorgan where he was educated and later ordained a priest.

St Illtyd's nephews were jealous of the affection he received from their uncle, and as soon as he became aware of this, Samson withdrew to live as a monk in a community on Caldey Island. When he was chosen to be abbot after the previous incumbent died, his uncle, Umbrafel, and his father, Amon, came to join him there. However, Samson felt the need to retreat once again and, accompanied by Amon, who had been cured of a severe illness through Samson's ministrations, and two others, he set up a hermitage on the banks of the river Severn.

During a trip to Cornwall, Samson was consecrated a bishop and again appointed as an abbot. He left England and travelled to Brittany via the Channel Islands, one of which is named after him. He spent the rest of his life as a roving missionary bishop in the style of the early Celtic Church, and founded monasteries in Normandy before dying peacefully in the company of his monks.

St Saturninus *Feast day: 11 February. Born in North Africa; died in 304.* St Saturninus was a priest at Abitina, a city 40 miles inland from Carthage in northern Africa. One Sunday a troop of soldiers disrupted the morning worship of his congregation of 49 people; the Emperor Diocletian, on discovering the important role that the Holy Scriptures held for the Christian faith, had commanded that all Church manuscripts be handed over under pain of death. Saturninus was among those who held out against this demand to the end, although others argued that lives were more precious than manuscripts or books, and therefore complied with the order. Saturninus' four children, young Saturninus, Felix, Mary, and Hilarianus were in the congregation that day and were arrested with him.

At the trial, the accused confessed Jesus Christ so bravely that even the judges applauded their courage, but still felt compelled to condemn them to death. The faithful group were shackled and sent to the proconsul in Carthage. They sang hymns and canticles all the way, praising and thanking God. The entire congregation died in prison as a result of privations or torture.

St Sava of Serbia *Feast day: 14 January. Born in Rastko in Serbia, 1173; died in 1235.* Patron of Serbia. Sava, the son of the Serbian King Stephen I, fled to Mount Athos when he was 17 to avoid marriage. He became a monk and founded the Hilander Monastery. In 1196, his father abdicated, took the name Simeon and went to join his son. Together they founded Khilandrai Monastery on Mount Athos for Serbian monks and Sava became the first abbot. St Simeon died three years later, and Sava, by now Archbishop of Serbia, took his father's relics back to their native land in 1208.

When his brothers, Stephen II and Vulkan, began to quarrel, Sava returned home once again in order to help resolve their dispute, bringing with him many of his monks from Mount Athos. He founded several monasteries and began the reformation and education of his homeland. Sava wrote a history of his father's reign, a Serbian hymnography in Church Slavonic and had liturgical documents translated from Greek into Serbian.

Sava opposed the pro-Roman policies and eventually persuaded the patriarch of Constantinople to grant the Serbian and Bulgarian Churches separate headship. Through his patient diplomacy, he was able to unite of his people, a process that his father had begun.

He resigned as archbishop in 1230 and then made a pilgrimage to the Holy Land where he visited various monasteries. He died at Tirnovo, Bulgaria, on his way back from a second visit there on an ecclesiastical mission.

St Scholastica *Feast day: 10 February. Died in 543*. Scholastica was the sister of **St Benedict**. After he had established the monastery at Monte Cassino, she founded a nunnery five miles away at Plombariola and Scholastica and her brother arranged to meet once a year at a house some distance from the monastery, to discuss spiritual matters.

On the occasion of their final meeting St Scholastica begged her brother to remain longer and tell her about the joys of heaven but St Benedict felt unable to stay. In order to delay his departure, Scholastica prayed for rain and a furious thunderstorm broke out which forced St Benedict to spend the whole night with his sister, which they spent in intense and joyful spiritual discussion. Three days later, St Scholastica died and her brother arranged for her to be laid in the tomb he had prepared for himself. St Benedict died a few years later.

St Sebastian *Feast day: 20 December. Born in Narbonne, Gaul; died in 300*. Patron of archers, athletes, and soldiers, and is appealed to for protection against plagues.

Sebastian's family originated from Milan, which was where he spent his childhood. He was a fervent Christian and, though not naturally inclined to the life of a soldier, he joined the Roman army in 283, with a view to aiding those who had been imprisoned for their faith.

Sebastian was able to maintain close contact with **Sts Mark and Marcellian**, and to encourage them to remain faithful. There were numerous converts among the guards and prison staff around the time of their imprisonment, and several significant healings are recorded.

Emperor Diocletian admired the courage and character of Sebastian and, unaware that he was a Christian, promoted him to the privileged position of captain in the praetorian guards. When it was discovered that he was indeed a Christian, Diocletian accused him of ingratitude and handed him over to a group of archers from Mauritania to be shot to death.

His body was pierced through with arrows and he was left for dead, but the widow of St Castulus found him still breathing and nursed him back to health. Rather than retreat into hiding, Sebastian took up his stance on a stairway where the emperor was known to pass and confronted him concerning his cruel treatment of Christians. After a brief moment of surprise, the emperor recovered himself and gave the order that Sebastian be beaten to death. The order was obeyed without question.

St Sebbi *Feast day: 29 August. Born in Essex, England; died in 694.* Sebbi became the King of Essex (or the East Saxons) following the conversion of the kingdom by **St Cedd** in 664. Sebbi had a gentle disposition and was a wise ruler, more suited to being a bishop than a king. He encouraged the missionary enterprise of Bishop Jaruman of Mercia in the subsequent period of relative peace. After ruling for 30 years, Sebbi abdicated and became a monk in London. He died there and was buried by the north wall of the old cathedral of St Paul's in London.

St Senan *Feast day: 8 March. Born in Munster, Ireland; died in 544.* Senan was born of Christian parents, and served as a soldier for a time. He became a monk under Abbot Cassidus, who sent him to Abbot St Natalis at Kilmanagh.

Known for his holiness and miracles, his sermons attracted great crowds. He made a pilgrimage to Rome and on his return passed through Wales. Here he spent some time with **St David**, and on his departure David presented him with his own staff, which Senan brought back to Ireland. He built several churches and monasteries, including one on Scattery Island which became his permanent residence.

Aware that he was close to death, Senan undertook one final visit to St Cassidus' monastery. On the return journey, in a field near Killeochailli, he heard a voice saying, 'Senan, servant of God, thou art called to heaven,' and he passed away soon after.

St Seraphim of Sarov *Feast day: 2 January. Born near Moscow, 1759; died in 1833. Canonized in the Orthodox Church in 1903.* Seraphim was the son of a builder and was originally named Prokhor Moshnin. He adopted his new name upon entering a monastery at Sarov in 1777. Soon after his ordination to the priesthood in 1793, he began to live as a solitary in a forest hut two hours from the abbey. He imitated **St Simeon the Stylite** for a time, living on top of a high rocky outcrop.

In 1804, robbers attacked him with his own axe, and left him for dead. Seraphim managed to drag himself to the monastery and, after being nursed for five months, he recovered well enough to return to the forest. Following this incident he had a permanent stoop and was unable to walk properly with out the help of a stick.

After 25 years of the solitary life, and as a result of a vision, he began to give time to the spiritual direction of others, and disciples from far and wide flocked to him.

His teachings have been the source of many books and he has become well known in the Western Churches as an example of the ideal spiritual leader. Seraphim is best known for his clear teaching on the transforming love of the Holy Spirit.

St Serf *Feast day: 1 July. Born in Fife, Scotland in the sixth century.* Serf was a Scottish bishop who founded a monastery at Culross in the West Fife region. There is a cave at nearby Dysart where Serf wrestled with the devil and won. He is associated with mission work in the Orkney Islands.

St Sergius *Feast day: 25 September. Born in Rostov, Russia, 1315; died in 1392. Canonized in 1449 by Pope Nicholas V.* Sergius, originally know as Bartholomew, was born into a noble family. At the age of 15, he fled with his family to Radonezh, near Moscow, to escape political persecution.

The family lost everything and became peasant farmers until 1335, when his parents died. He and his brother became hermits together at Makovka, and his reputation for spiritual wisdom and holiness spread widely. Sergius was a big-bearded man said to 'smell of fresh fir wood' and to be a 'befriender of bears'. He attracted followers and organized them into a community, which soon became established as the monastery of the Holy Trinity.

Sergius became abbot, was ordained priest at Pereyaslav Zalesky and set about restoring the monastic tradition that had been destroyed by Mongol invasions. His brother Stephen soon joined him, but opposed his extreme rule of life and was elected as leader in his stead. Sergius left to become a hermit again, but the monastery declined rapidly and he was asked to return by Alexis, Metropolitan of Moscow, which he did.

In 1380, during a time of great national danger, Prince Dimitri Donskoi came to consult Sergius as to whether he should fight the superior Tatar army or withdraw. After prayerful consideration, Sergius advised the former, and Donskoi won a famous victory at Kulikovo.

He resigned as abbot in 1392 and died six months later.

St Silas *Feast day: 13 July. Born in the first century.* Silas was a leader in the Jerusalem Church. He was sent to Antioch with **Sts Paul** and **Barnabas**, to pass on the decisions of the Council of Jerusalem to the Gentile community in Syria. Paul chose Silas to accompany him on his second missionary journey to Syria, Cilicia and Macedonia.

He was beaten and imprisoned with Paul at Philippi, and was caught up in the riot of Jews at Thessalonica which drove Paul and himself from the city to Beroea. Silas remained there with **Timothy** when Paul left, but later rejoined him at Corinth. He was the first Bishop of Corinth and died in Macedonia.

St Simeon Metaphrastes *Feast day: 28 November. Born in the tenth century.* Simeon was a civil servant who became a monk in old age. He was a meticulous recorder and careful scribe who was appointed by the Emperor Constantine VII to make a compilation of the lives of the saints from the oral tradition and the various written sources. He copied some lives as written, rewrote others and arranged the lives in the order of their feast days. He also wrote a history of the world and a collection of the sayings of the Church fathers.

St Simeon Stylites *Feast day: 5 January. Born in Sis, Cilicia (Syria), 390; died at Telenissus in 459.* Simeon was the devout son of a Cilician shepherd. He was given permission to join a monastery near his home but after two years found the discipline too lax for him. He became a monk at a stricter monastery ruled by Heliodorus at Eusebona near Antioch.

While there, Simeon nearly died through extreme austere practice of wearing a tight rope of palm leaves around his waist. This had to be cut out of him over three days and he was dismissed for his unwillingness to curb his extreme practices.

After sleeping rough for many years he made a cell for himself out of stones on top of Mount Teleanissae near Antioch. His reputation for holiness spread and crowds flocked to him.

In 423 Simeon erected a pillar three meters high and two meters in diameter and lived on top of it for about four years. In following years he lived on successively higher pillars ('stylos' in Greek). Simeon's last pillar was 20 meters high. He preached twice daily exhorting his listeners to greater holiness and many who heard him were converted. He also sorted out disputes among individuals and even whole tribes.

Full of kindliness and compassion Simeon spoke out in particular against swearing and usury. His body was buried at Antioch, accompanied by bishops and many of the faithful.

St Simon Stock *Feast day: 16 May. Born in Aylesford, England; died in Bordeaux, 1265.* The reference to 'stock', meaning tree trunk, in Simon's name comes from the fact that from the age of 12 he lived as a hermit in the hollow trunk of an ancient tree.

As a young man, he went on a pilgrimage to the Holy Land where he joined a group of Carmelites and returned with them to Europe. He founded many Carmelite Communities in England and France and helped transform the Carmelites from hermits into wandering monks before being elected superior-general in 1254.

The distinctive brown woollen garment known as a scapular that is worn by the Carmelites was communicated to him in a vision; in it the Virgin Mary promised that any who died wearing this garment would be saved.

St Simon the Zealot *Feast day: 28 October. Born in Palestine in the first century.* Simon was one of the original followers of Christ who was known as 'the Zealot' because of his strict and fervent adherence to the Jewish and Canaanite law. After the resurrection of Christ, he preached in Egypt and then went to Persia with St Jude, where both suffered martyrdom.

St Sixtus II *Feast day: 6 August. Born in Greece of Roman descent; died in 258.* Sixtus II was elected to the papacy in 257.

Sixtus mediated in the dispute between Rome and Carthage that had developed over the issue of baptism and rebaptism. While holding to the orthodox belief on baptism, he was persuaded by three letters from **St**

Dionysius of Alexandria not to act hastily and to be prepared to tolerate rebaptism. The matter was finally settled by the decision of a plenary council which is recorded by **St Augustine**.

The Emperor Valerian published his first decree against Christians in the same year that Sixtus was made pope, and persecutions soon followed. Though Sixtus was forbidden to hold services, he continued to do so, worshipping in the chapel in the cemetery of Prætextatus. One day, during one of the pope's sermons, soldiers broke into the chapel and beheaded him. Four of his eight attendant deacons were also beheaded, the others being executed later.

St Stanislaus *Feast day: 11 April. Born in Szczepanow near Cracow, Poland; died in 1079. Canonized in 1253 by Pope Innocent IV.* Patron of Cracow.

Stanislaus was born of noble parents and educated at Gnesen. He was later ordained and given a canonry by Bishop Lampert Zula of Cracow, where he became noted for his preaching, spiritual advice and reforms.

In 1072 Stanislaus was named Bishop of Cracow and expressed his disapproval of King Boleslaus the Bold, who had kidnapped the wife of a nobleman, by formally excommunicating him. Stanislaus enraged the king by stopping services at the Cathedral whenever he entered, and Boleslaus arranged to have the bishop murdered while he was saying Mass in a chapel outside the city. When his guards refused to comply, he carried out the deed himself.

St Stephen *Feast day: 26 December. Born in Palestine; died in the first century.* Patron of stonemasons.

Stephen, whose name means 'crown', was the first of Jesus' disciples to be martyred. He was one of the seven helpers or deacons appointed to look after the widows in the daily distribution of alms in the early Jerusalem Church.

He preached with such great power and grace that many who heard him became followers of Jesus. Those in authority were furious at Stephen's success and, being unable to counter his arguments, they arranged for false accusations to be made about him. Stephen, his face shining like an angel, chastised his enemies for not having believed in Jesus, and they rose in anger, dragged him outside the city of Jerusalem and stoned him to death.

The saint prayed, 'Lord Jesus, receive my spirit,' then he fell to his knees and begged God not to punish his enemies for killing him.

St Stephen I *Feast day: 2 August. Born in Rome; died in 257.* Stephen was a priest when elected to the papacy in 254. He believed that baptism was a sacrament that needed to be administered only once, even if heretics had done the baptizing. He had a disagreement with **St Cyprian of Carthage** over this issue as well as over the pope's decision to reinstate two Spanish bishops who had been synodically deposed. Stephen I defended the right of the bishops to appeal to Rome and was the first pope to use St Peter as an argument for Rome's primacy. He died a martyr during the persecutions of Emperor Valerian.

St Stephen the Great *Feast day: 16 August. Born in Hungary in 975; died in 1038. Canonized in 1083 by Pope Gregory VII.* Patron of Hungary.

Stephen was the son of the Magyar chieftain Geza, whom he succeeded as leader in 997. He was raised as a Christian and in 996 married the daughter of Duke Henry II of Bavaria and devoted much of his energy to promoting the Christian faith.

He supported Church leaders, and helped build churches, completing the monastery at Martinsberg that his father had begun. Stephen treated the clergy with great honour and respect, gradually establishing Sees and appointing clergy as bishops. Every tenth town had to build a church and support a priest, while the king himself furnished the churches. He forcibly converted rebels and repressed blasphemy, murder, theft, adultery and other public crimes.

Stephen was anointed king of Hungary in 1000, receiving the cross and crown from Pope Sylvester II. These were to become beloved symbols of the Hungarian nation, and Stephen was venerated as the ideal Christian king.

St Susanna *Feast day: 11 August. Born in Romè; died in 295.* Susanna was the daughter of a well-educated priest named Gabinius, and a niece of Pope Caius. She not only refused Emperor Diocletian's request that she marry his son-in-law, Maximian, but also converted two of her uncles, Claudius and Maximus, who had been sent to her by the emperor to persuade her to marry.

Diocletian was so angry about this that he sent Julian, who was one of his court favourites, to deal with the matter. Julian had the newly converted officials and their families burnt at Cumae, following which both Susanna and her father were beheaded.

St Swithun *Feast day: 15 July. Born in Wessex, England; died in 862.* Swithun was educated at the old monastery at Winchester, where he was also ordained. He became chaplain to King Egbert of the West Saxons, and tutor to the king's son, Ethelwulf.

When Ethelwulf succeeded his father as king in 852, Swithun was named Bishop of Winchester. He was known for his charity and humility, and built several churches.

Many miraculous signs followed his death and when the first monastic chapter was introduced into the cathedral of Winchester, St Swithun's remains were transferred there. This event was accompanied by an extreme thunderstorm and gave rise to the popular folk myth that if it rains on St Swithun's day, it will rain for the next 40 days.

St Sylvester *Feast day: 31 December. Born in Rome; died in 335.* Sylvester lived through the years of persecution by Diocletian and survived to see the triumph of Constantine in the year 312. Two years later, he succeeded St Melchiades as Bishop of Rome. The Council of Nicea was assembled during his reign in the year 325, and although he was unable to attend due to his advanced age, his delegated advisors headed the list of those subscribing to its decrees. St Sylvester was pope for almost 25 years.

St Sylvia *Feast day: 5 November. Born in Sicily; died in 593.* Sylvia was the mother of **St Gregory the Great**, his father being St Gordian. They came from a region near Rome. When his father died in 573, St Gregory converted his paternal home into a monastery and Sylvia retired to a solitary life in a small house near the Church of St Sava on the Aventine.

Sylvia's practice of sending fresh vegetables to her son on a silver platter ended on the day that St Gregory found himself with nothing to give a poor beggar, and gave him the plate instead.

After his mother's death, St Gregory arranged for a picture of both his parents to be placed in the Church of St Andrew in Rome.

St Symeon the New Theologian *Feast day: 12 March. Born in Galatia, in 949; died in 1022.* Symeon was born into a Byzantine provincial noble family. When he was 14 years old he met St Symeon the Pious who was to become his spiritual father. He advised him not to enter monastic life straight away, but to wait and prepare himself properly, which he obediently did.

During this period while Symeon was busy building a successful career for himself in the world, even to the extent of rising to the rank of imperial senator, he was also living a secret life as a monk. One of his elders had wisely advised him, 'Pay heed to your conscience and without fail do what it will instil in you.'

He eventually entered the monastery at Studios at the age of 27, so he could continue his studies and be closer to his mentor. However, Symeon's perceived dependence on his teacher caused friction with the authorities and he was instructed to move to another monastery in order to allow some space to develop between them. When this reverence continued even after the death of his spiritual guide, Symeon was exiled to a small hermitage on the Bosphorus.

It was here that he wrote his greatest works of theology and poetry, and in a short time others had come to join him until the hermitage had grown into a full monastery.

T

St Tarasius *Feast Day: 10 March. Born in Constantinople; died in 806.* Tarasius was born into an affluent Christian family, received an excellent education, and became a senator at a young age. In 783 when Patriarch Paul died, Tarasius was elected to succeed him. Tarasius agreed, but on condition that an Ecumenical Council was called to suppress the heresy of Iconoclasm*. The Empress Irene fully supported him and a council of over 300 bishops was convened in 787. It recommended that icons be given a special place in Orthodox worship.

Tarasius died peacefully after serving the Church as bishop for 22 years.

St Tatwin *Feast day: 30 July. Born in Mercia, England; died in 741.* Tatwin became a monk at Bredon and eventually, in 731, was named Archbishop of Canterbury in succession to Brithwald. **St Bede** thought highly of him, and he was the author of several works, including an improved grammar, a book of riddles written in acrostic style, and some poetry.

St Teilo *Feast day: 9 February. Born in Penally in Pembrokeshire, Wales in the sixth century.* Teilo studied under Sts Dyfrig and Dubricius. He accompanied **St David** of Wales to Jerusalem and was a friend and assistant to **St Samson** in Brittany for seven years.

On his return to Wales in 554 he proved to be an effective preacher and founded Llandaff monastery in Dyfed, Wales, serving as abbot-bishop there. He was buried in Llandaff Cathedral.

St Teresa de los Andes *Feast day: 13 July. Born in Santiago, Chile, 1900; died in 1920. Canonized 1993 by Pope John Paul II.* Teresa was baptized Juanita Fernandez Solar and was devoted to Christ from a very young age. She made a private vow of celibacy at 15 and, having read the life of **St Teresa of Avila**, she entered the Discalced Carmelite monastery at Los Andes in 1919. She had just begun to write spiritual letters, which showed the depth of her insight and wisdom, when she caught typhus and, having made her religious profession, died soon after. She was the first Chilean to be beatified or canonized.

St Teresa of Avila *Feast day: 15 October Born in Avila in Spain, 1515; died in 1582. Canonized in 1622 by Pope Gregory XV.* Patron of headache sufferers.

Teresa's father, who was rigidly pious, told her never to lie; her mother, who loved to read romantic novels, asked her to keep this a secret. Thus, as a child, she experienced great tensions and at the age of five attempted to run away from home, having persuaded her elder brother to go with her as her companion. Their plan had been to go to Morocco and die as martyrs.

As a teenager she was convinced that she was a horrible sinner, finding that she cared deeply only about worldly things. When she was 16, her father arranged for her to be educated in a local convent, and following this Teresa chose to enter a Carmelite convent. However, things had become very lax and Teresa found it all too easy to become involved in flattery and gossip.

She fell ill with malaria, and after being unconscious for four days was left partly paralyzed for three years and never completely recovered. Following her sickness she stopped praying completely and for years she hardly prayed at all. It was not until she was 41, though still finding it difficult, that she began to pray again and profound spiritual experiences followed. For example, if she felt God was going to levitate her body, she stretched out on the floor and called the nuns to sit on her and hold her down. She begged God not to give her any more public manifestations.

Teresa cut off all connections with her friends without explanation in the belief that she had to be friends with God alone. She explained that Jesus had told her, 'Teresa, that's how I treat my friends.' Teresa responded, 'No wonder you have so few friends.'

In the face of much opposition, she set about reforming her Carmelite order and began by founding a new convent based on the simple contemplative life. She saw spiritual life as an attitude of love, not a rule, and she believed in work, not in begging.

Some in authority began to question the reality of her experiences and actions and Teresa was ordered to write an account of her life; after reading it, the Inquisition cleared her of all charges.

The leader of the Carmelite order excommunicated the nuns of Teresa's former convent when they elected her prioress. However, many were eager to learn from Teresa, and soon she had many postulants entering her convents of reformed Carmelites. Her teaching about prayer spread far beyond Spain.

Teresa died at the age of 67, soon after returning from founding a new convent at Burgos. In 1970, Teresa was the first woman to be made a Doctor of the Church for her writing on prayer.

Mother Teresa of Calcutta *Feast day: 5 September. Born in Skopje, Macedonia 1910; died in 2001.* Teresa's father died when she was only eight years old and her mother, a devoutly religious woman, opened a clothes business to support the family. After being involved in parish activities in her youth, she was admitted as a postulant of the Loreto Convent in Rathfarnam (Dublin), Ireland, in 1928, where she received the name Teresa.

In 1929 she was sent by her order to work in Darjeeling, India, where she joined the Loreto novitiate, making her final profession as a Loreto nun in 1937. Hereafter she was called Mother Teresa and for many years worked as a teacher in St Mary's School, Calcutta.

In 1946, while on a train journey from Calcutta to Darjeeling, Mother Teresa received a 'call within a call', which was to give rise to the Missionaries of Charity. The aim of the mission was 'to quench the infinite thirst of Jesus on the cross for love and souls' by 'labouring at the salvation and sanctification of the poorest of the poor'.

Mother Teresa expanded the work of the Missionaries of Charity in Calcutta and across India, and the Society also branched out into Europe (the Tor Fiscale suburb of Rome) and Africa (Tabora, Tanzania). She also opened houses in Australia, the Middle East and North America, and the first novitiate outside Calcutta was in London.

In 1979, Mother Teresa was awarded the Nobel Peace Prize and by this time there were 158 Missionaries of Charity foundations. These reached into Communist countries, with houses in almost all Communist nations, but in spite of her very best efforts, Mother Teresa was never able to open a foundation in China.

She spoke at the 40th anniversary of the United Nations General Assembly, in 1985, and that same year, she opened her first house for AIDS patients in New York. In the coming years, this home was followed by others in the United States and elsewhere, all devoted specifically to those with AIDS.

New communities were founded in South Africa, Albania, Cuba and war-torn Iraq, and by 1997 her sisters numbered nearly 4,000 members, and were established in almost 600 foundations in 123 countries of the world. Following a period of intense world travel, Mother Teresa returned to Calcutta and died at the mother house.

She received a state funeral, her body being taken in procession on the same gun carriage that had borne the bodies of Mahatma Gandhi and Jawaharlal Nehru.

St Thecla *Feast day: 23 September. Born in Iconomium, Asia Minor in the first century.* Thecla was so influenced by the preaching of **St Paul** on virginity that she broke off her engagement and decided to live a celibate life. Paul was scourged and banished from the city for his teaching and the order was given to burn Thecla to death. A sudden rainstorm put the fire out, and she rejoined Paul at Myra in Lycia. Dressed as a boy she was commissioned by him to preach the Gospel, which she did for some time, before becoming a recluse in a cave at Meriamlik near Seleucia. She lived there until her death 72 years later.

St Theobald *Feast day: 30 June. Born in Provins, Brie in France, 1017; died in 1066. Canonized in 1073 by Pope Alexander II.* Theobald was the son of Count Arnoul of Champagne. He went into the army, but at the age of 18 he gave up his military career in order to live the life of a hermit at Sussy in the Ardennes, then at Pittingen in the Diocese of Trier in Luxembourg. He was joined in this way of life by his close friend Walter.

After several years, which included pilgrimages to Compostella in Spain, and to Rome, they settled at Salanigo, near Vicenza, Italy, where Theobald was ordained a priest. After two years Walter died, but others gathered around Theobald, including his mother, Gisela, who became a hermitess near his place of retreat. Before his death, Theobald became a member of the Camaldolese order.

St Theodore I *Feast day: 14 May. Born in Jerusalem; died in 649.* Theodore, the son of a bishop of Greek nationality, came to Rome to escape the Arab invasions of the Holy Land, and was elected to the papacy in 642. He opposed Monothelitism* and received the repentance of Patriarch Pyrrhus of Constantinople, whom **St Maximus the Confessor** had humiliated in public debate. However, Pyrrhus soon relapsed into his old ways. Theodore also called a council at the Lateran to condemn Monothelitism.*

St Theodore of Canterbury *Feast day: 19 September. Born in Tarsus in Turkey, 602; died in 690.* Theodore was of Greek descent and studied at Tarsus and Athens before going to Rome. He became highly respected by Pope Vitalian, who appointed him to the See of Canterbury in 667. However, this was rather a dubious honour since others had already declined this difficult role. Consecrated in 668, Theodore set out for England in the company of **St Benedict Biscop** and others.

He convened synods at Hereford in 673 and at Hatfield in 680, and was a successful and well-respected administrator who helped to organize the English Church into diocese and parishes for the first time. **St Bede** wrote that Theodore was 'the first archbishop obeyed by all the English Church'.

St Theodore of Studites *Feast day: 11 November. Born in Valis' evo near Kiev, 759; died in 826.* Theodore was the son of an imperial treasurer and the nephew of St Pluto, who was an abbot of a monastery at Saccudium in Bithynia, Asia Minor. He entered his uncle's community in 780 and succeeded him as abbot in 794.

Theodore and his brother monks opposed the adulterous marriage of Emperor Constantine VI and were banished. In 797 Constantine's mother Irene seized power, dethroned and then blinded her son, and Theodore and his community returned. Two years later, in order to escape the growing influence of the Arabs, they moved to the ancient rundown monastery of Studites. The monastery prospered under Theodore's care and grew to become one of the most important in the whole of the Eastern Church with over 1,000 members.

In 809 Theodore was exiled again by Emperor Nicephorus I but was recalled in 811, when he spoke out against the 'icon-smashing' policies of Emperor Leo V. In revenge, the emperor had him seized, cruelly abused, and banished. Nine years later he was once again recalled, this time by the Emperor Michael II, but this time Theodore didn't return and died some years later just outside Constantinople.

Theodore was remembered for his personal holiness, preaching skills and his prolific writings, which included over 500 letters, hymns and sermons.

St Theodore of Sykeon *Feast day: 22 April. Born in Sykeon in Galatia, Asia Minor; died in 613.* Theodore's father was a Byzantine imperial messenger and his mother a prostitute. He entered a monastery in

Jerusalem where he served for many years before becoming abbot of a number of monastic institutions.

He predicted the rise to power of Emperor Maurice and cured a royal prince of leprosy, later being appointed Bishop of Anastasiopolis, Galatia in 590.

St Theodosius Pechersky *Feast day: 10 July. Born in Russia; died in 1074. Canonized in 1108 by Pope Paschal II.* Theodosius gave up a comfortable existence as son of a wealthy family to work the fields with the humble peasants before entering the monastery of the Caves in Kiev in about 1032. He eventually became abbot of the community and introduced a less severe rule of life for the monks. He promoted a spiritual way of life in the region around Kiev, helping the poor, establishing hospitals, and taking a lively interest in local politics.

Theodosius established 'the Caves' which was to become one of the leading monastic institutions in Russia.

St Theophan *Feast day: 6 January. Born in Russia, 1815; died in 1891.* Theophan, whose father was a priest, studied under harsh conditions to become a monk. As a young man he was counselled by the Elder Hieromonk Partheny 'to pray unceasingly in your mind and heart to God'.

In 1859 he was consecrated Bishop of Tambov where he established a school for girls. In the summer of 1863 he was transferred to Vladimir and opened another school for girls there. However, in 1866, much disturbed by human corruption, he asked to be relieved of his position as Bishop of Vladimir. His simple trust in people, which he found to be often abused, made it very difficult for him to be a bishop.

He also felt the call to spiritual writing and over the years produced numerous volumes. In 1872 Theophan stopped going to the monastery church, and built a small church in his own room. He painted excellent icons and was skilled as a woodcarver and locksmith.

Every day Bishop Theophan received between 20 and 40 letters, and he answered them all. In 1891 he was found lying lifeless on his bed.

St Theresa of Lisieux *Feast day: 1 October. Born in Alençon, 1873; died in Algeria, 1897. Canonized in 1925 by Pope Pius XI.* Patron of African missions and people with AIDS.

Theresa's father was a watchmaker and her mother died of breast cancer when Theresa was four. She and her three sisters all became Carmelite nuns. Though she was the youngest, Theresa was the third to do so at the age of 15.

She discovered a natural and simple way of holiness and piety early in life. Known to be extremely sensitive to criticism she found loud and aggressive behaviour most distressing and was known to cry easily. Theresa believed that love showed itself best by actions, and that while she could not do great deeds, she could at least make every glance, word and action as full of love as possible.

In 1896, she began to cough up blood, the first sign of the tuberculosis which was to prove fatal, but kept this secret for a year. In obedience, she agreed to dictate her autobiography *The Story of a Soul*. It was edited by one of her sisters, and 2,000 copies were circulated to other convents. In the book Theresa described simple and childlike ways in which to find holiness in ordinary life. It proved to be very popular and within a short time it had been translated into several languages. She died in the convent infirmary at the age of 24.

St Thomas *Feast day: 3 July. Born in Palestine in the first century.* Patron of architects.

Thomas, known as Didymus (meaning 'the twin'), was of Jewish ancestry and a dedicated but impetuous follower of Christ. He encouraged the other disciples to accompany Jesus on the trip that involved certain danger and possible death. At the Last Supper, Thomas pleaded that they did not understand how to proceed and received the assurance from Jesus that he was the Way, the Truth, and the Life.

Thomas was absent when the other disciples first saw the risen Lord on the evening of the first Easter Sunday and his scepticism earned him the title of 'doubting Thomas'. A week later when Christ appeared a second time, he gently rebuked Thomas for his lack of faith, and showed him the evidence that he had asked for – the nail prints in his hands and spear wound in his side.

He was also present at the resurrection appearance of Jesus at Lake Tiberias.

After Pentecost, Thomas was sent to evangelize the Parthians, Medes, and Persians and went on to share his faith in India. He was speared to death at Calamine.

St Thomas Aquinas *Feast day: 28 January. Born in Rocca Secca near Aquino in Italy, 1225; died in 1274. Canonized in 1323 by Pope John XXII.* Declared a Doctor of the Church by Pope Pius V (1566–72).

Thomas was the son of Landulph, Count of Aquino, and at the age of five he was placed in the care of the Benedictines of Monte Casino by his father. Despite family opposition, he decided to join the Dominicans of Naples when he was 17.

He studied at Cologne under the celebrated **St Albert the Great** and was nicknamed the 'dumb ox' because of his huge frame and reticence, although he was in reality a brilliant student. At the age of 22 he was appointed as a teacher and began to publish his writings. After four years he was sent to Paris, where he received his doctorate and frequently dined with King Louis IX.

In 1261 Urban IV called him to Rome as a teacher, but he also preached very powerfully and productively. By this time he had filled 20 large volumes with his writings but he never completed his greatest work, the *Summa Theologica*. In 1274, on his way to the second Council of Lyon, he fell sick and died at the Cistercian monastery of Fossa Nuova.

Thomas was one of the greatest and most influential theologians of all time.

St Thomas Becket *Feast day: 29 December. Born in London, 1118; died in Canterbury, 1170. Canonized in 1173 by Pope Alexander III.* Thomas was the son of the sheriff of London and both of his parents were of Norman blood. He was educated at a school of canons regular at Merton Priory in Sussex, and later at the University of Paris. His parents had died when he returned from France and he found a job as clerk to the sheriff's court, at which he excelled.

He was strongly built and loved the outdoors, spending his leisure time in hawking and hunting. He was given a post in the household of St Theobald, Archbishop of Canterbury, and in due course was given permission to study canon law at the University of Bologna, and at Auxerre, France.

On his return to England, Thomas became provost of Beverley, and a canon at Lincoln and St Paul's cathedrals. He was appointed Archdeacon of Canterbury, the highest ecclesiastical office in England, and then chancellor, or chief minister to the king.

Thomas was ambitious and had a taste for the finer things in life. He was a close personal friend of the young monarch and when, in 1159, King Henry raised an army of mercenaries in France to regain a part of the inheritance of his wife, Eleanor of Aquitaine, Thomas actively supported him.

Two years later, the king appointed Thomas Primate of England, despite warnings from Thomas, that he could not simply be the king's puppet. In fact, Thomas rejected the post until he was persuaded to accept by the papal legate, Cardinal Henry of Pisa.

In 1162 Thomas rode to Canterbury to be ordained and shortly after was consecrated archbishop. From that day on, Thomas' way of life changed dramatically. He adopted an ascetic lifestyle, spending much time in the distribution of alms, reading and study, while overseeing the work of the Church.

Relations between Archbishop Thomas and the King slowly deteriorated and finally broke down completely over the tax payments demanded of the Church by the king.

Canon Philip de Brois was accused of murdering a soldier but, when he was tried and acquitted in an ecclesiastical court, King Henry was deeply dissatisfied with the outcome and demanded that, from then on, the clergy should be subject to the civil court system.

The king also ordered Thomas to give up certain castles and honours, and attempted to discredit him with charges of financial dishonesty. He commanded Thomas to submit his accounts, which he refused to do, saying that he was under God's (and his earthly representative the Pope's) judgement alone. The quarrel dragged on for three years, until an uneasy truce was finally agreed between Thomas and Henry. However, one day soon after, the King, in a fit of rage, pronounced, 'Who will rid me of this troublesome priest?' Several of his hearers took this to be a genuine request for action, and four of his knights at once set off for Canterbury.

They found Thomas in the Cathedral and slew him with their swords, before rushing away, waving their weapons excitedly.

When the King learned of what had happened he was grief stricken to think that his remark should have been so misconstrued. He shut himself away and fasted for 40 days, later performing public penance in Canterbury Cathedral before receiving formal absolution.

St Thomas Garnet *Feast day: 23 June. Born in Southwark, England; died in 1608. Canonized in 1970 by Pope Paul VI.* Thomas, the nephew of a Jesuit priest called Henry Garnet, studied for the priesthood at St Omer, France, and Valladolid, Spain. He was ordained as a secular priest, later joined the Jesuits and was instructed to go to England to do missionary work. Thomas, who had been staying in the home of one of the conspirators implicated in the Gunpowder Plot, was arrested. After months of torture during which he could not be persuaded to give any useful information to the authorities he was deported to Flanders. He returned to England the following year but was arrested within six weeks, charged with high treason, found guilty and hanged at Tyburn.

St Thomas More *Feast day: 22 June. Born in London, 1478; died in 1535.* Patron of lawyers.

Thomas studied law at Oxford and then began a legal career which eventually led him to enter Parliament. In 1505 he married Jane Colt and they had four children, but when Jane died young he married a widow called Alice Middleton.

He wrote a famous book entitled *Utopia* and became a friend of Henry VIII, who finally made him Lord Chancellor in 1529. He resigned in 1532, having disagreed with the king's planned divorce from Catherine of Aragon, and defended the supremacy of the pope in spiritual matters. He spent his remaining years writing mostly in defence of the Church.

Thomas was imprisoned in the Tower of London and was later tried and convicted of treason after telling the court that he could not go against his conscience. On the scaffold, he told the crowd of spectators that he was dying as 'the King's good servant, but God's first'. He was beheaded on July 6, 1535.

St Thomas of Villanueva *Feast day: 22 September. Born in Fuentellana in Spain, 1486; died in 1555. Canonized in 1658 by Pope Alexander VII.*

Thomas, the son of a miller, went to study theology at the University of Alcala, becoming a professor there at the age of 26. In 1516 he declined the chair of philosophy at the University of Salamanca and instead became an Augustinian Friar in that same town. Following his ordination in 1520, he served as prior to several houses including Salamanca and Burgos, and then became court chaplain to the Holy Roman Emperor Charles V.

He sent the first Augustinian missionaries to the New World, where they subsequently helped evangelize the area of modern Mexico. Thomas reluctantly accepted the appointment as Archbishop of Valencia in 1544, a See that had been vacant for nearly a century. He devoted much effort to restoring the spiritual and material life, caring deeply for the poor, and founding colleges for the children of new converts.

He organized priests to serve amongst the Moors, many of whom had been converted but were then left uncared for both spiritually and practically. He was renowned for his personal holiness and while he was excused attendance at the Council of Trent, he strongly supported that council's reforms.

St Thorfinn *Feast day: 8 January. Born in Trondheim, Norway; died in 1285.* Fifty years after his death, Thorfinn's tomb was opened during some building work and it was discovered that his remains gave out a strong and pleasing smell.

The Abbot made inquiries, and found an old monk named Walter de Muda who remembered Bishop Thorfinn and his gentle goodness. On Thorfinn's death, Walter had written a poem about him, and he was able to find this parchment, just where he had left it. Walter, who was a Canon of the Cathedral of Nidaros, was instructed to write down his memories of Thorfinn.

He recalled that King Eric had repudiated an earlier agreement between Church and state, thus causing a fierce dispute. The King outlawed the Archbishop, John, and his two chief supporters, Bishop Andrew of Oslo and Bishop Thorfinn of Hamar. Bishop Thorfinn, after many hardships, including shipwreck, travelled to the Abbey of Ter Doest in Flanders. This abbey had a number of links with the Norwegian Church.

Following a visit to Rome, he was taken ill and, aware that he was close to death, willed all his possessions to his immediate family and certain monasteries, churches and charities in his dioceses. He died shortly after.

Miracles were reported at his tomb and St Thorfinn was venerated by the Cistercians around Bruges.

St Thorlac Thorhallsson *Feast day: 23 December. Born in Iceland, 1133; died in 1193. Canonized in 1198 at the Iceland Athling.* Thorlac became a deacon when he was 15 and was ordained at 18 years of age. He studied in London before returning to Iceland in 1161 to found a monastery at Thykkviboer, becoming its first abbot. In 1178, he was named Bishop of Skalholt. He insisted on clerical discipline and celibacy, and fought simony.

St Timothy *Feast day: 26 January. Born in Lystra, Lycaenia in the first century.* Timothy was the son of a Greek father and Eunice, a converted Jewess, and he replaced **Barnabas** as **Paul**'s companion at Lystra. He grew to be one of Paul's closest friends and confidantes, accompanying him on his second missionary journey. When Paul was forced to flee Berea, Timothy remained behind but was later sent to Thessalonica to encourage those who were under persecution. Timothy and **Erastus** were sent to Macedonia in 58 AD and travelled on to Corinth to remind the Church of Paul's teaching. They then accompanied Paul into Macedonia and Achaia, and Timothy was with Paul when the Apostle was imprisoned at Caesarea and then Rome.

After being set free, Timothy went to Ephesus and became its first bishop. He was stoned and clubbed to death there when he opposed a pagan festival in honour of the goddess Diana.

Paul wrote two letters to him that are now in the New Testament, one written about 65 AD from Macedonia and the second from Rome while he was in prison, awaiting execution.

Sts Timothy, Thecla, and Agapius *Feast day 19 August. Born in the Holy Land; died in 304*. Urban, the president of Palestine during Diocletian's reign, cruelly oppressed the Christians. He ordered St Timothy, Bishop of Gaza, to be scourged, racked and finally to be burnt to death on a slow fire. Sts Agapius and Thecla were sentenced to be set before the wild beasts in the amphitheatre at Caesarea. Thecla was killed but Agapius escaped both the animals and the executioners.

Agapius was imprisoned for a further two years, remaining faithful, and when he was eventually thrown into the amphitheatre, he was torn by a bear but not mortally wounded. The next day his captors threw him into the sea and he drowned.

St Titus *Feast day: 26 January. Died in 96*. **St Paul** addressed one of his letters to Titus, who was his disciple and companion, calling him 'a true child in our common faith', and makes reference to him in his letter to the Galatians. He travelled to Jerusalem with Paul and **Barnabas** and was then sent on to Corinth in Greece, where he succeeded in reconciling the Christians and Paul.

Titus was later left behind on the island of Crete to help organize the Church there, after which he travelled on to Dalmatia, Croatia.
He served as the first bishop of Crete and was buried in Cortyna (Gortyna), Crete. His head was later taken to Venice during the invasion of Crete by the Saracens in 832 and was housed in St Mark's in Venice.

St Trophimus of Arles *Feast day: 29 December. Born in Rome: died in 280*. Trophimus was one of six bishops sent from Rome to preach and found churches in Gaul. **St Denis** was one of his companions. In 417, Pope **St Zosimus** described Trophimus' preaching as 'the source from which all the waters of the faith spread over all the land'. He became the first Bishop of Arles.

St Tudwal *Feast day: 30 November. Born in Wales; died in 564*. Tudwal was a Welsh monk who, along with his mother, sisters and other relatives, journeyed to Brittany, France. Welsh speakers easily understood the

Celtic language of Brittany. Tudwal's cousin, Deroc, was a king of Dumnonia and he worked to promote the faith in his cousin's domain, founding Lan Paku at Leon, Spain. He became Bishop of Treher with King Childebert I as his patron. He was known as Pabu (Father) among the Bretons.

St Turibius of Mogroveio *Feast day: 16 April. Born in Mayorga, Spain,1538; died at Santa, in Lima, Peru in 1606. Canonized in 1726 by Pope Benedict XIII.* Turibius was a lay professor of law at Salamanca University. Philip II appointed him principal judge of the Inquisition in Granada. In 1581, he resisted being appointed Bishop of Lima out of humility but eventually, in obedience, agreed to take up the position.

On his arrival in his new diocese, he found many abuses and scandals as well as a lack of clergy to provide adequate care and instruction for the many thousands of native Peruvians who had been baptized. This presented an immense challenge but Turibius set to work, building churches and hospitals, and opening the first-ever seminary for priests in South America in Lima.

He learned local dialects and, despite the poor roads, diligently travelled to the remotest parts of his diocese. His dedicated care for the native peoples caused some problems with the civil authorities although he also managed to provide aid secretly for impoverished Spaniards. He continued to work hard right up to the end, and died while visiting the district of Pacasmayo.

St Tutilo *Feast day: 28 March. Born in Ireland, 850: died in 915.* Tutilo was a large and powerful man and was educated at St Gall's monastery in Switzerland. He stayed on there after his education had finished to become a Benedictine monk.

An excellent student, Tutilo became a fine teacher, poet and hymn writer. He played several instruments including the harp. Though he was also gifted as a painter, sculptor, metal worker and mechanic, he preferred the solitude and prayers of his beloved monastery above any of his artistic pursuits.

St Tysilio *Feast day: 8 November. Born in Wales in the seventh century.* Tysilio was the son of a Welsh prince. He left home at a young age to become a monk at Meifod in Powys, Wales, later serving as abbot.

In 671 he left Wales for Brittany in an effort to escape the relentless attentions of the widow of his deceased brother and his father's demands that he leave the monastery and come home.

In Brittany he settled on the site that became known as St Suliac.

U

St Ubald Baldassini *Feast day: 16 May. Born in Gubbio Italy; died in Gubbio, 1160. Canonized in 1192 by Pope Celestine III.* Ubald was born into a noble family but was orphaned in his youth. He was educated by his uncle, the Bishop of Gubbio. Ubald was ordained and appointed dean of the cathedral in the hope that he might be able to reform the canons amongst whom there had arisen grave irregularities. He persuaded three of the canons to join him in a common life and this later extended to the entire chapter although Ubald left after a few years to become a hermit.

He was dissuaded from continuing his solitary life by Peter of Rimini and returned to Gubbio where, in 1126, he was proposed for the Bishopric of Perugia. Ubald hid himself from the party who were sent to find him and went straight to the pope to plead that he might be excused from having to accept the position. The pope agreed, but two years later the pope himself ordered that Ubald be appointed Bishop of Gubbio, and this time he agreed. When the Emperor Frederick II and his army approached Gubbio, Ubald went out to meet him and persuaded him not to sack the town, as he had Spoleto during one of his earlier forays into Italy.

St Ulrich *Feast day: 14 July. Born in Ratisbon, Germany; died in 1093.* Ulrich was a page at the court of Empress Agnes who chose to enter the religious life. His uncle, Bishop Notker of Freising, ordained him a deacon and he later became Archdeacon and provost of the Cathedral.

After he had been on pilgrimage to Rome and Jerusalem, he became a Benedictine monk at Cluny in France in 1052. He was appointed chaplain to the nuns at Marcigny but returned to Cluny after he lost the sight in one eye.

He served as Prior at Peterlingen and was the founding Friar of Ruggersberg Priory although he did return again to Cluny.

He opposed Bishop Burchard of Lausanne for his support of Henry IV against the pope and was founding abbot of the monastery at Zell in the Black Forest. Ulrich was the author of *Consuetudines Cluniacences*, which gave instruction on the liturgy and the direction of monasteries and novices. He became totally blind in 1091 and died two years later at Augsburg.

St Ultan *Feast day: 4 September. Born in Ireland; died in 657.* Ultan became Bishop of Ardbraccan, Ireland and was well know for his care of the poor, orphans, and the sick. He collected the writings of **St Brigid**, and also wrote her biography. He was a skilled copyist and illustrator of manuscripts.

St Urban *Feast day: 25 May. Born in Rome; died in 230.* St Urban succeeded St Calixtus as pope in the year 223 and although the Church enjoyed relative peace under his mild reign, there were frequent local disturbances raised by the people or governors. Urban suffered greatly in the persecution of the Emperor Alexander Serverus. While encouraging the martyrs and converting many idolaters, he was himself eventually arrested and beheaded.

St Ursula *Feast day: 21 October. Born in Britain in the fourth century.*
Ursula was the daughter of a Christian king in Britain and was permitted a three-year postponement of marriage to a pagan prince. She then set off with a company that included ten ladies in waiting on a pilgrimage that took her across the North Sea, up the river Rhine to Basle, Switzerland, and then on to Rome.

In 383, on their return journey, they were taken prisoner by the Huns at Cologne, and when Ursula refused to marry one of their chieftains she was put to death, her companions suffering the same fate.

Clematius, a senator, rebuilt a fourth-century basilica in Cologne, to honour this group of virgins who had been martyred.

V

St Valentine *Feast day: 14 February. Born in Rome: died in 269.* Patron of love, young people and happy marriages.

Valentine was a priest in Rome who, with **St Marinus** and others, assisted fellow Christians during the persecution under Claudius II. He was arrested and sent by the emperor to the Prefect of Rome where, in the year 269, still refusing to renounce his faith, he was condemned to be beaten with clubs and afterwards, to be beheaded. One legend says that while awaiting his execution Valentine restored the sight of his jailer's blind daughter and, on the eve of his death, he penned a farewell note to the jailer's daughter, signing it 'From your Valentine'.

St Venantius Fortunatus *Feast day: 14 December. Born in Treviso near Venice, 530; died in 610.* Venantius was afflicted with an eye ailment, but thanks to **St Martin of Tours** he was able to undertake a pilgrimage in 565 that took him to various Christian centres in Germany and France. During his time at King Sigebert's court at Metz, he received high praise for his poetic eulogies.

Venantius' next journey took him to Tours where he prayed at the tomb of St Martin, before moving on to Poitiers. Here, Venantius entered the service of Queen Rodegunda who was living as a nun, and he became her personal secretary until her death in August 587.

Shortly before he died at the age of 80, he was named Bishop of Poitiers.

He wrote 11 books of poems, a metrical life of St Martin of Tours, and the prose lives of 11 Gallic saints, including the *Vita Rodegundis*.

St Vénard Theophane *Feast day: 2 February. Born in Saint-Loup-sur-Thouet in France, 1829; died in 1861. Canonized in 1988 by Pope John Paul II.* Vénard was the son of a schoolmaster who joined the society of foreign missions in Paris. He was ordained in 1854 and sent to Vietnam in a time of extreme persecution in that land. He was expelled from Namdiuh two years later and travelled to Hanoi, where he was obliged to go into hiding in caves and sampans.

He was eventually captured and placed in a bamboo cage before being beheaded for refusing to deny the Christian faith.

His example and letters inspired **St Theresa of Lisieux** to offer herself for missionary service.

St Veronica *Feast day: 12 July. Born in Jerusalem in the first century.* Veronica is the name of the woman who wiped the face of Christ with a veil while he was on the way to Calvary. The image of Christ's face became miraculously imprinted on the material. While there is no historical evidence or scriptural reference to this event, the legend of Veronica became very popular in Christian tradition. Veronica is said to have carried the relic away from the Holy Land and used it to cure Emperor

Tiberius of some illness. The veil subsequently turned up in Rome in the eighth century, and was transferred to St Peter's Basilica in 1297, on the instructions of Pope Boniface VIII.

St Vicelin *Feast day: 12 December. Born in Hemeln in Germany, 1086; died in 1154.* Vicelin was a student in the cathedral school of Paderborn and Laon, France, before being appointed a canon at Bremen, Germany, and head of the local school there.

He was ordained by **St Norbert** at Magdeburg and became a missionary to the Wends in northern Germany, founding monasteries at Holstein, Segeberg, and Hogersdorf. In 1147 marauding pirates laid waste to the church buildings but in spite of this Christianity survived and grew.

Vicelin escaped with some of his priests to the safety of the Holy Roman Empire. He was named Bishop of Staargard in 1149, but Emperor Frederick I Barbarossa prevented him from returning to his missionary work.

He was paralyzed for the last three years of his life, and died at Neumunster in France.

St Victor I *Feast day: 28 July. Born in Africa; died in 198.* Victor was an African who became pope in 189. He was a favourite of Marcia, the mistress to the Emperor Commodus, and would regularly give her lists of imprisoned Christians, whom she arranged to be released. Victor excommunicated several Asian bishops who were resident in Rome for celebrating Easter on the same day as the spring full moon (14 Nisan) even if it fell on a weekday. Following criticism of undue severity from **St Irenaeus of Lyon,** he relented and simply insisted on uniformity of observance within his own province.

During his papacy he made Latin the official language of the Roman Church. Victor also fought Gnosticism* and wrote a treatise on the throwing of dice.

St Victorius *Feast day: 24 February. Born in Africa; died in Carthage, 259.* Victorius was a disciple of **St Cyprian of Carthage**. During a period of persecution by Valerian, violence erupted in Carthage and the Christians were blamed. Victorius was arrested, tortured and beheaded along with nine others.

St Victor of Marseilles *Feast day: 21 July. Born in the third century.* Victor was a soldier in the Roman army at Marseilles. During the preparations for a visit by the Emperor Maximian to the area, Victor exhorted Christians to stand firm in their faith, and to resist any attempts to compel them to sacrifice to idols. He was brought before the Emperor and found guilty of treachery.

Though he was dragged through the streets, racked and imprisoned, he still converted three guards while in prison. The guards were beheaded when it was discovered that they had converted to Christianity and Victor was tortured again. When he refused to offer incense to Jupiter, he was crushed in a millstone and beheaded.

St Victor the Moor *Feast day: 8 May. Born in Mauritania; died in Milan, 303.* Victor was a Christian from his youth and became a soldier in the elite Praetorian Guard. After a long life of faithful obedience in perilous times, Victor was taken prisoner and tortured by having molten lead poured onto his skin. Despite old age, infirmity and declining health, he remained steadfast, and was beheaded.

A church was erected over his grave and St Gregory of Tours recorded many of the miracles which occurred at the shrine.

St Vincent Ferrer *Feast day: 5 April. Born in Valencia, Spain, 1350; died in 1419. Canonized in 1485 by Pope Innocent VIII.* Patron of builders.

Vincent was the son of an Englishman who had settled in Spain. In 1374 he entered the Order of **St Dominic**, and was soon appointed to lecture on philosophy. He was sent to Barcelona to continue his studies and began to preach there, going on to receive a doctorate from the University of Lerida in the city of Catalonia.

In 1394 Pedro de Luna became Pope at Avignon and appointed Vincent as Master of the sacred palace. Vincent worked tirelessly to end the great schism in the Church and even though he was unsuccessful, supporters of both sides honourably received him.

He began to evangelize widely across Spain and went on to preach in France, Italy, Germany, Flanders, England, Scotland and Ireland. Numerous conversions followed, accompanied by miracles.

Though Vincent lived to see the end of the Great Schism, he died not many years later, having been totally worn out by his exertions.

St Vincent of Lerins *Feast day: 14 May. Born in Gaul (modern France); died in 445.* Vincent was born into a noble family and was the brother of St Lupus of Troyes.

He joined the army but gave up this career to become a monk on the island of Lerins near Cannes, off the south coast of France. He was ordained in 434 and wrote the *Commonitorium*, which included his famous Vincentian Canon, or test of orthodoxy which he expressed as 'that which has been believed everywhere, always, by all'.

He believed that the ultimate source of Christian truth was Holy Scripture, interpreted through the historic Church. Vincent favoured Semi-Pelagianism*, and was strongly opposed to any suggestion of pre-destination.

St Vincent de Paul *Feast day: 27 September. Born in Pouy in Gascony, France, 1580; died in Paris, 1660. Canonized in 1737 by Pope Clement XII.* Patron of charitable societies.

Vincent first studied under the Franciscan Fathers at Dax. Following this, Philip of Gondi, Count of Joingy, chose him as tutor to his children, thus enabling him to continue his studies at the University of Toulouse until he was ordained priest in 1600.

In 1605, on a voyage from Marseilles to Narbonne, he was captured by African pirates and was held as a slave in Tunisia for about two years, before escaping to Avignon.

In 1617 he returned to France after briefly visiting Rome and began to conduct preaching missions. Eight years later he laid the foundations of what was to become the Congregation of the Mission of Lazarists. This was a community of priests who renounced promotion and who all drew from a common fund in order to serve all those in need. Vincent founded the congregation of the Sisters of Charity which was the first women's congregation of unenclosed women to minister specifically to the poor and destitute.

St Vincent Saragossa *Feast day: 22 January. Born in Spain; died in 304.* Vincent was a deacon who was arrested along with his bishop, Valerius of Saragossa, during a persecution under Dacian the Governor of Spain. Valerius was banished but Vincent was subjected to fierce tortures including being pierced with iron hooks, being bound upon a red-hot gridiron and roasted, and being thrown into a prison, laid on a floor strewn with broken pottery and starved. Vincent's unwavering faithfulness led to his jailer's conversion. He was fatally injured, but survived long enough to see his friends before he died.

St Vincent Yen *Feast day: 30 June. Born in Vietnam; died in 1838. Canonized in 1988 by Pope John Paul II.* Vincent joined the Dominicans in 1808 and worked as a missionary until he was arrested in the general anti-Christian persecutions that took place throughout Vietnam. He spent six years in hiding before finally being caught and beheaded.

St Vincenza Mary Lopez y Vicuna *Feast day: 18 January. Born in Cascante, Navarre in Spain, 1847; died in Madrid, 1890. Canonized in 1975 by Pope Paul VI.* Vincenza was the daughter of a lawyer. She refused an arranged marriage and took a vow of chastity before establishing the Daughters of Mary Immaculate for the protection of vulnerable female domestic servants.

Papal approval for this Order was secured in 1888 and Vincenza died two years later after a long illness.

St Virgil of Arles *Feast day: 5 March. Born in Gascony, France; died in 610.* Virgil became a monk on the Lerins islands, two miles off the coast of Cannes, where he had been educated. He later became Abbot of St-Symphonien at Autun and was then appointed Archbishop of Arles in 580. His friend **St Gregory the Great** rebuked him for trying to force conversion upon the Jews and recommended that he confine his efforts to prayer and preaching.

St Bede records that, at Gregory's request, Virgil consecrated **St Augustine** as Archbishop of Canterbury and appointed him apostolic vicar to the court of Childebert II. When Virgil died he was buried at the monastery of St Saviour, which he founded.

St Virgil of Salzburg *Feast day: 27 November. Born in Ireland; died in 784. Canonized in 1233 by Pope Gregory IX.* Virgil travelled to mainland Europe in 743 and spent two years at the court of Pepin the Short before travelling to Bavaria to act as an arbitrator between the French king and Duke Odilo.

Odilo appointed Virgil Abbot of St Peter's, and St Boniface of Mainz twice complained to Pope Zachary of Virgil's supposedly unorthodox views. The pope censured Virgil for believing that people existed in the Antipodes, but took no drastic action.

Virgil was appointed Bishop of Salzburg, dedicating the first cathedral in the area and re-siting the relics of St Rupert there. Virgil was one of the more learned men of his day and went on to establish monasteries in his diocese and to send missionaries to Carinthia and Styria.

St Vitus *Feast day: 15 June. Born in Sicily; died in 303.* Patron of epileptics and nervous diseases, dancers and actors, and protector against storms.

Vitus, the only son of a senator in Sicily, became a Christian when he was 12. His reputation for making conversions came to the attention of the administrator of Sicily, who had him brought before him and tried unsuccessfully to shake his faith.

Vitus escaped to Rome along with his tutor, Modestus, and his servant, Crescentia. While in Rome he freed Emperor Diocletian's son of an evil spirit, but when Vitus refused to sacrifice to the gods, the cure was attributed to sorcery, and they were arrested and ill-treated.

Vitus, Modestus and Crescentia emerged unscathed from various tortures and were freed when a violent storm destroyed some pagan temples. They were eventually re-arrested and martyred at Lucania.

Vitus is one of a group known as the Fourteen Holy Helpers.

St Vladimir *Feast day: 15 July. Born in Kiev, 956; died in Beresyx, Russia, 1014.* Vladimir was the grandson of **St Olga** and illegitimate son of Sviastoslav, Grand Duke of Kiev and his mistress, Malushka. His early life was violent and brutal. He was given Novgorod to rule but war broke out between him and his half-brothers and in 977 Vladimir was attacked and forced to flee from Novgorod to Scandinavia.

In 980 Vladimir returned with an army, captured Novgorod and slew his half-brother at Rodno. This made Vladimir the sole ruler of Russia where he was notorious for his barbarism and immorality, having at least five wives and numerous female slaves.

After his conquest of Kherson in the Crimea in 988, Vladimir became impressed by the progress of Christianity and, in return for aid from Byzantium, agreed to become a Christian. His conversion was politically motivated but in due course he became wholehearted in his commitment to Christianity, reformed his life and married Ann, the daughter of Emperor Basil II.

On his return to Kiev he invited Greek missionaries to Russia and led his people to Christianity. While he was mainly influenced by the Byzantine traditions, Vladimir felt free to borrow features from the Western Church. He built several schools and churches.

His two sons by Ann, Sts Romanus and David, became martyrs.

In 1014 he fell ill and died on the way to fight his rebellious half-brother in Novgorod.

Sts Votus and Felix *Feast day 29 May. Born in Saragossa, Spain; died in 750.* Votus and Felix were brothers who left their home to live as hermits. They found a suitable place in the Pyrenees under a huge rock, but discovered that another hermit had already made his home there. All three agreed to share the cave and the Benedictine monastery of Saint John de la Peña was built near to the site of their hermitage soon after their deaths.

W

St Walburga *Feast day: 25 February. Born in Devonshire, England, 710; died in 779.* Walburga was the daughter of a West Saxon chieftain and the sister of **St Willibald** and **St Winebald**. She became a nun at Wimborne Monastery in Dorset, where she had been educated. In 748 she was sent to Germany to the Abbey of Bishofsheim, which her brother Winebald had founded, to help **St Boniface**.

Willibald became Bishop of Eichstadt and appointed Walburga as abbess of the double monasteries for both men and women. Upon her death she was buried first at Heidenheim, but later her body was interred next to that of her brother, St Winebald, at Eichstadt. In Germany this transfer is commemorated on the first day of May and is known as '*Walpurgisnacht*', and many superstitions are associated with this festival.

St Waldebert *Feast day: 5 February. Died in 668.* Waldebert was a Frankish knight who became a monk at **St Columban**'s monastery of Luxeuil, donating all his wealth to the work there. In 628 he was appointed the third abbot and introduced the Benedictine Rule two years after his appointment. During his 40 years as abbot, Luxeuil monastery flourished and became a highly influential religious centre. Numerous miracles are attributed to Waldebert and objects he had touched were venerated for their healing properties. When he first entered the abbey Waldebert had surrendered his weapons; they were suspended from the roof of the church and remained there for centuries.

St Walfrid *Feast day: 15 February. Died in 765.* Walfrid was a prosperous and well-respected citizen of Pisa who married and raised five sons and a daughter. After many years, both he and his wife decided to enter the religious life and with a friend, Fortis, and a relative, Gunduald, he founded a monastery at Palazzuolo near Volterra. A convent for their wives and Walfrid's daughter was established 18 miles away. Gunduald's only son, Gimfrid, was ordained as a priest but ran off with some valuable objects belonging to the monastery.

Walfrid was greatly distressed and sent out a search party for him. He prayed for Gimfrid's repentance and that he would be given a sign of the error of his ways. That same day, Gimfrid was brought back penitent, and he had miraculously been given a permanent reminder: the middle finger of his right hand was so mutilated that he could never use it again.

St Walter of Pontoise *Feast day: 8 April. Born in Picardy, France, 1030; died in 1095.* Walter was a professor of philosophy and rhetoric who entered the Benedictine abbey of Rebais-en-Brie. He was chosen to be the first abbot of a new monastery at Pontoise by King Philip I but, seeking solitude, he tried more than once to escape.

One night he climbed over the abbey wall and for a brief time was blissfully happy in a small hermitage that he had constructed on an island in the Loire, but his brother monks soon tracked him down and led him back to the abbey.

On another occasion he walked to Cluny Abbey in the hope of gaining anonymity among the hundreds of other monks there. He was quickly recognized, however, and ordered back to Pontoise. Walter eventually travelled to Rome to ask Pope **St Gregory** VII to relieve him of his responsibilities, but the pope turned down his request and instructed him to use the talents that God had given him.

Walter protested against simony and lax behaviour among the clergy, but he was criticized for his outspokenness and even beaten and thrown into prison. On being released he continued to live a life of extreme asceticism and deep prayer, and established a new convent in honour of Mary, at Bertaucourt.

St Waltheof of Melrose *Feast day: 3 August. Born in Northumbria, England: died in 1160.* Waltheof was the second son of Earl Simon of Huntingdon and Matilda, the great-niece of William the Conqueror. He was gentle and peace-loving and was drawn towards the religious life from an early age.

On the death of his father, King Henry I gave Waltheof's mother in marriage to **St David I**, usually known as King David of Scotland. He also went to the Scottish court and became a close friend of **St Aelred of Rievaulx**.

In 1130 Waltheof took the decision to leave Scotland and entered an Augustinian monastery at Nostell, near Pontefract in Yorkshire and was soon chosen prior of a new monastery at Kirkham. In 1140 Waltheof was chosen to be Archbishop of York, but King Stephen refused to accept this because he was fearful of Waltheof's Scottish connections.

Waltheof tried to unite his entire community with the Cistercian monks of Rievaulx, where his friend and mentor St Aelred had become abbot. Failing to accomplish this he went ahead and entered the Cistercian order alone at Waldron in Bedfordshire and finally moved to Rievaulx. Within four years he was chosen by King David to be the Abbot of Melrose. He proved to be a great success, and was widely known for his kindness and humility.

In 1154 Waltheof was chosen to be Archbishop of Saint Andrew's, but he persuaded St Aelred to oppose this and was able to continue his work at Melrose for several more years until his death in 1160.

St Wenceslaus *Feast day: 28 September. Born near Prague, Czechoslovakia in 903; died in 929.* Patron of Bohemia.

Wenceslaus was the son of Duke Wratislaw. He was taught Christianity by his grandmother, St Ludmila. An anti-Christian faction murdered the Duke and St Ludmila and took over the government, but after a coup in 922 Wenceslaus was declared the new ruler and actively encouraged Christianity.

However, after Wenceslaus' wife had a son, his brother, Boleslaus, became jealous since he was no longer the direct successor to the throne, and joined a group of noble Czech dissenters. They invited Wenceslaus to take part in a local patronal festival. The morning after this Boleslaus and his friends waylaid Wenceslas as he made his way to church and killed him.

St Wilfrid *Feast day: 12 October. Born in Ripon, Northumbria, 634; died at Ripon, 709.* Wilfrid was educated at Lindesfarne, which was at that time the centre of Celtic worship in the north. He went on to spend some time broadening his horizons in Lyon and Rome, before returning to England. He was elected Abbot of Ripon in 658 and introduced the Roman rules and practices into northern England.

In 664 Wilfrid opposed the Celtic date for Easter at the Synod of Whitby and ultimately was on the winning side of the debate on the accepted form of Church structure and authority. He was appointed Bishop of York, but since he regarded the northern bishops who had refused to accept the decrees of Whitby as schismatic, he went to Compiègne, France, to be ordained and, after some difficulty, finally took possession of his See in 669.

He founded many monasteries of the Benedictine Order and was very diligent in his work but, in order to prevent the subdivision of his diocese by **St Theodore**, Archbishop of Canterbury, he appealed to Rome. Forced into exile, he worked hard to evangelize the pagan south Saxons until the affair was settled in his favour in 686. In 691 he was suspended until Rome once again vindicated him. In 703, Wilfrid resigned and retired to his monastery at Ripon where he died six years later.

Wilfrid spent a short time in Friesland in 678–9 and his good work proved to be the starting point of a great English mission to the Germanic peoples.

St Willehad *Feast day: 8 November. Born in Northumbria, England; died in 789.* Willehad studied at York and became a monk in Yorkshire. In 766 he set out on a mission to the Netherlands, but was forced to give up because of the violent opposition that he met.

In 780 Charlemagne asked him to become a missionary among the Saxons, but again he was forced to withdraw in the face of a Saxon uprising. He went to Rome to make a report to Pope Adrian I and then spent two years at Echternach monastery in Luxembourg.

After Charlemagne's re-conquest of Saxony, Willehad was appointed Bishop of Worms in 787, and began his missionary work again, this time with much more success.

He died at Bremen two years later, a few days after dedicating the cathedral of St Peter.

St William of Maleval *Feast day: 10 February. Died in 1157.* As a young man, William led a licentious life in the army. Having experienced conversion, he made a pilgrimage to Rome to the Apostles' tombs and in

1145 asked for pardon and penance from Pope Eugenius III. The pope instructed him to make a pilgrimage to the Holy Land, and when William returned eight years later, he was a changed man.

William took up residence as a hermit at Lupocavio near Pisa before going on to become the head of a nearby monastery. Failing to bring about serious reforms among the monks there, he left and once more became a hermit at Maleval near Siena. He lived in a cave until the local landowner discovered him some months later and built him a small hermit's cell. William was noted for his gifts of prophecy and miracles in his later years and was joined by two others. Soon after his death, others also came to study his teachings and enter a similar life of prayer and austerity. They received papal approval and developed to become the Hermits of St William (the Gulielmites).

St William of Rochester *Feast day: 23 May. Born in Perth, Scotland; died in 1201.* Patron of adopted children.

William, a fisherman by trade, experienced conversion as a young man and committed himself to the care of orphans and the poor. Once he saved an infant that had been abandoned at the door of the church and raised him as his own, naming him David. He went on pilgrimage to Jerusalem taking with him his young adopted son. However, David diverted him onto a supposed short-cut and murdered him for his few possessions.

This happened not far from Rochester, England. His body was found by a mentally deranged woman who garlanded it with honeysuckle and was cured by her simple act of care. A shrine is dedicated to William at Rochester Cathedral.

St William of Roskilde *Feast day: 2 September. Born in England, 1067.* William was an Anglo-Saxon priest who went to Scandinavia as chaplain to Canute, King of England and Denmark.

He served as a missionary among the pagans and was appointed Bishop of Roskilde on Zeeland Island. He publicly rebuked King Sven Estridsen for his lack of contrition after having several men stoned to death in a church without trial. The king came to William's cathedral with a troop of armed men, but was refused entry by the courageous bishop who, carrying only his crozier, offered them his neck in readiness to die for his faith.

The king withdrew and in due course confessed his crime and donated land to the Church at Roskilde. From then on the king and William worked well together to promote political and religious unity. Despite being very different, they were the best of friends and William died, broken-hearted, while going out to meet the funeral procession of the king. They were buried together in Roskilde Cathedral, which had recently been completed.

St William of York *Feast day: 8 June. Born in England; died in 1154. Canonized in 1226 by Pope Honorius III.* William's father was Count

Fitz Herbert, treasurer to Henry I, and his mother Emma was King Stephen's half-sister. He became treasurer of the Church of York at an early age and was elected Archbishop of York in 1140.

His election was challenged on the grounds of simony and unchastity, but he was cleared by Rome. However, a short time later, when Eugene III became pope, he suspended William and in 1147, deposed him as Archbishop of York. William retired to Winchester to live the life of a monk.

Following the death of Pope Eugene III, Pope Anastastius IV restored William to his position as archbishop, but after only one month back in the See of York, he died.

St Willibald *Feast day: 7 June. Born in Wessex, England; died in 786.* Willibald was the brother of **Sts Winebald** and **Walburga**. He studied in a monastery at Bishops Waltham, Hampshire, before going on pilgrimage to Rome with his father, St Richard the Saxon, who died on the way. Willibald continued on to Rome and then to Jerusalem. After being held for a time by Saracens on suspicion of being a spy, he continued to visit the holy places and then went to Constantinople where he visited numerous monasteries.

On his return to Italy, he went to Monte Cassino and lived there for ten years. **St Boniface** requested Pope **St Gregory III** to send Willibald to Germany to help with his missionary work. Boniface ordained him in 741 and soon appointed him Bishop of Eichstatt, in Franconia.

Willibald served as bishop for some four decades, and in his later years dictated an account of his journeys in the Holy Land to Hugeburc, a nun of Heidenheim.

St Willibrord *Feast day: 7 November. Born in Northumbria in England, 658; died in 739.* Willibrord studied at Ripon monastery under **St Wilfrid** and spent 12 years studying in Ireland at the abbey of Rathmelsigi in County Louth under **Sts Egbert** and Wigbert. Following his ordination in 690, he set out with a dozen companions for Frisia and in 693 Willibrord visited Rome to seek papal approval for his work. He received this, and during a second visit in 696, Pope Sergius I consecrated him archbishop to the Frisians, his See based at Utrecht.

Willibrord also received great encouragement from the Frankish leader, Pepin of Heristal. He founded the monastery of Echternach, Luxembourg, to serve as a centre for missionary work in Denmark and Upper Friesland, although he experienced setbacks and was nearly murdered by angry pagans after he tore down a pagan idol. In 714 he watched his life's work all but undone when Duke Radbod reclaimed the extensive territories from Pepin.

After Radbod's death, Willibrord began his mission work again with renewed vigour with the help of **St Boniface**. He died while on retreat at Echternach.

St Willigis *Feast day: 23 February. Born in Schoningen, Germany; died in 1011.* Willigis was the son of a wheelwright. After ordination, he was named a canon at Hildesheim and then chaplain to Emperor Otto II, who made him Chancellor of Germany in 971 and then Archbishop of Mainz in 973.

Pope Benedict VII appointed him vicar apostolic for Germany. In 983, he crowned the infant emperor Otto III at Aachen and along with Otto's mother was one of the powers behind the throne. Willigis was a gifted statesman, and also a patron of the arts; his motto was 'by art to the knowledge and service of God'. When Otto died in 1002, he played a key role in the election of Henry of Bavaria, whom he consecrated.

He had a long-running dispute with **St Bernward** of Hildesheim about jurisdiction over the convent of Gandersheim. At long last, Willigis admitted that he was in the wrong and withdrew his claims with good grace. He sent missionaries to Scandinavia, founded churches, and rebuilt the cathedral of Mainz.

St Winebald *Feast day: 18 December. Born in Wessex, England; died at Heidenheim, Germany, 761.* St Richard the Saxon, an important landowner in eighth-century Britain, embarked with his two sons, **Sts Willibald and Winebald**, on a pilgrimage to the Holy Land, but died at Lucca, Italy. From Rome, Willibald went on to the Holy Land (the first Englishman in recorded history to go there), but Winebald did not have his brother's stamina; he was ill by the time they reached Rome so he decided to stay there as a student and remained there for seven years. He then returned to England, but made two further pilgrimages to Rome in the company of friends, and became a Benedictine monk. Winebald was in Rome for his third visit in 739 when his kinsman **St Boniface** arrived.

Although Winebald was still in poor health, Boniface persuaded him to join his mission to the Germans. He was ordained a priest and took responsibility for the care of seven churches. He was harried by the German Saxons but persevered and worked in Bavaria for several years. He finally went to join his brother who had been appointed Bishop of Eichstatt.

With his brother's agreement Winebald built a Benedictine double monastery in a remote place. The two brothers decided that their sister Walburga should be placed in charge of the community of women. This location, not far from Heidenheim (Würtemburg), became an important centre for evangelization and prayer. Their sister **St Walburga** came from England to lead a community of nuns.

Winebald spent his last three years in great physical pain but bore this with patience and, when he died, his brother and sister were at his side.

St Winoc *Feast day: 6 November. Born in Brittany, France; died in 717.* Winoc was a Welshman who was raised in St Peter's monastery at Sithiu (Saint-Omer) under **St Bertinus**, and he eventually became a monk there. With the help of three friends, he later founded a monastery near Dunkirk which became a missionary centre for outreach to the Morini people at Wormhoult.

St Wiro *Feast day: 8 May. Born in Northumbria, England; died in 753.* Wiro was, like **St Willibrord**, an apostle to Frisia. He was sent to Rome to be consecrated bishop and appointed to the See of Utrecht by **St Boniface**. In 746, he joined Boniface in writing a letter of correction to King Ethelbald of Mercia.

Wiro helped to build a small church in Friesland in the Netherlands and also the monastery at Peterkosler on land granted by Pepin of Herstal. He was martyred while preaching the Gospel.

St Withburga *Feast day: 8 July. Born in East Anglia, England; died in 743.* Withburga, the youngest daughter of King Anna, led a life of simplicity and solitude at Holkham near Norfolk. After her father was killed in battle, Withburga moved to Dereham, where she established a nunnery and a church.

She died with the church unfinished and her remains were later stolen by monks who enshrined her in Ely. Following this, a fresh spring, known as Withburga's Well, sprang up beside her grave in Dereham.

St Wolfgang *Feast day: 31 October. Born in Swabia in Germany, 924; died near Linz, Austria, in 994. Canonized in 1052 by Pope Leo IX.* Wolfgang studied at Reichenau on Lake Constance under the Benedictines and at Wurzburg before moving to Trier as a teacher in the cathedral school.

He entered the Benedictine monastery at Einsiedeln in 964 where he was appointed head of the monastery school and ordained in 971. He then set out with a group of monks to preach in the region of Pannonia (Hungary), but had little success.

The following year he was named Bishop of Regensburg by Emperor Otto II. The Church prospered due to his reforming zeal and diplomatic skills. The clergy in his diocese supported his reforms as he restored monasteries and preached enthusiastically.

Wolfgang served for a time as tutor to Emperor Henry II of Bavaria. He never gave up wearing his monastic habit, was known for his care for the poor, and was given the title the Grand Almoner.

Taken ill while travelling down the Danube into Austria, Wolfgang died in the small town of Puppingen.

St Wulfhilda *Feast day: 9 September. Born in England; died in 988.* King Edgar sought Wulfhilda's hand in marriage while she was a novice at Wilton Abbey. Her aunt Wenfelda, who was Abbess of Wherwell, tricked her into coming to that convent with the supposed aim of becoming her successor, but when Wulfhilda arrived, she found the king waiting for her and her aunt ready to allow him to take her as his wife.

She managed to escape through the drains, despite the presence of chaperons inside the convent and guards outside. Edgar pursued her to Wilton, caught up with her and grabbed hold of her in the cloister, but Wulfhilda managed to escape once more and sought sanctuary in the church.

The king gave up any hope of marrying her, and in due course appointed her Abbess of Barking Abbey, re-endowing it with several other institutions. He took her cousin Wulftrudis as his mistress instead.

St Wulfric *Feast day: 20 February. Born in Compton Martin near Bristol in England, 1080; died in 1154.* Wulfric was ordained a priest but his love of hunting and hawking led him to be attracted to a materialistic and worldly lifestyle. He experienced a personal conversion after a chance encounter with a beggar, and became a hermit at Haselbury in Somerset, devoting his remaining years to an austere life as a hermit. His rigid routine involved strict periods of fasting, wearing chain mail, and frequently immersing himself in cold water.

Wulfric worked at copying and binding books for church use and made various other articles of use in worship, being widely known for his miracles and prophecies.

Wulfric was buried at his cell at Haselbury, and this became a popular pilgrimage site in the Middle Ages.

St Wulfstan *Feast day: 19 January. Born in Long-Itchington in Warwickshire, England, 1008; died in 1095. Canonized in 1203 by Pope Innocent III.*

Wulfstan studied at the abbeys of Evesham and Peterborough and, after ordination, joined the Benedictines at Worcester. He was known for his holiness of life and childlike innocence. He served the community as schoolmaster but also took a turn at various other positions in this small community of 12 monks.

In 1062 he was nominated as Bishop of Worcester and, while he initially refused, he finally accepted the post under obedience. Aldred of York consecrated him just four years before the Normans conquered England. For months on end, Wulfstan preached against the inhumanity of selling poor debtors into slavery at the slave market in Bristol, and eventually obtained the abolition of the Irish slave trade. Wulfstan encouraged devotion to the memory of **St Oswald**, whose abstinence and generosity to the poor he imitated and surpassed.

Initial doubts about his ability soon proved to be unfounded and, following the Norman Conquest, he was the only bishop to be kept in post by William the Conqueror. For the next 30 years, Wulfstan continued to care for the poor, to support the rebuilding of his cathedral, and to alleviate harsh oppression. Loved by his own people and respected by their Norman conquerors, Wulfstan was active in ministry to the end of his life. He died while he was conducting his daily routine of washing the feet of a dozen poor men.

St Wulmar *Feast day: 20 July. Born near Boulogne in Picardy, France; died in 689.* Wulmar married, but was separated from his wife by force and entered the Benedictine order as a lay brother at Haumont in Hainault. His daily work as a monk involved caring for cattle and forestry.

After a time he was ordained and founded the monastery of Samer near Boulogne where he served as abbot. He also founded a monastery for nuns about two kilometres away at Wierre-aux-Bois. The abbey at Samer was named after him.

Y

St Yrieix *Feast day: 25 August. Born at Limoges, France; died in 591.* Yrieix served for a time in the court of the Franks before going on to found the monastery of Atane in Limousin. The monastery, and also the surrounding village of Saint-Yrieix were named in his honour.

St Ywi *Feast day: 8 October. Died in 690.* Ywi was a Benedictine monk and hermit at Lindisfarne Abbey. **St Cuthbert** ordained him a deacon and he lived much of his life as a hermit. When he died, his relics were enshrined at Wilton, near Salisbury.

Z

St Zeno *Feast day: 12 April. Born in Africa; died in 371.* Zeno received an excellent classical education and became a hermit. In 362 he was named Bishop of Verona, Italy.

He was active in missionary work, converted many, and opposed Arianism*. He built a church at Verona, founded a convent that he directed, and was known for his charitable giving.

Zeno encouraged Christian virgins who lived at home to be consecrated and wrote widely on a variety of ecclesiastical topics, including the incarnation.

St Zenobius *Feast day: 25 May. Born in Florence, Italy; died in 390.* Zenobius was a member of the Geronimo family and was baptized by Bishop Theodore, at the age of 21. Sometime later, Theodore ordained him and appointed him his archdeacon. **St Ambrose of Milan** became acquainted with the character and gifting of Zenobius, and recommended him to Pope **St Damasus**.

Zenobius diligently served the pope in Rome and also travelled to Constantinople on his behalf. On his return to Italy, he was chosen to be Bishop of Florence and became widely known for his preaching and miraculous gifts. He is recorded as having resuscitated five dead people, including a child who was run over by a cart as he played in front of the Cathedral. St Zenobius died at the age of 80 and was buried first in San Lorenzo. His remains were later transferred to the Cathedral.

St Zephyrinus *Feast day: 26 August. Born in Rome; died in 217.* Zephyrinus was appointed pope in 199. His rival, Hippolytus, described him as a simple and avaricious man who placed too much reliance on his deacon, Callixtus. In spite of this, Zephyrinus faithfully combated the heresies of Adoptionism*, Modalism*, and Monarchianism*.

He died peacefully, but is considered a martyr because of his perseverance in the face of severe criticism and persecution.

St Zita *Feast day: 27 April. Born in Monte Sagrati near Lucca in Italy, 1218; died in 1278. Canonized in 1696 by Pope Innocent XII.* Patron of domestic workers.

Zita was born into a poor Christian family. Her older sister became a Cistercian nun and her uncle a hermit. At the age of 12, Zita became a housekeeper in the house of a rich weaver in Lucca. She attended church daily and regarded her employment as her Christian vocation, though Zita upset her employers by giving away food from the household store to the poor and destitute. In time, her evident goodness persuaded them of the value of her presence in the household.

Zita was allowed to arrange her housework around visits to the sick and those in prison. Her good deeds and heavenly visions became public knowledge and she was visited by both poor and rich. She stayed with the family until her death, 48 years later.

St Zoe *Feast day: 2 May. Born in Attilia, Asia Minor; died in 135.* Zoe was the Christian wife of Exsuperius. They were slaves of Catulus at Pamphylia, Asia Minor, during the reign of Emperor Hadrian. They and their two sons, Syriacus and Theodulus, were tortured and then roasted to death in a furnace because they refused to eat food offered to the gods.

St Zosimus *Feast day: 30 March. Born in Sicily; died in 418.* Zosimus was a Greek of Jewish descent who was offered to the monastery of **St Lucy** at the age of seven. Though he ran away, his parents returned him straight away to the monastery and he went on to experience several visions, both fearful and encouraging, and developed into a faithful monk, eventually being ordained a priest. **John Chrysostom** commended him to Pope Innocent I, and Zosimus was elected pope in 417.

Pelagius and his follower Celestine had become very popular and were well respected as compassionate and able teachers. They taught about the original goodness of Creation as opposed to the doctrine of original sin which prevailed in the Mediterranean understanding of the Christian faith at that time. Though they had been condemned as heretics, Zosimus agreed to re-hear their case and cleared them of all charges. However, when the North African bishops learned what had happened, they were deeply concerned about the consequences of Pelagius' teaching (see appendix on heresies: Pelagianism*) in their own divided dioceses. A fresh appeal was made to the pope, and as a result, a year later, Zosimus reversed his decision.

His decision to give the See of Arles primacy over other Sees in France caused much dissent in that land.

Zosimus had planned to excommunicate the people of Ravenna for plotting against him, but before he could do so he fell ill and died.

Heresies

The word 'heresy' derives from the Greek word *haireomai* which means 'to choose or prefer', and thus developed into the term for a private opinion. Such preferred opinions often grew out of a genuine desire to make the Christian faith more understandable, accessible or pure, and many heresies became popular movements within the Church.

The saints of the Church often found themselves in open conflict with the most prevalent and successful heresies of their day, and apart from a few notable exceptions, who seemed to thrive on conflict, the saints sought to live peaceably, holding firmly to the basic tenets of the Christian faith based on the Holy Scriptures and affirmed by the historic councils of the Church.

It should be noted that heresy often, if not always, precedes the orthodox statement on doctrine. The term orthodoxy, in Greek *ortho-doxis*, means 'right glory' or 'right belief', thus when the faithful find that someone such as Arius has made a statement that obscures something that is important in worship or faith, then an orthodox response is proposed.

Any disagreement on spiritual matters has the potential to be deeply divisive, but it may still be difficult to appreciate why such deep passions should be aroused by what might be considered by today's standards such obscure theological niceties. However, these disputes often involved clashes of personality and political considerations, which greatly magnified their latent potential to disintegrate relationships. Those seeking to keep hold of 'right glory' were deeply offended by false or incomplete versions of the truth. Thus the creeds, far from being doctrinal compendiums, were more glorious statements of confession of faith. The theological doctrines which the saints have felt continually called to affirm in the course of many historic struggles had one end in view; to maintain and promote 'right glory'.

The following brief account of the major heresies, while of necessity somewhat superficial, gives some idea as to the issues facing the saints in their battles for the soul of the Church.

Adoptionism

Adoptionism holds that Jesus was a human being who was adopted by God as his 'Son' at his baptism by John. Therefore, Jesus was not truly divine from birth but was filled with grace to the maximal degree, others to some lesser degree. The problem that St Athanasius (and other Orthodox Christians) identified with adoptionism is that if Jesus is not *fully divine* as well as human he cannot defeat death and corruption. The doctrine arose in the second century and was first condemned as a heresy by Pope St Victor (190–8).

Albigensians

Named after the region surrounding the ancient town of Albi in southern France, the Albigensians were 'Cathars' or 'pure ones'. They believed in the existence of two opposing forces: one good and the other evil. They associated Jesus and the New Testament with all things spiritual; and Satan, the Old Testament and the material world with all things evil. They believed in reincarnation and abstained from meat, milk, cheese, eggs, and sexual relations. Suicide was sometimes practised as a way to rid oneself of the 'evil' human body. The movement was wiped out by a fierce persecution in the 14th century.

The Catholic Cathedral in Albi, built as a response to the Albigensian heresy, has floor-to-ceiling murals of Gospel stories and the Last Judgment.

Arianism

Named after Arius, a priest of Alexandria in around 320, who taught that only God the Father was eternal and that He was too pure and infinite to appear on the earth. Jesus was therefore considered to be a lesser, created being. The Arians believed that the divine quality of the Son took the place of the human and spiritual aspect of Jesus, thus denying the incarnation.

One of the criticisms of the teaching of the Arians was that in asserting that Christ the Son, as a created thing, was to be worshipped, they were advocating idolatry. Athanasius fervently opposed Arianism, explaining that only God had the power to defeat death and corruption and only a human being could reverse the death and corruption of the human race.

Cathars

The word Cathar comes from the Greek *cathar* meaning 'pure one.' The Cathars first came into being in the eleventh century as an offshoot of a small surviving European Gnostic community that had emigrated to the Albigensian region in the south of France. They believed that the world was split along lines of matter and spirit, good and evil, and that they could achieve salvation by clean living, chastity and poverty.

Docetism

From the Greek *dokeo* meaning 'to seem', docetists shared a common perception in the ancient world that the body was associated with enslaving evil desires and that therefore it was impossible that the Redeemer (Christ) could have a human body. It followed then that Jesus only appeared to be human, but was in fact a divine being. Docetists did not believe that Jesus truly suffered or that he rose from the dead, and regarded matter as inherently evil.

Docetism was condemned at the Council of Chalcedon in 451.

Fraticelli

From the Italian *frati* meaning 'little brother', the Fraticelli were members of the Franciscan Order who fell into dispute with the leaders of their community over the proper application of the teaching of their founder. They desired to follow St Francis' strict requirements for holy poverty while those who had been given responsibility over them felt that these rules should be adapted to meet new circumstances.

Gnosticism

Gnosticism took its name from the Greek word *gnosis*, meaning 'knowledge'. Gnostics taught that all matter is evil, and that deliverance from the material form was attainable only through special secret knowledge. Gnosticism taught a dualism between a good and evil, spirit and matter, light and dark in the whole universe, and thus that Jesus could not atone for the sins of others. Gnostics claimed that Jesus was a great teacher, but they did not believe he was the incarnate Son of God.

Iconoclasm

From the Greek word meaning 'to break images', Iconoclasts believed that the making of any religious image was wrong and insisted that any that were in existence in churches should be destroyed. Iconodules disagreed and regarded the proper use of images and icons for veneration as a vital part of the mystery of the incarnation. The latter view eventually prevailed at the Council of Constantinople in 843.

Manichaeism

Manichaeism is based on the teachings of the Persian prophet Mani. It was an extreme form of dualistic Gnosticism that arose in the third century. It promised salvation through special knowledge of spiritual truths, and believed that the universe was founded on the opposing principles, good and evil, each of which had equal power. Its proponents frequently followed a lax moral code.

Marcionism

Named after the teachings of Marcion of Sinope, Marcionism was a dualistic belief system that rejected the writings of the Old Testament and taught that Christ was not the son of the God of the Jews but the son of the Christian God. They adopted Church structures very similar to those of the early Church and thus presented one of the most dangerous and confusing of the early heresies. Marcion's cosmology was much simpler than that of other gnostics (see above). Tertullian first denounced these views as heretical early in the third century.

Modalism

The name is taken from the Latin *modus* meaning 'measure' or 'manner'. Modalists taught that God was a single person who, throughout biblical history, has revealed Himself in three sequential modes or forms: in the mode of the Father in Old Testament times; then at the incarnation in the mode of the Son; and after Jesus' ascension, in the mode of Holy Spirit. These modes are consecutive and never simultaneous. Even though Modalism retains the divinity of Christ, it denies the distinctiveness of the three persons in the Trinity.

Monarchianism

Taken from the Greek *mono* meaning 'one' and *arche* meaning 'rule', Monarchianists taught that God maintained his sole authority even over Christ and the Holy Spirit. God was seen as the Father, Jesus only a man, and the Holy Spirit a force or presence of God.

Monophysitism

From the Greek *mono* meaning 'one' and *physis* meaning 'body', Monophysitism asserts that Jesus had only one mixed or composite nature and not two distinct natures, human and divine, as the historic creeds state. Monophysitism arose out of a reaction against Nestorianism, which taught that Jesus was two distinct persons rather than one. This teaching undermined the incarnation and Monophysitism was condemned as heresy at the Sixth Ecumenical Council in 680–1.

Nestorianism

Named after Nestorius, who was born in Syria and died in 451. Nestorius taught that Jesus was two distinct persons, divine and human, closely and inseparably united and thus that Mary was the mother of Christ only in respect to His humanity. The Council of Ephesus, convened in 431, refuted this and pronounced that Jesus was one person in two distinct and inseparable natures: divine and human.

Novatianism

Named for Novatian, a Roman priest of the third century. Novatian and his followers believed that Christians who had not maintained their confession of faith in times of persecution could not be received again into communion with the Church, and also that all second marriages were unlawful. This view was condemned by a synod in Rome in 251.

Pelagianism (and Neo Pelagianism, Semi-Pelagianism)

Named for Pelagius, who lived in the fifth century in Rome. Pelagianism taught that human beings had the ability to fulfil the commands of God by exercising the freedom of human will apart from the grace of God. They denied that sinful nature was inherited from Adam, but taught that human nature was spoiled rather than fatally flawed. It was therefore considered possible to choose God by the exercise of individual free will and rational thought.

Pelagius was condemned by the Ecumenical Council of Ephesus and excommunicated in 417 by Pope Innocent I.

Neo Pelagianism was a milder version of the above but was still believed to overemphasize the significance of human effort in the process of salvation.

Priscillianism

Named after the Spanish theologian Priscillian of Avila, the Priscillianists believed in the existence of two kingdoms, one of Light and one of Darkness. Both kingdoms were thought to be represented in human beings, symbolized on the side of light by the Twelve Patriarchs, and on the side of darkness by the Signs of the Zodiac. They believed that salvation consisted in liberation from the domination of matter. This gave rise to an extreme system of asceticism. Those among their number who were believed to be truly enlightened were even permitted to tell lies for the sake of a holy end.

The Apostles' Creed

In response to various heresies the church developed creeds in order to set out its beliefs in a clear and definite way. One of the earliest forms of this was known as the Apostles' Creed. Even though this was not written by the immediate followers of Jesus, but developed over several centuries, as far as the Church was concerned it carried the full weight of apostolic authority.

It is still the most popular creed used in worship by Western Christians and contains within it a reference to the communion of saints, this being the belief that, as a result of the resurrection of Jesus Christ, death has been overcome (1 Corinthians 15) and no longer separates Christians in this life from the saints of earlier ages.

In its earliest version, known as the Interrogatory Creed of **St Hippolytus**, it was used during baptismal services and took the form of a series of questions and answers. The full creed, almost as we have it today, is contained in the writings of **St Caesarius of Arles**.

The Apostles Creed[8]

I believe in God, the Father Almighty,
Creator of heaven and earth.
I believe in Jesus Christ, God's only Son, our Lord,
Who was conceived by the Holy Spirit,
Born of the Virgin Mary,
Suffered under Pontius Pilate,
Was crucified, died, and was buried;
He descended to the dead.
On the third day he rose again;
He ascended into heaven,
He is seated at the right hand of the Father,
And he will come to judge the living and the dead.
I believe in the Holy Spirit,
The holy catholic Church,
The communion of saints,
The forgiveness of sins,
The resurrection of the body,
And the life everlasting. Amen.

Symbols of the Saints

The following is a list of some of the symbols associated with the names of specific saints.

St Agatha	Carrying her breasts in a dish
St Agnes	A peacock feather, with lamb at her side
St Anastasia	A palm branch
St Andrew	A saltire cross
St Anthony	A tau cross, a pig by his side
St Apollonia	A tooth and palm branch
St Asaph	A crozier
St Barbara	A book and palm branch
St Barnabas	A staff in one hand and an open book in the other; also a rake
St Bartholomew	A knife, or a processional cross
St Blaise	Iron wool combs
St Bridget	A crozier and book
St Catherine	An inverted sword, or large wheel
St Cecilia	Playing on a harp or organ
St Christopher	A gigantic figure carrying Christ over a river
St Clare	A palm branch
St Clement	A papal crown, an anchor or a pot
St Crispin and Crispian	Two shoemakers at work
St Cuthbert	St Osbald's head in his hand
St David	A leek
St Denis	His mitred head in his hand
St Dorothy	Carrying a basket of fruit
St Edward the Confessor	Holding a sceptre
St Elizabeth	St John and the lamb at her feet

St Faith	A gridiron
St Felix	An anchor
St Francis	A seraph inflicting the stigmata or a lily on a trampled globe
St George	On horseback spearing a dragon
St Giles	A hind, its head in the saint's lap
St Ignatius Loyola	'I.H.S.' in the sky, circled with a glory
St James the Greater	A pilgrim's staff or a scallop shell
St James the Less	A fuller's pole
St John the Divine	A young man with an eagle in the background
St Jerome	A blue hat, and studying a large book
St Jude	A club or lance
St Lawrence	A book and gridiron
St Luke	At a reading-desk, or an ox's head
St Mark	Seated writing, a lion at his feet
St Martin	On horseback, dividing his cloak
St Mary Magdalene	A box of ointment
St Mary the Virgin	Carrying the child Jesus and a lily
St Matthew	Holding a pen, a man's face
St Michael	In armour, with a cross, or holding scales
St Nicholas	A tub with naked infants in it
St Paul	A sword and a book
St Peter	Keys and an inverted cross, a boat or a cock
St Philip	A pastoral staff with a cross
St Sebastian	Bound to a tree, shot through with arrows
St Simon	A saw
St Stephen	A book and a stone in his hand
St Thomas	With a builder's rule, or a stone in his hand
St Thomas of Canterbury	Kneeling, a man striking him with a sword from behind
St Ursula	A book and arrows

Saints in Waiting

'They also serve who only stand and wait.'
John Milton, Sonnet 16, On his Blindness

The stories of modern-day saints still circulate and I include a brief account of three that I have come across during the compiling of this dictionary. While not as yet officially recognized as saints, their lives exhibit the carelessness about physical death and the devotion to life in all its fullness. **St Ignatius of Loyola** describes this as cultivating a sense of indifference to the consequences of their faithful actions. For them, death appears to have been grave but not serious.

Jane Haining
Born in Dunscore in Dumfries Scotland, 1897; died in Auschwitz, 1945.

Brought up in southwest Scotland, Jane was the youngest of three daughters of devout Christian parents. She trained for a career in business and became a private secretary before receiving a call to mission work. When told that she lacked the suitable qualifications, she refused to be put off and set about attaining a diploma in Domestic Science, learning German and piano in her spare time. In 1932 after training at St Colm's college in Edinburgh, she was sent to Budapest to help in a hostel for Jewish girls.

During the rise of Nazism in the 1930s she resisted requests to return to Scotland. Budapest was invaded in March 1944, and Jane was arrested by the Gestapo in May of that year. One of the main charges against her was that she had wept when obeying the order to sew yellow stars on the dresses of the girls in her care.

During her trial Jane again wept profusely at the recollection of having to do this.

She was placed in Auschwitz concentration camp. Once there, her parents received just one postcard from Jane asking for food to be sent.

No more was heard of Jane until some years later a death certificate was discovered which itemized the cause of demise as cachexia, a general collapse of the body due to starvation.

Robin Lindsay
Born in Papua New Guinea; died in the Solomon Islands 2003.

Brother Robin Lindsay from Papua New Guinea was assistant head brother of the Melanesian Brotherhood, an Anglican Community based in the Solomon Islands. During his 20 years in the community he showed great dedication, wise leadership and a remarkable gift for resolving conflicts.

In April 2003 a member of their community, Brother Nathaniel Sado, disappeared while seeking to help resolve the guerrilla war by meeting with the rebel leader Harold Keke. Robin and five other brothers, Francis Tofi, Alfred Hill, Ini Paratabatu, Patteson Gatu and Tony Sirihi, travelled to the remote Weathercoast of Guadalcanal to find out exactly what had happened. They also hoped to bring back Nathaniel's body for burial, if the rumours that he had been killed proved to be correct.

Several weeks later news came that three of the brothers had been shot and killed upon arrival and had been buried in a single grave. The bodies of the other three, who had been shot on the following day, showed signs of torture. They too were buried in a single grave. Harold Keke was soon arrested, charged with murder and found guilty. He was jailed for life in 2005.

At the funeral service of the brothers the words 'Blessed are the peace-makers for they shall be called the sons of God' was placed in front of each coffin next to the name of each brother.

Matrionushka

During the 1930s I[1] was imprisoned in a concentration camp and, since I was already a doctor, they put me in charge of the camp hospital. The majority of the prisoners were in such a bad state that my heart couldn't stand it, and so I let many off from work so as to help them at least a little, and took the weakest into hospital.

Then one day, during the time we saw the sick, a nurse who was working with me and was also a prisoner, said to me: 'Doctor, I have heard that someone has denounced you for being too soft-hearted in dealing with the prisoners. They are threatening to extend your sentence by 15 years.' My companion was a serious person, well-acquainted with camp-life, and therefore I was terrified by what she said. I had already been condemned for three years, which were now coming to an end, and I was counting the months and days that separated me from my long-awaited freedom. And suddenly – another 15 years!

I didn't sleep the whole night, and when I went to work in the morning, the nurse shook her head sadly at the sight of my haggard face. After we had seen the sick, she said in a hesitant manner: 'Doctor, I would like to give you some advice, but I'm afraid that you will laugh at me.' 'Please, tell me,' I replied. 'In Penza, the town where I was born lives a woman called Matrionushka. The Lord has given her a special power of prayer, and once she begins to pray for someone, her prayer is answered without fail. Many people call upon her, and she refuses no one's request. You, too, should ask for her help.' I smiled sadly: 'While my letter is getting to her, they'll have time to give me 15 more years.'

[1]The person who recorded the story of Matrionushka explains that it was told to him by Bishop Stefan (Nikitin), who was then a layman and a doctor. The Russian text can be found in *Nadezhda* 7 (Frankfurt/Main 1982), 241–5. The present translation was made by Bishop Bazil of Sergievo and is used with his permission.

With some embarrassment the nurse replied: 'There's no need to write, in fact. You just call her.' 'Call her?' I said. 'From here? But she lives hundreds of kilometres away from us!' 'I knew you would laugh at me,' she said, 'but it's true that she does hear people from everywhere. Do this: when you go out for a stroll in the evening, lag a little behind everyone else and cry out three times: "Matrionushka, help me! I am in trouble!" She will hear you and help you.'

Although all this seemed strange to me and a bit like magic, nevertheless, when I went out for my evening walk, I did what my assistant said. One day passed, a week, a month ... They didn't send for me. Meanwhile, certain changes took place in the administration of the camp: one person was dismissed, another appointed ... Finally, six months went by, and the day of my departure from camp arrived. When they issued me my papers at the commandant's office, I asked them to give me a warrant to stay in the town where Matrionushka lived, since before I cried out to her I had promised myself that, if she helped me, I would remember her each day in my prayers and make my first task on leaving the camp to go and thank her.

Having obtained my papers, I heard that two young men, who were also being set free, were going to the town to which I had been given permission to go. I joined up with them and we set off together. On the way I began to question my companions to see if they knew about Matrionushka. 'We know her very well,' they replied. 'But then everyone knows her – both in town and throughout the district. We could take you to her if you really needed it, but we live in the country, not in town, and very much want to get home. This is what you should do. When you get there, just ask the first person you meet where Matrionushka lives and they will point it out to you.'

On arrival I did as my companions had said and made enquiries of a young boy, who was the first person I met. 'Go down this street,' he told me, 'and then, by the post office, turn down the lane. Matrionushka lives there, in the third house.' With trepidation I approached the house, intending to knock on the door. But it was not shut and opened easily. Standing on the threshold, I looked around the almost empty room. In the middle stood a table, and on the table was a large box.

'May I come in?' I asked in a fairly loud voice. 'Come in, Seriozhenka,' replied a voice from the box. I gasped with surprise, and then hesitantly moved forward towards the voice. Looking into the box, I saw inside it a tiny woman, lying there motionless on the table. She was blind and had undeveloped, rudimentary arms and legs. But her face was astonishingly radiant and gentle. After greeting her, I asked, 'How did you know my name?' 'How could I not know it,' came her faint but clear, pure voice. 'You called me, and I prayed to God for you. That is how I know you. Sit down, be my guest.'

I sat for a long time with Matrionushka. She told me that she had been taken ill in childhood with some sort of disease and had stopped growing or being able to move about. At birth she was able to see, but she caught smallpox when she was two years old and lost her sight. Her family was poor, and her mother packed her into a little tub when she went to work and took her to the church. There she would put the tub with the little girl in it on a bench, and would leave her until the evening. Lying there in the tub Matrionushka would hear all of the church services and all the sermons. The priest felt sorry for her, and would spend time with her. The parishioners also felt sorry for the child and would bring her things, now a little bite to eat, now a piece of clothing, while others simply caressed her and made her comfortable.

And so in this way she grew up in a deeply spiritual atmosphere of prayer.

Then the two of us talked about other things – about the purpose of life, about faith, about God. And as I listened, I was staggered by the wisdom of her judgement, and by her spiritual discernment. As I was saying goodbye, she said: 'When you stand before the altar of God, remember the servant of God, Matrona.' At that time the idea of Episcopacy had never occurred to me, and I was not yet even a priest. Of herself, however, she said that she would die in prison. Sitting beside her, I realized that in front of me lay not simply a sick woman, but someone who was great in the eyes of God. I found it hard to tear myself away, it was so good and comforting to be with her, and I promised myself that I would visit her again as soon as possible.

But it didn't happen. Soon they took Matrionushka off to prison in Moscow, where she died.

Alphabetical Index of Saints

St Abban	16 March
St Abbo	13 November
Sts Abdon and Sennen	30 July
St Abel	5 August
St Abercius Marcellus	22 October
St Abraham	15 June
St Abraham Kidunaja	16 March
St Abraham of Rostov	29 October
St Abraham of Smolensk	21 August
St Acacius	31 March
St Acca	20 October
St Acepsimas	3 November
St Acestes	2 July
St Achatius	31 March
St Achillas	7 November
St Adalbert of Prague	23 April
St Adamnan	23 September
St Adelaide	16 December
St Adrian	4 March
St Aelred of Rievaulx	3 February
St Agatha	5 February
St Agnes	21 January
St Agnes of Assisi	16 November
St Aidan of Lindisfarne	31 August
St Ailbhe	12 September
St Alban	22 June
St Alberic	26 January
St Albert the Great	15 November
St Aldhelm	25 May
St Alexander	18 March
St Alexander of Constantinople	28 August
St Alexander Nevski	30 August

St Alexis	17 July
St Alfrick	16 November
St Alfwold	26 March
St Alipius	15 August
St Alphege	12 March
St Alphonsus Marie Liguori	1 August
St Altman	8 August
St Alto	9 February
St Alvarez	19 February
St Amalberga	10 July
St Amand	6 February
St Amata	20 February
St Amator	1 May
St Amatus	13 September
St Ambrose of Milan	7 December
St Ammon	20 December
St Amphianus	2 April
St Amphilocus	23 November
St Anastasius I	19 December
St Anatolia	9 July
St Anatolius	3 July
St Andochius	24 September
St Andrew	30 November
Sts Andrew Kim Taegon, Paul Chong Hasang, and Companions	20 September
St Andronicus	9 October
St Angadresma	14 October
St Angela de'Merici	27 January
St Angelo	5 May
St Angilbert	18 February
St Annemund	28 September
St Ansanus	1 December
St Anselm of Canterbury	21 April
St Antoninus	2 September
St Antony of Egypt	17 January
St Antony of Padua	13 June
St Anysia	30 December
St Aphraates	7 April
St Apollinaris	8 January

St Apollo	25 January
St Armogastes and Companions	29 March
St Arnulf	18 July
St Arnulf	15 August
St Arsacius	16 August
St Arsenius the Great	19 July
St Artaldus	7 October
St Artemius	20 October
St Asaph	1 May
St Asclas	23 January
St Asicus	27 April
St Astius	7 July
St Athanasia	15 August
St Athanasius	2 May
St Athenodorus	18 October
St Attalas	10 March
St Atticus	8 January
St Atto	22 May
St Attracta	11 August
St Aubin	1 March
St Augustine of Canterbury	28 May
St Augustine of Hippo	28 August
St Austreberta	10 February
St Autbert	10 September
St Auxentius	14 February
St Aventanus	25 February
St Babylas	24 January
St Bagnus	20 June
St Baldomerus	27 February
St Baldred	6 March
St Balin	3 September
St Bandaridus	9 August
St Barbara	4 December
St Barbasymas	14 January
St Barbatus	19 February
St Bardo	15 June
St Barhadbescaba	20 July
St Barlaam	6 November
St Barlaam	19 November

St Barnabas	11 June
St Barnard	23 January
St Barsanuphius	11 April
St Bartholomew	24 August
St Basil the Great	14 June
St Bathildis	30 January
St Baudelius	20 May
St Bavo	1 October
St Beatus	9 May
The Venerable Bede	25 May
St Bega	31 October
St Begga	17 December
St Benedict	21 March
St Benedict II	7 May
St Benedict Biscop	12 January
St Benedict the Black	4 April
St Benedict the Hermit	23 March
St Benignus	9 November
St Benjamin	31 March
St Bercharius	16 October
St Berhtwald	9 January
St Bernadette	16 April
St Bernard of Clairvaux	20 August
St Bernard of Parma	4 December
St Bernardino Realino	2 July
St Bernardino of Siena	20 May
St Bernward	20 November
St Bertharius	22 October
St Berthold	29 March
St Bertinus	5 September
St Bessarion	17 June
St Bettelin	9 September
St Bibiana	2 December
St Bilfrid	6 March
St Blaise	3 February
St Blandina	2 June
St Blane	11 August
St Bonaventure	15 July
St Boniface (Wynfrith)	5 June
St Bosa	9 March

St Botulph	17 June
St Braulio	26 March
St Brendan	16 May
St Brice	13 November
St Bridget	23 July
St Brigid	1 February
St Bruno	6 October
St Bruno of Würzburg	27 May
St Burchard	14 October
St Cadoc	24 January
St Cadwallader	12 November
St Caedmon	11 February
St Caesaria	12 January
St Caesarius of Arles	27 August
St Caesarius of Nazianzus	25 February
St Cajetan	7 August
St Calepodius	10 May
St Calimerius	31 July
St Callistus	14 October
St Camillus de Lellis	18 July
St Canice	11 October
St Canute IV	19 January
St Canute Lavard	7 January
St Caprasius	20 October
St Caradoc	14 April
St Carpus, Papylus, Agathonica and Agathodorus	13 April
St Casimir	4 March
St Cassian	3 December
St Cassian of Imola	13 August
St Catherine of Alexandria	25 November
St Catherine Labouré	28 November
St Catherine de Ricci	13 February
St Catherine of Siena	30 April
St Catherine of Sweden	24 March
St Catherine de Vigri	9 March
St Cecilia	22 November
St Cedd	26 October
St Celestine I	6 April
St Celsus	7 April

St Ceolfrid	25 September
St Chad	2 March
St Charbel	24 December
St Charles Borromeo	4 November
The Venerable Charles de Foucauld	1 December
St Charles Garnier	19 October
St Christina	24 July
St Christina the Astonishing	15 December
St Christopher	25 July
St Christopher Magallenes	15 July
St Clare	11 August
St Claudia	7 August
St Clement I	23 November
St Clement of Okhrida	17 July
St Clotilde	3 June
St Cloud	7 September
St Colette	7 February
St Colman of Dromore	7 June
St Colman of Lindisfarne	18 February
St Columba	9 June
St Columba of Cordova	17 September
St Columban	23 November
St Comgall	10 May
St Cornelius	2 February
St Cornelius	16 September
Sts Cosmas and Damian	27 September
Sts Crispin and Crispinian	25 October
St Crispin of Viterbo (Peter Fioretti)	19 May
St Cuthbert	20 March
St Cuthman	8 February
St Cyprian	9 December
St Cyprian of Carthage	6 September
St Cyril of Alexandria	27 June
St Cyril of Jerusalem	18 March
Sts Cyril and Methodius	14 February
St Damasus	11 December
St Daniel	16 February
St Daniel the Stylite	11 December

St David I	24 May
St David Lewis	27 August
St David of Wales	1 March
St Declan	24 July
Sts Denis, Rusticus, and Eleutherius	9 October
St Derferl-Gadarn	5 April
St Desiderius	23 May
St Dionysios	17 December
St Disibod	8 September
St Dismas	25 March
St Dominic	4 August
St Dominic of Silos	20 December
St Donald	15 July
St Donan	17 April
St Dorothy	6 February
St Drithelm	17 August
St Drostan	11 July
St Dunchad	24 May
St Dunstan	19 May
St Dymphna	15 May
St Eata	26 October
St Ebbe	25 August
St Ebbe the Younger	22 June
St Edbert	6 May
St Edburga	12 December
St Edgar	8 July
St Edith of Wilton	16 September
St Edmund Arrowsmith	28 August
St Edward the Confessor	13 October
St Edward the Martyr	18 March
St Edwin	12 October
St Egbert	24 April
St Egilo	28 June
St Egwin	30 December
St Eleanora	21 February
St Elfleda	8 February
St Elizabeth of Hungary	19 November
St Elizabeth of Portugal	4 July
St Elizabeth Seton	4 January

St Eloi	25 June
St Emily de Vialar	17 June
St Emma	27 June
St Emmeramus	22 September
St Enda	21 March
St Ephraem	9 June
St Erastus of Corinth	26 July
St Eric IX	18 May
St Ethbin	19 October
St Ethelbert	20 May
St Ethelburga	11 October
St Ethelreda	23 June
St Ethelwold	1 August
St Eugene de Mazenod	21 May
St Eulalia of Merida	10 December
St Eulogius of Cordova	11 March
St Euphemia	16 September
St Euphrosyne of Polotsk	23 May
St Eusebius of Vercelli	2 August
St Eustace	20 September
St Eustochium Calafato	20 January
St Everild	9 July
St Exuperius	2 May
St Fabian	20 January
St Fabiola	27 December
St Fara	3 April
Sts Faustinus and Jovita	15 February
St Faustus	28 September
Sts Felix and Audactus	24 October
Sts Felix and Augebert	6 September
St Felix of Nola	14 January
St Ferdinand III of Castile	30 May
St Fergus	27 November
St Fiacre	12 October
St Fillan	19 January
St Finbar	25 September
St Finnian	17 February
St Fintan	17 February
St Flavian of Acquapendente	22 December
St Flavian of Constantinople	18 February

St Frances of Rome	9 March
St Frances Xavier Cabrini	13 November
St Francis of Assisi	4 October
St Francis Borgia	10 October
Bl Francis Pacheco	20 June
St Francis of Paola	2 April
St Francis de Sales	24 January
St Francis Xavier	3 December
St Frideswide	19 October
St Fridolin	6 March
St Fructuosus	21 January
St Frumentius of Ethiopia	27 October
St Fursey	16 January
St Fulk	22 May
St Gabriel the Archangel	29 September
St Gaius of Korea	15 November
St Gall	1 July
St Galla	5 October
St Gelasius I	21 November
St Geminian	31 January
St Genesius	25 August
St Genevieve	3 January
St George	23 April
St Gerald of Aurillac	13 October
St Gerard	3 October
St Gerard Majella	16 October
Sts Gerard Miles and Francis Dickenson	30 April
St Gerasimus	5 March
St Germaine of Pibrac	15 June
St Germanus of Auxerre	31 July
St Gertrude	16 November
Sts Gervase and Protase	19 June
St Gilbert of Sempringham	16 February
St Gildas	29 January
St Godric	21 May
St Gregory III	10 December
St Gregory VII (Hildebrand)	25 May
St Gregory the Enlightener	30 September
St Gregory the Great	3 September

St Gregory of Nazianzus	2 January
St Gregory of Nyssa	9 March
St Gregory Palamas	14 November
St Gregory the Sinaite	8 August
St Gregory Thaumaturgus	17 November
St Gundisalvus Garcia	6 February
St Guthlac	11 April
St Guy of Anderlecht	12 September
St Gyavire	13 June
St Hallvard	15 May
St Hedda	7 July
St Hedwig	28 February
St Hedwig	16 October
St Helena	18 August
St Helen of Skovde	31 July
St Helier	16 July
St Heliodorus	6 May
St Henry	13 July
St Henry of Sweden	19 January
St Herbert	20 March
St Heron	14 December
St Hervé	17 June
St Hilarion	21 October
St Hilary of Arles	5 May
St Hilary of Poitiers	13 January
St Hilda	17 November
St Hildegard of Bingen	17 September
St Hippolytus	13 August
The Holy Innocents	28 December
St Honoratus	16 January
St Hope	1 August
St Hubert	3 November
St Hugh the Great	29 April
St Hugh of Grenoble	1 April
St Hugh of Lincoln	17 November
St Hyacinth	17 August
St Hypatius	17 June
Sts Hypatius and Andrew	29 August
St Ia	4 August
St Ibar	23 April

St Ignatius of Antioch	1 February
St Ignatius Loyola	31 July
St Illtyd	6 November
St Ingrid of Sweden	2 September
St Irenaeus	28 June
St Irene	26 February
St Isaac the Great	9 September
Sts Isaac Jogues and Rene Goupil	19 October
St Isadore the Farmer	15 May
St Isadore of Seville	4 April
St Ita	15 January
St Ivo of Brittany	19 May
St Jambert	12 August
St James the Less	3 May
St James of the Marches	28 November
St James of Nisibis	15 July
St Jane Frances de Chantal	21 August
St Jan Sarkander	17 March
St Januarius	19 September
St Jeanne de Lestonnac	2 February
St Jerome	30 September
St Joan of Arc	30 May
St John-Baptist de la Salle	7 April
St John Bosco	31 January
St John Cassian	23 July
St John Chrysostom	14 September
St John of the Cross	24 November
St John the Divine	26 September
St John of Egypt	27 March
St John Fisher	22 June
St John Ogilvie	10 March
St Josémaria Escriva de Balageur	26 June
St Joseph	19 March
St Joseph Calasanz	25 August
St Joseph of Copertino	18 September
St Joseph Cottolongo	29 April
St Joseph Tommasi	1 January
St Joseph of Volokolamsk	9 September

St Julian of Norwich	13 May
St Justin Martyr	1 June
Bl Kateri Tekakwitha	14 July
St Katherine Drexel	3 March
St Kenelm	17 July
St Kentigern (Mungo)	14 January
St Kessag	10 March
St Kevin	3 June
St Keyna	18 October
St Kiernan	22 March
St Kilian	8 July
St Kunegunda	24 June
St Lanfranc	24 May
St Laserian	18 April
St Lawrence	14 November
St Lawrence of Brindisi	21 July
St Lawrence of Canterbury	2 February
St Lawrence (martyr)	10 August
St Lawrence Ruiz	28 September
St Lebuin	11 November
St Leger	2 October
St Leo III	12 June
St Leo IX	19 April
St Leocritia of Cordova	15 March
St Leo the Great	10 November
St Leonard of Port Maurice	20 December
St Leonides of Alexandria	22 April
St Longinus the Centurion	15 March
St Lucy of Syracuse	13 December
St Ludan	12 February
St Luke	14 October
St Macanisius	3 September
St Macarius of Jerusalem	10 March
St Machar	12 November
St Macrina the Elder	14 January
St Macrina the Younger	19 July
St Madeleine Sophie	25 May
St Maelruain	7 July
St Magnus of Orkney	16 April
St Maharsapor	10 October

St Maieul	11 May
St Malachy O'More	3 November
St Malchus	27 July
St Malo	15 November
St Marcellina	17 July
Sts Marcellinus and Peter	2 June
St Marcellus the Centurion	30 October
St Marcian of Chalcis	2 November
St Marek Krizin	7 September
St Margaret of Antioch	20 July
St Margaret of Cortona	22 February
St Margaret of Hungary	26 January
St Margaret of Scotland	16 November
St Margaret Ward	25 October
St Marguerite Bourgeoys	12 January
St Marguerite d'Youville	16 October
St Maria Crocifissa di Rosa	14 December
St Maria-Domenica Mazzarello	14 May
St Maria Goretti	6 July
St Maria Skobtsova	20 July
St Maria Soledad	11 October
St Marinus	3 March
St Mark	25 April
Sts Mark and Marcellian	18 June
St Maro	14 February
St Martha	28 July
St Martin de Aguirre	6 February
St Martin of Braga	20 March
St Martinian	13 February
St Martin de Porres	3 November
St Martin of Tours	11 November
St Mary	8 December
St Mary of Egypt	2 April
St Mary Magdalene	22 July
St Mary Magdalene de Pazzi	25 May
St Mary the Slave	1 November
St Matilda	14 March
St Matthew	21 September
St Matthias	14 May

St Maurice	22 September
St Maurus	25 January
St Maximilian	14 August
St Maximilian Kolbe	14 August
St Maximus	10 June
St Maximus the Confessor	13 August
St Maximus of Jerusalem	5 May
St Mel	6 February
St Mellitus of Canterbury	24 April
St Mennas	10 December
St Mercurius of Caesarea	25 November
St Mesrop	19 February
St Michael the Archangel	29 September
St Michael Ghebre	1 September
St Miguel Cordero de la Salle	9 February
St Mildred	14 July
St Miltiades	10 December
St Mirin of Benchor	15 September
St Modwenna	5 July
St Monica	27 August
St Moses the Ethiopian	28 August
St Narcissus	29 October
St Nathalan	19 January
St Nectan	17 June
St Nectarius	11 October
St Nektarios of Pentapolis	9 November
St Nerses	20 November
St Nerses the Great	19 November
St Nicasius of Rheims	14 December
St Nicephorus	13 March
St Nicetas	22 June
St Nicetius	5 December
St Nicholas	6 December
St Nicholas I	13 November
St Nicholas Cabasilas	20 June
St Nicholas Pieck	9 July
St Nicholas Studites	4 February
St Nicholas of Tolentino	10 September
St Nicholas von Flue	21 March

St Nicodemus of the Holy Mountain	14 July
St Nikon	26 November
St Nilus the Elder	12 November
St Nilus the Younger	26 September
St Nina	14 January
St Ninian	16 September
St Noel Chabanel	26 December
St Non	3 March
St Norbert	6 June
St Notburga	14 September
St Numidicus	9 August
St Odilo	1 January
St Odo	18 November
St Olaf of Norway	29 July
St Olaf of Sweden	30 July
St Olga	11 July
St Oliver Plunkett	11 July
St Olympias	17 December
St Omer	9 September
St Osmund	4 December
St Oswald	4 August
St Otto of Bamberg	2 July
St Ouen	24 August
St Pabo	9 November
St Pachomius	9 May
St Palemon	11 January
St Palladius	7 July
St Pancras	12 May
St Pantaenus	7 July
St Pantaleon	27 July
St Panteleimon the All-Merciful	27 July
St Paschal Baylon	17 May
St Paschasius	26 April
St Paternus	15 April
St Patiens	11 September
St Patrick	17 March
St Paul	29 June
St Paula	26 January

St Paul of Constantinople	7 June
St Paul the Hermit	15 January
St Paulinus of Aquileia	28 January
St Paulinus of Nola	22 June
St Paulinus of York	10 October
St Paul Miki	6 February
St Paul Tong Buong	23 October
St Pelagia	8 October
St Pelagia of Antioch	8 June
St Peregrine Laziosi	3 May
Sts Perpetua and Felicity	7 March
St Peter	29 June
St Peter of Alicante	13 October
St Peter Canisius	21 December
St Peter of Canterbury	6 January
St Peter Celestine	19 May
St Peter Chrysologus	30 July
St Peter Damian	23 February
St Peter of Mount Athos	12 June
St Peter Nolasco	28 January
St Peter of Tarantaise	8 May
St Peter of Verona	29 April
St Petroc	4 June
St Petronella of Rome	31 May
St Phileas	26 November
St Philemon	8 March
St Philibert	22 August
St Philip	3 May
St Philip Benizi	23 August
St Philip Evans	22 July
St Philip Neri	26 May
St Phocas the Gardener	23 July
St Pio of Pietrelcina (Padre Pio)	23 September
St Pionius	1 February
St Pius V	30 April
St Pius X	21 August
St Placid	5 October
St Polycarp	23 February
St Praejectus	25 January

St Praxedes	21 July
Sts Processus and Martinian	2 July
St Prosper	7 July
St Prudentius	28 April
St Quadratus	26 May
St Quentin	31 October
St Quintian	23 May
Sts Quiricus and Julitta	16 June
St Quodvultdeaus	19 February
St Radbod of Utrecht	29 November
St Rainerius Scacceri	17 June
St Raphael	29 September
St Raphael Kalinowski	19 November
St Raymond Nonnatus	31 August
St Raymond of Pennafort	7 January
St Raymond of Toulouse	8 July
St Raymund Palermo	27 July
St Realino	3 July
St Reineldis	17 July
St Remigius	1 October
St Richard of Chichester	3 April
St Richard Gwyn	17 October
St Richardis	18 September
St Richard Reynolds	4 May
St Rita of Cascia	22 May
St Robert of Molesmes	29 April
St Robert of Newminster	7 June
St Roch	16 August
Sts Romanus and Barula	18 November
St Romanus the Melodist	1 October
St Romuald	19 June
St Roque Gonzalez de Santa Cruz	17 November
St Rose of Lima	30 August
St Sabas	5 December
St Salvatore	18 March
St Samson	28 July
St Saturninus	11 February
St Sava of Serbia	14 January
St Scholastica	10 February

St Sebastian	20 December
St Sebbi	29 August
St Senan	8 March
St Seraphim of Sarov	2 January
St Serf	1 July
St Sergius	25 September
St Silas	13 July
St Simeon Metaphrastes	28 November
St Simeon Stylites	5 January
St Simon Stock	16 May
St Simon the Zealot	28 October
Sixtus II	6 August
St Stanislaus	11 April
St Stephen	26 December
St Stephen I	2 August
St Stephen the Great	16 August
St Susanna	11 August
St Swithun	15 July
St Sylvester	31 December
St Sylvia	5 November
St Symeon the New Theologian	12 March
St Tarasius	10 March
St Tatwin	30 July
St Teilo	9 February
St Teresa de los Andes	13 July
St Teresa of Avila	15 October
Mother Teresa of Calcutta	5 September
St Thecla	23 September
St Theobald	30 June
St Theodore I	14 May
St Theodore of Canterbury	19 September
St Theodore of Studites	11 November
St Theodore of Sykeon	22 April
St Theodosius Pechersky	10 July
St Theopan	6 January
St Theresa of Lisieux	1 October
St Thomas	3 July
St Thomas Aquinas	28 January
St Thomas Becket	29 December

St Thomas Garnet	23 June
St Thomas More	22 June
St Thomas of Villanueva	22 September
St Thorfinn	8 January
St Thorlac Thorhallsson	23 December
St Timothy	26 January
Sts Timothy, Thecla, and Agapius	19 August
St Titus	26 January
St Trophimus of Arles	29 December
St Tudwal	30 November
St Turibius of Mogroveio	16 April
St Tutilo	28 March
St Tysilio	8 November
St Ubald Baldassini	16 May
St Ulrich	14 July
St Ultan	4 September
St Urban	25 May
St Ursula	21 October
St Valentine	14 February
St Venantius Fortunatus	14 December
St Vénard Theophane	2 February
St Veronica	12 July
St Vicelin	12 December
St Victor I	28 July
St Victorius	24 February
St Victor of Marseilles	21 July
St Victor the Moor	8 May
St Vincent Ferrer	5 April
St Vincent of Lerins	14 May
St Vincent de Paul	27 September
St Vincent Saragossa	22 January
St Vincent Yen	30 June
St Vincenza Mary Lopez y Vicuna	18 January
St Virgil of Arles	5 March
St Virgil of Salzburg	27 November
St Vitus	15 June
St Vladimir	15 July
Sts Votus and Felix	29 May

APPENDIX VI

Index of Feast Days[10]

January

1 St Joseph Tommasi, St Odilo
2 St Gregory of Nazianzus, St Seraphim of Sarov
3 St Genevieve
4 St Elizabeth Seton
5 St Simeon Stylites
6 St Peter of Canterbury, St Theopan
7 St Canute Lavard, St Raymond of Pennafort
8 St Apollinaris, St Atticus, St Thorfinn
9 St Berhtwald
11 St Palemon
12 St Benedict Biscop, St Caesaria, St Marguerite Bourgeoys
13 St Hilary of Poitiers
14 St Barbasymas, St Felix of Nola, St Kentigern, St Macrina the Elder, St Nina, St Sava of Serbia
15 St Ita, St Paul the Hermit
16 St Fursey, St Honoratus
17 St Antony of Egypt
18 St Vincenza Mary Lopez y Vicuna
19 St Canute IV, St Fillan, St Henry of Sweden, St Nathalan, St Wulfstan
20 St Eustochium Calafato, St Fabian
21 St Agnes, St Fructuosus
22 St Vincent Saragossa
23 St Asclas, St Barnard
24 St Babylas, St Cadoc, St Francis de Sales
25 St Apollo, St Maurus, St Praejectus
26 St Alberic, St Margaret of Hungary, St Paula, St Timothy, St Titus
27 St Angela de'Merici
28 St Paulinus of Aquileia, St Peter Nolasco, St Thomas Aquinas
29 St Gildas
30 St Bathildis
31 St Geminian, St John Bosco

February

1 St Brigid, St Ignatius of Antioch, St Pionius
2 St Cornelius, St Jeanne de Lestonnac, St Lawrence of Canterbury, St Vénard Theophane

St Walburga	25 February
St Waldebert	5 February
St Walfrid	15 February
St Walter of Pontoise	8 April
St Waltheof of Melrose	3 August
St Wenceslaus	28 September
St Wilfrid	12 October
St Willehad	8 November
St William of Maleval	10 February
St William of Rochester	23 May
St William of Roskilde	2 September
St William of York	8 June
St Willibald	7 June
St Willibrord	7 November
St Willigis	23 February
St Winebald	18 December
St Winoc	6 November
St Wiro	8 May
St Withburga	8 July
St Wolfgang	31 October
St Wulfhilda	9 September
St Wulfric	20 February
St Wulfstan	19 January
St Wulmar	20 July
St Yrieix	25 August
St Ywi	8 October
St Zeno	12 April
St Zenobius	25 May
St Zephyrinus	26 August
St Zita	27 April
St Zoe	2 May
St Zosimus	30 March

3 St Aelred of Rievaulx, St Blaise
4 St Nicholas Studites
5 St Agatha, St Waldebert
6 St Amand, St Dorothy, St Gundisalvus Garcia, St Martin de Aguirre, St Mel, St Paul Miki
7 St Colette
8 St Cuthman, St Elfleda
9 St Alto, St Miguel Cordero de la Salle, St Teilo
10 St Austreberta, St Scholastica, St William of Maleval
11 St Caedmon, St Saturninus
12 St Ludan
13 St Catherine de Ricci, St Martinian
14 St Auxentius, Sts Cyril and Methodius, St Maro, St Valentine
15 Sts Faustinus and Jovita, St Walfrid
16 St Daniel, St Gilbert of Sempringham
17 St Finnian, St Fintan
18 St Angilbert, St Colman of Lindisfarne, St Flavian of Constantinople
19 St Alvarez, St Barbatus, St Mesrop, St Quodvultdeaus
20 St Amata, St Wulfric
21 St Eleanora
22 St Margaret of Cortona
23 St Peter Damian, St Polycarp, St Willigis
24 St Victorius
25 St Aventanus, St Caesarius of Nazianzus, St Walburga
26 St Irene
27 St Baldomerus
28 St Hedwig

March

1 St Aubin, St David of Wales
2 St Chad
3 St Katherine Drexel, St Marinus, St Non
4 St Adrian, St Casimir
5 St Gerasimus, St Virgil of Arles
6 St Baldred, St Bilfrid, St Fridolin
7 Sts Perpetua and Felicity
8 St Philemon, St Senan
9 St Bosa, St Catherine de Vigri, St Frances of Rome, St Gregory of Nyssa
10 St Attalas, St John Ogilvie, St Kessag, St Macarius of Jerusalem, St Tarasius
11 St Eulogius of Cordova
12 St Alphege, St Symeon the New Theologian
13 St Nicephorus
14 St Matilda
15 St Leocritia of Cordova, St Longinus the Centurion
16 St Abban, St Abraham Kidunaja
17 St Jan Sarkander, St Patrick

18   St Alexander, St Cyril of Jerusalem, St Edward the Martyr,
     St Salvatore
19   St Joseph
20   St Cuthbert, St Herbert, St Martin of Braga
21   St Benedict, St Enda, St Nicholas von Flue
22   St Kiernan
23   St Benedict the Hermit
24   St Catherine of Sweden
25   St Dismas
26   St Alfwold, St Braulio
27   St John of Egypt
28   St Tutilo
29   St Armogastes and Companions, St Berthold
30   St Zosimus
31   St Acacius, St Achatius, St Benjamin

April
1   St Hugh of Grenoble
2   St Amphianus, St Francis of Paola, St Mary of Egypt
3   St Fara, St Richard of Chichester
4   St Benedict the Black, St Isadore of Scville
5   St Derferl-Gadarn, St Vincent Ferrer
6   St Celestine I
7   St Aphraates, St Celsus, St John-Baptist de la Salle
8   St Walter of Pontoise
11   St Barsanuphius, St Guthlac, St Stanislaus
12   St Zeno
13   St Carpus, Papylus, Agathonica and Agathodorus
14   St Caradoc
15   St Paternus
16   St Bernadette, St Magnus of Orkney, St Turibius of Mogroveio
17   St Donan
18   St Laserian
19   St Leo IX
21   St Anselm of Canterbury
22   St Leonides of Alexandria, St Theodore of Sykeon
23   St Adalbert of Prague, St George, St Ibar
24   St Egbert, St Mellitus of Canterbury
25   St Mark
26   St Paschasius
27   St Asicus, St Zita
28   St Prudentius
29   St Hugh the Great, St Joseph Cottolongo, St Peter of Verona,
     St Robert of Molesmes
30   St Catherine of Seina, St Gerard Miles and Francis Dickinson,
     St Pius V

May

1 St Amator, St Asaph
2 St Athanasius, St Exuperius, St Zoe
3 St James the Less, St Peregrine Laziosi, St Philip
4 St Richard Reynolds
5 St Angelo, St Hilary of Arles, St Maximus of Jerusalem
6 St Edbert, St Heliodorus
7 St Benedict II
8 St Peter of Tarantaise, St Victor the Moor, St Wiro
9 St Beatus, St Pachomius
10 St Calepodius, St Comgall
11 St Maieul
12 St Pancras
13 St Julian of Norwich
14 St Maria-Domenica Mazzarello, St Matthias, St Theodore I,
    St Vincent of Lerins
15 St Dymphna, St Hallvard, St Isadore the Farmer
16 St Brendan, St Simon Stock, St Ubald Baldassini
17 St Paschal Baylon
18 St Eric IX
19 St Crispin of Viterbo, St Dunstan, St Ivo of Brittany, St Peter
    Celestine
20 St Baudelius, St Bernardino of Siena, St Ethelbert
21 St Eugene de Mazenod, St Godric
22 St Atto, St Fulk, St Rita of Cascia
23 St Desiderius, St Euphrosyne of Polotsk, St Quintian, St William of
    Rochester
24 St David I, St Dunchad, St Lanfranc
25 St Aldhelm, The Venerable Bede, St Gregory VII (Hildebrand),
    St Madeleine Sophie, St Mary Magdalene de Pazzi, St Urban,
    St Zenobius
26 St Philip Neri, St Quadratus
27 St Bruno of Würzburg
28 St Augustine of Canterbury
29 Sts Votus and Felix
30 St Ferdinand III of Castile, St Joan of Arc
31 St Petronella of Rome

June

1 St Justin Martyr
2 St Blandina, Sts Marcellinus and Peter
3 St Clotilde, St Kevin
4 St Petroc
5 St Boniface (Wynfrith)
6 St Norbert
7 St Colman of Dromore, St Paul of Constantinople, St Robert of
    Newminster, St Willibald
8 St Pelagia of Antioch, St William of York

 9 St Columba, St Ephraem
10 St Maximus
11 St Barnabas
12 St Leo III, St Peter of Mount Athos
13 St Antony of Padua, St Gyavire
14 St Basil the Great
15 St Abraham, St Bardo, St Germaine of Pibrac, St Vitus
16 St Quiricus and Julitta
17 St Bessarion, St Botulph, St Emily de Vialar, St Hervé, St Hypatius,
    St Nectan, St Rainerius Scacceri
18 Sts Mark and Marcellian
19 St Gervase and St Protase, St Romuald
20 St Bagnus, Bl Francis Pacheco, St Nicholas Cabasilas
22 St Alban, St Ebbe the Younger, St John Fisher, St Nicetas,
    St Paulinus of Nola, St Thomas More
23 St Ethelreda, St Thomas Garnet
24 St Kunegunda
25 St Eloi
26 St Josémaria Escriva de Balageur
27 St Cyril of Alexandria, St Emma
28 St Egilo, St Irenaeus
29 St Paul, St Peter
30 St Theobald, St Vincent Yen

July
 1 St Gall, St Serf
 2 St Acestes, St Bernardino Realino, St Otto of Bamberg,
    Sts Processus and Martinian
 3 St Anatolius, St Realino, St Thomas
 4 St Elizabeth of Portugal
 5 St Modwenna
 6 St Maria Goretti
 7 St Astius, St Hedda, St Maelruain, St Palladius, St Pantaenus,
    St Prosper
 8 St Edgar, St Kilian, St Raymond of Toulouse, St Withburga
 9 St Anatolia, St Everild, St Nicholas Pieck
10 St Amalberga, St Theodosius Pechersky
11 St Drostan, St Olga, St Oliver Plunkett
12 St Veronica
13 St Henry, St Silas, St Teresa de los Andes
14 Bl Kateri Tekakwitha, St Mildred, St Nicodemus of the Holy
    Mountain, St Ulrich
15 St Bonaventure, St Christopher Magallenes, St Donald, St James of
    Nisibis, St Swithun, St Vladimir
16 St Helier
17 St Alexis, St Clement of Okhrida, St Kenelm, St Marcellina,
    St Reineldis
18 St Arnulf, St Camillus de Lellis

19 St Arsenius the Great, St Macrina the Younger
20 St Barhadbescaba, St Margaret of Antioch, St Maria Skobtsova, St Wulmar
21 St Lawrence of Brindisi, St Praxedes, St Victor of Marseilles
22 St Mary Magdalene, St Philip Evans
23 St Bridget, St John Cassian, St Phocas the Gardener
24 St Christina, St Declan
25 St Christopher
26 St Erastus of Corinth
27 St Malchus, St Pantaleon, St Panteleimon the All-Merciful, St Raymund Palermo
28 St Martha, St Samson, St Victor I
29 St Olaf of Norway
30 Sts Abdon and Sennen, St Olaf of Sweden, St Peter Chrysologus, St Tatwin
31 St Calimerius, St Germanus of Auxerre, St Helen of Skovde, St Ignatius Loyola

August

1 St Alphonsus Marie Liguori, St Ethelwold, St Hope
2 St Eusebius of Vercelli, St Stephen I
3 St Waltheof of Melrose
4 St Dominic, St Ia, St Oswald
5 St Abel
6 St Sixtus II
7 St Cajetan, St Claudia
8 St Altman, St Gregory the Sinaite
9 St Bandaridus, St Numidicus
10 St Lawrence (martyr)
11 St Attracta, St Blane, St Clare, St Susanna
12 St Jambert
13 St Cassian of Imola, St Hippolytus, St Maximus the Confessor
14 St Maximilian, St Maximilian Kolbe
15 St Alipius, St Arnulf, St Athanasia
16 St Arsacius, St Roch, St Stephen the Great
17 St Drithelm, St Hyacinth
18 St Helena
19 Sts Timothy, Thecla & Agapius
20 St Bernard of Clairvaux
21 St Abraham of Smolensk, St Jane Frances de Chantal, St Pius X
22 St Philibert
23 St Philip Benizi
24 St Bartholomew, St Ouen
25 St Ebbe, St Genesius, St Joseph Calasanz, St Yrieix
26 St Zephyrinus
27 St Caesarius of Arles, St David Lewis, St Monica
28 St Alexander of Constantinople, St Augustine of Hippo, St Edmund Arrowsmith, St Moses the Ethopian

29 Sts Hypatius and Andrew, St Sebbi
30 St Alexander Nevski, St Rose of Lima
31 St Aidan of Lindisfarne, St Raymond Nonnatus

September

1 St Michael Ghebre
2 St Antoninus, St Ingrid of Sweden, St William of Roskilde
3 St Balin, St Gregory the Great, St Macanisius
4 St Ultan
5 St Bertinus, Mother Teresa of Calcutta
6 St Cyprian of Carthage, Sts Felix and Augebert
7 St Cloud, St Marek Krizin
8 St Disibod
9 St Bettelin, St Isaac the Great, St Joseph of Volokolamsk, St Omer, St Wulfhilda
10 St Autbert, St Nicholas of Tolentino
11 St Patiens
12 St Ailbhe, St Guy of Anderlecht
13 St Amatus
14 St John Chrystostom, St Notburga
15 St Mirin of Benchor
16 St Cornelius, St Edith of Wilton, St Euphemia, St Ninian
17 St Columba of Cordova, St Hildegard of Bingen
18 St Joseph of Copertino, St Richardis
19 St Januarius, St Theodore of Canterbury
20 Sts Andrew Kim Taegon, Paul Chong Hasang and Companions, St Eustace
21 St Matthew
22 St Emmeramus, St Maurice, St Thomas of Villanueva
23 St Adamnan, St Pio of Pietrelcina (Padre Pio), St Thecla
24 St Andochius
25 St Ceolfrid, St Finbar, St Sergius
26 St John the Divine, St Nilus the Younger
27 Sts Cosmas & Damian, St Vincent de Paul
28 St Annemund, St Faustus, St Lawrence Ruiz, St Wenceslaus
29 St Gabriel the Archangel, St Michael the Archangel, St Raphael
30 St Gregory the Enlightener, St Jerome

October

1 St Bavo, St Remigius, St Romanus the Melodist, St Theresa of Lisieux
2 St Leger
3 St Gerard
4 St Francis of Assisi
5 St Galla, St Placid
6 St Bruno
7 St Artaldus
8 St Pelagia, St Ywi

 9 St Andronicus, Sts Denis, Rusticus, and Eleutherius
10 St Francis Borgia, St Maharsapor, St Paulinus of York
11 St Canice, St Ethelburga, St Maria Soledad, St Nectarius
12 St Edwin, St Fiacre, St Wilfrid
13 St Edward the Confessor, St Gerald of Aurillac, St Peter of Alicante
14 St Angadresma, St Burchard, St Callistus, St Luke
15 St Teresa of Avila
16 St Bercharius, St Gerard Majella, St Hedwig, St Marguerite
    d'Youville
17 St Richard Gwyn
18 St Athenodorus, St Keyna
19 St Charles Garnier, St Ethbin, St Frideswide, Sts Isaac Jogues and
    Rene Goupil
20 St Acca, St Artemius, St Caprasius
21 St Hilarion, St Ursula
22 St Abercius Marcellus, St Bertharius
23 St Paul Tong Buong
24 Sts Felix and Audactus
25 Sts Crispin and Crispinian, St Margaret Ward
26 St Cedd, St Eata
27 St Frumentius of Ethiopia
28 St Simon the Zealot
29 St Abraham of Rostov, St Narcissus
30 St Marcellus the Centurion
31 St Bega, St Quentin, St Wolfgang

November
 1 St Mary the Slave
 2 St Marcian of Chalcis
 3 St Acepsimas, St Hubert, St Malachy O' More, St Martin de Porres
 4 St Charles Borromeo
 5 St Sylvia
 6 St Barlaam, St Illtyd, St Winoc
 7 St Achillas, St Willibrord
 8 St Tysilio, St Willehad
 9 St Benignus, St Nektarios of Pentapolis, St Pabo
10 St Leo the Great
11 St Lebuin, St Martin of Tours, St Theodore of Studites
12 St Cadwallader, St Machar, St Nilus the Elder
13 St Abbo, St Brice, St Frances Xavier Cabrini, St Nicholas I
14 St Gregory Palamas, St Lawrence
15 St Albert the Great, St Gaius of Korea, St Malo
16 St Agnes of Assisi, St Alfrick, St Gertrude, St Margaret of Scotland
17 St Gregory Thaumaturgus, St Hilda, St Hugh of Lincoln, St Roque
    Gonzalez de Santa Cruz
18 St Odo, Sts Romanus and Barula
19 St Barlaam, St Elizabeth of Hungary, St Raphael Kalinowski,
    St Nerses the Great

20 St Bernward, St Nerses
21 St Gelasius I
22 St Cecilia
23 St Amphilocus, St Clement I, St Columban
24 St John of the Cross
25 St Catherine of Alexandria, St Mercurius of Caesarea
26 St Nikon, St Phileas
27 St Fergus, St Virgil of Salzburg
28 St Catherine Labouré, St James of the Marches, St Simeon Metaphrastes
29 St Radbod of Utrecht
30 St Andrew, St Tudwal

December

1 St Ansanus, The Venerable Charles de Foucauld
2 St Bibiana
3 St Cassian, St Francis Xavier
4 St Barbara, St Bernard of Parma, St Osmund
5 St Nicetius, St Sabas
6 St Nicholas
7 St Ambrose of Milan
8 St Mary
9 St Cyprian
10 St Eulalia of Merida, St Gregory III, St Mennas, St Miltiades
11 St Damasus, St Daniel the Stylite
12 St Edburga, St Vicelin
13 St Lucy of Syracuse
14 St Heron, St Maria Crocifissa di Rosa, St Nicasius of Rheims, St Venantius Fortunatus
15 St Christina the Astonishing
16 St Adelaide
17 St Begga, St Dionysios, St Olympias
18 St Winebald
19 St Anastasius I
20 St Ammon, St Dominic of Silos, St Leonard of Port Maurice, St Sebastian
21 St Peter Canisius
22 St Flavian of Acquapendente
23 St Thorlac Thorhallsson
24 St Charbel
25 Christmas Day
26 St Noel Chabanel, St Stephen
27 St Fabiola
28 The Holy Innocents
29 St Thomas Becket, St Trophimus of Arles
30 St Anysia, St Egwin
31 St Sylvester

Index of Patron Saints

Actors	St Genesius and St Vitus
Adopted children	St William of Rochester
African Americans	St Benedict the Black
African missions	St Theresa of Lisieux
Against snake bites	St Hilary of Poitiers
AIDS sufferers	St Theresa of Lisieux
Animals	St Francis of Assisi
Apulia	St Nicholas
Archers	St Sebastian
Architects	St Thomas
Artists	St Luke and St Catherine de Vigri
Astronomers	St Dominic
Athletes	St Sebastian
Aviators, flying	St Joseph of Copertino
Bakers	St Nicholas
Bankers	St Matthew
Barbers	St Martin de Porres
Bell-founders	St Agatha
The blind	St Raphael
Bohemia	St Wenceslaus
Brewers	St Augustine of Hippo
Brittany, France	St Hervé
Builders	St Vincent Ferrer
Bulls	St Luke
Cancer patients	St Peregrine Laziosi
Canonists	St Raymond of Pennafort
Cars	St Frances of Rome
Castrofuli	St Fulk
Catalonia	St George
Charitable societies	St Vincent de Paul
Chemically addicted	St Maximilan Kolbe
Childbirth	St Margaret of Antioch
Childlessness	St Henry

Children	St Nicholas
Choirboys	St Gregory the Great
Cooks	St Martha
Cracow	St Stanislaus
Dancers	St Vitus
Difficult marriages	St Edward the Confessor
Doctors	St Luke and St Camillus de Lellis
Domestic workers	St Zita
Drivers	St Frances of Rome
Dukes	St Henry
Ecology	St Francis of Assisi and Bl Kateri Tekakwitha
Educators	St Gregory the Great
Engineers	St Ferdinand III of Castile
England	St George and St Gregory the Great
Environment	Bl Kateri Tekakwitha
Epileptics	St Vitus
Europe	St Benedict
Expectant mothers	St Gerard Majella and St Raymond Nonnatus
Families	St Maximilian Kolbe
Finland	St Henry of Sweden
Fishermen	St Andrew
France	St Denis
Germany	St Boniface (Wynfrith)
Glasgow, Scotland	St Kentigern (Mungo)
Gout	St Gregory the Great
Greece	St Nicholas
Grocers	St Michael the Archangel
The handicapped	St Henry
Happy marriages	St Valentine
Happy meetings	St Raphael
Hartland, Devonshire	St Nectan
Hat makers	St James the Less
Headache sufferers	St Teresa of Avila
Hopeless causes	St Rita of Cascia
Hungary	St Stephen the Great
Immigrants	St Frances Xavier Cabrini
Inquisitors	St Peter of Verona
Internet	St Isadore of Seville
Invalids	St Roch
Ireland	St Patrick and St Brigid

Journalists	St Francis de Sales and St Maximilian Kolbe
Kings	St Edward the Confessor
Lace makers	St Luke
Latin America	St Rose of Lima
Lawyers	St Thomas More
Lawyers and judges	St Ivo of Brittany
Learning and the arts	St Charles Borromeo
Librarians	St Jerome
Lithuania	St Casimir
Locksmiths	St Baldomerus
Lost objects	St Anthony of Padua
Love	St Valentine
Marble-workers	St Clement I
Mariners	St Michael the Archangel
Merchants	St Francis of Assisi
Midwives	St Raymond Nonnatus
Modern stenographers	St Cassian
Motorists	St Christopher
Munster	St Ailbhe
Nervous and mental afflictions	St Dymphna
Nervous diseases	St Vitus
Norway	St Olaf of Norway
Notaries	St Mark
Nurses	St Raphael
Nurses and nursing groups	St Camillus de Lellis
Oslo	St Hallvard
Oxford University	St Frideswide
Paratroopers	St Michael the Archangel
Parents of large families	St Matilda and St Michael the Archangel
Paris	St Genevieve
Parish missions	St Leonard of Port Maurice
Pawnbrokers	St Nicholas
Philosophers	St Catherine of Alexandria
Physicians	St Raphael
Poland	St Casimir
Police	St Michael the Archangel
Postal workers	St Gabriel the Archangel
Preachers	St Catherine of Alexandria

Prisoners	St Maximilian Kolbe
Pro-life movement	St Maximilian Kolbe
Protection against plagues	St Sebastian
Protector against storms	St Vitus
Purity	St Maria Goretti
Race relations	St Martin de Porres
Rome	St Philip Neri
Russia	St Nicholas and St Andrew
Sailors	St Nicholas and St Phocas the Gardener
Scotland	St Andrew
Separated spouses	St Edward the Confessor
Serbia	St Sava of Serbia
Shepherds	St Paschal Baylon
Sickness	St Michael the Archangel
Silesia region of Eastern Europe	St Hedwig
Soldiers	St Gabriel the Archangel, St Martin of Tours and St Sebastian
Speliologists (cave explorers)	St Benedict
Stafford, England	St Bettelin
Stonemasons	St Stephen
Studying	St Joseph of Copertino
Sweden	St Eric IX
Swineherds	St Anthony of Egypt
Switzerland	St Nicholas von Flue
Travellers	St Christopher and St Raphael
Telephone workers	St Gabriel the Archangel
The Philippines	St Rosa of Lima
Those rejected by religious orders	St Henry
Throat illnesses	St Blaise
Victims of child abuse	St Germaine of Pibrac
Victims of rape	St Maria Goretti
Wales	St David
West Indies	St Gertrude
Widows	St Paula
Wild animals	St Blaise

Wives and
   abuse victims   St Monica

Young girls   St Blandina
Young people   St Valentine
Young women   St Maria Goretti
Youth   St Maria Goretti

Notes

1   N.T. Wright, *Scripture and the authority of God* (London: SPCK, 2004), 20.

2   Donald Attwater with Catherine Rachael John, *The Penguin Dictionary of Saints* (London: Penguin Books, 1995), 77

3   Ibid., 86.

4   Ken Kesey, *One Flew Over the Cuckoo's Nest* (London: Methuen & Co. Ltd., 1973), 42.

5   P. Chamberas (ed.), *Nicodemus of the Holy Mountain* (New York: Paulist Press, 1989), 18.

6   For the first thousand years of the Christian church, saints were recognized as such by local and regional assent. Little by little however, beginning with St Ulrich in the late tenth century, the papacy played a more important role in recognizing and officially 'canonizing' individuals. By 1634 the process had become fairly well established and requirements for sainthood were further clarified by Pope Urban VIII in a series of edicts. This is a complex matter, but dates for the canonization of those officially designated as saints by the papacy in the last millennium have been included where available.

7   Cardinal Suenens, *A New Pentecost?* (New York: Seabury Press, 1975), 66.

8   English translation of the Apostles' Creed copyright © 1988, by the English Language Liturgical Consultation.

9   The person who recorded the story of Matrionushka explains that it was told him by Bishop Stefan (Nikitin), who was then a layman and a doctor. The Russian text can be found in Nadezhda 7 (Frankfurt/Main 1982), 241-245. This present translation was made by Bishop Bazil of Sergievo and is used with his permission.

10 The major saints' feast days were established to coincide with the death of the saint where it was known. In the case of major saints these dates were generally agreed in the Western Church, though the Eastern Church regularly commemorates the same saints on different days. In the case of less well-known saints and where the date of death is unknown then, not infrequently, different dates have been adopted. Where applicable the dates shown here are based on those given in Butler's *Lives of Saints*.

Maps

The maps that follow show the location of places and principal districts referred to in the dictionary.

Ireland

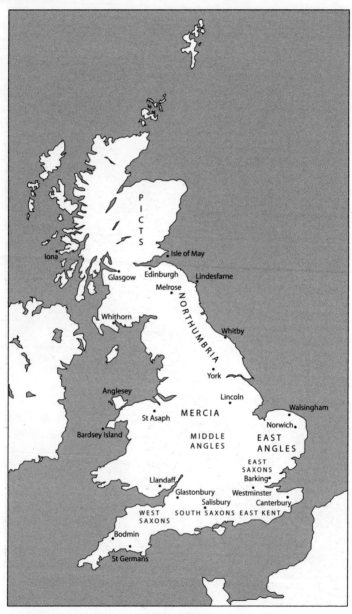

Mainland Britain

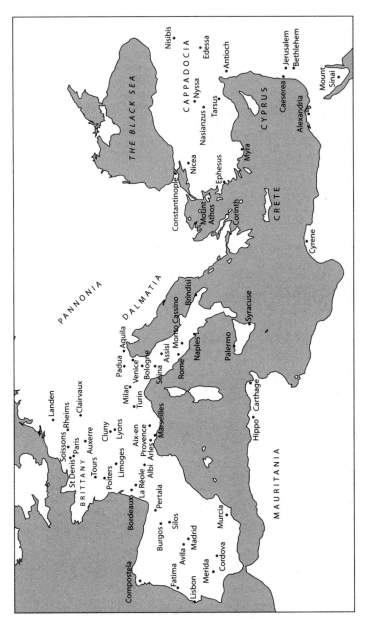

Europe, the Mediterranean and Asia Minor